T0211051

Communications in Computer and Information Science   1593

More information about this series at https://link.springer.com/bookseries/7899

Lorna Uden · I-Hsien Ting ·
Birgit Feldmann (Eds.)

Knowledge Management in Organisations

16th International Conference, KMO 2022
Hagen, Germany, July 11–14, 2022
Proceedings

 Springer

Editors
Lorna Uden
Staffordshire University
Stoke-on-Trent, UK

I-Hsien Ting
University of Kaohsiung
Kaohsiung, Taiwan

Birgit Feldmann
FernUniversität in Hagen
Hagen, Germany

ISSN 1865-0929   ISSN 1865-0937 (electronic)
Communications in Computer and Information Science
ISBN 978-3-031-07919-1   ISBN 978-3-031-07920-7 (eBook)
https://doi.org/10.1007/978-3-031-07920-7

This Springer imprint is published by the registered company Springer Nature Switzerland AG
The registered company address is: Gewerbestrasse 11, 6330 Cham, Switzerland

Preface

Welcome to the proceedings of the 16th International Conference on Knowledge Management in Organisations (KMO 2022). The conference focused on emerging trends of knowledge management in organisations and knowledge management in the post pandemic era, and was held at the FernUniversität in Hagen, Germany, during July 11–14 July, 2022. KMO 2022 was held in conjunction with the 10th International conference on Learning Technology for Education Challenges (LTEC 2022).

The conference was preceded by a day of free tutorials for participants who wished to learn about the state of the art of research relating to the topics of KMO and LTEC. The tutorials were held on July 11, 2022. The conference itself commenced on July 12, 2022.

Knowledge management (KM) identifies and globalises knowledge to facilitate access for all collaborators. Businesses depend on a reliable knowledge management system for smooth information sharing and internal operations. Technology has a tremendous impact on knowledge management, inspiring the development of robust software platforms to leverage knowledge management strategies.

Knowledge management solutions have sustained momentum and even accelerated their growth during the COVID-19 pandemic. Effective knowledge management supported by technology enables organisations to become more innovative and productive. There is increased use of cloud technology, AI, language processing solutions, and graph databases which have all contributed to a robust environment for knowledge management. Technology is undoubtedly a big part of the growing need for more effective knowledge management. In addition, knowledge sharing is a pervasive challenge. With the rapid advance of Industry 4.0., knowledge management will play an important role in organisations of all sizes.

KM today is developing a more robust approach that includes vendors, clients, and customers. Newer knowledge management options must allow for external integration so that internal and external parties can share information more easily. Blockchain and cryptographic technologies allow users in KM to own and control their data, and for data to be trusted by the third parties they choose to interact with. There are potential benefits of automating routine knowledge tasks and using powerful algorithms to recommend relevant content and colleagues based on users' personas and the context of their work.

The importance of KM as a strategic knowledge resource during the COVID-19 crisis cannot be overstated. It plays a critical role in guiding decision makers to make strategic decisions not only on behalf of organisations but for countries globally. Optimal use of knowledge resources is critical in ensuring that organisations survive in uncertain times such as the recent pandemic. What form will knowledge management take in the post-COVID-19 era?.

Although technology plays crucial roles in the advance of KM, it is important to remember that KM will always fail if the end users and stakeholders are not at the centre of strategy, design, implementation, and operation. KM should also be concerned with human-centered approaches, taking into consideration the core components of people, process, content, and culture along with new design methodologies such as design for users' experiences. To effectively manage knowledge in organisations, it is necessary that we address many of these issues.

KMO aims to encourage research into the various aspects of knowledge management to address many of the challenges facing organisations. The objective is to create a better understanding of knowledge management practices, research, and practical applications. To this end, KMO 2022 brought together leading academic researchers and research scholars to exchange and share their experiences and research from all aspects of knowledge management. It also provided an interdisciplinary platform for researchers, practitioners, and educators to present and discuss their most recent work, trends, innovation, and concerns as well as practical challenges encountered, and solutions adopted in the field of knowledge management in organisations.

This proceedings consists of 29 papers covering various aspects of knowledge management. All published papers underwent a rigorous review process involving at least four reviewers per paper. The authors of these papers come from 22 different countries or regions comprising Argentina, Austria, Brazil, China, Colombia, Ecuador, Finland, France, Germany, Hong Kong, Indonesia, Italy, Japan, Malaysia, Poland, Russia, South Africa, Switzerland, Taiwan, Tunisia, UAE, and the UK.

The papers are organised into the following thematic sections:

- Knowledge Transfer and Sharing
- Knowledge and Organisation
- Knowledge and Service Innovation
- Industry 4.0
- Information and Knowledge Systems
- Intelligent Science
- AI and New Trends in Knowledge Management

Besides the papers, KMO 2022 also featured invited keynote speakers and tutorials.

We would like to thank our reviewers and the Program Committee for their contributions and the FernUniversität in Hagen, Germany, for hosting the conference. Special thanks go to the authors and participants at the conference. Without their efforts, there would be no conference or proceedings.

We hope that this proceedings will be beneficial for your reference and that the information in this volume will be useful for further advancements in both research and industry in the field knowledge management.

Lorna Uden
Derrick I-Hsien Ting

Organisation

Conference Chair

Lorna Uden   Staffordshire University, UK

Program Chair

Derrick I-Hsien Ting   National University of Kaohsiung, Taiwan

Local Chair

Birgit Feldmann   FernUniversität in Hagen, Germany

Program Committee

Akira Kamoshida   Hosei University, Japan
Reinhard C. Bernsteiner   Management Center Innsbruck, Austria
Derrick I-Hsien Ting   National University of Kaohsiung, Taiwan
Costas Vassilakis   University of the Peloponnese, Greece
Dai Senoo   Tokyo Institute of Technology, Japan
Eric Kin-Wai Lau   City University, Hong Kong
George Karabatis   University of Maryland, USA
Fernando De la Prieta   University of Salamanca, Spain
Lorna Uden   Staffordshire University, UK
Luka Pavlič   University of Maribor, Slovenia
Marjan Heričko   University of Maribor, Slovenia
Remy Magnier-Watanabe   University of Tsukuba, Japan
Victor Hugo Medina Garcia   Universidad Distrital Francisco José de Caldas,
                                      Colombia
William Wang   University of Waikato, New Zealand
Yuri Zelenkov   Higher School of Economics, Russia
Pei-Hsuan Hsieh   National Chengchi University, Taiwan
Marta Silvia Tabares   Universidad EAFIT, Colombia
Gan Keng Hoon   Universiti Sains Malaysia, Malaysia
Stephan Schlögl   Management Center Innsbruck, Austria
Jari Kaivo-Oja   University of Turku, Finland
Christian Ploder   Management Center Innsbruck, Austria
Hércules Antonio do Prado   Catholic University of Brasília, Brazil

Contents

Knowledge and Service Innovation

Industry 4.0

Information and Knowledge Systems

Intelligent Science

AI and New Trends in KM

Knowledge Transfer and Sharing

The Effect of Telework Frequency on Communication Media and Knowledge Sharing in Japan

Remy Magnier-Watanabe[✉]

Graduate School of Business Sciences, University of Tsukuba, Tokyo, Japan
magnier-watanabe.gt@u.tsukuba.ac.jp

Abstract. Covid-19 has forced millions of office workers to telework without proper training or job redesign. This paper investigates how telework frequency has affected the use of communication media, and subsequently knowledge sharing. A large sample of full-time Japanese employees with no prior telework experience is examined using mediation analysis.

Results suggest that telework resulted in a lower use of face-to-face meetings and phone calls, and in a higher use of chat and virtual meetings, and had no effect on email use. Moreover, phone call, chat, and virtual meeting frequencies were found to mediate the relationship between telework frequency and knowledge sharing.

These findings highlight the importance of both existing and newer communication media in offsetting the loss of face-to-face meeting opportunities, and show that companies have found ways to achieve effective knowledge sharing during mandatory telework. Firms should therefore invest in tools and training to speed up the adoption of instant messaging and virtual meeting solutions.

Keywords: Telework · Knowledge sharing · Communication media · Japan

1 Introduction

COVID-19 has now become a major epidemic, resulting in excess mortality of at least 5.5 million deaths as of January 2022 (WHO 2022). Early on, it triggered exceptional preventive measures, such as the mandatory confinement of several billion people. In Japan, Tokyo and surrounding prefectures decreed a fourth state of emergency from July 12 to September 28, 2021, during which a large number of office employees had to work from home. Legally, the central government in Japan only has limited authority imposing a state of emergency, whose enforcement is left to each prefecture and municipality. The government and prefectures counted on large companies to support the stay-at-home order by directing their employees to switch to home-based telework when possible. A large number of employees in Japan switched to 100% telework in April 2020, with an even higher number in the service industry. Such a turnaround was unimaginable just a few weeks earlier since company management was very reluctant to let employees telework and prior agreements were often limited to one or two days a week.

© Springer Nature Switzerland AG 2022
L. Uden et al. (Eds.): KMO 2022, CCIS 1593, pp. 3–15, 2022.
https://doi.org/10.1007/978-3-031-07920-7_1

According to the Japanese Ministry of Health, Labor, and Welfare, telework from home can be done from a few days a month to several days a week (MHLW 2020). It warns that when working from home, working hours and daily life can become mixed up, therefore encouraging employers to discuss with their employees how to evaluate and manage their work to ensure peace of mind. In July 2021, a survey of 1,100 people showed that about 20% of respondents were teleworking at least some time over a recent week, of which about 12% every day, down from 19% in April 2021 (Japan Times 2021). The same survey found that 13%, against 16% previously, felts their efficiency had improved thanks to telework. The issue of efficiency is important as telework has deeply affected how employees work, especially with their colleagues with whom they no longer share a common time and place.

While telework is not new, most people experiencing it today are thrust into this work style without having chosen to. This large-scale experiment has seen millions of people provide services, produce content, organize meetings, teach courses, and more, all from home. Improvised telework with no prior experience or training can involve more work than in the office as interactions must be planned and initiated through technical means rather than quick and ad-hoc face-to-face chats. An earlier survey of about 1,000 people 18 or older conducted in May 2020 stressed that 36% of respondents had experienced difficulties communicating with bosses and coworkers (Japan Times 2020).

Already some firms have announced they will make flexible work permanent once COVID-19 is under control. Yahoo Japan announced in January 2022 it is planning to let its 8,000 employees work from anywhere in the country, even providing a monthly commuting budget of up $1,300 per employee to drop in the office when needed, mindful of in-person communication (Nonomiya 2022). And the government is pushing more businesses to further promote telework in preventing the spread of the omicron variant of the virus (Japan Times 2022). Thus, the pandemic can be said to have accelerated changes in work styles in Japan, and it is therefore critical to foresee problems and propose corrective actions, especially when it comes to job communication and knowledge sharing.

2 Literature Review and Hypotheses Development

2.1 Telework from Home

Telework from home is defined as regular salaried employment conducted at the employee's home. It is also referred to as home-based teleworking or home-working. Its frequency can be from 1 day to 5 days or more per week, leaving aside less recurrent occurrences (Aguilera et al. 2016). There is abundant research on the factors affecting the adoption of home-based telework, which are primarily related to the nature of work, its perceived benefits and drawbacks, and fit with the company or national cultures (Peters and Batenburg 2015; Aguilera et al. 2016). It follows that telework from home is better suited for highly skilled and autonomous workers who consider it to be advantageous to their professional and personal lives, and is better suited in cultures and firms where it has gained general acceptance (De Graaf and Rietveld 2007). The frequency, or intensity, of telework has been found to play an important role for employee satisfaction, performance, relationships with colleagues, as well as outcomes related to those employees who do not telework (Allen et al. 2015).

In Japan, the Ministry of Health, Labor, and Welfare has been sharing public guidelines for telework since 2004, and updated them in 2008 highlighting the pros and cons of such work arrangement (MHLW 2008). Some of the merits of telework for companies include: business operations can continue in the event of a natural disaster, in accordance with a Business Continuity Plan; obtaining and retaining talent by enabling flexible working styles; promoting work-life balance and corporate social responsibility; reducing costs for office space and for commuting allowances (in Japan, the employer bears the totality of the commuting cost between home and office for regular employees). And some merits for employees comprise: working while raising children or caring for a parent; increase in free time due to the lack of commuting; expanding employment opportunities for the elderly and disabled who have difficulty commuting; working in a quieter environment allowing better concentration and therefore productivity. The guidelines also detail the demerits of telework based on employee data: separating work from non-work activities; working long hours; evaluating one's work; accessing dispersed work documents; noise disturbances; communicating with one's superior; managing one's health; feeling lonely or estranged; pressure to produce results; improving one's skills; and drop in salary (MHLW 2008).

We label working from home as 'mandatory' telework since employees were forced to do so by their firm, which needed to comply with the state of emergency orders decreed by the prefectures in which their offices are located, in order to prevent the spread of COVID-19. In this setting, home-based telework was implemented without any regard for suitability, as long as jobs could be carried out from home with a computer and a phone. Past literature has contrasted voluntary from involuntary telework, on the basis of whether employees' personal preferences dictated their particular work arrangement (Lapierre et al. 2016).

2.2 Communication Modes

Daft and Lengel (1984, 1986) proposed the media richness theory at a time when electronic communication was starting to spread. Their theory posits that a communication channel, or medium, is effective if it can match the richness of the original medium. Richness is a function of immediate feedback, multiple cues, language variety, and personal focus. The main criteria in picking a communication medium for a given message or meeting should be to minimize equivocality or the possibility of misinterpretations or multiple interpretations of a message. When a message is difficult to decipher and interpret, multiple cues and more data will be required to understand it as intended. The more likely a message is to be challenging to decode and understand, the more cues and data will be needed to interpret it correctly. As explained by Suh (1999), "a lean medium (e.g. a memo) is sufficient to exchange an unequivocal message (e.g. a routine communication), while a rich medium (e.g. a face to-face meeting) is recommended to resolve an equivocal situation (e.g. negotiation)" (p. 296). Besides the four original criteria of richness, Carlson and Zmud (1999) added social influence and experience (with a particular channel, topic, communicator, and organizational context).

Face-to-face is deemed the richest medium, then phone, written addressed documents, and last unaddressed documents (bulk emails, flyers). Since the theory was introduced almost 40 years ago, chat (instant messaging/texting) and virtual meetings have been introduced and widely accepted. Virtual meetings (such as those using Zoom, Microsoft Teams, Webex) have been judged as rich media, one notch below face-to-face communication since they still prevent manipulating objects together, physical contact, and more generally grasping non-verbal cues, as long a video is on (Reed and Allen 2021). Instant messaging, although a viable alternative way to interact in real-time, is more problematic and considered much leaner because of its lack of support for nonverbal cues (Tang and Bradshaw 2020). In short, media richness theory posits that leaner personal communication media (email, text, or phone) are less effective for communicating complex issues in comparison to richer media. Specifically, Reed and Allen (2021) maintain that "scheduling a meeting is typically fairly straightforward and can be done via email, a lean form of media [...] but a detailed message about a person's work performance on a recent project probably needs a richer medium, such as a face-to-face meeting" (p. 108).

2.3 Knowledge Sharing

Knowledge sharing is considered a critical phase of knowledge management, along with creation, storage, and application (Heisig 2009). Knowledge sharing is the most frequent KM process studied, followed by knowledge acquisition and knowledge application (Al-Emran et al. 2018). Knowledge sharing consists of movements of knowledge between organizational agents (Kianto et al. 2018), and it can be formal or informal. While knowledge donation refers to giving one's knowledge to others, knowledge collection denotes receiving knowledge from another unit or actor. Knowledge sharing is considered to occur once knowledge has been given and received freely (Hooff and De Ridder 2004).

Knowledge sharing is predicated on trust, intrinsic and extrinsic motivation, job satisfaction, norms and values of an organization and leadership support (Hooff and De Ridder 2004). Because not all knowledge is easily verbalized or conveyed, Polanyi distinguished two types of knowledge, tacit and explicit (1966). Tacit knowledge is cognitive knowledge that is highly individual and difficult to express with language or numbers; for example, beliefs, points of view, technical skills and know-how are all part of tacit knowledge. Explicit knowledge, on the other hand, is objective and rational knowledge, and can be expressed with words or numbers; texts, equations, specifications and manuals. It is therefore fairly easy to identify, store, and retrieve (Wellman 2009).

2.4 Hypotheses and Research Model

Past research on telework and knowledge management has focused on consultants who have historically engaged in work activities away from the office on the road and at clients' sites (Hislop et al. 2007). For them working from home allowed higher levels of concentration than working on the road or even in the office better suited for deep in-person communication. Peters and Batenburg (2015) state that firms allow telework for high-value personnel in order to lower knowledge transfer risk and increase retention and performance.

Some recent research has explored the implications for knowledge management following the outbreak of COVID-19. For instance, Ammirato et al. (2021) have catalogued a number of issues such as knowledge integration for contact tracing or the integration of emergency KM systems. Taskin and Bridoux (2010)'s research investigated the damaging effect of telework on knowledge transfer in organizations. They reviewed the literature on the cognitive and relational components of organizational socialization in their role as facilitators of knowledge transfer. They showed that telework may negatively affect some of these cognitive and relational components, based on frequency, location, and perception.

In Japan, Hosoda (2021) has looked at how COVID-19 affected the use of telework. He found that while the pandemic was instrumental in the adoption of telework in the country, it has been lower than expected. Communication, especially that which is frequent and face-to-face, as well as technological issues among small and medium enterprises, have been identified as being responsible for such low telework implementation (Mori and Hayashi 2020). However, little research to date has focused on the effect of mandatory telework on communication modes and knowledge sharing.

The link between communication medium and knowledge sharing has therefore already been established. For instance, communication patterns have been found to be affected by collaborative technology, resulting in an increase in explicit knowledge sharing and a decrease in tacit knowledge sharing (Bélanger and Allport 2008). And considering media richness theory, effective knowledge sharing will depend on the type of knowledge to be shared, and thus on the selection of an appropriate communication medium. Previous research has indeed ascertained that, in general, tacit knowledge is better shared using richer media, whereas explicit knowledge is more effectively transferred using leaner media (Murray and Peyrefitte 2007). And overall, organizational actors select communication media based on their richness and the nature of knowledge to be shared.

In this research, we focus on the relationships between telework frequency, communication modes, and knowledge sharing. We do not directly differentiate between tacit and explicit knowledge but inferences will be made later based on communication modes. We predict that communication modes fully mediate the relationship between telework frequency and knowledge sharing, except for face-to-face communication. Telework will surely negatively affect face-to-face frequency, which will be replaced by other modes of communication, especially virtual meetings, the closest in terms of media richness. We therefore expect a substitution effect whereby other communication modes become alternatives to face-to-face meetings. In turn, because firms are rational actors incurring costs only for value-adding activities, such as knowledge sharing, we hypothesize that higher frequencies of communication modes are related to higher knowledge sharing. Below are detailed hypotheses (Fig. 1).

H1a: Higher telework frequency is related to lower face-to-face frequency.
H1b: Higher telework frequency is related to higher phone call frequency.
H1c: Higher telework frequency is related to higher email frequency.
H1d: Higher telework frequency is related to higher chat frequency.
H1e: Higher telework frequency is related to higher virtual meeting frequency.

H2a: Higher face-to-face frequency is related to higher knowledge sharing.
H2b: Higher phone call frequency is related to higher knowledge sharing.
H2c: Higher email frequency is related to higher knowledge sharing.
H2d: Higher chat frequency is related to higher knowledge sharing.
H2e: Higher virtual meeting frequency is related to higher knowledge sharing.

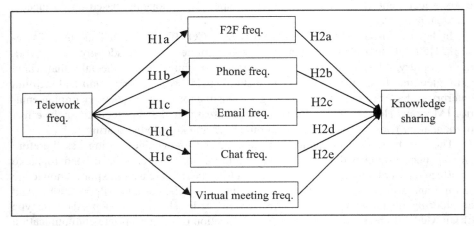

Fig. 1. Research model

3 Methodology

3.1 Survey and Sample

The survey was conducted in December 2021 by an Internet survey company with a sample of full-time Japanese employees living and working in the Tokyo area. By design, the respondents had no prior experience with telework from home, and had all engaged in some degree of telework over the period of interest. The questionnaire inquired about the respondents' frequency of telework, as well as their frequency for different types of communication for face-to-face, phone, email, chat, and virtual meeting during the state of emergency orders (between July 12 and September 28, 2021). This retrospective design allows the evaluation of a specific unforeseen event such as COVID-19 and the resulting state of emergency orders and mandatory telework from home, which rule out the use of prospective instruments (Pratt et al. 2000).

In this sample of 575 respondents, we have a majority of male employees (76%), most with a university degree (73%), having subordinates (59%), working as general employees (55%) in very large companies with more than 500 employees (56%) for more than 10 years (64%), living (57%) and working (82%) in Tokyo, with an average commute one-way between 30 and 60 min (51%) (Table 1).

Table 1. Sample demographics

Indicator	N	%	Indicator	N	%
Gender			Company size		
Men	437	76.0	<10	22	3.8
Women	138	24.0	10–49	48	8.3
Age			50–249	115	20.0
20–24	10	1.7	250–499	67	11.7
25–29	51	8.9	500+	323	56.2
30–34	37	6.4	Tenure		
35–39	51	8.9	2–5 yrs	102	17.7
40–44	62	10.8	5–10 yrs	106	18.4
45–49	108	18.8	10 yrs+	367	63.8
50–54	80	13.9	Domicile		
55–59	69	12.0	Tokyo	326	56.7
60–64	107	18.6	Kanagawa	123	21.4
Education			Saitama	76	13.2
High school	39	6.8	Chiba	50	8.7
Professional school	34	5.9	Workplace		
Associate degree	18	3.1	Tokyo	471	81.9
University degree	419	72.9	Kanagawa	58	10.1
Master degree	53	9.2	Saitama	28	4.9
PhD degree	10	1.7	Chiba	18	3.1
Other	2	.3	Commute (one-way)		
Function			0–30 mn	89	15.5
Gen. employee	314	54.6	31–60 mn	294	51.1
Section chief	122	21.2	61–90 mn	147	25.6
Manager	68	11.8	91–120 mn	36	6.3
Senior manager	15	2.6	120 mn+	9	1.6
Top management	22	3.8	Telework frequency		
CEO	7	1.2	1 day a week	55	9.6
Other	27	4.7	2 days a week	116	20.2
Subordinates			3 days a week	150	26.1
0	233	40.5	4 days a week	92	16.0
1–5	168	29.2	5 days a week	162	28.2
6–10	58	10.1			
11–30	63	11.0			
31+	53	9.2			

3.2 Survey and Measures

Three questions were used to assess knowledge sharing, based on Kianto et al. (2018) on a 7-point scale; those asked for the respondents' level of agreement with the following: "we have systems to capture new ideas and experiences"; "the management motivates us to share our knowledge"; "we spend time to share ideas and experiences with each other". For telework frequency: 1: none; 2: 1–3 times a month; 3: 1 day a week; 4: 2 days a week; 5: 3 days a week; 6: 4 days a week; 7: 5 days a week. And for communication frequency: 1: never; 2: once a year; 3: once a month; 4: once a week; 5: 2–3 times a week; 6: once a day; 7: several times a day.

For the 3 questions on knowledge sharing, Cronbach's alpha was 0.899 thus denoting internal consistency. A factor analysis of those same 3 questions yielded a single factor explaining 83% of the variance with loading above 0.9, thus confirming convergent validity. The other variables in the survey use only a single survey item each, and therefore making tests of validity and consistency unsuitable.

During the fourth state of emergency, on average, respondents teleworked between 3 and 4 days a week, and used face-to-face communication between once and 2–3 times a week, phone 2–3 times a week, email between once and several times a day, chat between 2–3 times a week and once a day, and virtual meetings between once and 2–3 times a week. Correlations, all below 0.5, reveal no issues with collinearity (Table 2).

4 Results

The following statistical tests use SPSS and PROCESS, a freely-available computational tool for SPSS that specifically addresses mediation, moderation, or conditional process analyses (Hayes 2018). The results are depicted in Table 3 and Fig. 2.

H1a, whereby higher telework frequency is related to lower face-to-face frequency (-0.486, p = 0.000) is supported. Unexpectedly, higher telework frequency is related to lower phone call frequency (-0.241, p = 0.000), the opposite of H1b. H1c, about the relationship between telework and email frequency is not supported (0.054, p = 0.092). H1d, whereby higher telework frequency is related to higher chat frequency 0.388, p = 0.000) is supported. And H1e, whereby higher telework frequency is related to higher virtual meeting frequency 0.413, p = 0.000) is supported.

As for H2 hypotheses, only H2b phone call frequency (0.129, p = 0.000), H2d chat frequency (0.083, p = 0.004), and H2e virtual meeting frequency (0.095, p = 0.002) are positively and significantly related to knowledge sharing, and are therefore supported.

In the model, neither the total effect (0.052, t(573) = 1.180, p = 0.238) nor the direct effect are significant (0.009, t(573) = 0.187, p = 0.852). However, several indirect effects are significant, as indicated by the asymmetric bootstrap confidence intervals which do not contain zero (Hayes 2018): through phone call frequency (-0.028, bootstrap confidence interval between -0.053 and -0.009), through chat frequency (0.032, bootstrap confidence interval between 0.009 and 0.060), and through virtual meeting frequency (0.039, bootstrap confidence interval between 0.010 and 0.068) chat frequency to knowledge sharing (0.037, bootstrap confidence interval between 0.015 and 0.068).

As expected, telework has resulted in a lower use of face-to-face meetings and a higher use of chat and virtual meetings during the fourth state of emergency in the Tokyo

Table 2. Means, standard deviations and correlations of survey variables

	Mean	SD	1	2	3	4	5	6	7	8	9	10	11	12	13
1. Gender	1.2	0.4	1												
2. Age range	7	2.3	-.373**	1											
3. Education	3.8	1	-.106*	0.02	1										
4. Tenure	4.5	0.8	-.244**	.457**	0.031	1									
5. Subordinates	2.2	1.3	-.128***	.088*	.108**	.172**	1								
6. Company size	4.1	1.2	-.109***	0.072	.171**	.170**	.131**	1							
7. Commute one-way	2.3	0.9	-.123**	.135**	0.04	0.017	-0.042	0.059	1						
8. Telework freq	5.3	1.3	-0.023	-0.02	0.039	-0.067	-.090*	0.04	0.025	1					
9. F2F freq.	4.3	1.6	0.001	0.02	0.046	0.035	.112**	0.077	-0.011	-.412**	1				
10. Phone freq.	5.3	1.8	0.022	-.098*	0.075	0.009	.190**	-0.025	-0.009	-.161**	.270**	1			
11. Email freq.	6.5	1	-0.002	0.035	.172**	0.019	.094*	.151**	-0.039	0.07	.130**	.369**	1		
12. Chat freq.	5.5	2.2	0.068	-.251**	0.05	-.164***	0.081	.149***	0.009	.239**	-0.029	.135**	.220**	1	
13. Virt. meet. freq.	4.3	2.1	-0.037	-.160**	.158**	-0.051	.145**	.248**	-0.046	.262**	0.007	.155**	.255**	.392**	1

Gender: 1 = male; 2 = female.

Age range: 2 = 20–24; 3 = 25–29; 4 = 30–34; 5 = 35–39; 7 = 40–44; 7 = 45–49; 8 = 50–54; 9 = 55–59; 10 = 60–64.

Education: 1 = High school; 2 = Prof. school; 3 = Associate degree; 4 = University; 5 = Master degree; 6 = PhD; 7 = Other.

Tenure: 3 = 2–5 yrs; 4 = 5–10 yrs; 5 = 10 yrs+

Subordinates: 1 = 0; 2 = 1–5; 3 = 6–10; 4 = 11–30; 5 = 31 +

Company size: 1 = <10; 2 = 10–49; 3 = 50–249; 4 = 250–499; 5 = 500+

Commute once-way: 1 = 0–30 mn; 2 = 31–60 mn; 3 = 61–90 mn; 4 = 91–120 mn; 5 = 120 mn+

Telework freq.: 1 = never; 2 = 1–3 times a month; 3 = 1 day a week; 4 = 2 days a week; 5 = 3 days a week; 6 = 4 days a week; 7 = 5 days a week.

Comm. freq.: 1 = never; 2 = once a year; 3 = once a month; 4 = once a week; 5 = 2–3 times a week; 6 = once a day; 7 = several times a day.

Table 3. Regression coefficients, standard errors, and model summary information

Antecedent	Consequent					
	M1 (F2F)			M2 (Phone)		
	Coeff.	SE	P	Coeff.	SE	P
X (TW Freq)	−0.486	0.045	**0.000**	−0.241	0.055	**0.000**
Constant	6.857	0.246	**0.000**	6.399	0.302	**0.000**
	R2 = 0.170 **F(1,573) = 117.384, p = 0.000**			**R2 = 0.026** **F(1,573) = 15.156, p = 0.000**		
	M3 (Email)			M4 (Chat)		
Antecedent	Coeff.	SE	P	Coeff.	SE	P
X (TW Freq)	0.054	0.032	0.092	0.388	0.066	**0.000**
Constant	6.235	0.177	**0.000**	3.382	0.361	**0.000**
	R2 = 0.005 F(1,573) = 2.852, p = 0.092			**R2 = 0.057** **F(1,573) = 34.699, p = 0.000**		
	M5 (Virt. meet.)			Y (Knowledge sharing)		
Antecedent	Coeff.	SE	P	Coeff.	SE	P
X (TW Freq)	0.413	0.064	**0.000**	0.009	0.049	0.852
M1 (F2F)				0.009	0.040	0.832
M2 (Phone)				0.129	0.035	**0.000**
M3 (Email)				0.046	0.060	0.440
M4 (Chat)				0.083	0.029	**0.004**
M5 (Virt. meet.)				0.095	0.030	**0.002**
Constant	2.103	0.349	**0.000**	2.592	0.464	**0.000**
	R2 = 0.069 **F(1,573) = 42.271, p = 0.000**			**R2 = 0.103** **F(6,568) = 10.844, p = 0.000**		

area. However, telework has also caused a lower use of phone calls, indicating that they may be used in combination of face-to-face meetings, or at least in their organization. Moreover, telework had no effect on email use, suggesting that whether employees work from the office or from home, they rely on email to the same degree.

As for the predictors of knowledge sharing, the data identified the higher use of only phone calls, chat, and virtual meetings, but not face-to-face meetings or email. These results, considered in conjunction with the mediations through phone call, chat, and virtual meeting frequencies, of telework frequency and knowledge sharing, unequivocally highlight their importance.

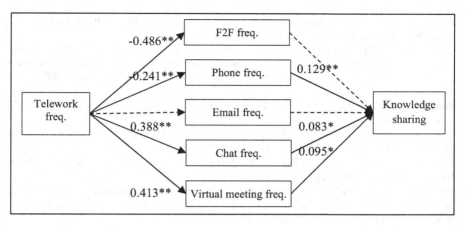

Fig. 2. Empirical model

5 Conclusion

These findings highlight the importance of both existing (phone) and newer communication media (chat and virtual meetings) in offsetting the loss of face-to-face meeting opportunities, and show that companies have found ways to achieve effective knowledge sharing during mandatory telework. Firms should therefore invest in tools and training to speed up the adoption of instant messaging and virtual meeting solutions.

References

Aguilera, A., Lethiais, V., Rallet, A., Proulhac, L.: Home-based telework in France: characteristics, barriers and perspectives. Transp. Res. Part A: Policy Pract. **92**, 1–11 (2016)

Al-Emran, M., Mezhuyev, V., Kamaludin, A., Shaalan, K.: The impact of knowledge management processes on information systems: a systematic review. Int. J. Inf. Manag. **43**, 173–187 (2018)

Allen, T.D., Golden, T.D., Shockley, K.M.: How effective is telecommuting? Assessing the status of our scientific findings. Psychol. Sci. Public Interest **16**(2), 40–68 (2015)

Ammirato, S., Linzalone, R., Felicetti, A.M.: Knowledge management in pandemics. A critical literature review. Knowl. Manag. Res. Pract. **19**(4), 415–426 (2021)

Bélanger, F., Allport, C.D.: Collaborative technologies in knowledge telework: an exploratory study. Inf. Syst. J. **18**(1), 101–121 (2008)

Carlson, J.R., Zmud, R.W.: Channel expansion theory and the experiential nature of media richness perceptions. Acad. Manag. J. **42**(2), 153–170 (1999)

Daft, R.L., Lengel, R.H.: Information richness: a new approach to managerial behavior and organizational design. Res. Organ. Behav. **6**, 191–233 (1984)

Daft, R.L., Lengel, R.H.: Organizational information requirements, media richness and structural design. Manag. Sci. **32**(5), 554–571 (1986)

De Graaff, T., Rietveld, P.: Substitution between working at home and out-of-home: the role of ICT and commuting costs. Transp. Res. Part A: Policy Pract. **41**(2), 142–160 (2007)

Hayes, A.F.: Introduction to Mediation, Moderation, and Conditional Process Analysis: A Regression-Based Approach, 2nd edn. Guilford Press, New York (2018)

Heisig, P.: Harmonisation of knowledge management – comparing 160 KM frameworks around the globe. J. Knowl. Manag. **13**(4), 4–31 (2009)

Hislop, D.: Knowledge processes and communication dynamics in mobile telework. In: McInerney, C.R., Day, R.E. (eds.) Rethinking Knowledge Management: From Knowledge Objects to Knowledge Processes, pp. 187–207. Springer, Berlin (2007). https://doi.org/10.1007/3-540-71011-6_8

Hofstede, G., Hofstede, G.J.: Cultures and Organizations: Software of the Mind. McGraw-Hill, New York (2005)

Hosoda, M.: Telework amidst the COVID-19 pandemic: effects on work style reform in Japan. Corp. Gov. Int. J. Bus. Soc. **21**(6), 1059–1071 (2021)

Ishii, K., Lyons, M.M., Carr, S.A.: Revisiting media richness theory for today and future. Hum. Behav. Emerg. Technol. **1**(2), 124–131 (2019)

Japan Times: 70% in Japan want telecommuting to continue after pandemic, survey finds. The Japan Times (June 22, 2020) (2020). https://www.japantimes.co.jp/news/2020/06/22/business/japan-telecommuting-continue/#.XvFDa-eRVtR

Japan Times: 'Telework fatigue' sees more Japanese workers going back to the office. The Japan Times (July 11) (2021). https://www.japantimes.co.jp/news/2021/07/17/business/telework-fatigue-sees-japanese-workers-going-back-office/

Japan Times: Economic revitalization minister urges business groups to further promote telework. The Japan Times (January 13) (2022). https://www.japantimes.co.jp/news/2022/01/13/business/economy-business/government-business-groups-omicron-telework/

Kianto, A., Shujahat, M., Hussain, S., Nawaz, F., Ali, M.: The impact of knowledge management on knowledge worker productivity. Balt. J. Manag. **14**(2), 178–197 (2018)

Kwak, H.: Self-disclosure in online media: an active audience perspective. Int. J. Advert. **31**(3), 485–510 (2012)

Lapierre, L.M., Van Steenbergen, E.F., Peeters, M.C., Kluwer, E.S.: Juggling work and family responsibilities when involuntarily working more from home: a multiwave study of financial sales professionals. J. Organ. Behav. **37**(6), 804–822 (2016)

MHLW: Guidelines for proper labor management in telework [Terewāku ni okeru tekisetsuna rōmu kanri no tame no gaidorain]. Ministry of Health, Labor, and Welfare (2008). https://www.mhlw.go.jp/content/000553510.pdf

MHLW: Work style called "telework from home" ['Jitaku de no terewāku' to iu hatarakikata]. Ministry of Health, Labor, and Welfare (2020). https://www.mhlw.go.jp/bunya/roudoukijun/dl/pamphlet.pdf

Mori, T., Hayashi, H.: 60% feel teleworking has obstacles, but they also feel benefits—difficulties in introducing telework for Japanese companies as seen from business culture. Nomura Research Institute, NRI Group Urgent Proposals Regarding Measures for Covid-19, vol. 31, pp. 1–9 (2020)

Murray, S.R., Peyrefitte, J.: Knowledge type and communication media choice in the knowledge transfer process. J. Manag. Issues **19**(1), 111–133 (2007)

Nonomiya, L.: Yahoo tells Japan employees they can work anywhere and commute by plane when necessary. The Japan Times (January 12) (2022). https://www.japantimes.co.jp/news/2022/01/12/business/corporate-business/yahoo-japan-telework-anywhere/

Peters, P., Batenburg, R.: Telework adoption and formalisation in organisations from a knowledge transfer perspective. Int. J. Work Innov. **1**(3), 251 (2015)

Polanyi, M.: Tacit Dimension. Peter Smith, Gloucester (1966)

Reed, K.M., Allen, J.A.: Suddenly Virtual: Making Remote Meetings Work. Wiley, Hoboken (2021)

Suh, K.S.: Impact of communication medium on task performance and satisfaction: an examination of media-richness theory. Inf. Manag. **35**(5), 295–312 (1999)

Tang, C.M., Bradshaw, A.: Instant messaging or face-to-face? How choice of communication medium affects team collaboration environments. E-learn. Digital Media **17**(2), 111–130 (2020)

Taskin, L., Bridoux, F.: Telework: a challenge to knowledge transfer in organizations. Int. J. Hum. Resour. Manag. **21**(13), 2503–2520 (2010)

Van Den Hooff, B., De Ridder, J.A.: Knowledge sharing in context: the influence of organizational commitment, communication climate and CMC use on knowledge sharing. J. Knowl. Manag. **8**(6), 117–130 (2004)

Wellman, J.L.: Organizational Learning: How Companies and Institutions Manage and Apply Knowledge, 1st edn. Palgrave Macmillan, Ltd. (2009)

WHO: Weekly epidemiological update on COVID-19 - 25 January 2022. World Health Organization (2022). https://www.who.int/publications/m/item/weekly-epidemiological-update-on-covid-19---25-january-2022

Efficacy of Knowledge and Skills in Teaching and Learning and Research in Higher Education Institution

Rexwhite Tega Enakrire[✉] and Hanlie Smuts

Department of Informatics, School of Information Technology, University of Pretoria, Pretoria, South Africa
rexwhite.enakrire80@gmail.com, hanlie.smuts@up.ac.za

Abstract. The activities of teaching and learning and research are core functions that require adequate knowledge and skills to master the tricks of the game in higher education institutions. These have helped to strengthen the complexity and uncertainty, that makes many academics not attain the expected height. Adequacy of knowledge and skills are critical success factors for organizational productivity among academics, irrespective of the context. The question that prompted this discussion is how knowledge and skills have enforced/enhanced the effectiveness and efficiency of transformation in work performance in organizations. The purpose of this study is to examine the efficacy that knowledge and skills in mastering the tricks of the game in research, teaching, and learning among academics. The qualitative research approach was adopted in this study, using interpretive content analysis of articles harvested from different online databases of Scopus and Web of Science. Findings indicate that academics possess a tacit type of knowledge, which support academics to master the tricks of the game in teaching and learning, research, community engagement, and citizenship activities. Certain skills of search strategies to access online sources required for teaching, learning, and research; technical skills to use different systems; decision-making skills; change management skills; and evaluation of job performance, were enablers to academics. The study recommends active training and exposition among academics, to advance their knowledge and skills for best practices in the teaching profession. The support of the organization to staff members is paramount, as it would bring productivity among colleagues.

Keywords: Information · Knowledge · Skills · Higher education institutions (HEIs) · Teaching · Learning and research · Higher education institutions (HEIs)

1 Introduction

The activities carried out in academia or higher education institutions (HEIs) depends largely on the existence of human beings, doing diverse work operations. The diverse work operations were the essence of academic participation in activities of teaching, learning, and research being core functions in HEIs. These core functions require adequate knowledge and skills to master the tricks of the game. These help to strengthen the

L. Uden et al. (Eds.): KMO 2022, CCIS 1593, pp. 16–24, 2022.
https://doi.org/10.1007/978-3-031-07920-7_2

complexity and uncertainty, which makes many academics not attain the expected height [1]. The question that prompted this crucial discussion is how knowledge and skills have enhanced the effectiveness and efficiency of transformation in work performance in organizations. The capabilities and skills demonstrated by academics in providing solutions to specific and general problems have helped HEIs globally and specifically in South Africa and Nigeria to become more productive.

This paper argues that knowledge and skills have become pivotal to excellence in job performance of academics on daily basis. The critical success factor demonstrated implies the execution of operations, using knowledge, ideas, insight, experience, skills, and attitude of academics in a manner that is unexplainable to what the academics believes. The view that academics have is essential to how their knowledge and skills activate effectiveness and efficiency of transformation in the execution of work operation/performance in higher education institutions (HEIs). In this ever-changing world of digital technology [2], the application of knowledge and skills stand as prerequisites in every space of human endeavors. Higher Education Institutions (HEIs) being a viable organization in today's world require constant use of knowledge and skills by academics to drive their teaching, learning, research, and other related activities in the organization. The organizational productivity seen among academics in HEIs today results in the different academic's knowledge and skills embedded in their brain [3, 4]. The authors of this study established that the capabilities and skills demonstrated among academics through the provision of solutions for specific and general problem solving have helped HEIs to become a better organization in the world where South African and Nigerian HEIs are not left out.

In Sect. 2, the background of the study was presented, followed by the purpose of the study. While looking at the background, consideration of knowledge and skills were presented, followed by the methodology applied for the study. Section 4, represent the implication of using knowledge and skills in teaching, learning, and research among academics in HEIs. Section 5 is the concluding part of the paper.

2 Background

HEIs continue to thrive to sustain competitive superiority over their competitors through the support which academics give using their knowledge and skills in teaching, learning, and conducting research in the institutions [5, 6]. Previous arguments by [7–13] extended the understanding of knowledge to be an invisible entity, though can act dependent on the distinction between the behavioural potential, either directly observed, or the observable performance or behaviour of the individual [1]. [1] notes that, the knowledge possessed by an individual gives power to successful work performance. Such an individual could possess considerable knowledge as a result of learning; however, the knowledge of that individual remains hidden power, except the person uses the knowledge to do something like performing some tasks, understand a situation, decide or solve a problem. Despite its inaccessibility, its power over work performance can be overwhelming [1].

In the next section, the purpose of the study, which considers the perceived usefulness of knowledge and skills was conceptualized.

2.1 Purpose of the Study

The purpose of this study was to conceptualize the efficacy of knowledge and skills in the productivity of work performance and how it has helped academics to master the tricks of the game in conducting research using different strategies/approaches, teaching, and learning among academics. This has become crucial considering the evolving nature of the phenomena and changes happening in the workplace of learning. The knowledge and skills of academics require in-depth articulation and imagination of their intuitive/tacit knowledge for proper decision making and planning. The essence of such imagination of their intuitive/tacit knowledge is to enable the academics to develop resourceful lecture notes/modules required to support students' teaching and learning and at the same come up with resounding research papers published in high-impact journals. Mastering the trick of the game in research, teaching, and learning would put academics ahead in this world of competition, such that, having advantages over their counterpart bring good result to every economic growth.

2.2 Concept of Knowledge

[14] note that knowledge is fluids of insights, exposure, and experiences acquired over a long period. Knowledge is crucial in the execution of any task. Knowledge is viewed as finished products of information categorized as new economic factors of production in this knowledge economy. In support of this, [15] unfolds that knowledge is acquired through learning processes and social interrelations. Another remark made by [43] revealed that knowledge is the capabilities and skills applied by individuals to provide solutions for specific problems. Several studies in knowledge management [16, 17], and [18] gave instances of two types of knowledge, which are explicit and tacit. The explicit are those found in books or documents which can also be accessed with ease and transferred among individuals, while the tacit is hidden in the individual mind, thoughts, capacities, insight, and experiences [19].

2.3 Concept of Skill

Previous studies by [20–22], allude to skill as the ability to perform the tasks. It could further be affirmed that skills are very crucial in whatever a man does. Diverse studies as stipulated by [23–26] and [27] note that skills are capabilities in physical or psychological attributes of an individual, by content and context, to be acquired and mastered through activity related approaches of professional and non-professional training. Another dimension, of e-skills, is categorized as ICT skills being a prerequisite of informal education, work experience, training (on-the-job or external), self-training, or non-formal learning. The acquisition of ICT skills/e-skills relies heavily on the strategic ability of the individual to have the basic knowledge, skills, and qualifications necessary to compete in the labor market. These knowledge, skills, and qualification are acquired through the various stages of formal education in schools, vocational training, universities, and so on. The essence of the above analogy was based on the understanding of the authors that, skills and knowledge cannot be acquired without following some of the routes or principles of formal or informal education, work experience, training (on-the-job or external), and self-training. It therefore means that knowledge and skills are fundamental in every sphere of human endeavors. They both work together, as someone could have knowledge about a particular thing but might not have the necessary skills to execute it. Skills are hidden compartments of knowledge and both can be acquired through diverse means.

In this study, the interpretive content analysis of documents/literature harvested from different databases of Scopus and Web of Science was considered. In doing this, the authors harvested literature or articles using key terms of 'knowledge', 'skills', and 'how they support teaching, learning, and research in HEIs. The selection of documents/articles in knowledge and skills was carried out within three weeks, thereafter, each of the articles was separated according to their different variables. The content analysis was performed by internalizing the discourse of the concept of knowledge and skills, bringing out findings that speak to how knowledge and skills were used to support teaching and learning, and research in HEIs.

3   Methodology Applied

The objective of the paper is to conceptualize how knowledge and skills of academics could be more in-depth such that, improving service delivery in teaching and learning and research in HEIs becomes a priority. The reason for this assertion is that many students have proven not to perform to expectation after graduating from HEIs. This results in many becoming half-baked in terms of having inadequate knowledge for application in service delivery in workplace learning. The half-baked graduates could be that they were not impacted by much knowledge and skills of the lecturer. This study employed interpretive content analysis of literature harvested from different online databases of Web of Science and Scopus. The literature harvested was harnessed using the following sub-themes of 'knowledge' and 'skills' and how they support teaching, learning, and research. The set of documents/articles was selected according to the themes and variables used in the study. These were the sub-themes through which the paper was developed. The research investigation which was developed for this study was carried out within three-week intervals by reading through the various articles harvested from the online databases. To strengthen the discussion surrounding knowledge and skills required in teaching and learning and research, the authors consulted over twenty research papers/articles in this study. There were a lot of commonalities and differences in what was found in the study through internalization of the interpretive content analysis of articles used in the study. [28] was of the view that interpretive content analysis is another important strategy used in most research investigations because it unveils hidden understanding that would have been difficult to find out ordinarily. Many researchers today now prefer to internalize the outcome of research already published since going about collecting data is not an easy task. Besides, many respondents do not even give room for them to interact in any research project.

4 Implication

In this study, there were a lot of commonalities and differences regarding how knowledge and skills become imperative in sustaining HEIs. The sustenance depends largely on in-depth knowledge and skills which academics possess in developing their module, tutorials lectures, and writing articles among other factors too numerous to mention. Knowledge and skills are required to execute activities that involve research, teaching, and learning due to how evolving the processes and practices is essential. Without it, no academics would be able to flourish, even amid the adequacy of material resources. The notion with those who no longer want to learn is that it is possible they are tired of being alive because, for every individual that is alive, the expectation is that, you must learn at one point or the other. The idea of reskilling is very important, as it helps to build an organizational culture so as to support individual growth and that of the organization. Another important factor that could propel one's knowledge and skills in competition. When there is no rival, it is expected that people or individuals would not be motivated to advance in their thoughts or imagination of acquiring more knowledge and skills required to function better in their job descriptions in the organization. Interestingly, acquired knowledge and skills of academics through formal and informal phase is believed to assist them in their personal career growth, where they become top scholars known globally in their areas of expertise. Most students who graduate with excellent grades in HEIs today result in how much impact, in terms of transfer of knowledge and skills on the subject/modules taught by the academics. There are scenarios where the academics/lecturer had to spoon-feed the students by engaging them through interactive and presentation approaches, group discussion, and giving of continuous assignments and term papers. These measures have helped both the students and academics/lecturers to have a better grasp of the modules taught. The reason for this approach was due to some students who are slow learners but require support in HEIs. The reason for the efficacy of knowledge and skills of academics/lecturers in HEIs is to showcase every confronting situation in the workplace, such that, the academics become more versatile and sounder in applying their knowledge and skills to execute appropriate teaching, learning, and research practices in HEIs. The authors of this paper believed that many students have demonstrated not to perform to expectations at the workplace learning after graduating from HEIs, due to their half-baked nature. The half-baked nature results in graduates not being well or fully impacted with much knowledge and skills of the academics/lecturer.

Several studies by [29–41] and [42] which lay claim to best practices on skills and knowledge application as essential components in diverse contexts and content, did not consider knowledge and skills of academics to be a critical success factor for organizational productivity in HEIs, hence the imperatives of this study. Knowledge and skills are required for work performed in the present-day organizational learning interface.

Academics possess a tacit type of knowledge, which has made them master the tricks of the game of teaching and learning, research, community engagement, and citizenship activities. Certain skills of search strategies to access online sources required for teaching, learning, and research; technical skills to use different systems; decision-making skills; change management skills; and evaluation of job performance, were enablers to academics. With this in mind, academics need to acquire certain tools of personal computers to ease their workflow even though they might have the ones they are using at the office.

The rationale that brought this assertion is that the authors of this paper reiterate that, based on personal experiences having worked in the university environment for over fourteen years, saw that especially in the context of Africa, some academics do not have suitable personal computers that would ease their workflow and the knowledge, skills, experience, exposure, and attitude in the performance of their job explanation, especially in areas of research, teaching, and learning. This could be more simplified in a scenario where academics who was supposed to teach a particular course/module do not have much content of the subject being taught. The authors of this paper have seen similar cases of academics/lecturers in HEIs not qualified to teach but were employed due to godfatherism and political influence. The reason is that they would do worse than expected because they do not have a passion for academic positions. Therefore, for any individual to become an academic/lecturer, there is a need to have passion for the profession and at the same be prepared to acquire adequate knowledge and skills for the job performance. Such knowledge and skills acquisition could be through attending formal and informal training like short courses, seminars, and conferences. The authors of this paper would like to note that, when academic knowledge and experience oppose the internal vision of HEIs, there is a tendency that, fitting into the HEI system would be difficult.

The use of experience and knowledge for teaching and learning and research can be accommodated when the mental cognitive of the user aligns with the outside world. This could be related to having more to do with the academics/lecturer, thus bringing the result of advanced considerable knowledge required to pass on to students in their learning process. Academics should act with the hope that their best in teaching and learning and research has a lot to do with the growth of the HEIs and students' academic performance. As academics remain steadfast in their learning curve, thus working towards the growth of the institution, there is the tendency that HEIs, will improve on their goal performance. The importance of knowledge and skills remain crucial in every organization, irrespective of the geographical location. Therefore, academics need to remain steadfast to act upon transforming the existing experiences and skills. Based on this analogy, the authors reinvigorate the drive for strengthening the acquisition of knowledge and skills of academics for organizational growth and enhanced teaching and learning and research regularly.

5 Conclusion

It was established from this study that, different articles consulted gave diverse views on which academics use knowledge and skills for teaching and learning, and research. Some of the factors identified in the articles consulted indicate the development of their modules, writing research papers/articles, execution of teaching and learning processes, disentangling uncertainty, presentation of papers in conferences, seminars, and workshops, socialization, and interactions, supporting students in their academic work and pursuit, solving the organizational problem and personal growth and development among others. The basic types of knowledge used by academics are tacit and explicit in the transformation of HEIs and personal growth in their career. It was further emphasized that certain skills of search strategies to access online sources cannot be devoid when it comes to teaching, learning, and research, as academics need all of these at all times even while updating their lecture notes. Another important skill is technical skills which are used in navigating diverse information systems, especially when facilitating and projecting substance in the classroom environment. Another form of skills includes change management skills; and evaluation of job performance, which allow academics to execute their responsibilities on daily basis. Amidst all these, High costs of personal computers and software required by academics to run their system are not easy to come by, because the expectation of using the library is not always there. Lack of support from some HEIs in Africa is rare due to constraints in budgetary allocation. The study recommends practical ongoing education to update academic knowledge and skills since current trends in the teaching profession have advanced in the most developed world, thus requiring the use of digital technologies.

References

1. Hunt, D.P.: The concept of knowledge and how to measure it. J. Intellect. Cap. **4**(1) (2003)
2. Petersen, A.W., et al.: ICT, and e-business skills and training in Europe: towards a comprehensive European e-skills reference framework: final synthesis report. Luxembourg (2005)
3. Castelli, A.: ICT practitioner skills and training: banking and financial services. Office for Official Publications of the European Communities, Luxembourg (2004) (Cedefop Panorama series, 95). http://www2.trainingvillage.gr/etv/publication/download/panorama/5151_en.pdf. Accessed 26 Jan 2022
4. Chigona, A., Chigona, W.: An investigation of factors affecting the use of ICT for teaching in the Western Cape schools. In: 18th European Conference on Information Systems (2010)
5. Pears, D.: What is Knowledge, pp. ix–106. Harper & Row, New York (1971)
6. SkillScan, Three types of skills classification (2012). http://www.skillscan.com/sites/default/files/Three%20Types%20of%20Skills%20Classification.pdf. Accessed 01 Sept 2021
7. O'Dell, C., Grayson, C.: If only we knew what we know: identification and transfer of internal best practices. Calif. Manag. Rev. **40**, 154–174 (1998). https://doi.org/10.2307/41165948
8. Sveiby, K.E.: The New Organizational Wealth: Managing and Measuring Knowledge Based Assets. Berett-Koehler Publisher, San Francisco (1997)
9. Ayer, A.J.: The Problem of Knowledge. Macmillan and Company, London (1958)
10. Agarwal, N.K., Poo, D.C.C.: Capturing tacit knowledge across different domains: knowledge community (K-Comm). In: Mitra, A. (ed.) Special Issue on KM. Int. J. Bus. Inf. Syst. **3**(6), 668–685 (2008). https://doi.org/10.1504/IJBIS.2008.018997
11. Zhang, X., Gao, S.: A study of the features and mechanism of knowledge innovation in university based on triple helix theory. Manag. Eng. **3**, 1838–5745 (2011)
12. O'dell, C., Hubert, C.: The New Edge in Knowledge: How Knowledge Management is Changing the Way We Do Business. Wiley, Hoboken (2011)
13. Kidwell, J., Linde, K., Johnson, S.: Applying corporate knowledge management practices in higher education. Educ. Q. **4**, 28–33 (2000)
14. Gill, A.: Knowledge management initiatives at a small university. Int. J. Educ. Manag. **23**(7), 604–616 (2009). https://doi.org/10.1108/09513540910990834

15. Alazmi, M., Zairi, M.: Knowledge management critical success factors. Total Quality Manag. Bus. Excell. **14**(2), 199–204 (2003)
16. Polanyi, M.: The Tacit Dimension. Routledge & Kegan Paul, London (1966)
17. Polanyi, M.: Knowing and Being. Chicago University Press, Marjorie Grene (1969)
18. Farnese, M.L., Barbieri, B.: Chirumbolo A and Patriotta G managing knowledge in organizations: a Nonaka's SECI model operationalization. Front. Psychol. **10**, 2730 (2019). https://doi.org/10.3389/fpsyg.2019.02730
19. Moffett, S., McAdam, R.: The effects of organizational size on knowledge management implementation: opportunities for small firms? Total Quality Implementation **17**(2), 221–241 (2006). https://doi.org/10.1080/14783360500450780
20. Mohayidin, M.G., Azirawani, N., Kamaruddin, M.N., Margono, M.L.: The application of knowledge management in enhancing the performance of malaysian universities. Electron. J. Knowl. Manag. **5**(3), 301–312 (2007)
21. OECD. ICT skills and employment. In OECD Information technology outlook 2004: Chapter 6 (2005). http://www.oecd.org/dataoecd/31/53/34238722.pdf
22. IFIP; OECD; WITSA. Meeting global IT skills needs: the role of professionalism: joint working conference. 25–27 October 2002. Gorse Hill Executive Centre. Woking: IFIP 2002. http://www.globalitskills.org/proceedings.pdf
23. Empirica. E-skills and e-security statistics: revised final draft prepared by Empirica for Eurostat. Bonn, Empirica (2002). http://www.empirica.biz/empirica/projekte/laufende-details_en.htm
24. Dixon, M.: Information technology practitioner skills in Europe: study of the labour market position, in particular for Germany, Ireland, Sweden and the United Kingdom. Frankfurt
25. ICT skills monitoring group. E-business and ICT skills in Europe: synthesis report. Brussels: European Commission (2002). http://europa.eu.int/comm/enterprise/ict/policy/ict-skills/wshop/synthesis-report-v1.pdf
26. Head, D., Raz, N., Gunning-Dixon, F., Williamson, A., Acker, J.D.: Age-related differences in the course of cognitive skill acquisition: the role of regional cortical shrinkage and cognitive resources. Psychol. Aging **17**(1), 72 (2002)
27. Behringer, F., Coles, M.: The Role of National Qualifications Systems in Promoting Lifelong Learning. OECD Education Working Papers, No. 3. 2003, OECD Publishing (NJ1)
28. Polanyi, M.: Personal Knowledge: Towards a Post-Critical Philosophy. University of Chicago Press, Chicago (1974)
29. Rastogi, A., Molhorta, S.: Determinants of ICT pedagogy integration. Society for Information Technology and Teacher Education International Conference. Association for the Advancement of Computing in Education (AACE), Chesapeake, VA (2012). http://www.editlib.org/p/40287
30. Kesdek, M., Yildirim, E.: Contribution to the knowledge of Carabidae fauna of Turkey. Part 5: Brachinini (Coleoptera: Carabidae, Brachininae). na. (2007)
31. Gulbahar, Y.: ICT Usage in Higher Education: A Case Study on Preservice Teacher and Instructions. Online Submission **7**(1) (2008)
32. Mumtaz, S.: Factors affecting teachers' use of information and communications technology: a review of the literature. J. Inf. Technol. Teach. Educ. **9**(3), 319–342 (2000)
33. Streep, P.: Confucius: The Wisdom, Bowker, Ingram, East Grinstead (1995)
34. Woodrow, J.E.: The influence of programming training on the computer literacy and attitudes of preservice teachers. J. Res. Comput. Educ. **25**(2), 200–219 (1992)
35. Yildirim, S.: Current utilization of ICT in Turkish basic education schools: a review of teacher's ICT use and barriers to integration. Int. J. Instr. Media **34**(2), 171–186 (2007)
36. Jimoyiannis, A., Komis, V.: Exploring secondary education teachers' attitudes and beliefs towards ICT adoption in education. Themes Educ. **7**(2), 181–204 (2006)

37. Ertmer, P.A., et al.: Professional development coaches: Perceptions of critical characteristics. J. School Leadersh. 15(1), 52–75 (2005)
38. Gobbo, C., Girardi, M.: Teachers' beliefs and integration of information and communications technology in Italian schools. J. Inf. Technol. Teach. Educ. 10(1–2), 63–85 (2001)
39. Gilakjani, A.P., Leong, L.M.: EFL. Teachers" attitudes toward using computer technology in English language teaching. Theory Pract. Lang. Stud. 2(3) (2012)
40. Bordbar, F.: English teachers' attitudes toward computer-assisted language learning. Int. J. Lang. Stud. 4(3), 27–54 (2010)
41. Chigona, A., Chigona, W.: An investigation of factors affecting the use of ICT for teaching in the Western Cape schools (2010)
42. Buabeng-Andoh, C.: An exploration of teachers' skills, perceptions and practices of ICT in teaching and learning in the Ghanaian second-cycle schools. Contemp. Educ. Technol. 3(1), 36–49 (2012)
43. Filstad, C.: Learning and knowledge as interrelations between CoPs and NoPs. The Learning Organization (2014)

Information Technology Outsourcing Success: A Knowledge Sharing Conceptual Model

Willem Pienaar and Hanlie Smuts[(⊠)] [iD]

Department of Informatics, University of Pretoria, Pretoria, South Africa
hanlie.smuts@up.ac.za

Abstract. There is an increasing dependency and spend on Information Technology (IT) by organisations to maintain a competitive edge in a digitised society. In order to optimise application of control and monitoring through computer-based algorithms, cognitive computing, on-demand availability of computing power and data storage, organisations make use of IT outsourcing (ITO). However, scholars report that organisations are failing to realise value from ITO, due to failure of ITO projects. Reasons for such failure are reported to be lack of future direction and requirements of the organisation, lack of top management support, poor cultural fit and wrongly selected ITO vendor. Therefore, the purpose of this study is to consider critical success factors (CSFs) for ITO projects. By considering such CSFs for ITO projects, organisations may focus on the specific knowledge sharing factors required to ensure project success. This study was conducted as a single case study in a regulatory financial services organisation. CSFs were identified from the literature and ranked according to importance by IT employees of the case study organisation. A conceptual model was proposed in support of organisations' ITO efforts.

Keywords: Information technology outsourcing · Critical success factors · Knowledge sharing · Conceptual model

1 Introduction

Organisations are increasingly dependent on IT, and, as a result, invest more in IT and in particular ITO as ITO allows the organisation to focus on its core business [1, 2] and enables organisations to gain access to technical expertise [3, 4]. Organisations are also looking for ways to cut IT costs due to limited capital to invest [5–7]. A longitudinal study conducted in The Netherlands regarding ITO deals found that only 18 out of 30 were successful [8]. A report by the Standish Group [9]. On average, only 16.2% of projects are delivered on time and within budget [9]. Controllable factors (things that can be changed in the early stages of the ITO process that influence project success were working according to a transition plan, demand management and communication at the ITO vendor [8].

Lack of success of ITO in recent years encouraged research to determine the knowledge sharing factors that influence ITO success [10]. Therefore, it would be highly

© Springer Nature Switzerland AG 2022
L. Uden et al. (Eds.): KMO 2022, CCIS 1593, pp. 25–40, 2022.
https://doi.org/10.1007/978-3-031-07920-7_3

beneficial for organisations to gain a better understanding of the factors in their environment that influence the success rate of ITO. The purpose of this study is firstly to identify the CSFs relevant to ITO in organisations, and secondly, to determine the importance ranking of CSFs. Hence, the research was guided by the following main research question: *"What are the critical success factors that influence ITO knowledge sharing in organisations?"* The CSFs were reported through creating a knowledge sharing conceptual model for ITO that may assist organisations to create ITO awareness and focus on the particular knowledge sharing factors that would support ITO implementation success.

In Sect. 2 we present the background to the study followed by the research approach in Sect. 3. Section 4 details the data analysis and findings, while Sect. 5 concludes the paper.

2 Background

Organisations are searching for ways to grow and maintain their competitive edge by using ITO, as a global business practice, strategically in order to achieve their goals [3, 11]. The market value for ITO is increasing and more organisations are deciding to outsource some, or all of their IT operations and responsibilities [5]. Even though ITO is a well-established and large market, a considerable amount of failed projects can be witnessed [4].

In the next sections we consider ITO as a business phenomenon and the application of CSFs in an ITO context, as well as ITO processes.

2.1 Information Technology Outsourcing

ITO can be defined as "a long-term contractual arrangement in which one or more service providers are assigned the responsibility of managing all or part of a client's information systems (IS) infrastructure and operations" [5: 1052]. According to research, reasons to outsource include focusing on strategic issues, increasing the IT department's flexibility, improving quality, getting rid of routine tasks, getting access to new technology, renewing technology, staff costs saving [4, 6]. Other reasons include technology costs saving, access to alternate IT resources and joining the global trend [6]. Internal IT operations, not part of the organisation's core competency, are outsourced in an effort to cope with constant technological evolution and constant increase of internal IT competence [12, 13].

The decision to outsource involves many factors, categorised as internal and external [14]. Internal determinants refer to factors where the source is internal to the organisation, while external determinants refer to factors external to the organisation [14]. The internal motivation to outsource includes cost reduction, allowing the organisation to focus on its core capabilities, gaining access to skills or expertise, and improving business processes [4, 14]. Other ITO relationship determinants include top management support, trust, commitment, cooperation, communication quality, and knowledge and information sharing [4]. External determinants, include IT labour shortage, volatility in the IT job market and labour costs. Industry factors include market influence, supplier competition and industry maturity, while sociocultural external factors point to language, cultural distance and ethnocentrism (judging another culture based on one's own) [14]. Other external ITO factors include regulations and restrictions, intellectual property rights, legal and political uncertainty, sustainability and the human environmental impact [14].

2.2 Knowledge Sharing Critical Success Factors in the Context of ITO

A CSF is a set of key areas of activity that yields favourable results specific to a certain goal [15, 16] and is a mechanism to ensure success when applied [17]. It includes factors that influence the ITO relationship between the organisation and ITO vendor and affects or determines outsourcing relationships and their outcome [4]. Risks may arise in the organisations-vendor relationship such as cultural incompatibility and a low degree of shared values and goals [18, 19]. Other reported risks include the loss of technical knowledge in the organisation, underqualified vendor staff, weak partnership management, hidden costs, not a value-for-money relationship, low security and possible organisational staff resistance [12]. In terms of the ITO contract management, insufficient formal warranties, lack of a communication plan, unclear statements about objectives, processes and timelines are highlighted as risks [12]. The risk of ineffective coordination and knowledge transfer relates to the lack of adequate relevant information availability [12, 20].

In the context of ITO, knowledge is transferred beyond organisational boundaries and knowledge from different organisations interacts to create new knowledge [21]. Through a process of dynamic interaction, knowledge created by the organisation can trigger the mobilisation of knowledge held by the ITO vendor, which in turn triggers a new round of product and process innovation in the organisation [21]. A broad range of mechanisms is employed by organisations to facilitate knowledge transfer with ITO vendors, and organisations with both explicit and tacit knowledge transfer processes exhibit higher levels of shared knowledge than organisations utilising only one of the processes [22].

2.3 ITO Processes

Many scholars have attempted to understand ITO processes [23–27]. Alborz et al. [25] proposed 3 phases: architect (scoping, business case compilation, design and outsourcing requirements), engage (ITO vendor procurement process) and govern (outsource contract management and agreement deliverables) [25]. Chou & Chou [24] suggested 3 phases: pre-contract (focuses on identifying the need to outsource, planning and strategy setting and selecting an ITO vendor), contract (contracting, transitioning and execution of the ITO project) and post-contract (assesses the success of the ITO and gives input to a decision whether to renew the contract or look for a new ITO vendor) [24]. The model proposed by Perunovic & Pedersen [26], contained 5 phases, namely preparation (should the organisation consider ITO), vendor selection (procurement and ITO partner selection), transition (vendor takes over service delivery), managing relationship (communication, service level agreement, performance management) and reconsideration (reviews options to extend or terminate). Lee et al. [27] recommended 7 steps, make-or-buy dilemma, motivation, scope, performance, insource or outsource, formal contract, and informal partnership. For the purpose of this study, we followed the 3-step model [24], to report the findings from this study.

3 Research Approach

The overall objective of this paper was to understand the particular factors that would support ITO implementation success in organisations. In order to achieve this outcome, an interpretive, single case study was used in the development of the proposed conceptual ITO model and ranking of CSFs [28–30]. The case study [31] organisation is a regulatory financial services organisation that adopted a strategy of using technical partners to supplement internal IT resources or completely outsource IT. The technical partners consist of multiple vendors. At the time of the study, multiple outsourcing agreements were in effect, providing an ideal environment to consider CSFs for ITO. Two data collection methods were applied for this paper. Firstly, CSFs were identified through a systematic literature review (SLR), where after an online questionnaire was used to collect respondent opinions and CSF ranking as perceived in the case study organisation.

A literature search in academic databases and peer-reviewed sources was performed with the keywords "information technology outsourcing" and "critical success factors". The search returned 1270 results that was screened based on title and abstract. Results with "critical success factors" or "success" and "IT outsourcing" in the title, and English journal articles and conference proceedings were considered. Fifty-one papers were identified from the initial screening where after 21 papers that specifically dealt with CSFs were identified for analysis. A list of CSFs for ITO was compiled using the descriptions from the identified literature (Data set extract A.1 in the Appendix). Axial coding was used on the complete list of CSFs to identify emerging themes [30] as illustrated in the extract for one theme shown in Table 1.

Table 1. Knowledge management theme after coding process

CSF for knowledge management theme	N	CSF for knowledge management theme	N
Knowledge sharing	9	Market knowledge	1
Retain key knowledge	3	Knowledge of the various cost factors	1
Knowledge repository	2	Knowledge of service level agreements	1
Knowledge of organisation	3	Knowledge of required scope of outsourcing	1
Knowledge of operations	3	Knowledge of outsource model risk	1
Supplier knowledge	1	Knowledge infrastructure	1
Negotiation skills and knowledge of negotiation position	1	Bidirectional transfer of knowledge	1
		Knowledge management theme total	**29**

In Table 2, an overview is provided of the CSF themes identified through the coding process. For each theme a brief description is provided as well as the total frequency count contribution of CSFs to that theme. The themes and CSFs obtained were utilised to design a questionnaire to facilitate the second step in the research approach i.e. to collect the opinion of IT resources in the case study organisation and to rank the CSFs. The questionnaire consisted of an introduction, consent, respondent demographic information and the questions divided into sections - each section represented a CSF theme and CSF questions. Respondents had to indicate the importance of the CSF statements according to a scale ranging from 1 (not important) to 5 (critical). A final open-ended question at each section and at the end of the questionnaire, enabled respondents to provide comments with regard to CSFs for ITO in general. Research study participants were selected based on their involvement with ITO, and the type of work performed, which represented different roles and different corporate levels within the case study organisation. The questionnaire was self-administered, and was distributed in an electronic format over the internet. Fifty-nine questionnaires were distributed and 43 questionnaires were completed, yielding a response rate of 72%.

Table 2. Total number of themes identified

	Theme	Description	Count	
1	People	People-themed CSFs, e.g. trust, cultural awareness, skills, shared values, shared principles	54	19%
2	Business	Business-themed CSFs, e.g. quality production, success ITO track record, degree of ITO	47	16%
3	Management	Management-themed CSFs, e.g. effective ITO relationship management, management support	44	15%
4	Strategy	Strategy-themed CSFs, e.g. commitment, continuous improvement, win-win strategy	33	11%
5	Knowledge management	Knowledge management-themed CSFs, e.g. knowledge sharing, knowledge of operations	29	10%
6	Financial	Financial-themed CSFs, e.g. minimise IT costs, sufficient funding, value-for-money relationship	23	8%
7	Communication	Communication-themed CSFs, e.g. ongoing effective communication, frequent engagements	19	7%
8	Technology	Technology-themed CSFs, e.g. appropriate infrastructure, utilisation of proper tools	14	5%
9	Security	Security-themed CSFs, e.g. vendor governance mechanism, security assurance, protection of knowledge	8	3%
10	Legal	Legal-themed CSFs, e.g. proper contract, structuring, contract flexibility, properly structured contract	7	2%

(continued)

Table 2. (*continued*)

	Theme	Description	Count	
11	Project	Project-themed CSFs, e.g. sensitivity to needs of stakeholders, ITO vendor responsiveness, compile detailed plan, advertising	5	2%
12	Regulatory	Regulatory-themed CSFs, e.g. tax allows remote work, customs laws support overseas work	3	1%
13	Political	Political-themed CSFs, e.g. political stability, travel restrictions	2	1%
	Total number of knowledge sharing CSFs identified through SLR		288	

The profile of respondents are summarised in Table 3. The –3 respondents consisted of 2 members of senior management, 13 management members and 27 technical specialists. In terms of the profile of the respondents related to the number of years' IT experience, 36 respondents (84%) had 12 or more years' IT experience. In general, the sample was very experienced in IT and ITO, and could influence ITO at a decision-making level. The quantitative data provided by the respondents was analysed using statistical analysis to determine the mean, mode and median and the CSFs were ranked according to the highest mean. Table 4 shows the 12 highest-ranking CSFs for ITO based on the feedback provided by the respondents, presenting the theme, CSF, mean, median and mode. Quality production was the highest-ranked CSF, followed by trust and knowledgeable resources.

Table 3. Respondent profile

Years of IT experience	Count		Years of ITO experience	Count		Job level	Count	
1–5	1	2%	1–3	11	26%	IT Specialist	24	56%
8–11	6	14%	3–5	5	12%	Management	13	30%
11+	36	84%	5–7	6	14%	Senior management	2	5%
			7+	21	49%	FC upper	1	2%
						Functional contributor	1	2%
						Intermediate	1	2%
						Software developer	1	2%

Table 4. Top 12 ranked knowledge sharingCSFs for ITO based on respondent feedback

Rank	Theme	Critical success factor	Mean	Median	Mode
1	Business	Quality production	4.70	5	5
2	People	Trust	4.63	5	5
3	People	Knowledgeable resources	4.56	5	5
4	Management	Performance monitoring	4.49	5	5
5	Strategy	Commitment	4.44	5	5
6	Strategy	Vendor selection process	4.44	5	5
7	People	Technical skills	4.42	5	5
8	Management	Poor performance consequence	4.37	4	4
9	Knowledge management	Knowledge repository	4.37	5	5
10	Management	Efficient relationship management	4.26	4	5
11	Knowledge management	Knowledge sharing	4.26	4	5
12	Financial	Value-for-money relationship	4.26	4	5

The open-ended questions feedback was analysed through thematic analysis with regard to CSFs for ITO in general (Data extract Table A.2 in the Appendix). The respondents listed the following CSFs for the people-themed open-ended question: close relationship, correct skills, share skills, goals oriented, understanding goals, fulfil contractual obligation, agreed-upon scope, scope flexibility, preference of local ITO vendor and take accountability. The organisation should have a close relationship with the vendor. The ITO vendor should have the correct skills, and should be willing to share those skills with the organisation. There should be a goals-oriented approach. The ITO vendor should also understand the ITO goals. For the business-themed open-ended questions, respondents listed the costing model and defined benefits as additional CSFs. "*The costing model and benefits should be outlined clearly,*" a respondent stated. For the management-themed CSFs, six respondents stressed that a service-level agreement (SLA) should be in place. A respondent mentioned that an "*SLA should be discussed upfront*". The setting of timelines and milestones was also mentioned under this theme. For knowledge management, only one additional CSF was mentioned, namely collaboration: "*Collaboration is key for successful implementation,*" the respondent stated. A cost-benefit analysis was the only additional financial-themed CSF mentioned. Frequent communication, open communication and communication to relevant stakeholders was the additional communication-themed CSF mentioned. With the technology-themed open-ended question, the respondents felt strongly that organisation-led technology direction and security can be added to the list of CSFs. General comments about ITO included previously mentioned CSFs like common goals, quality service, selective ITO, no operational issues, SLA in place, relationship management, knowledge sharing, IT cost savings, strategy, knowledge management, ITO vendor dependency and ITO vendor product support.

The study set out to determine which knowledge sharing CSFs influence the success rate of ITO and to propose a conceptual model for CSFs for ITO. In order to report the findings, the 3-step model (Chou & Chou.) consisting of the pre-contract phase, the contract phase and the post-contract phase (Sect. 2.3) were used to map the 12 highest ranked CSFs from the questionnaire, depicted in Fig. 1. Mapping was done by considering in which phase the specific CSF is relevant based on the definition of the particular phase.

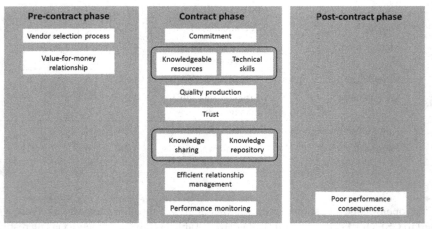

Fig. 1. Knowledge sharing CSF conceptual model for ITO based on the SLR and respondent feedback

The proposed conceptual model presents three phases. The pre-contract stage includes the vendor selection process and the value-for-money relationship CSF. The contract phase starts with commitment from the ITO vendor and the organisation, followed by knowledgeable resources assigned to the ITO project running parallel with the technical skills of the knowledgeable resources. With technical skills, quality production is possible. Quality production brings trust to the ITO relationship. Knowledge sharing and repository follow. The relationship should be managed efficiently, and the ITO vendor's performance should be monitored. Finally, poor performance should have a consequence. The ITO contract should be renewed or the organisation should seek a new ITO vendor with which to partner.

Vendor Selection Process: Before the ITO service agreement can be signed, a proper vendor selection process should be followed to ensure that the right vendor is selected. The organisation should "undertake a due diligence on itself to understand, quantify and qualify its outsourcing needs before starting with a request for information" [32: 24] to make the vendor selection process easier for the organisation.

A respondent felt that *"appointments are done too easily"*, and another felt that the ITO vendor resources should go through a thorough interview process. Another note was made that some ITO vendor resources are selected without the proper selection criteria, and continue to provide a service. This is clearly an instance where the CSF is not performed at the right time, and will ultimately lead to failure.

Value-for-Money Relationship: Before the organisation decides to proceed with the ITO agreement, the proposed ITO relationship should be seen as good value for money. A respondent mentioned that *"it is a misconception that outsourcing is cheaper. It often turns out to be more expensive"*. Another comment was that the organisation is *"paying too much"*. *"Value for money is non-negotiable"* was commented by another respondent. The ITO vendor should deliver quality to the organisation. In order for the ITO vendor to deliver value to the organisation there should be trust, confidence, clear objectives and regular performance monitoring [33]. The clear objectives form part of the due diligence the organisation has to go through before ITO to understand, quantify and qualify the organisation's ITO needs.

Commitment: Once an agreement is signed with the selected ITO vendor following the vendor selection process, the organisation and the ITO vendor must commit to a long-term relationship. This commitment should exceed the mere contractual obligations stated in the signed ITO agreement. This commitment should be long term and both the organisation and the ITO vendor must *"collaboratively work towards shared goals, while sharing both risks and rewards"* [34]. Commitment will lead to the success of ITO [35]. There will be delays in the ITO project if the ITO vendor does not show commitment [35].

Knowledgeable Resources: The organisation benefits from the ITO vendor, using the vendor's knowledgeable resources. "Knowledge skills of outsourced workers (read, write well, good overall knowledge of processes and work) support the ability of the company to do work" [36: 31]. It is not just the ITO vendor resources that should be knowledgeable, but the organisation's contact as well, in order to communicate the requirements to the ITO vendor [36]. The ITO vendor should provide technical knowledge or resources if the knowledge cannot be found internally. A respondent noted that some ITO vendors *"often send amateurs"*. This is definitely reason for concern, and can lead to the failure of ITO projects.

Technical Expertise: The organisation should benefit from the variety of technical expertise the ITO vendor offers. "There are many outsourced resources that do not have special skills and do not understand the business", and this should be avoided. A respondent noted that *"skills should be transferred continuously"*. Technical expertise contributes to the success of the ITO relationship [37]. The success of ITO might be affected if the right technical expertise is not available. As noted by a respondent, sometimes the ITO vendor cannot provide technical expertise with business knowledge.

Quality Production: *"Quality delivered should be high"*, *"business service provided by the outsourcer needs to be of a high quality"*, *"vendor needs to deliver quality and within the time frames"*, *"quality and timeous deliverables are more important than time management"* and *"the drivers for outsourcing are of utmost importance as the contract at the end should not compromise quality"* were some of the comments made by respondents that relate to quality production. Quality production was the highest-ranked CSFs, thus was considered the most important CSF. Quality management should ensure a quality product, service, resources and infrastructure [38].

Trust: Trust is earned when the ITO vendor delivers a quality product. The trust should also be mutual. One respondent stated that *"the relationship between the two companies will be very strong if the outsourcing company is seen as a trusted advisor by the client organisation"*. Other comments include *"trust, skills and shared values are pivotal to a good relationship"*, *"people should be trustworthy and trusted, share values and principles, and be reliable"*, *"the two parties need to build a professional trust relationship"* and *"trust is key and should be matured for the vendor's longevity"*. The organisation should have confidence in the ITO vendor's reliability and integrity [35]. Many failures are reported due to a lack of trust [35].

Knowledge Sharing and Knowledge Repository: Skills transfer in the form of knowledge sharing and creating a knowledge repository is important for the ITO agreement to continue. A respondent stated that *"there needs to be a commitment to knowledge sharing in the organisation and with the partners. Projects should not be signed off if high-quality business and technical documentation does not exist"*. Another respondent stated that there should be tangible evidence. This tangible evidence should be in the form of a knowledge repository. Another felt that *"the extent of knowledge sharing and approach are then of the utmost importance"*. Knowledge sharing is important for the success of ITO [35].

Efficient Relationship Management: The ITO vendor and organisation should effectively manage the relationship. The organisation *"should have a very close relationship with the vendor"*, and *"there must be a working relationship between the two parties"*. Another respondent noted that *"trust, skills and shared values are pivotal to a good relationship"*. Efficient relationship management is important for the success of ITO [39].

Performance Monitoring: The performance of the ITO vendor should be monitored and *"communication should be used not only to share objectives, but to provide feedback on the ITO's performance or lack thereof"*. Performance monitoring provides input to the final phase and *"without proper monitoring, the vendor could deliberately waste time in delivering the product or service required; which could result in additional costs"*. The ITO service needs regular performance monitoring in order to deliver value to the organisation [33, 40].

Poor Performance Consequence: Poor performance should have a consequence. A respondent noted that "_if there is no evidence of knowledge transfer, then the IT vendor should be deemed as 'failed' and its contract should not be renewed._" There should also be an incentive for performance that exceeds expectation. The ITO agreement should be terminated if the ITO vendor did not perform according to expectation. One respondent said that "_there are no consequences and something should be put in place if a contractor/consultant does not deliver to the standards_". Another respondent noted that some ITO vendors do not perform, but there is no consequence. This is definitely reason for concern, and can lead to critical factors for ITO project failure. The organisation should impose penalties to motivate the ITO vendor if its performance is low [32].

We applied the proposed conceptual model in a proof of concept. The application and subsequent findings of the ITO conceptual model application are discussed in the next section.

4   Application of the Conceptual Model

The aim of this study was to consider knowledge sharing CSFs for ITO projects and propose a conceptual model. By applying the conceptual model, IT resources involved in ITO may influence the success rate of ITO. In order to collect feedback on the application of the conceptual model, one of the ITO project management teams of the case study organisation was requested to consider how it may be applied. The case study organisation's ITO project management team referenced one of their ITO projects and used a typical red-amber-green (RAG) status tracking to consider the proposed conceptual model. According to the organisation's RAG status application, the top four CSFs to be addressed have a red status, the next four have an amber status, and the last four have a green status as depicted in Fig. 2.

The areas for concern are highlighted after applying the RAG status to the conceptual model. CSFs for immediate action (the red CSFs) include knowledgeable resources, quality production, trust and performance monitoring. The organisation should act on these CSFs first. CSFs with less concern (the amber CSFs) include the vendor selection process, commitment, technical skills and poor performance. The organisation should focus on these CSFs once the red CSFs have been addressed. The CSFs of least concern (the green CSFs) include a value-for-money relationship, knowledge sharing, knowledge repository and efficient relationship management. These can be addressed last. All 12 CSFs are regarded as important, but the RAG status application prioritised the CSFs to be addressed first.

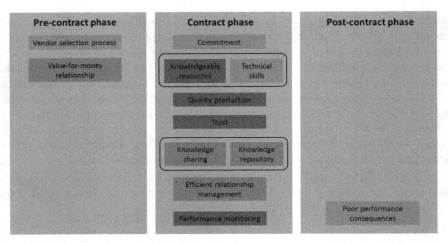

Fig. 2. ITO project team application of the knowledge sharing conceptual model

The proposed knowledge sharing conceptual model may be applied from two perspectives. Firstly, the model guides decision makers through each phase of the ITO in terms of what particular aspects to address to achieve better ITO results. Secondly, by applying the model to an existing project, an indicative prioritisation of the key aspects to be addressed may be derived.

5 Conclusion

The study set out to determine which knowledge sharing CSFs influence the success rate of ITO in the regulatory financial services sector, and proposed a conceptual model of the highest ranked CSFs for ITO. The CSFs were derived through an SLR process where after the identified CSFs were ranked by respondents in the case study organisation. The CSF for ITO that was regarded as the most important was quality production within the business theme. In order to report the ranked CSFs, the top 12 CSFs were considered and mapped to the 3 phases of ITO according to Chou and Chou (year). An exemplary presentation as instantiation of the proposed conceptual model was also presented, showing which specific CSF to be addressed first in order to focus on ITO success.

As this study was concluded in a single case study environment, further research is required to generalise the findings. Research with a focus on the quality management of ITO can also be done within the organisation, since quality production was identified as the highest-ranking CSF for ITO. Research can also be expanded to include the phase before vendor selection that focuses on scoping, business case compilation, design and outsourcing requirements.

Appendix

Table A1. SLR execution – CSF identification (extract only)

[36] Jennex, M. & Adelakun, O., 2003. Success factors for offshore information system development. *Journal of Information Technology Case and Application Research*, 5(3), pp. 12–31

Theme	CSF	Description
People	Knowledgeable resources	"Knowledge skills of outsource workers (read, write well, good overall knowledge of processes and work) support ability of company to do work"
Communication	Communication language	"Language skills of outsource workers (know the language of the client) support ability of company to do work with other nations"
People	Cultural awareness	"Cultural awareness of outsource workers (understand the culture of the client and how it differs from yours)"
Management	Management people	"Project management people skills (managers know how to manage workers and users)"

[41] Khan, S. U., Niazi, M. & Ahmad, R., 2011. Factors influencing clients in the selection of offshore software outsourcing vendors: An exploratory study using a systematic literature review. *Journal of Systems and Software*, 84(4), pp. 686–699

Theme	Critical success factor	Description
Technology	Appropriate infrastructure	
Business	Company size	
Security	Protection of knowledge	
Management	Efficient contract management	
Management	Efficient relationship management	
Management	Efficient project management	
Financial	Sufficient Funding	"Financial stability"

Table A.2. Analysis of qualitative comments (extract only)

Respondent	Any comments with regards to the People (e.g. trust, cultural awareness, skills, shared values, shared principles) component of IT outsourcing	Emerging CSF
3.	The employees in the organisation that will be outsourcing should have a very close relationship with the vendor, for the purpose of maintenance after the service has been rendered	- Close relationship
5.	It is important to get vendors with the correct skills and whom are willing to share their skills with permanent employees of the company	- Correct skills - Share skills
9.	People skills should be up to date	- People skills
10.	There should be a mutual trust between the two parties. The skill set that the vendor is assigning to the contract should be able to meet the clients need. The values and principles can always be adopted as and when required	- Mutual trust - Shared values and principles
11.	There should be a common level of understanding or goals-oriented approach between an organisation and its vendors	- Goals oriented - Understanding goals

References

1. Mohiuddin, M., Su, Z.: Offshore outsourcing of core and non-core activities and integrated firm-level performance: an empirical analysis of Québec manufacturing SMEs. M@n@gement **16**(4), 454–478 (2013)
2. Yu, T.-Y.: An empirical study of collaborative partnering among enterprises and government organizations for information system outsourcing. Appl. Econ. **46**(3), 312–322 (2014)
3. Alexandrova, M.: IT outsourcing partnerships: empirical research on key success factors in Bulgarian organizations. Manag. J. Contemp. Manag. Issues **17**(2), 31–50 (2012)
4. Vorontsova, A., Rusu, L.: Determinants of IT outsourcing relationships: a recipient–provider perspective. Procedia Technol. **16**, 588–597 (2014)
5. Chang, Y.B., Gurbaxani, V.: Information technology outsourcing, knowledge transfer, and firm productivity: an empirical analysis. MIS Q. 1043–1063 (2012)
6. González, R., Gascó, J., Llopis, J.: Information systems outsourcing reasons and risks: review and evolution. J. Glob. Inf. Technol. Manag. **19**(4), 223–249 (2016)
7. Jafari, S.M.: Strategic cost-cutting in information technology: toward a framework for enhancing the business value of IT (2014)
8. Delen, G.P., et al.: Lessons from Dutch IT-outsourcing success and failure. Sci. Comput. Program. **130**, 37–68 (2016)
9. Standish Group: The Standish Group Report-CHAOS. The Standish Group (2019)
10. Gonzalez, R., Gasco, J., Llopis, J.: Information systems outsourcing: an empirical study of success factors. Hum. Syst. Manag. **29**(3), 139–151 (2010)
11. Mann, A., et al.: Spatial and temporal trends in information technology outsourcing. Appl. Geogr. **63**, 192–203 (2015)

12. Alexandrova, M.: Risk factors in IT outsourcing partnerships: vendors' perspective. Glob. Bus. Rev. **16**(5), 747–759 (2015)
13. Kivijärvi, H., Toikkanen, J.: Measuring the business value of IT outsourcing: a systems approach. Strateg. Outsourcing: Int. J. (2015)
14. Rajaeian, M.M., Cater-Steel, A., Lane, M.: IT outsourcing decision factors in research and practice: a case study. arXiv preprint arXiv:1606.01454 (2016)
15. Alazmi, M., Zairi, M.: Knowledge management critical success factors. Total Qual. Manag. Bus. Excell. **14**(2), 199–204 (2003)
16. Rockart, J.F.: The changing role of the information systems executive: a critical success factors perspective (1980)
17. Munro, M.C., Wheeler, B.R.: Planning, critical success factors, and management's information requirements. MIS Q. 27–38 (1980)
18. e Silva, L.C., et al.: Analysis of IT outsourcing services failures based on an existing risk model. In: 2015 IEEE International Conference on Systems, Man, and Cybernetics. IEEE (2015)
19. Lin, T., Vaia, G.: The concept of governance in IT outsourcing: a literature review (2015)
20. Gorla, N., Somers, T.M.: The impact of IT outsourcing on information systems success. Inf. Manag. **51**(3), 320–335 (2014)
21. Nonaka, I., Toyama, R., Byosiere, P.: A theory of organisational knowledge creation: understanding the dynamic process of creating knowledge. In: Dierkes, M., et al. (eds.) Handbook of Organizational Learning & Knowledge, pp. 491–517. Oxford University Press, New York (2001)
22. Blumenberg, S., Wagner, H., Beimborn, D.: Knowledge transfer processes in IT outsourcing relationships and their impact on shared knowledge and outsourcing performance. Int. J. Inf. Manag. **29**, 342–352 (2009)
23. Moon, J., et al.: Innovation in IT outsourcing relationships: where is the best practice of IT outsourcing in the public sector? Innovation **12**(2), 217–226 (2010)
24. Chou, D.C., Chou, A.Y.: Information systems outsourcing life cycle and risks analysis. Comput. Stand. Interfaces **31**(5), 1036–1043 (2009)
25. Alborz, S., Seddon, P., Scheepers, R.: A model for studying IT outsourcing relationships. In: 7th Pacific Asia Conference on Information Systems. Adelaide, South Australia (2003)
26. Perunovic, Z., Pedersen, J.L.: Outsourcing process and theories. In: Proceedings of the 18th Annual Conference of the Production and Operations Management Society, Dallas, Texas (2007)
27. Lee, J., et al.: The evolution of outsourcing research: what is the next issue? In: Proceedings of the 33rd Annual Hawaii International Conference on System Sciences, Maui, Hawaii. IEEE (2000)
28. Oates, B.J.: Researching Information Systems and Computing. Sage, Thousand Oaks (2005)
29. Saunders, M., Lewis, P., Thornhill, A.: Research Methods for Business Students. Pearson Education, London (2009)
30. Leedy, P.D., Ormrod, J.E.: Practical Research: Planning and Design, 10th edn. Pearson Education Limited, New Jersey (2014)
31. Yin, R.K.: Case Study Research Design and Methods. Sage, Thousand Oaks (2014)
32. Hodosi, G., Rusu, L.: How do critical success factors contribute to a successful IT outsourcing: a study of large multinational companies. J. Inf. Technol. Theory Appl. **14**(1), 17–43 (2013)
33. Smuts, H., et al.: Threats and opportunities for information systems outsourcing. In: 2015 International Conference on Enterprise Systems (ES). IEEE (2015)
34. Ali, S., Khan, S.U.: Critical success factors for software outsourcing partnership (SOP): a systematic literature review. In: 2014 IEEE 9th International Conference on Global Software Engineering. IEEE (2014)

35. Qi, C., Chau, P.Y.: Relationship, contract and IT outsourcing success: evidence from two descriptive case studies. Decis. Support Syst. **53**(4), 859–869 (2012)
36. Jennex, M.E., Adelakun, O.: Success factors for offshore information system development. J. Inf. Technol. Case Appl. Res. **5**(3), 12–31 (2003)
37. Blaskovich, J., Mintchik, N.: Information technology outsourcing: a taxonomy of prior studies and directions for future research. J. Inf. Syst. **25**(1), 1–36 (2011)
38. Khan, A.W., Khan, S.U.: Critical success factors for offshore software outsourcing contract management from vendors' perspective: an exploratory study using a systematic literature review. IET Softw. **7**(6), 327–338 (2013)
39. Moon, J., et al.: IT outsourcing success in the public sector: lessons from e-government practices in Korea. Inf. Dev. **32**(2), 142–160 (2016)
40. Smuts, H., et al.: Critical success factors for information systems outsourcing management: a software development lifecycle view. In: Proceedings of the 2010 Annual Research Conference of the South African Institute of Computer Scientists and Information Technologists (2010)
41. Khan, S.U., Niazi, M., Ahmad, R.: Factors influencing clients in the selection of offshore software outsourcing vendors: an exploratory study using a systematic literature review. J. Syst. Softw. **84**(4), 686–699 (2011)

Critical Obstacles of Knowledge Sharing in Organizational Knowledge Management System from an Exploratory Case Study

Eric Kin Wai Lau[✉]

Lee Shau Kee School of Business & Administration, Hong Kong Metropolitan University, Kowloon, Hong Kong
ekwlau@hkmu.edu.hk

Abstract. The paper begins with a brief review of previous empirical studies on knowledge sharing. Then, it presents a business case study in China where a KM system is poorly implemented. Three main research questions identified in the next phase of the quantitative study. This paper also lessons to other organizations to implement their KM system effectively.

Keywords: Knowledge sharing · Knowledge management system · Top management support · Business case study

1 Introduction

Managing organizational knowledge is important in every organization [1]. According to Garg, Pandey and Vashisht, "The management of knowledge is promoted as an important and necessary factor for organisational survival and maintenance of competitive strength" [2]. Knowledge management consists of knowledge acquisition, knowledge conversion and knowledge application [3]. Therefore, information technology (IT) can help to facilitate organizational knowledge management (KM). Frappaolo and Capshaw identified those four basic functions of KM system as intermediation, externalization, internalization, and cognition [4]. Interestingly, Brown, Dennis, Burley and Arling appreciated the person-to-person transfer of knowledge than the organizational knowledge management system [5].

It is important to assess the knowledge sharing behaviors in organizations. The paper begins with the review of previous empirical studies on organizational knowledge sharing. The second section of this paper discusses a business case of knowledge share and identifies some obstacles of the IT based KM system implementation. Finally, the paper concludes with the theoretical and managerial implications.

2 The Importance of Organizational Knowledge Sharing

In today's highly competitive business environments, knowledge sharing is a key for the success of organization as it helps gaining the competitiveness [6]. Defined by Davenport

© Springer Nature Switzerland AG 2022
L. Uden et al. (Eds.): KMO 2022, CCIS 1593, pp. 41–48, 2022.
https://doi.org/10.1007/978-3-031-07920-7_4

and Prusak, knowledge is "A fluid mix of framed experience, values, contextual information, and expert insight that provides a framework for evaluating and incorporating new experiences and information. It originates and is applied in the minds of knowers" [7]. Knowledge, therefore, is created, stored and processed with individual employee in organization.

Knowledge sharing in an organization becomes the most important element of the knowledge management. Accordingly to Paulin and Suneson, knowledge sharing is "An exchange of knowledge between two individuals: one who communicates knowledge and one who assimilates it. In knowledge sharing, the focus is on human capital and the interaction of individuals. Strictly speaking, knowledge can never be shared. Because it exists in a context; the receiver interprets it in the light of his or her own background" [8]. Lehesvirta found that it is necessary for individuals to appreciate the importance of their knowledge sharing in the learning processes [9]. Radaelli, Mura, Spiller and Lettieri found that knowledge-sharing climate in an organization is important for knowledge-sharing behavior [10]. Wickramasinghe and Widyaratne constructed a research model and proposed that interpersonal trust, team leader support, rewards and knowledge sharing mechanisms have positive effects on knowledge sharing [11]. With a sample of 150 employees in different software development firms, they found that interpersonal trust and rewards have significant positive effect on knowledge sharing.

Knowledge sharing culture is another important domain for organizations to investigate [12]. Yasir and Majid tried to investigate those enablers for the trust in organizational knowledge sharing [13]. With a sample of 1036 Pakistan respondents, they found that top management support, organizational culture, KM system quality and openness in communication have positive association between trust and knowledge sharing. Similarly, Ouakouak and Ouedraogo also tested the affective commitment, continuance commitment, personal trust and professional trust on the knowledge sharing [14]. With a sample of 307 Canadian employees, they found that affective commitment and professional trust have significant impacts on knowledge sharing.

In a recent study, Ouakouak, AlBuloushi, Ouedraogo & Sawalha identified factors that affect knowledge sharing [15]. With a sample of 237 bank employees in Kuwait, receiver's openness to receive knowledge and their openness to share knowledge have positive and significant relationships with their knowledge-sharing behavior.

Information technology can facilitate knowledge sharing in organizations [16]. In an earlier study, Bart and de Ridder suggested that computer-mediated communication is important in the knowledge sharing processes [17]. Refer to the definition by Buckland, "a key characteristics of "information-as-knowledge" (knowledge is that it is intangible: one cannot touch it or measure it in any direct way. Knowledge, belief, and opinion are personal, subjective, and conceptual. Therefore, to communicate them, they have to be expressed, described, or represented in some physical way, as a signal, text, or communication. Any such expression, description or representation would be "information-as-thing" (information)" [18]. With the help of information technology, knowledge can be stored, transferred and shared in an organization.

Al-Busaidi and Olfman conducted a detailed investigation about the factors affecting the use of information system in knowledge sharing [19]. They ranked the usefulness of different IT applications in organizational knowledge system (Table 1). With a sample of 101 of users of IOKSS knowledge system in US, they found that individual factors and peer factors are significant factors with knowledge workers' knowledge sharing intention.

Table 1. The usefulness of IT applications in organizational knowledge system

Rank	IT application	Usefulness
1	Best practice databases	4.32
2	Expertise locator systems	4.28
3	Lessons learned systems	4.26
4	Knowledge maps	4.19
5	Team collaboration tools	4.18
6	Email	4.17
7	Information repositories	4.13
8	Teleconferencing	4.12
9	Video-conferencing	4.03
10	Wikis	4.00

3   Preliminary Case Study

3.1   Qualitative Interviews

Company ABC established in 1997 by two Chinese electrical engineers in Shenzhen China. It is an upstream manufacturer in display industry and its products are mainly micron-level refined molds for the lamination and formation of IC/TFT/OLED and other refined circuits. The company vision is become one of the top OEM and ODM display manufacturers and providing high-quality products to its customers all over the world. They provide top quality display boards at competitive prices. The company received ISO9001 quality assurance certificate in 2004 and comply with RoHS and CE standards. It has about 60 employees in its head office for research and development (R&D), product testing, sales and after sale services. The company employs 150 workers in its 15,000 square meters production facilities.

Due to the keen market competition and the changes of customer demand, the company need to shorten the R&D and product testing processes from original average 1 year to 6 months for each product. It is a great challenge to the company. In addition, compared to other competitors in Shenzhen, an employee turnover rate of the Company ABC is extremely high (Table 2). The company conducted the annual employee survey by its human resource department in 2021, the survey results show employees are feeling upset about the high job pressure, poor engagements, poor communication and lacking of top management supports in the Company ABC (Table 3).

For Company ABC, a lot of technical knowledge involves in the business operations and production processes. Such as business intelligence and industry knowledge,

Table 2. Employee turnover in Company ABC and its major competitors in 2020

Department	Company ABC	Competitor A	Competitor B
Office administration	20%	10%	8%
R&D	55%	40%	35%
Product testing	20%	25%	10%
Sales & marketing	15%	8%	5%
Production line	65%	40%	36%

Table 3. Recent employee satisfaction survey results in Company ABC

Focus area average score	Office administration	R&D	Product testing	Sales & marketing	Production line
Rewards	85%	70%	80%	65%	80%
Training opportunities	75%	45%	40%	70%	75%
Respect	80%	60%	60%	80%	75%
Job pressure*	20%	70%	85%	70%	35%
Engagement	70%	60%	60%	65%	60%
Leadership	75%	60%	75%	80%	85%
Communication	60%	50%	40%	70%	80%
Management supports	80%	65%	60%	70%	70%
Overall job satisfaction	80%	65%	50%	75%	70%

Remarks: Reverse coding

product and business knowledge, customer requirements and technical specifications, employees' work experience. In-depth qualitative interviews conducted in the Company ABC on its knowledge management system and employees' knowledge sharing behaviors in 2021. Five respondents from all departments in the company participated. Table 4 shows the current IT applications for knowledge transfer in different departments.

3.2 Failure Factors of Knowledge Sharing in the Case Study

It was noted that peer attitudes had an effect on employees' actual knowledge sharing behaviors and their usage of the KM system in the Company ABC. Some interview dialogues were very negative. An emotional department head who rated the importance of KM system poorly gave the following comment: "It is completely meaningless of our KM system. None of my colleagues appreciate the importance our KM system and the knowledge sharing. They all keep their knowledge and never share with other colleagues

Table 4. Top three IT applications use in Company ABC for knowledge transfer and share

Department	Rank 1	Rank 2	Rank 3
Office administration	E-mail	Video conference	Team collaboration tools
R&D	Team collaboration tools	E-mail	Video conference
Product testing	Team collaboration tools	E-mail	Video conference
Sales & marketing	Video conference	E-mail	Best practice databases
Production line	E-mail	Best practice databases	Knowledge maps

in the department due to the afraid of losing their know-how and only storing the outdated information in the KM system."

Another department head mentioned: "No one in my department consider knowledge management is important for their works."

Another department head added: "We don't have any incentive for people using the system, no systematic approach for the important corporate knowledge share within the department and inter-departmental communication. People insist on their own work practices and never share with other colleagues."

It was observed that there is no well-written guidelines on the use of KM system in the Company ABC. One department head mentioned a recent product design failure case to illustrate the problem. "I still remember an incident happened last year. One product engineer made the same design fault that appeared in another product design by another product engineer a year ago. Our engineers keep the trial-and-error style in product design without referring the lesson learnt in other projects."

Dramatically, a conclusion made by a department head: "I guess only 5% to 10% of our knowledge can be shared in our KM system!".

When reviewed the contents shared in the Company ABC's KM system, one department head commented that: "I just found that one of our departmental databases was damaged in the server and no one in the department noted."

Interestingly, another department head found that he does not has the access rights of his departmental KM system. Without the access rights, he can't able to read the departmental shared folders in the system and update any data in the KM system.

3.3   Research Questions Identified in the Case Study

After reviewing the interview data collected in the case study, following research questions identified for the further investigation.

- Research Question 1. Do the majority of employees in the Company ABC use the KM system improperly?
- Research Question 2. Which factors are important in motivating employees in Company ABC for the use of KM system?
- Research Question 3. What amount and category of knowledge can be shared in Company ABC?

4   Quantitative Study

A structural questionnaire was developed and an quantitative study will be conducted in the Company ABC as to investigate factors affecting knowledge sharing behavior in the company. Figure 1 shows the conceptual framework of the study. The study builds on those factors identified in previous empirical research on knowledge sharing (Table 5).

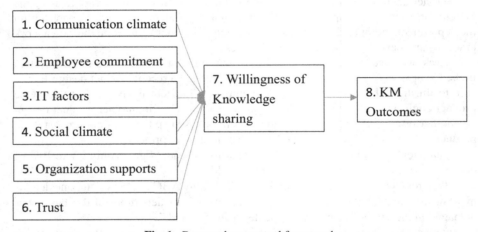

Fig. 1. Proposed conceptual framework

Table 5. Supporting literature for the constructs

Construct	KM literature	Measurement
Communication climate	Yasir and Majid (2017)	Scale
Employee commitment	Ouakouak and Ouedraogo (2019)	Scale
IT factors	Al-Busaidi and Olfman (2017)	Scale
Social climate	Al-Busaidi and Olfman (2017)	
Organization supports	Wickramasinghe and Widyaratne (2012)	Scale
Trust	Wickramasinghe and Widyaratne (2012) Ouakouak and Ouedraogo (2019)	Scale
Willingness of knowledge sharing	Wickramasinghe and Widyaratne (2012) Ouakouak and Ouedraogo (2019)	Scale
KM usage and outcomes	Ouakouak and Ouedraogo (2019) Ouakouak, AlBuloushi, Ouedraogo & Sawalha (2021)	Scale

5 Conclusion

A successful knowledge-based company captures, spreads, integrates, and manages its knowledge capital to achieve its business objectives and goals. An effective KM system can allow everyone in the organization to learn the lessons from experiences and improve their decisions in future. In this regard, it is important to investigate the knowledge barrier in the processes of knowledge sharing and knowledge transfer [8]. Knowledge workers would always be supported with the appropriate management styles, and if a change in style occurs, they should be informed and responded. Poor KM system and knowledge share behavior can be a disaster of every organization. The first phase of this study reviewed the current KM practice of Company ABC and its knowledge sharing problems. Organizations can use the lessons learnt in the Company ABC to identify the potential areas that they need to improve in their KM implementations.

References

1. Nonaka, I., Takeuchi, H.: The Knowledge-Creating Company: How Japanese Companies Create the Dynamics of Innovation. Oxford University Press, New Your NY (1995)
2. Garg, S., Pandey, D.K., Vashisht, A.: Importance of knowledge management for organizational management. Delib. Res. **37**(1), 41–45 (2018)
3. Gold, A.H., Malhotra, A., Segars, A.H.: Knowledge management: an organizational capabilities perspective. J. Manag. Inf. Syst. **18**(1), 185–214 (2001)
4. Frappaolo, C., Capshaw, S.: Knowledge management software. Inf. Manag. J. **33**(3), 44–49 (1999)

5. Brown, S.A., Dennis, A.R., Burley, D., Arling, P.: Knowledge sharing and knowledge management system avoidance: the role of knowledge type and the social network in bypassing an organizational knowledge management system. J. Am. Soc. Inf. Sci. Technol. **64**(10), 2013–2023 (2013). https://doi.org/10.1002/asi.22892. Accessed 31 Mar 2022

6. Hameed, Z., Khan, I.U., Sheikh, Z., Islam, T., Rasheed, M.I., Rana, M.N.: Organizational justice and knowledge sharing behavior: the role of psychological ownership and perceived organizational support. Pers. Rev. **48**(3), 748–773 (2019)

7. Davenport, T.H., Prusak, L.: Working knowledge: How organisations manage what they know. Harvard Business School Press, Boston (1998)

8. Paulin, D., Suneson, K.: Knowledge transfer, knowledge sharing and knowledge barriers - three blurry terms in KM: EJKM. Electron. J. Knowl. Manag. **10**(1), 81–91 (2012)

9. Lehesvitra, T.: Learning processes in a work organization: From individual to collective and/or vice versa? J. Work. Learn. **16**(12), 92–100 (2004)

10. Radaelli, G., Mura, M., Spiller, N., Lettieri, E.: Intellectual capital and knowledge sharing: the mediating role of organisational knowledge-sharing climate. Knowl. Manag. Res. Pract. **9**(4), 342–352 (2011)

11. Wickramasinghe, V., Widyaratne, R.: Effects of interpersonal trust, team leader support, rewards, and knowledge sharing mechanisms on knowledge sharing in project teams: very informal newsletter on library automation. Vine **42**(2), 214–236 (2012)

12. Halisah, A., Jayasingam, S., Ramayah, T., Popa, S.: Social dilemmas in knowledge sharing: an examination of the interplay between knowledge sharing culture and performance climate. J. Knowl. Manag. **25**(7), 1708–1725 (2021)

13. Yasir, M., Majid, A.: Impact of knowledge management enablers on knowledge sharing: is trust a missing link in SMEs of emerging economies? World J. Entrep. Manag. Sustain. Dev. **13**(1), 16–33 (2017)

14. Ouakouak, M.L., Ouedraogo, N.: Fostering knowledge sharing and knowledge utilization: the impact of organizational commitment and trust. Bus. Process. Manag. J. **25**(4), 757–779 (2019)

15. Ouakouak, M.L., AlBuloushi, N., Ouedraogo, N., Sawalha, N.: Knowledge sharing as a give-and-take practice: the role of the knowledge receiver in the knowledge-sharing process. J. Knowl. Manag. **25**(8), 2043–2066 (2021)

16. Davison, R.M., Ou, C.X.J., Martinsons, M.G.: Information technology to support informal knowledge sharing. Inf. Syst. J. **23**(1), 89–109 (2013)

17. Van Den Hooff, B., De Ridder, J.A.: Knowledge sharing in context: the influence of organizational commitment, communication climate and CMC use on knowledge sharing. J. Knowl. Manag. **8**(6), 117–130 (2004)

18. Buckland, M.K.: Information as thing. J. Am. Soc. Inf. Sci. **42**(5), 351–360 (1991)

19. Al-Busaidi, K., Olfman, L.: Knowledge sharing through inter-organizational knowledge sharing systems: Very informal newsletter on library automation. VINE J. Inf. Knowl. Manag. Syst. **47**(1), 110–136 (2017)

Value of the Influence of Research Highlights on Academic Papers

Yue Liu[1], Dejun Zheng[1(✉)], Haichen Zhou[2], and Shaoxiong Fu[1]

[1] School of Information Management, Nanjing Agricultural University, Nanjing 210095, Jiangsu, China
zdejun@njau.edu.cn
[2] Chengdu Library of the Chinese Academy of Sciences, Chengdu 610041, Sichuan, China

Abstract. This study explores the differences between highlight papers and non-highlight papers from the perspective of academic influence as a crucial insight for evaluating scientific research. Three dimensions are considered: journals, papers, and research highlights. We selected 8 academic journals in the field of library and information science, which are published by Elsevier and indexed by SSCI, and analyzed 5,020 academic papers published therein from 2011 to 2020. The results of our empirical study demonstrate that all journals acknowledge the existence of research highlights, although not all online academic papers provide them. In recent years, the number of highlight papers has increased annually, and more importantly, the proportion has also grown steadily. The ETA square coefficient of citations is higher for highlight papers compared to non-highlight papers. Furthermore, in the training of the innovation recognition model, the effect of the training model that uses the research highlights of academic papers with high citation frequency is better, although the PRF value has a smaller difference.

Keywords: Research highlights · Academic value · Academic influence

1 Introduction

Research highlights were officially initiated by the Elsevier Publishing Group in 2010, independently prepared, and submitted by the author of the academic paper. They consist of three to five key points to help readers quickly understand the paper. They are generally called "research highlights" and are independent of the abstract. Each research highlight generally does not exceed 85 characters and only appears in the online version of the academic paper. Furthermore, the use of jargon or abbreviations should be avoided as much as possible [1, 2].

Academic and publishing circles have begun to discuss the value and function of research highlights. However, most of them introduce the concept and value of research highlights in a descriptive way. For example, Tse P (2012) believes that research highlights are accompanying content for research papers that can support a clear academic position and a credible academic image [3]. Yang (2016) provides a linguistic analysis of the research highlights of 240 journal papers, exploring characteristics of the evaluative language and interactive discourse, and further investigates the opinions of editors

© Springer Nature Switzerland AG 2022
L. Uden et al. (Eds.): KMO 2022, CCIS 1593, pp. 49–64, 2022.
https://doi.org/10.1007/978-3-031-07920-7_5

and authors on research highlights by means of a questionnaire survey [4]. By tagging 385 journal papers in XML format, Chuanjun and Guoxin (2020) built a research corpus, examined the language features of research highlights by keyword analysis, and explored the distribution features of research highlights using natural language processing algorithms [2].

Yet to date, there has been no research on the influence and academic value of research highlights for academic papers. Therefore, this study takes up the topic. We selected SSCI academic journals and papers in the field of library and information science as the research data. The journals all belong to Elsevier. We then linked the journals and papers with advanced metrics. Focusing on academic influence, we use quantitative indicators to investigate the differences between academic papers with and without research highlights. The value of research highlights for the evaluation of academic innovation is also the focus of our attention. This study is of theoretical value and practical significance for understanding the academic value of research highlights, exploring the innovative discovery mechanism of academic papers, and promoting the research of humanities and social sciences.

The rest of the paper is organized as follows: The second part summarizes the research status of evaluation indexes of journals, evaluation indexes of papers and innovation indexes of research highlights. The third part introduces the process of data collection and the methods of analysis. The fourth part shows the experimental process comparative analysis. The conclusion was given in the fifth part and the implications and limitations were introduced in the last part.

2   Related Works

2.1   Influence Evaluation Indexes of Journals

Academic journals are an important link between authors, reviewers, and readers in the paper-dissemination ecosystem and are the most important and authoritative carriers of academic papers [5]. They not only play an important role in promoting the exchange and dissemination of scientific knowledge but also make great contributions to the innovation of science and technology. Since Eugene Garfield completed the scientific citation index (SCI) in 1964 [6], the journal impact factor (IF) has become the main index to evaluate the quality of academic journals [7]. While the IF has been a serious bone of contention, often criticized as not being a good measure of academic quality, it is, despite these criticisms, the dominant metric in academic publishing since its inception in the 1960s, dominating academic publishing for the better part of approximately 60 years [8, 9].

Elsevier launched a new citation metric in 2016: CiteScore [10]. It has been argued that CiteScore might represent a wider or more realistic perspective of a journal's published content and portfolio and thus a more congruent (or "realistic") method of journal evaluation than the IF [8]. However, CiteScore represents another method of journal evaluation within vanity publishing that competes with but also supplements the IF, its use, its effects, and its actual or potential abuse [11, 12].

Therefore, to observe whether the number of papers with research highlights influences the evaluation indexes of journals, this research uses the IF and CiteScore as the evaluation indexes of the academic influence of journals to measure the relationship between them and research highlights.

2.2 Influence Evaluation Indexes of Papers

Since Garfield (2006) put forward the citation analysis method in the 1950s, the paper citation has been used as a measure to gauge the influence of papers, despite their well-known lack of predictive power for future impact: current citations capture only past accomplishments [13, 14]. Typically, researchers seek to publish articles that have a greater impact on science by receiving more citations. Citation counts reflect the degree of usage and authority of papers to a certain extent [15].

Altmetrics are a new type of metrology that analyzes and disseminates academic research based on social networks [16]. PlumX Metrics is a platform for integrating and presenting altmetrics. The PlumX Metrics platform is divided into five indicators: citations, usage, captures, mentions, and social media, which mainly present the public's views on an academic research achievement (article, meeting minutes, book chapters, etc.) in the network environment in a quantitative form [17]. They may reflect non-scholarly types of impacts that are ignored by citations from other journal articles and that may appear more quickly than citations, allowing earlier evidence of impact.

Based on this, this paper takes citation data of Web of Science and metric data of PlumX as indicators to measure the role of research highlights on the academic influence of a single academic paper.

2.3 Innovation Indexes of Research Highlights

Innovation plays a very important role in academic departments [18]. The essence of academic paper influence evaluation is reflected in the measurement of academic paper innovation [19]. In the existing research, most of the methods of machine learning used to measure the innovation of academic papers, based on the breakthrough articles identified, used SVM, TextCNN, and BERTto train the models to identify abstracts with breakthrough evaluations [20]. Zhang and Fan (2021) developed a novel ensemble embedding method to generate semantic and contextual representations of the words in review sentences [21]. The resultant representations in each sentence are then used in a long short-term memory (LSTM) model for innovation-sentence identification.

The originality or breakthrough of academic achievements is the main purpose of academic activities. Similarly, the selection of indicators based on the content characteristics of research highlights the innovative identification of academic papers. Although the innovation of academic papers is not completely equal to the influence, as influence is the comprehensive result of various factors, the innovation of academic papers has a certain predictive significance for academic influence.

3 Data and Methods

3.1 Dataset

In 2010, Elsevier proposed the concept of research highlights. This paper selects academic papers published in eight academic journals in the field of library and information science collected by SSCI under Elsevier as research data from 2011 to 2020. The reasons include the following: first, access to basic data is convenient. Second, the author is familiar with this discipline. The basic information of the eight academic journals is shown in Table 1. The data collection and processing are mainly divided into the following four steps.

Table 1. Sample journal information

No.	Journaltitle	Abr	ISSN	Publishername	WebofScienceCategories
1	GovernmentInformationQuarterly	GIQ	0740-624X	elsevierinc	informationscience&libraryscience
2	InformationandOrganization	IO	1471-7727	elseviersciltd	management|informationscience&libraryscience
3	Information&Management	IM	0378-7206	elsevier	management|informationscience&libraryscience
4	InformationProcessing&Management	IPM	0306-4573	elseviersciltd	informationscience&libraryscience
5	InternationalJournalofInformationManagement	IJIM	0268-4012	elseviersciltd	informationscience&libraryscience
6	JournalofAcademicLibrarianship	JAL	0099-1333	elsevierscienceinc	informationscience&libraryscience
7	JournalofStrategicInformationSystems	JSIS	0963-8687	elsevier	management|informationscience&libraryscience
8	Library&InformationScienceResearch	LISR	0740-8188	elsevierscienceinc	informationscience&libraryscience

1) First, we used crawler technology to collect title information and alternative measurement information on the official websites of the eight academic journals from 2011 to 2020.see Fig. 1. The data collection period was from June 13, 2021, to June 16, 2021, with a total of 7,025 papers obtained.
2) Second, the missing research highlight data were manually supplemented from June 17, 2021, to June 19, 2021.
3) Then, the data were cleaned to ensure the relative accuracy of the research data. The remaining 5,020 data were used as the research data.
4) The last step was to collect the citation data of the academic papers. The citation data were obtained from the Web of Science and matched with the academic papers using the Vlookup formula in Excel.

3.2 Analysis Methods

Exploring the differences between highlight papers (i.e., papers with research highlights) and non-highlight papers (i.e., papers without research highlights) from the perspective of academic influence is crucial for evaluating scientific research. We conducted a comparative analysis using three dimensions: descriptive statistical analysis based on journal and single paper indicators, correlation analysis based on citation and alternative indicators, and innovation identification analysis based on research highlights.

1) Descriptive statistical analysis based on journal and single paper indicators: The analysis investigated the number and proportion of highlight papers and non-highlight papers from the journal dimension and time dimension to explore the popular degree of research highlights. Specific indicators of this part include: Distribution of highlight papers and non-highlight papers, the proportion of highlight papers with the trend of journal IF and CiteScore in the time dimension, the R^2 between IF, CiteScore

Government Information Quarterly
Volume 31, Issue 4, October 2014, Pages 660-668

Technology knowledge and governance:
Empowering citizen engagement and
participation ☆

Highlights

- We examine the extent to which an extended Technology Acceptance
  Model (TAM) facilitates technology knowledge (t-knowledge).

Abstract

The term technology knowledge (T-knowledge) is used to describe knowledge about
and the ability to operate specific technologies such as the internet. T-knowledge
also includes the ability required to operate particular technologies. T-knowledge

42	33	219	2	1
Citations	Usage	Captures	Mentions	Social Media

Metric Options: ◉ Counts ○ 1 Year ○ 3 Year ⓘ

Fig. 1. Bibliographic information and metrical information

and Proportion of highlight papers, and the average and median of citation, captures, usage, mention and social media.

2) Correlation analysis based on citation and alternative indicators: As IF and CiteScore did not conform to a normal distribution [22], we tested various statistical data through the Kolmogorov–Smirnov method before selecting the correlation analysis method. Hence, the Spearman correlation analysis method was used to test the correlations among the indicators [5]. In addition, according to the results and the data types of this paper, the correlation ratio measurement method (also known as the ETA square coefficient) was used to measure the correlation. So specific indicators of this part include: Spearman correlation coefficients, t-test and ETA correlation coefficient.

3) Innovation identification analysis based on research highlights: We carried out innovative identification model training on the research highlights of academic papers with both high and low citation frequency and further explored the relationship between the research highlights and the academic influence of the papers through the comparative analysis of the model training effect. Therefore, the evaluation index used in this part is the PRF of the BiLSTM model.

4 Results and Discussion

4.1 Descriptive Statistical Analysis of Academic Journals and Papers

4.1.1 Descriptive Statistical Analysis in the Journal Dimension

To evaluate a journal's recognition of research highlights, we identified the quantity distribution and proportion of highlight papers and non-highlight papers in the journal dimension. The specific analysis results are shown in Fig. 2. In addition, we calculated the proportion of the number of highlight papers in the total number of papers for each year. To explore the relationship between the proportion of highlight papers and journal evaluation indicators (IF, CiteScore), we made a trend analysis chart of the proportion of highlight papers and journal evaluation indicators from 2011 to 2020 and the specific analysis results are shown in Fig. 3. To further explore the correlation between IF, CiteScore and Proportion of highlight papers in each journal, We conducted a trend analysis of those datas using the trend lines function of offices software. The results are as shown in Fig. 4.

Figure 2 illustrates the differences between highlight papers and non-highlight papers in the journal dimension, namely, that journals have different attitudes toward research highlights. First, all journals recognize the existence of research highlights, although not all online papers provide them. Second, the proportion of highlight papers in most journals is 74%–87%, which shows that since the concept of research highlights was put forward, an increasing number of journals have taken a positive attitude toward it.

From Fig. 3, IF and CiteScore are both indicators to evaluate the quality of academic journals. Although the scope of journals and the algorithm cycle covered by them are different, they have the same results in measuring the changing trend of disciplinary journals in the time dimension. For a single journal, the proportion of highlight papers in GIQ, IJIM, LISR, JAL, IO, and JSIS shows an upward trend, as do the corresponding journal IF and CiteScore. The proportion of highlight papers in IPM fluctuates in a specific period, but the rising trend in the later period is also roughly similar to that of IF and CiteScore. IM papers are special. In a certain period of time, the proportion of highlight papers in this journal and the corresponding IF and CiteScore show an upward trend followed by an opposite trend.

More interestingly, the CiteScores of IM and IPM in 2011 was above 5, while the CiteScores of other journals were below 4.5. There may be a few reasons for this phenomenon. First, with the rapid growth of scientific paper output, researchers have accelerated the browsing speed of papers to read as many professional journal papers as possible. Highlight papers are first retrieved by researchers, which will naturally increase the number of reading and alternative scores and then affect the IF and CiteScore of journals. Second, the IF and CiteScore are evaluation indicators not only for journals but also for authors. Therefore, an increasing number of authors are willing to provide research highlights to increase the exposure of the paper. Third, similar to late development advantage theory [23], journals with low CiteScores in the initial stage may have less influence, and the overall structure and content of journals are relatively easy to adjust, including adding research highlights.

R^2 represents degree of relevance, and the higher R^2, the higher correlation. From Fig. 4, the R^2 between IF and Proportion of highlight papers is mostly higher than 0.5, except the LISR journal. Similarly, except IO LISR and JAL journal, the R2 between CiteScore and Proportion of highlight papers is all higher than 0.5. The analysis results demonstrate that there is a strong correlation between IF, CiteScore and Proportion of highlight papers, showing that highlight have a positive effect on IF and CiteScore.

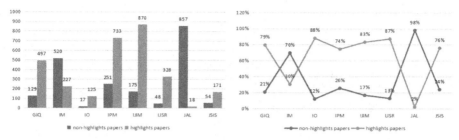

Fig. 2. Distribution of highlight papers and non-highlight papers in the journal dimension

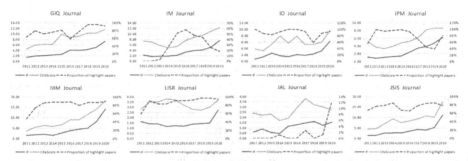

Fig. 3. Comparison of the proportion of highlight papers with the trend of journal IF and CiteScore in the time dimension

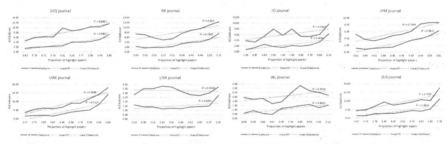

Fig. 4. Correlation between IF, CiteScore and Proportion of highlight papers in the time dimension.

4.1.2 Descriptive Statistical Analysis in the Time Dimension

We use two datasets for analysis in this paper, the times cited of all databases in WoS and the altmetrics data in PlumX Metrics. To distinguish the data sources during the analysis, we refer to the times cited of all databases in WoS as traditional citations and the altmetrics data in PlumX Metrics as altmetrics citations, usage, captures, mentions, and social media. When comparing the specific data of highlights papers and non-highlights papers, we prefix specific indicators to prevent mixed dishes: e.g., highlight_traditional_citation refers to the number of times the highlight paper is cited in Wos, and non-highlight_usage refers to the frequency of usage of non-highlight papers.

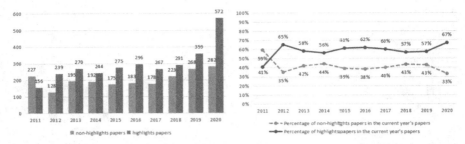

Fig. 5. Annual distribution of papers with highlight papers and non-highlight papers

From Fig. 5, we see that the number of highlight papers has exceeded the number of non-highlight papers since 2012, and the number and proportion of highlight papers had an obvious increasing trend from 2014 to 2016. However, the proportion of highlight papers decreased from 2017 to 2019. Then, by 2020, it had increased to the highest level in the previous ten years. There are two reasons for this trend. First, when research highlights first appeared, authors were willing to provide them for reasons of novelty, curiosity, and so forth. However, due to the focus on reading papers at that time [24], the role of research highlights was not fully reflected, which led to the low enthusiasm of subsequent authors in providing highlights. On the other hand, with the popularity of the Internet and the appearance of various alternative indicators, an increasing number of scholars are aware of the role of studying highlights, so their enthusiasm for providing highlights has increased [25].

Figure 6 shows the difference in the average and median of indicators between highlight papers and non-highlight papers from 2011 to 2020. First, the average and median of highlight_traditional_citation were higher than those of non-highlight_traditional_citation, indicating that research highlights can promote the citation of papers and expand their academic influence in the academic ecosystem. Second, the indicator of capture refers to the number of times a paper has been saved, read, marked, and tracked and to the number of people who have subscribed for renewal and have paid attention to updates of the paper. The indicator of usage provides insight into whether people are reading papers and calls attention to the nature of access to the papers (e.g., full-text view, download, or recommendation). Both are a product of social network behavior and play a fundamental role in scientific interaction. Therefore, in terms of capture and usage indicators, the average and median of highlight papers gradually exceed those of non-highlight papers with time. This demonstrates that highlight papers may receive more attention. There is also trend that the average and median of citation, captures and usage both for highlight and non-highlight papers falls with time. Most notably,This trend conforms to the variation law, which states that the longer the time since publication, the higher the cumulative count of citation, captures and usage.

Finally, regarding the indicators of mention and social media, both are products of social media, which is characterized by high timeliness and low sustainability. Therefore, the newer the papers, the higher the mention and social media indicators. As presented in Fig. 6, the average and median of the mention and social media indicators of highlight papers were higher than those of the corresponding non-highlight papers in the past year.

This verifies that research highlights can promote the dissemination of papers on social media to a certain extent and expand their academic influence in public social space.

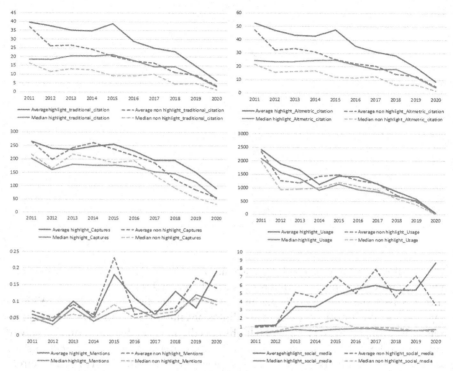

Fig. 6. Annual average and median of citations, usage, captures, mentions, and social media indicators of highlight papers and non-highlight papers from 2011 to 2020

4.2   Correlation Analysis of Academic Journals and Papers

4.2.1   Correlation Analysis with Journals Evaluation Indicator

Spearman correlation coefficients between the IF, CiteScore, and research highlights of eight academic journals were measured, and the results are shown in Table 2. Research highlights correlated with the CiteScore of GIQ journals, and the correlation coefficient was 75%, indicating a strong correlation between them. There was a negative correlation with IPM journals, which is consistent with the data in Fig. 3. There were no correlations in other journals.

4.2.2   Correlation Analysis with Academic Paper Indicators

We analyzed the difference between the indicators of the highlight papers and non-highlight papers. The correlation analysis used an independent sample t-test and was carried out within the confidence interval with a difference of 95%. The specific analysis

Table 2. Correlation analysis with journal evaluation indicator

Journal	Indicator	sample size	Mean difference	Standard error difference	p	rho
GIQ	IF	10	3. 499	1. 809	0. 06	0. 612
	CiteScore	10	8. 270	2. 383	0. 012	. 750*
IM	IF	10	3. 373	1. 886	0. 424	0. 286
	CiteScore	10	7. 960	2. 439	0. 973	0. 012
IO	IF	10	2. 356	1. 559	0. 254	-0. 399
	CiteScore	10	6. 030	1. 957	0. 549	0. 216
IPM	IF	10	2. 640	1. 864	0. 043	-. 648*
	CiteScore	10	5. 760	2. 041	0. 006	-. 793**
IJIM	IF	10	4. 542	3. 951	0. 162	0. 479
	CiteScore	10	8. 950	4. 491	0. 098	0. 552
LISR	IF	10	1. 499	0. 455	0. 446	0. 273
	CiteScore	10	3. 270	0. 422	0. 485	-0. 251
JAL	IF	10	1. 077	0. 426	0. 377	0. 314
	CiteScore	10	2. 610	0. 637	0. 366	0. 321
JSIS	IF	10	3. 887	2. 779	0. 159	0. 482
	CiteScore	10	8. 860	3. 673	0. 057	0. 618

results are shown in Table 3. The ETA correlation coefficient is calculated for the index data with significant impact, and the results are shown in Table 4.

Table 3 lists the impact of paper indicators data in the last ten years. With the passage of time, the impact of research highlights on citations and altmetrics is becoming increasingly stronger. In 2011, research highlights did not establish any connection with the relevant index data of academic papers. It can be reasonably inferred that this was because research highlights had only been proposed fairly recently, and academic circles were not paying much attention to them at the time. Since 2011, however, research highlights have had a continuous impact on both traditional citations and altmetrics citations, and the effect is significant. Moreover, research highlights have a significant but discontinuous impact on the two indicators of usage and capture, as well as a significant impact on mention and social media in the past two years.

As shown in Table 4, on the whole, the correlation coefficients between research highlights and citation and altmetrics measures are less than 50%. This indicates that research highlights have some influence on traditional citation and altmetrics measures, but this influence is not particularly obvious at present. Indicated by the single paper index, the correlation coefficient between research highlights and traditional citations and altmetrics citations grew steadily from 2013 to 2018. The correlation coefficient between research highlights and traditional citations gradually increased from 9% to 22%, and similarly, that between research highlights and altmetrics citations gradually increased from 10% to 21%. The overall increasing trend of the curve in Table 4 illustrates that research highlights have had a continuous impact on traditional citations and altmetrics citations, and the degree of this impact is increasing. It should be noted that the correlation coefficient between research highlights and usage shows a downward trend year by year, and research highlights had no impact on usage in approximately 2016. The correlation coefficient between research highlights and capture fluctuates greatly over the years. The influence period of research highlights on mention and social media is short, and the influence intensity is weak.

Table 3. Correlation analysis with academic paper indicators

Year	Indicator	sample size	Mean difference	Standard error difference	F	t	P	Year	Indicator	sample size	Mean difference	Standard error difference	F	t	P
2011	traditional_citation		-2.560	5.942	0.121	-0.431	0.667	2016	traditional_citation		-11.238	2.764	9.722	-4.066	0*
2011	Altmetric_citation		-5.172	7.605	0.000	-0.680	0.497	2016	Altmetric_citation		-13.151	3.510	7.810	-3.746	0*
2011	Usage	383	-71.059	216.589	0.062	-0.328	0.743	2016	Usage	479	-131.957	114.665	6.666	-1.151	0.250
2011	Captures		-0.474	23.238	0.136	-0.020	0.984	2016	Captures		-17.533	15.983	12.875	-1.097	0.273
2011	Mentions		0.006	0.042	0.096	0.152	0.879	2016	Mentions		-0.051	0.034	7.275	-1.527	0.128
2011	social_media		-0.151	0.394	0.633	-0.384	0.701	2016	social_media		-0.528	1.794	0.688	-0.294	0.769
2012	traditional_citation		-11.408	6.049	3.147	-1.886	0.060	2017	traditional_citation		-8.481	2.399	7.855	-3.536	0*
2012	Altmetric_citation		-14.740	7.490	3.720	-1.968	0.050	2017	Altmetric_citation		-10.528	2.979	7.683	-3.534	0*
2012	Usage	367	-620.634	142.897	0.486	-4.343	0*	2017	Usage	445	18.148	85.654	0.048	0.212	0.832
2012	Captures		-40.547	19.929	6.320	-2.035	0.043*	2017	Captures		-9.507	17.072	0.003	-0.557	0.578
2012	Mentions		0.009	0.023	0.592	0.397	0.691	2017	Mentions		0.017	0.026	1.712	0.646	0.519
2012	social_media		-0.121	0.336	1.313	-0.360	0.719	2017	social_media		1.903	1.932	2.504	0.985	0.325
2013	traditional_citation		-8.526	4.281	2.470	-1.992	0.047*	2018	traditional_citation		-11.894	2.197	14.601	-5.414	0*
2013	Altmetric_citation		-9.951	5.273	2.420	-1.887	0.060	2018	Altmetric_citation		-13.939	2.682	13.037	-5.196	0*
2013	Usage	465	-470.566	109.591	2.026	-4.294	0*	2018	Usage	514	-141.207	68.467	4.578	-2.062	0.04*
2013	Captures		6.802	19.670	2.487	0.346	0.730	2018	Captures		-70.514	14.317	13.635	-4.925	0*
2013	Mentions		-0.013	0.039	0.354	-0.333	0.739	2018	Mentions		-0.053	0.065	2.754	-0.824	0.410
2013	social_media		1.737	1.195	3.797	1.454	0.147	2018	social_media		-0.902	1.862	1.467	-0.485	0.628
2014	traditional_citation		-10.443	4.340	3.096	-2.406	0.017*	2019	traditional_citation		-5.165	1.500	5.807	-3.444	0.001*
2014	Altmetric_citation		-11.821	5.457	2.466	-2.166	0.031*	2019	Altmetric_citation		-6.726	2.029	4.164	-3.315	0.001*
2014	Usage	436	297.144	132.398	19.016	2.244	0.026*	2019	Usage	627	-103.960	37.722	2.171	-2.756	0.006*
2014	Captures		13.466	21.504	0.000	0.626	0.532	2019	Captures		-64.821	11.309	14.037	-5.732	0*
2014	Mentions		0.017	0.024	2.058	0.714	0.476	2019	Mentions		0.090	0.044	17.205	2.037	0.042*
2014	social_media		1.151	1.157	0.343	0.995	0.320	2019	social_media		1.637	2.535	1.518	0.646	0.519
2015	traditional_citation		-18.493	5.906	4.947	-3.131	0.002*	2020	traditional_citation		-2.826	0.588	15.532	-4.810	0*
2015	Altmetric_citation		-22.222	7.468	4.347	-2.976	0.003*	2020	Altmetric_citation		-3.600	0.729	18.224	-4.937	0*
2015	Usage	450	45.331	121.315	0.843	0.374	0.709	2020	Usage	854	-11.517	8.184	6.930	-1.407	0.160
2015	Captures		-18.007	33.658	0.829	-0.535	0.593	2020	Captures		-33.560	6.648	19.671	-5.048	0*
2015	Mentions		0.056	0.106	0.959	0.528	0.598	2020	Mentions		-0.043	0.122	0.588	-0.356	0.722
2015	social_media		2.267	1.964	0.615	1.154	0.249	2020	social_media		-5.063	1.761	14.059	-2.875	0.004*

Table 4. ETA correlation coefficient analysis of indicators with significant impact

year	traditional_ citation	Altmetric_ citation	Usage	Captures	Mentions	social_ media
2011	–	–	–	–	–	–
2012	–	–	22%	9%	–	–
2013	9%	–	20%	–	–	–
2014	12%	10%	11%	–	–	–
2015	13%	12%	–	–	–	–
2016	17%	16%	–	–	–	–
2017	15%	15%	–	–	–	–
2018	22%	21%	9%	20%	–	–
2019	14%	13%	11%	21%	9%	–
2020	15%	15%	–	15%	–	8%

4.3   Innovation Identification Analysis Based on Research Highlights

The essence of scientific activities is seeking truth and innovation. The influence of academic papers is the result of the comprehensive influence of many factors. Although this influence is not completely equal to academic innovation, it can reflect academic innovation. In this part of the research, we believe that academic innovation models trained on corpora with academic papers of higgh influence are more effective. Therefore, we selected two parts of the data for experiments based on the number of traditional citations. We call the number of traditional citations greater than 100 "high traditional citations" and that equal to 0 "low traditional citations." Our analysis of the innovation of research highlights that high traditional citations and low traditional citations helped in understanding the value of the content characteristics of research highlights on academic impact.

Liu (2018) thinks academic innovation can be measured from four aspects [26]: (1) what breakthroughs have been made in academic research; (2) In what way; (3) What is the conclusion of the research; (4) The application prospect of the research. Therefore, if highlights have the above feature (it can be one feature or multiple features), it is considered to be academic innovation. For example, this is the first research study in competitive intelligence which combines meta-synthesis and Delphi methods. The underlined places reveal the main innovations of academic research.

We first selected 118 high traditional citation papers and 125 low traditional citation papers from the highlight papers. Then, the research highlights with innovation sentences were marked as positive example 1, and those without innovation sentences were marked as negative example 0. Finally, Given the effect and sample size of the recognition algorithm, we chose BiLSTM model to train the academic innovation identification model and judged the correlation between academic innovation and its impact according to the effect index of the model. The effect data of the model training are shown in Fig. 8.

As shown in Fig. 7, there were 76 positive examples and 433 negative examples in the high traditional citation papers and 71 positive examples and 457 negative examples in the low traditional citation papers. The proportion of innovative sentences in the high traditional citation papers was 14.93%, which is slightly greater than that in the low traditional citation group. This shows that the high traditional citation papers had a larger number of innovative sentences in their research highlights in comparison to the low traditional citation papers.

As presented in Fig. 8, in five rounds of training of the BiLSTM model with labeled data, the precision rate, recall rate, and F-measure (PRF) values of the data-trained model marked with the research highlights of high traditional citation papers were higher than those of the data-trained model marked with the research highlights of low traditional citation papers, and the PRF value was relatively stable. More importantly, the precision rate and F-measure trained by the data-trained model marked with the research highlights of high traditional citation papers were generally on the rise. Although the recall rate fluctuated greatly in the model training, the recall rate trained by the data-trained model marked with the research highlights of high traditional citation papers was 17% higher than for low traditional citation papers. This shows that the research highlights of high traditional citation papers are standardized and focused and can help users quickly

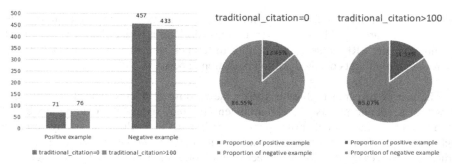

Fig. 7. Comparative analysis of the labeled data of research highlights with different citation frequencies

understand the paper contents. This attracts users to download, browse, and promote the dissemination of papers.

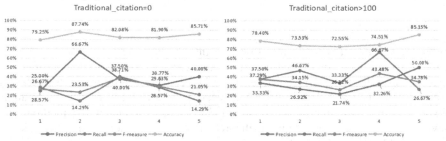

Fig. 8. Comparative analysis of the model effects of labeled data training of research highlights with different citation frequencies

5   Conclusions

Several important conclusions are drawn.

1) The eight academic journals selected in this paper have research highlights, the number of highlight papers has increased year by year, and the proportion among all papers has also increased steadily. From 2011 to 2020, the proportion of research highlights increased by 26%, showing an upward trend.

2) An independent sample t-test was conducted on the index data between the highlight papers and non-highlight papers. The results showed a significant positive correlation between highlights papers and citations and some indicators of altmetrics. Different from the non-highlight papers, for the highlight papers, the eat square coefficient of citations was relatively high, and the eat square coefficient of some indicators of altmetrics was also relatively high, showing that the research highlights had a strong correlation with citation and some indicators of altmetrics.

3) Furthermore, in the training of the innovation recognition model, the model trained by the research highlights of high traditional citation papers had a better effect, although the PRF value had a smaller difference from the model trained by the research highlights of low traditional citation papers.

The use of research highlights solves the reading obstacles caused by the rapid growth of academic papers to a certain extent and may reduce the reading anxiety of scholars facing a large number of papers. According to the results of this study, research highlights also show a positive correlation with classic journal indicators and paper indicators. However, the positive effect of the correlation is not strong enough, and some data fluctuate and need to be observed more widely. Overall, research highlights can help attract users to read a paper and may increase the frequency of citations. It can be concluded that they promote effective communication.

6 Implications and Limitations

6.1 Implications

The findings of this study offer novel insights into the influence of research highlights on the academic value of journal papers. The research makes two key contributions. First, it contributes to existing work on the influence of research highlights, including academic influence and social influence. Specifically, this study proves the relationship between research highlights and paper influence using a quantitative method. This view is very important because it has theoretical value for understanding the value of research highlights, exploring the innovative discovery mechanism of academic papers, and promoting humanities and social science research.

On a practical front, our research provides important insights for editors and authors wishing to expand the influence of academic papers. That is, our findings can help editors and authors understand the value of research highlights for the influence of papers. Editors should clearly explain the concept of research highlights to help authors understand their importance so as to increase authors' willingness to write them. Then, to increase the influence of their academic papers, authors can also better reflect the innovation of a paper in the research highlights.

6.2 Limitations and Further Research Directions

There are two main limitations to this study. First, the papers in the analysis are from magazines in the field of library and information science. Further analysis of journals in other fields, such as computer science, medicine, and biology, is needed to verify our conclusions. Moreover, the differences between highlight papers and non-highlight papers should be examined from multiple dimensions, such as the topics these papers cover. Additional research is needed to identify the communication characteristics and laws of highlight papers, improve the existing research conclusions, and provide a more scientific theoretical basis for paper writing, journal publishing, and the scientific research evaluation of academic institutions and funding institutions.

References

1. Elsevier Systems. Highlights. https://www.elsevier.com/authors/tools-and-resources/highlights. Accessed 10 Oct 2021
2. Chuanjun, S., Guoxin, Y.: Exploration of the research "highlights" in academic papers. Libr. Inf. Serv. **64**(9), 104 (2020). https://doi.org/10.13266/j.issn.0252-3116.2020.09.012
3. Tse, P.: Stance in academic bios. In: Stance and Voice in Written Academic Genres, pp. 69–84. Palgrave Macmillan, London (2012)
4. Yang, W.: Evaluative language and interactive discourse in journal article highlights. Engl. Specif. Purp. **42**, 89–103 (2016). https://doi.org/10.1016/j.esp.2016.01.001
5. Kong, L., Wang, D.: Comparison of citations and attention of cover and noncover papers. J. Informetrics **14**(4), 101095 (2020). https://doi.org/10.1016/j.joi.2020.101095
6. Schubert, A., Schubert, G.: Whatever happened to Garfield's constant? Scientometrics **114**(2), 659–667 (2018). https://doi.org/10.1007/s11192-017-2527-3
7. Kaltenborn, K.F., Kuhn, K.: The journal impact factor as a parameter for the evaluation of researchers and research. Rev. Esp. Enferm. Dig. **96**(7), 460–476 (2004). https://doi.org/10.1007/s00063-003-1240-6
8. da Silva, J.A.T., Memon, A.R.: CiteScore: a cite for sore eyes, or a valuable, transparent metric? Scientometrics **111**(1), 553–556 (2017). https://doi.org/10.1007/s11192-017-2250-0
9. On impact. Nat. Methods **12**, 693 (2015). https://doi.org/10.1038/nmeth.3520
10. Fernandez-Llimos, F.: Differences and similarities between journal impact factor and citescore. Pharm. Pract. (Granada) **16**(2) (2018). https://doi.org/10.18549/pharmpract.2018.02.1282
11. da Silva, J.A.T.: The journal impact factor (JIF): science publishing's miscalculating metric. Acad. Quest. **30**(4), 433–441 (2017). https://doi.org/10.1007/s12129-017-9671-3
12. da Silva, J.A.T., Bernès, S.: Clarivate analytics: continued omnia vanitas impact factor culture. Sci. Eng. Ethics **24**(1), 291–297 (2018). https://doi.org/10.1007/s11948-017-9873-7
13. Garfield, E.: Citation indexes for science: a new dimension in documentation through association of ideas. Int. J. Epidemiol. **35**(5), 1123–1127 (2006)
14. Xiao, S., et al.: On modeling and predicting individual paper citation count over time. In: IJCAI, pp. 2676–2682, July 2016
15. Yang, J., Liu, Z.: The effect of citation behaviour on knowledge diffusion and intellectual structure. J. Informetrics **16**(1), 101225 (2022). https://doi.org/10.1016/j.joi.2021.101225
16. Priem, J., Hemminger, B.H.: Scientometrics 2.0: new metrics of scholarly impact on the social web. First Monday **15**(7), 16 (2010). https://doi.org/10.5210/fm.v15i7.2874
17. Plum analytics. About PlumX metrics. https://plumanalytics.com/learn/about-metrics/. Accessed 11 Oct 2021
18. Heaton, J.P.: The vital role of creativity in academic departments. BJU Int. (Papier) **96**(3), 254–256 (2005). https://doi.org/10.1111/j.1464-410X.2005.05613.x
19. Zhuoran, L., Yuqi, W., Wei, Q.J.L.: Research review on innovation evaluation of academic papers. J. China Soc. Sci. Tech. Inf. **40**(7), 780–790 (2021). https://doi.org/10.3772/j.issn.1000-0135.2021.07.010
20. Wang, X., Yang, X., Du, J., Wang, X., Li, J., Tang, X.: A deep learning approach for identifying biomedical breakthrough discoveries using context analysis. Scientometrics 1–19 (2021). https://doi.org/10.1007/s11192-021-04003-z
21. Zhang, M., Fan, B., Zhang, N., Wang, W., Fan, W.: Mining product innovation ideas from online reviews. Inf. Process. Manag. **58**(1), 102389 (2021). https://doi.org/10.1016/j.ipm.2020.102389
22. Bornmann, L.: Usefulness of altmetrics for measuring the broader impact of research: a case study using datafrom PLOS and F1000Prime. Aslib J. Inf. Manag. **67**(3), 305–319 (2015). https://doi.org/10.1108/AJIM-09-2014-0115

23. Li, G.: The advantage of backwardness's revolution and enlightenment. Contemp. Econ. Res. **4**, 57–60 (2009)
24. Cole, J., Suman, M., Schramm, P., Zhou, L., Reyes-Sepulveda E., Lebo, H.: The World Internet Project. World Internet Project, University of Southern California (2012)
25. Digital Future. World Internet Project Report: Ninth Edition (2018). https://www.digitalce nter.org/world-internet-project/. Accessed 30 July 2021
26. Liu, Y.D.: An open evaluation in academia promotes the scholarly creativity. J. Beijing Normal Univ. (Soc. Sci.) (2018)

Effective Researcher Collaboration: A Taxonomy of Key Factors Impacting Knowledge Sharing

Hanlie Smuts[1]([✉]) [iD], Vladimir Sudakov[2] [iD], and Ester Luna Colombini[3] [iD]

[1] Department of Informatics, University of Pretoria, Pretoria, South Africa
hanlie.smuts@up.ac.za
[2] Department of Mathematical Modeling Problems and High-Performance Computing, Keldysh Institute of Applied Mathematics, Russian Academy of Sciences, Moscow, Russia
sudakov@ws-dss.com
[3] Department of Information Systems, University of Campinas (Unicamp), Campinas , SP, Brazil
esther@ic.unicamp.br

Abstract. Collaborative research practices are a means to solve significant challenges faced by the modern-day world. In the quest to provide efficient and effective solutions, societies are challenged with how to manage the knowledge created by such solutions. In addition, there are differences in the roles and approaches applied by different research team members of a research collaboration project related to ways of work, as well as knowledge sharing as a multifaceted concept and contextual in practice. Therefore, the aim of this study is to consider the key factors impacting knowledge sharing in researcher collaboration projects. The taxonomy development process defined by Nickerson et. al. was utilized to analyze academic, peer-reviewed papers and derive a taxonomy of key factors impacting researcher collaboration knowledge sharing consisting of 8 dimensions and 31 characteristics. Such a taxonomy is useful not only for describing key factors impacting knowledge sharing in researcher collaboration, but also as an assessment and development tool for researchers to increase efficacy of knowledge sharing. This was illustrated through application of the taxonomy with one exemplary study.

Keywords: Researcher collaboration · Knowledge sharing · Taxonomy

1 Introduction

The contemporary world is facing a significant number of challenges, of which the COVID pandemic is but one [1, 2]. Although revolutionary advances in science, research, and technology may provide efficient and effective solutions to better solve complex problems, societies are challenged with how to manage the created knowledge of such solutions [1]. In this regard, emerging collaborative research practices have emphasized the need to bring together researchers, to harness a variety of expertise, and to enable

L. Uden et al. (Eds.): KMO 2022, CCIS 1593, pp. 65–76, 2022.
https://doi.org/10.1007/978-3-031-07920-7_6

them to work together towards achieving a common goal [1, 3]. Furthermore, building on a foundation of such a collaborative team helps to connect the talent of team members, enhance effectiveness, promote individual skills, accelerate solution finding, and increase job satisfaction [4].

Regardless of the position and experience of researchers in a collaborative team, they all provide valuable knowledge to share, as well as to receive [5]. However, there are differences in the roles and approaches applied by different team members of a research collaboration project [6–8], not only as it relates to ways of work, but also as it pertains to knowledge sharing as a multifaceted concept and contextual in practice [6, 9]. In order to investigate this multifaceted notion towards effective researcher collaboration, this study aims to consider the key factors impacting knowledge sharing in researcher collaboration projects. The primary research question that this study aims to address is: *"What are the key factors impacting knowledge sharing in researcher collaboration projects?"*. This was achieved by reviewing the literature focusing on critical success factors pertinent to researcher collaboration projects and by applying Nickerson et al.'s classification method for developing a taxonomy [10]. By applying the taxonomy of the key factors impacting knowledge sharing in researcher collaboration projects, researchers will be able to increase the efficacy of their engagement, as well as deliver optimal research outputs.

Section 2 of this paper provides the background to the study and presents an overview of knowledge sharing and researcher collaboration. The approach to this study is discussed in Sect. 3, while Sect. 4 provides an overview of the taxonomy development process, as well as the taxonomy of the key factors impacting knowledge sharing in research collaboration projects. Section 5 illustrates the application of the taxonomy and Sect. 6 concludes the paper.

2 Background

The scientific performance of research universities is impacted by inter-organizational collaboration across the universities, research institutes, and industries [11]. The success of such inter-organizational research projects is impacted by many key factors related to the intention of the knowledge creators, the interactive nature of engagement in the research project team, and the shared vision subscribed to by all members of the research team [11, 12].

In the following sections, we consider knowledge sharing and researcher collaboration at universities.

2.1 Knowledge Sharing

Knowledge sharing refers to the voluntary process of exchanging tacit and explicit knowledge from one person to another person or group in an organization [13, 14]. A greater extent of knowledge sharing secures success in the face of uncertainty because it facilitates a shared interpretation of unexpected alterations, emerging problems, and potential solutions [15]. The accumulation of practical skills by an individual encompasses the transition from explicit forms of knowledge to more tacit forms through a process of cognitive processing. Cognitive processing transforms information into knowledge [16, 17]. The codification and articulation of knowledge make the knowledge explicit, enabling knowledge exchange with another individual, which, in turn, transforms information into knowledge interpreted in the individual's mental model [18]. Shared knowledge is created on the basis of such knowledge integration, which is required for individuals to come to the same understanding of an issue [19].

However, several factors impede knowledge sharing, such as lack of top management support and participation [20], hierarchy (inequality of project team members) [20–23], human nature (the notion that sharing one's data, understanding, and opinion with others diminishes one's personal competitive advantage) [24–28], geographical barriers [21, 28] and personality (strong preference for analysis discourages offering ideas without hard facts) [21, 23, 25, 28, 29]. Therefore, one of the initial steps towards creating shared knowledge is to construct a common language, as different domains speak and understand a different domain language. This will ensure that the goals and requirements of one domain are not perceived as unreasonable by another domain [19]. Another mechanism that enables a shared knowledge base is frequent interaction. This creates a mutual understanding, alleviates cooperation barriers, and creates a common frame of reference [19].

2.2 Researcher Collaboration

Research universities are recognized as knowledge-based organizations [6] that revolve around knowledge creation and - dissemination, leading to consequential advancement and growth advantage [20]. Such research collaboration is the incubator for new knowledge, placing knowledge sharing at the center [9]. Knowledge sharing is therefore vital to universities in general and specifically for the career advancement, self-empowerment and reputation of faculty members [3]. Faculty members have contributed to research projects based on their extensive knowledge and work experience in research [9].

However, faculty members tend to be autonomous, independent and individualistic, impacting their willingness to share knowledge and ultimately potentially affecting institutional goals and objectives [12]. Therefore, research universities must focus on approaches that foster collaboration, which is an essential enabler of knowledge sharing among team members [14]. In particular, the SECI model [30] presents a process spiral based on tacit and explicit knowledge interchange among individuals, eventually becoming group knowledge [30]. The 4 modes of knowledge conversion in the knowledge spiral include socialization (sharing experience to create new knowledge), externalization (articulating and converting knowledge), combination (restructuring and aggregating knowledge), and internalization (reflecting on knowledge and internalizing it) [30]. Multiple factors impacting these modes of knowledge conversion must therefore be considered by research universities and research teams [14, 31].

3   Research Approach

The objective of this paper was to design a taxonomy of the key factors impacting knowledge sharing in researcher collaboration projects. Next, we present an overview of the taxonomy development approach followed by the outline of the taxonomy development process.

3.1 Taxonomy Development Approach

Nickerson et al. studied classification methods and as a main contribution of their work, they defined a taxonomy, as well as proposed a classification method for a taxonomy [10]. They formally define a taxonomy T as a set of n dimensions D_i ($i = 1, ..., n$), each consisting of k_i ($k_i \geq 2$) mutually exclusive and collectively exhaustive characteristics C_{ij} ($j = 1, ..., k_i$) such that each object under consideration has one and only one C_{ij} for each D_i, or $T = \{D_i, i = 1, ..., n \mid D_i = \{C_{ij}, j = 1, ..., k_i; k_i \geq 2\}\}$. They specified additional characteristics of taxonomies that need to be adhered to, including that taxonomies should be mutually exclusive (an object in a dimension cannot have two different characteristics) and collectively exhaustive (each object must have one of the characteristics in a dimension). Together these conditions imply that each object has exactly one of the characteristics in a dimension. The classification approach defined by Nickerson et al. [10] consists of an iterative method that starts with establishing the meta-characteristics (informed by the overall purpose of the taxonomy) and determining the ending conditions, that may be subjective or objective. Subjective ending conditions relate to conciseness, robustness, comprehensiveness, extendibility and explanatory factors of the classification. Objective ending conditions included confirmation that a representative sample of objects has been examined, that no object was merged or split, or new object added, during the last iteration of the taxonomy development steps and that no 'null' objects exist [10].

In a *conceptual-to-empirical* iteration, the dimensions of the taxonomy are conceptualized in a deductive or intuitive way that is based on the researcher's knowledge. These dimensions are then refined by adding characteristics that allow for the classification of objects. In an *empirical-to-conceptual* iteration, the researcher identifies a subset of objects that have to be classified, and from an investigation of the objects, characteristics are identified. These characteristics are then refined into dimensions. It is necessary to note that for the development of a taxonomy, both types of iterations may be adopted. For instance, the first iteration might be conceptual-to-empirical, and a next iteration that refines the taxonomy could be empirical-to-conceptual. The iterations are performed until the ending conditions are met.

3.2 Taxonomy Development Process

In order to develop the taxonomy, we followed a number of steps. Firstly, we identified potentially relevant articles using a keyword search with the terms "researcher collaboration" and "critical success factors". The keyword search was executed in common academic databases and 33 peer-reviewed papers were extracted. Secondly, we screened the identified set of papers and extracted 27 papers as we excluded non-English papers, duplicates, and papers that did not contribute any considered key factors impacting researcher collaboration projects. We concluded a detailed screening of abstracts and analysis of the full text of the prospective papers and based on citations highlighting relevant papers, added 5 additional papers to the dataset (Appendix 1) as shown in Fig. 1.

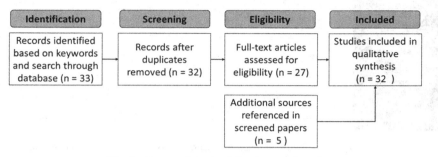

Fig. 1. Peer-reviewed publications analysed.

The dataset (Appendix 1) was utilized for the systematic development of the taxonomy dimensions and characteristics based on Nickerson et al.'s [10] taxonomy development method. This taxonomy development process [32, 33] was executed through a number of steps: firstly, we defined the meta-characteristics as the dimensions of key impacts on researcher collaboration knowledge sharing. We proceeded with the classification process until all the extracted papers in our dataset were classified and the ending conditions were fulfilled as specified by Nickerson et. al. [10].

In terms of the iterations, we initially adopted a conceptual-to-empirical iteration and integrated taxonomy dimensions identified in the literature review. The rest of the iterations were empirical-to-conceptual and led to classifying of all the extracted papers in our dataset guided by the key factors impacting knowledge sharing in research collaboration. We describe each dimension in the taxonomy in detail in the taxonomy in detail in the paper's results section.

Lastly, we performed a thematic analysis for each dimension of the taxonomy to identify, analyze and report patterns or characteristics within the data [34]. The purpose of thematic analysis is to interpret and organize the data in order to identify patterns or themes, emphasizing both organization and detailed description of the data set and theoretically inform the interpretation of meaning [35, 36]. We followed an iterative approach identifying patterns of themes until all characteristics in a particular taxonomy dimension were classified (Appendix 2).

In the next section, the taxonomy design of the key factors impacting knowledge sharing in research collaboration projects is discussed.

4   Results: Taxonomy for Key Factors Impacting Knowledge Sharing in Researcher Collaboration Projects

The purpose of this study is to present a taxonomy of the key factors impacting knowledge sharing in researcher collaboration projects. In Fig. 2 the taxonomy of key factors impacting researcher collaboration knowledge sharing is depicted consisting of 8 dimensions, and each dimension with 2 to 5 distinct characteristics.

DIMENSIONS	CHARACTERISTICS					
Motivation	Financial		Non-financial	Development		Recognition
Engagement	Culture	Soft skills	Team cohesion	Interaction		Communication
Governance	Commercial		Control			Project management
Purpose	Common goal		Clear expectations			Shared vision
Way of work	Role clarity	Structure	Environment		Evaluation	Operations
Resources	Technology	Allocation	Infrastructure		Human	Funding
Knowledge	Information management			Knowledge distribution		
Outcome	Academic reward		Spin-offs	Synergies		Performance

Fig. 2. Taxonomy of key factors impacting researcher collaboration knowledge sharing.

The *motivation* dimension refers to the characteristics that motivate researchers to collaborate in research projects and consists of 4 characteristics. *Financial* refers to financial rewards received by both universities and researchers for the execution or completion of research projects [5, 8], while the *non-financial* characteristic refers to e.g. promotion opportunity resulting from research outputs achieved [8]. The *development* characteristic refers to sufficient time spent in the research collaboration project in order to focus on team development [5]. The final characteristic, *recognition*, refers to local and global research community acknowledgment based on research collaboration outputs achieved [8].

The *engagement* dimension describes the level of enthusiasm and dedication a research team member feels toward their job and consists of 5 characteristics. *Culture* includes aspects such as the collective effort, mutual respect, trust and shared collaborative nature of the research team. In addition, it describes the application of a "common language" in the research collaboration team [5, 7, 9, 37–40]. *Soft skills* refer to adaptability, leadership, problem-solving and reflection [37, 38, 41, 42], while *team cohesion* includes the social interdependence of the research collaboration team, as well as team integration [38]. *Interaction* represents collaboration structure and processes, decision making, interpersonal relationships and partnerships. Furthermore, it signifies the researcher collaborators' jointly developed "rules of engagement" [5, 7, 38, 41, 43, 44]. The fifth characteristic, *communication*, denotes engagement with stakeholders, face-to-face interactions, shared communications, and well-elaborated communication etiquette [5, 7, 38, 40, 45]. Closed-loop communication enables effective communication processes that empower team members to better grasp the intent and relevance of information [5, 7, 37, 38, 41, 46–48]. *Governance* is the dimension that deals with commercial aspects (development of research agreements), control (good governance structure with the integrated research program and process) and project management (application of good project management principles and project prioritization) [5, 38, 40, 47, 49].

The *purpose* dimension points to creating a common understanding or *common goal* and priorities for the research project. *Shared vision* is created through shared mental models, while *clear expectations* ensure matching participants' expectations and objectives [5, 7, 37–40]. The *ways of work* dimension refer to the aspects that enable the research team to collaborate. *Role clarity* ensures clear roles and responsibilities and authentic task allocation [5, 38, 42], while *structure* points to the organizational design of the cross-functional, multi-disciplinary team [49]. *Environment* denotes working environment factors and change management [7, 50], aiding task performance strategies and *operations,* including policies, processes and procedures for collaboration and interoperability standards, and administrative processes that impact scientific productivity [5, 7, 38, 40, 51]. The *evaluation* characteristic represents mutual performance monitoring and output evaluation, as well as trials and pilots [38, 43, 52]. *Resource* denotes a source of supply or support and includes aspects such as *human* and *financial* resources [5, 7, 8, 38, 40, 53, 54], *infrastructure* (equipment) [5, 7] and *technology* [7, 40, 41], including media required to facilitate collaboration processes. *Allocation* refers to a balanced research across the researcher collaboration project [55]. *Knowledge* represents two characteristics, namely *information management* and *knowledge distribution* referring to the collective knowledge, skills and expertise of the research collaboration team, as well as the efficacy of knowledge transfer among team members [5, 38, 48, 56–58]. *Outcome* signifies some of the outcomes of the research collaboration project, such as *spin-offs* where research findings may be monetized, the design of the research collaboration as a *performing* unit and producing synergistic outcomes in accordance with the objectives. Finally, the *academic reward* is a key aspect once the research collaboration project is concluded [38, 40, 52, 59, 60].

In the next section, we share the application of the taxonomy with one exemplary study.

5   Using the Proposed Taxonomy of Key Factors Impacting Researcher Collaboration Knowledge Sharing

This study aimed to present a taxonomy of the key factors impacting knowledge sharing in research collaboration. The taxonomy presented in the previous section could be applied as an analysis tool to improve the knowledge-sharing efficacy in the research collaboration project. The South African team working as part of a multi-country BRICS research collaboration with Russia and Brazil, tested the application of the taxonomy as an analysis tool and applied a basic red-amber-green notation to denote their knowledge sharing experience in the research collaboration in Fig. 3.

The *recognition* and *evaluation* characteristics were rated amber as it is too early in the BRICS research collaboration and no recognition or integrated evaluation has been noted. Due to the COVID pandemic, the teams could not travel among the BRICS countries, and no face-to-face engagement has taken place yet, which impacted *team cohesion.* This also impacted the *structure* characteristic as an integrated organizational research collaboration structure has not been established. Although each country forms part of the research collaboration, no integrated *information management* and no *knowledge distribution* has been achieved. Information is managed in local country repositories. Due to the research collaboration project stage, only some *synergies* could be realized

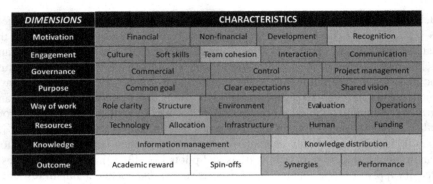

DIMENSIONS	CHARACTERISTICS				
Motivation	Financial		Non-financial	Development	Recognition
Engagement	Culture	Soft skills	Team cohesion	Interaction	Communication
Governance	Commercial		Control		Project management
Purpose	Common goal		Clear expectations		Shared vision
Way of work	Role clarity	Structure	Environment	Evaluation	Operations
Resources	Technology	Allocation	Infrastructure	Human	Funding
Knowledge	Information management			Knowledge distribution	
Outcome	Academic reward		Spin-offs	Synergies	Performance

Fig. 3. Exemplary study mapped with the proposed taxonomy using heat map notation.

and *performance* is monitored at the local country level. It was too early to assess *academic rewards* and *spin-offs* as the research collaboration is still in progress. Using the proposed taxonomy as an assessment tool, the researcher collaboration project team may now focus on closing the identified gaps and ensuring that knowledge sharing occurs optimally.

6 Conclusion

In this study, we presented a taxonomy of the key factors impacting researcher collaboration knowledge sharing. The taxonomy was developed by applying Nickerson et. al's [10] taxonomy development process.

A taxonomy of key factors impacting knowledge sharing in researcher collaboration, consisting of 8 dimensions, was defined. Each taxonomy dimension consists of two to five characteristics. Such a taxonomy is useful not only for describing key factors impacting knowledge sharing in researcher collaboration, but also as an assessment and development tool for researchers to increase efficacy of knowledge sharing. In order to illustrate the application of the taxonomy, an example assessment against the taxonomy using the heat map notation, was shared. One team within the broader multi-country BRICS researcher collaboration highlighted that the proposed taxonomy was a useful tool to identify where knowledge was shared optimally and what still needed further attention.

The characteristics of the first version taxonomy is quite coarse and further refinement of the classification may be implemented in future research. In addition, specific implications for practice, aimed at university administrators and Deans, would be useful, in order to increase collaboration among researchers. Finally, a study that specifically evaluates the applicability of the taxonomy related to knowledge shared in the entire research collaboration project (BRICS), may also be considered for further study.

Appendix 1. Dataset Created from Papers Identified (Extract Only)

Communication	Clear, effective communication	[5, 7, 37, 41, 46-48]
Communication	Face-to-face interactions	[5, 38, 40, 45]
Communication	Shared communications	[38]
Communication	Well elaborated communication etiquette	[40]
Development	Sufficient time for team development	[5]
Engagement	Adaptability	[38]
Engagement	Appropriate team orientation	[5]
Engagement	Closed-loop communication	[38]
Engagement	Collaboration structure	[7]
Engagement	Collaborative culture	[38]
Engagement	Collaborative processes	[43]
Engagement	Decision making	[41]
Engagement	Interaction processes	[38]

Appendix 2. Classification During Taxonomy Development Process (Extract Only)

Engagement	Communication	Clear, effective communication	[5, 7, 37, 41, 46-48]
Engagement	Communication	Closed-loop	[38]
Engagement	Communication	Engagement of stakeholders	[7]
Engagement	Communication	Face-to-face interactions	[5, 38, 40, 45]
Engagement	Communication	Shared communications	[38]
Engagement	Communication	Well elaborated communication etiquette	[40]
Engagement	Culture	Collective effort and motivation	[38]
Engagement	Culture	Mutual respect and trust	[5, 7, 9, 37, 38]
Engagement	Culture	Shared and collaborative culture	[7, 38, 39]
Engagement	Culture	Usage of common language	[40]
Engagement	Interaction	Collaboration structure and processes	[7, 43]
Engagement	Interaction	Decision making	[41]
Engagement	Interaction	Interpersonal relationships	[38]
Engagement	Interaction	Jointly develop "rules of engagement"	[5]
Engagement	Interaction	Researcher relationships and partnership	[5, 44]
Engagement	Soft skills	Adaptability	[38]

References

1. Zamiri, M., et al.: Knowledge management in research collaboration networks. In: 2019 International Conference on Industrial Engineering and Systems Management (IESM) (2019)
2. Gerard, G., Lakhani, K.R., Puranam, P.: What has changed? The impact of COVID pandemic on the technology and innovation management research agenda. J. Manage. Stud. **57**(8), 1754–1758 (2020)
3. CegarraNavarro, J.G., et al.: Turning heterogeneity into improved research outputs in international R&D teams. J. Bus. Res. **128**, 770–778 (2021)

4. Randrup, N., Druckenmiller, D., Briggs, R.: Philosophy of collaboration. In: 49th Hawaii International Conference on System Sciences. IEEE, Hawaii (2016)
5. Bowen, S., et al.: Beyond "two cultures": guidance for establishing effective researcher/health system partnerships. Int. J. Health Policy Manage. 6(1), 27–42 (2017)
6. Ibrahim, F., Ali, D.N.: Evaluating knowledge management practices in higher education institutions (HEIs): towards KMPro framework guidelines. In: Zyngier, S. (ed.) Enhancing Academic Research and Higher Education with Knowledge Management Principles, pp. 221–245. IGI Global, Hershey, PA, USA (2021)
7. Dok Yen, D.M., Adinyira, E., Dauda, A.M.: Imperatives for academia-industry collaboration in building construction research in Ghana. J. Build. Constr. Plann. Res. 6(4), 185–197 (2018)
8. Kharazmi, O.A.: Modelling the role of university-industry collaboration in the Iranian national system of innovation: generating transition policy scenarios. In: Stirling Management School. University of Stirling: United Kingdom, p. 514 (2011)
9. Tan, C.N.-L., Noor, S.: Knowledge management enablers, knowledge sharing and research collaboration: a study of knowledge management at research universities in Malaysia. Asian J. Technol. Innov. 21(2), 251–276 (2013)
10. Nickerson, R., Varshney, U., Muntermann, J.: A method for taxonomy development and its application in IS. Eur. J. Inf. Syst. 22, 336–359 (2013)
11. Chen, K., et al.: Do research institutes benefit from their network positions in research collaboration networks with industries or/and universities? Technovation 94–95, 102002 (2020)
12. Syed, A., et al.: The impact of knowledge management processes on knowledge sharing attitude: the role of subjective norms. J. Asian Fin. Econ. Bus. 8(1), 1017–1030 (2021)
13. Woo Bock, G., Way Siew, C., Jung Kang, Y.: Effects of extrinsic rewards on knowledge sharing initiatives. In: Khosrow-Pour, D.B.A.M., (ed.) Encyclopedia of Information Science and Technology, Second Edition, pp. 1287–1293. IGI Global, Hershey, PA, USA (2009)
14. Julpisit, A., Esichaikul, V.: A collaborative system to improve knowledge sharing in scientific research projects. Inf. Dev. 35(4), 624–638 (2018)
15. Stock, G.N., et al.: Coping with uncertainty: Knowledge sharing in new product development projects. Int. J. Project Manage. 39(1), 59–70 (2021)
16. Alavi, M., Leidner, D.E.: Review: knowledge management and knowledge management systems: conceptual foundations and research issues. MIS Q. 25(1), 107–136 (2001)
17. Jones, E., Chonko, L., Roberts, J.: Creating a partnership-orientated, knowledge creation culture in strategic sales alliances: a conceptual framework. J. Bus. Indus. Mark. 18(4), 336–352 (2003)
18. Nonaka, I., Takeuchi, H.: The Knowledge Creating Company. Oxford University Press, Oxford (1995)
19. Blumenberg, S., Wagner, H.-T., Beimborn, D.: Knowledge transfer processes in IT outsourcing relationships and their impact on shared knowledge and outsourcing performance. Int. J. Inf. Manage. 29, 342–352 (2009)
20. Tan, C.-L.: Enhancing knowledge sharing and research collaboration among academics: the role of knowledge management. High. Educ. 71(4), 525–556 (2016). https://doi.org/10.1007/s10734-015-9922-6
21. Kotelnikov, V.: Collecting, Leveraging and Distributing both Explicit and Tacit Knowledge Throughout Your Organisation (2001). www.1000ventures.com
22. Andrew, B., Westhuizen, J.: To share or not to share? In: Competing Effectively in the Information Economy: Knowledge Management, pp. 34–39 (1999)
23. Hosen, M., et al.: Individual motivation and social media influence on student knowledge sharing and learning performance: evidence from an emerging economy. Comput. Educ. 172, 104262 (2021)

24. Godbout, A.J.: Filtering knowledge: changing information into knowledge assets. J. Syst. Knowl. Manage. (J. Knowl. Manage. Pract.), **1**, 1 (1999)
25. Muller, R.M., Spiliopoulou, M., Lenz, H.J.: The Influence of incentives and culture on knowledge sharing. In: Proceedings of the 38th Hawaii International Conference on System Science. IEEE, Hawaii (2005)
26. Frappaolo, C.: Knowledge Management, 127p. Capstone Publishing Ltd, West Sussex (2006)
27. Krogh, G., Ichijo, K., Nonaka, I.: Enabling Knowledge Creation: How to Unlock the Mystery of Tacit Knowledge and Release the Power of Innovation, 292p. Oxford University Press Inc., New York (200)
28. Marwick, A.D.: Knowledge management technology. IBM Syst. J. **40**(4), 814–830 (2001)
29. McCullough, C.: What is Knowledge Management - Knowing What We Know? (2005). www.topicarticles.com/knowledge-management/
30. Nonaka, I., Toyama, R., Konno, N.: SECI, Ba and leadership: a unified model of dynamic knowledge creation. Long Range Plan. **33**, 5–34 (2000)
31. Chikh, A.: A knowledge management framework in software requirements engineering based on the SECI Model. J. Softw. Eng. Appl. **4**(12), 11 (2011)
32. Remane, G., et al.: The business model pattern database: a tool for systematic business model innovation. Int. J. Innov. Manage. **21**(1), 1–61 (2017)
33. Nakatsu, R.T., Grossman, E.B., Iacovou, C.L.: A taxonomy of crowdsourcing based on task complexity. J. Inf. Sci. **40**(6), 823–834 (2014)
34. Vaismoradi, M., Turunen, H., Bondas, T.: Content analysis and thematic analysis: implications for conducting a qualitative descriptive study. Nurs. Health Sci. **15**(3), 398–405 (2013)
35. Alhojailan, M.I.: Thematic analysis: a critical review of its process and evaluation. West East J. Soc. Sci. **1**(1), 39–47 (2012)
36. Leedy, P.D., Ormrod, J.E.: Practical Research: Planning and Design. 12th Edn. Pearson, London (2018)
37. Hansen, B.D., et al. Facilitation–a supporting approach towards successful University-Business knowledge collaboration. In: Proceedings of the University Industry Interaction Conference: Challenges and Solutions for Fostering Entrepreneurial Universities and Collaborative Innovation. University Industry Innovation Network, Amsterdam (2015)
38. Waruszynski, B.T.: Collaboration in Scientific Research: Factors That Influence Effective Collaboration During a Period of Transformational Change, p. 300. Royal Roads University (Canada), Ann Arbor (2017)
39. Wildridge, V., et al.: How to create successful partnerships—a review of the literature. Health Info. Libr. J. **21**(s1), 3–19 (2004)
40. Karume, S.M., Muchiri, G.: Accelerating research in africa through sustainable virtual research communities. In: Proceedings and report of the 5th UbuntuNet Alliance Annual Conference. UbuntuNet Alliance (2012)
41. Jääskä, E., Aaltonen, K., Kujala, J.: Game-based learning in project sustainability management education. Sustainability **13**(15), 8204 (2021)
42. Gazi, Z.A.: Implementing constructivist approach into online course designs in distance education institute at Eastern Mediterranean University. Turkish Online J. Educ. Technol. **8**(2), 7 (2009)
43. Fisher, J., Carberry, P.: Participative evaluation of learning and impacts (2008)
44. Walter, I., Davies, H., Nutley, S.: Increasing research impact through partnerships: evidence from outside health care. J. Health Serv. Res. Policy. **8**(2_suppl), 58–61 (2003)
45. Jagosh, J., et al.: A realist evaluation of community-based participatory research: partnership synergy, trust building and related ripple effects. BMC Public Health **15**(1), 725 (2015)
46. Sibbald, S.L., Tetroe, J., Graham, I.D.: Research funder required research partnerships: a qualitative inquiry. Implement. Sci. **9**(1), 176 (2014)

47. Salsberg, J., et al.: Successful strategies to engage research partners for translating evidence into action in community health: a critical review. J. Environ. Public Health **2015**, 191856 (2015)
48. Butler, P.: Marketing problems: from analysis to decision. Mark. Intell. Plan. **12**(2), 4–12 (1994)
49. Masara, B., van der Poll, J.A., Maaza, M.: A nanotechnology-foresight perspective of South Africa. J. Nanopart. Res. **23**(4), 1–22 (2021). https://doi.org/10.1007/s11051-021-05193-6
50. Casey, M.: Partnership – success factors of interorganizational relationships. J. Nurs. Manage. **16**(1), 72–83 (2008)
51. Liu, Z., et al.: A paradigm of safety management in Industry 4.0. Syst. Res. Behav. Sci. **37**(4), 632–645 (2020)
52. Cargo, M., Mercer, S.L.: The value and challenges of participatory research: strengthening its practice. Annu. Rev. Public Health **29**(1), 325–350 (2008)
53. Smits, P.A., Denis, J.-L.: How research funding agencies support science integration into policy and practice: an international overview. Implement. Sci. **9**(1), 28 (2014)
54. Tetroe, J.M., et al.: Health research funding agencies' support and promotion of knowledge translation: an international study. Milbank Q. **86**(1), 125–155 (2008)
55. Jiang, W., et al.: Political risk management of foreign direct investment in infrastructure projects. Eng. Constr. Archit. Manage. **28**(1), 125–153 (2021)
56. Purnomo, S., et al.: E-procurement research mapping: lesson from bibliometric approach (1975–2019). In: 2021 International Conference on Information Management and Technology (ICIMTech) (2021)
57. Purnomo, A., et al.: Mapping of business intelligence research themes: four decade review. In: 2021 IEEE International Conference on Communication, Networks and Satellite (COMNETSAT) (2021)
58. Kirschner, F., Paas, F., Kirschner, P.A.: A cognitive load approach to collaborative learning: united brains for complex tasks. Educ. Psychol. Rev. **21**(1), 31–42 (2009)
59. Stanton, T.K.: New times demand new scholarship: opportunities and challenges for civic engagement at research universities. Educ. Citizensh. Soc. Justice **3**(1), 19–42 (2008)
60. Carthey, J.: User group consultation: design quality and project success. HERD: Health Environ. Res. Des. J. **13**(2), 143–169 (2019)

Knowledge and Organization

Part II The Organization

Knowledge Communication in Government ICT Projects: A Cross-Case Analysis Study

Rohaizan Daud[1]($\boxtimes$), Surya Sumarni Hussein[2], Nor Zairah Ab Rahim[3],
Roslina Ibrahim[3], Suraya Ya'acob[3], and Nur Azaliah Abu Bakar[3]

[1] National Institute of Public Administration (INTAN) Public Service Department, Kuala
Lumpur, Malaysia
`rohaizan@intanbk.intan.my`
[2] Faculty of Computer and Mathematical Sciences, Universiti Teknologi MARA, Shah Alam,
Malaysia
`suryasumarni@uitm.edu.my`
[3] Advanced Informatics Department, Faculty of Technology and Informatics,
Universiti Teknologi Malaysia, Kuala Lumpur, Malaysia
`{nzairah,iroslina,suraya.yaacob,azaliah}@utm.my`

Abstract. This study proposes a model from the identified elements affecting knowledge communication during the decision-making process. This study also discusses in detail the findings from five case studies conducted in the Malaysian public sector. A comprehensive analysis of various works of literature outlined crucial elements that influence knowledge communication among IT experts and decision-makers. A conceptual model was developed and applied as a parameter for fifteen interviews at five agencies using the basis review. The cross-case analysis findings emerged a new digital communication element, besides four existing elements. At the end of this study, these elements will be summarised in a model of knowledge communication, particularly for decision-making purposes.

Keywords: Case studies · Knowledge communication · Decision making · IT experts · Decision-makers

1 Introduction

Recently, strategic proficiencies in decision making are strictly interrelated to the great prospect of success of an organization. To achieve this goal in the organization, numerous people whose obligations and parts are different must agree in making a decision. According to Ya'acob et al. [1], towards sustaining the organization's competitiveness, two elements which consist of humanity and non-humanity aspects, must complement each other to form the finest decision. Some examples of humanity are management, expertise, and obligation to work, whereas procedures, technology, and material are non-humanity elements.

However, since decision making in an organization is getting complex and dynamic, the collaboration of decision-makers and experts develops more critical factors to achieve

L. Uden et al. (Eds.): KMO 2022, CCIS 1593, pp. 79–90, 2022.
https://doi.org/10.1007/978-3-031-07920-7_7

high-quality decision making. This is in line with the study by Rogers et al. [3] and Abu Bakar et al. [4] that decision making is the process of incorporating different domains of knowledge by the decision-makers and experts into a complete form of group knowledge and applying it in an actual situation. The organization may face many challenges in collaborating knowledge between experts and decision-makers, such as developing common ground or mutual understanding of the topic.

In addition to that, through an appropriate support system, Knowledge Management (KM) also does an important part in continuing the organizations' competitive dominance towards making reliable decisions [2]. Therefore, knowledge communication (KC) is applied to manage and transfer knowledge across different domains. It is said that communication is more effective and productive when people share a better quantity of common knowledge [5]. Poor common ground will lead to a difficult path from information to knowledge and the decision-making process. KC significantly contributes to facilitating the decision-making process by improving the condition of work, spreading the insignificantly contributes to facilitating the decision-making process most by the system, and reducing amendment [6].

Recently, governments across the world are actively deploying various ICT projects to support citizen demands. Nevertheless, in the robust implementation of ICT projects, the KC aspect was often neglected as knowledge from IT experts and decision-makers was not transmitted, especially in a vital decision-making process. According to Patanakul [9], numerous researchers have been encouraged to review the problems of deprived performance due to the increasing statistic of unsuccessful ICT projects. However, there is still fewer back of review from the viewpoint of integrating ICT knowledge among experts and decision-makers. The integration in terms of communication is crucial as a study by Williams et al. [2] stated that during business analysis in the project initiation phase, IT experts need to sit together with decision-makers to assist with the project specification and finalize the expected project deliverable, project compliance conditions, and business demands. Since this interaction extensively focused on the initial stage of ICT project management [3], the challenge was to create mutual understanding on the communicated knowledge between IT experts and decision makers.

A study by Mengis [41] mentioned that the communication problems that existed between IT experts and decision makers could be different language use, various areas of expertise, use of jargon terms, and being too technical. Therefore, there is a need to explain how the communication takes place between the IT experts and decision makers so that the information communicated by them can be visualised understandably [1, 41]. Apart from the necessary information, knowledge communication also requires individual experience and judgment. It is more than just interacting via the materials such as charts, diagrams, and numbers or feelings (e.g., irritation, amazement, drowsy, and others) to convey the text, contextual, and expectations. Even though the direction has been established for relatively some period in several organizations, it is still new in academic study.

Therefore, this paper intends to explore the understanding of knowledge communication and describe five in-depth case studies conducted at agencies in the Malaysian public sector (MPS). The agencies selected based on these criteria have registered at least 100 ICT projects with a minimum of five functional projects; it has a workable ICT committee and is involved in the annual budget screening meeting (ABM). A detailed investigation was made on how KC is conducted in the ICT project management initial phase. In MPS, the initial phase includes the needs and details of the basics of ICT projects such as project scope, objectives, cost, and duration, as well as the benefits derived from project implementation; hence this phase is crucial to ensuring successful implementation of ICT projects.

2 Material and Method

2.1 The Concept of Knowledge Communication

KC occurs when the knowledge sender gives knowledge to the knowledge receiver. The process of conveying knowledge may be fitted into the communication model created by Shannon and Weaver in 1949 [44], which consists of a sender, message, and recipient. As mentioned earlier, KC is defined by Eppler [4] as the "activity of conveying and constructing insights, assessments, experiences, or skills through verbal and nonverbal means interactively in knowledge management". KC is many-to-many communication where knowledge is transferred and shared with many people in KM. These activities are called knowledge transfer and knowledge sharing [5]. KC is vital to make intra and inter knowledge transfers in knowledge management. KC is more than just communicating or interacting with information or emotions because it involves stating perception, primary hypotheses, individual thoughts, experiences, and contextual conditions. As noticed, interacting the proficient knowledge is the utmost competent transfer of experiences, thoughts, views, and skills among experts and decision makers.

2.2 KC in ICT Project

KC is critical in ensuring successful project management. This is aligned with research by Foong [42], Taherdoost, Kashavarzsaleh, and Wang [17], good communication among decision makers and experts can produce a reliable decision for an organisation. Hence, it upsurges the need for efficient communication. A systematic and well-defined KC will facilitate the clarity of project management. Communication in project management is a critically important element that can have a major impact on a team's performance. KC can help reduce the misunderstanding; the use of jargon terms and the project team will be able to develop mutual understanding and grasp the big picture. The significance of this field in this study was measured by observing thoroughly the cases of MPS where a comprehensive overview of IT experts and decision-makers differs in conditions and procedures. Decision-makers also have difficulties expressing the needs and requirements conditions to the IT experts. Hence, when IT experts and decision-makers debate an issue without appropriate procedures, they build a general image of the problems according to their judgment. The hesitation and the misunderstanding in creating a complete outline usually bring to activities that vary throughout the stage of scrutiny and synthesis. As a result, to overcome some problems, it is necessary to re-adjust all parties' intellectual models and maintain a shared understanding by arranging the criteria and objectives outline. The outline also acts as a proposal that develops the key driver to gain and improve interpretation and assist the organisation in making better principal decisions.

2.3 Research Model Formulation

The development of the KC-ICTPM model in MPS is principally derived from the dimensionally content model by Leavitt H in 1965 and the communication model by Waller and Polonsky in 1998 [14]. Waller and Polonsky [14] suggests that most communication models are based on the 'traditional model' of sender-message-receiver, with an examination of the models using different aspects of communication or in different contexts. Since KC was born "to reduce the existing weakness of KM like knowledge sharing and knowledge transfer respectively", then Hidayat [6] suggested that KC should consider the process of knowledge sharing as a form of communication and knowledge transfer as an act of communication. Therefore, both KS and KT framework is selected to construct this new KC-ICTPM model.

Based on the discussion about knowledge sharing frameworks, it is practical to choose the ShaRInk framework in this research [20]. This is because the ShaRInK framework is the most current with 12 interrelationships. All the elements are considered suitable and similar to the existing issues in KC in the MPS. These elements are from the enhancement of the study by Wang and Noe [17], which is an opportunity to explore the model in this study. On the other hand, the idea of the elected KT model by Liyanage [24] is mainly built upon two main elements; source and receiver, or known as "an act of communication". The type of knowledge in this model is based on Nonaka [26], namely, tacit and explicit. The KC-ICTPM conceptual model (Fig. 1) was used as a parameter during interview sessions with the experts.

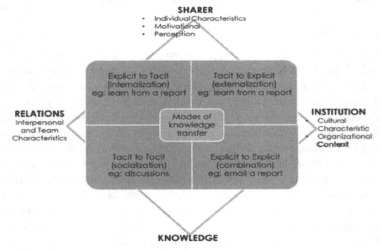

Fig. 1. KC-ICTPM conceptual model

The proposed conceptual model (Fig. 1) combines both knowledge sharing framework and knowledge transfer model with 12 interrelationships between elements that are sharer, relationship, institution, and knowledge. The first element, the sharer, contains three sub-elements: individual characteristics, motivation, and perceptions on shared knowledge. The second element emphasises the institution that performs as an incorporated unit that comprises cultural characteristics and organizational context. Next, the relationship element concentrates on the connotation between the sharer and another sharer with interpersonal and team characteristics as the sub-element. Finally, the knowledge element is pertinent only to itself.

The four elements are interconnected towards each other. Such interrelationships refer to the influence of each element's significance towards other elements and mode of knowledge communicated. For example, the elements of the relation are determined by the characteristics of the institution at which the sharers are attached; hence explicit knowledge is applied. The sharers' attitude is influenced by relation elements through the job position and education background. These elements and sub-elements were then mapped upon the proposed conceptual model. The modes of knowledge transfer from the receiver and source are separated into four types, namely: (1) explicit to tacit (e.g., learning from a report); (2) tacit to explicit (e.g., small dialogue session); (3) tacit to tacit (e.g., team meetings); and (4) explicit to explicit (e.g., email a report). The proposed KC-ICTPM model theoretically suggests numerous perspectives on the knowledge communication process in an organization.

2.4 Multiple Case Studies Methodologies

For this study, main data sources is in-depth case study interviews. The case study interviews were conducted with fifteen participants from five agencies that involve ICT projects. Case studies aim to gain a rich understanding of KC in the MPS ICT Project Management. In relation to this research, the researcher developed a start-list based on the prior issues addressed in the conceptual model. The themes refer to elements in KC, while sub-themes indicate sub-elements of KC. In the case study, the data gathered from the interviews were transcribed and translated before the relevant codes, or key findings were captured. Then, each of the key findings was then grouped according to the similarities and the themes. The key findings process for this research was simplified since the themes and sub-themes were identified earlier in the start list. These in-depth interviews were analysed using the thematic analytic method. The term thematic analysis method was coined by Javadi and Zarea [33] as "it provides core skills that will be useful for conducting many other kinds of analysis". The thematic analysis is used to identify themes, which consist of patterns in the data that are important or interesting to be used to address the research or raise concern over an issue. This method is more than just summarising the data; however, as a good thematic analysis, it is conducted to interpret and make sense of the data collected. The in-depth interviews with the KC-ICTPM model as a parameter were used in which experts or interviewees identified and explained the elements and sub-elements by themselves.

The in-depth interviews with all participants were conducted at their workplaces. Every interview session was held between 45 min to 1 h. The questions are divided into four sections; (1) involvement of participants in the ICT project; (2) awareness about the relevant Standard Operating Procedures (SOP) and the existing practice of ICT project management; (3) the challenges, problems, and recommendation to improve the quality of Malaysian Public Sector ICT project management; and (4) demographic questions. Since the participants were selected from both IT experts and decision-makers backgrounds, therefore this study can gain richer data, better understanding, and relevant information on KC in MPS.

3   Results and Discussion

3.1   Cross-Case Analysis

In line with the aim of this study, the objective is to enrich data on KC in MPS. Sufficient to this requirement, the data collected allow a comprehensive picture of how KC is conducted in MPS. The four elements in KC Conceptual Model identified earlier in the literature were used for data analysis and as the parameter during interview sessions. Within the elements, the sub-elements are identified. Based on case studies' interview data from 15 participants in MPS, five elements of influences that are fundamentally different emerged. Most participants agreed about four main elements that contribute to KC, namely, i) Sharer, ii) Institution, iii) Relationship, and iv) Knowledge. In addition to that, one element was found from the case studies' interviews: technology and digital communication as the sub-element. The enhanced KC model developed in this study is modelled in a pentagon-shaped configuration, as represented in Fig. 2 below.

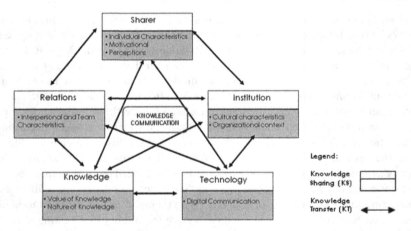

Fig. 2. An enhanced model of knowledge communication

To get a better idea of all the five elements above, each element is shortly discussed in the following sections.

3.1.1   Sharer

The first factor is concerning the sharer, which consists of three items. Sharer can be defined as an individual who can be the source or recipient who provides or receive knowledge [18, 20]. The sharer in these case studies refers to the decision-maker team and IT personnel, who consist of the IT team and IT experts. From Table 4, the initial influence of the KC process is the individual characteristics factor of the sharer. This coincides with Sanchez et al. [34], who mentioned that individual characteristics are essential to modernization and organizational success. However, in terms of motivational items, 11 respondents agreed with the motivation factor whilst four contended it. As for perception, among the response received from the interviews, only eight respondents agreed. When analysing the data, participants discussed the individual characteristics of other-sharer that formed their perceptions towards the decision-making process in the initial phase. One major difficulty of communicating knowledge between IT experts and decision makers is to get and uphold the big picture of the matter discussed. This is due to the different personnel backgrounds in the decision maker team. However, it is also noted that language is one of the main barriers. To minimize miscommunication, throughout the ICT project initial phase meeting with the top management, the presentation mostly applies the analogy model to achieve better understanding. This was mentioned by respondent E1 from the interview session.

3.1.2 Institution

The second element focuses on institutions that act as a united entity which includes cultural characteristics and organizational context as the items. It involves the whole organization from top-down and otherwise [20, 35]. The cultural characteristics factor of the institution element received 13 consents out of 15 respondents, and the organizational context factor received 14 consents out of 15 respondents. Organizational context includes involvement and practices of knowledge communication by the employees in the organization. As alluded to, MPS is an organization that has guidelines and laws to be followed for every project execution regardless of the project type. Since many MPS ICT projects are bound with law and regulation, both parties (IT experts and decision-makers) need to tolerate the responsibilities altogether. For instance, in Agency E, any changes to the requirements must follow the mission and vision of the agency. This was stated by one of the respondents, E1, during the interview:

"Any IT system in this agency must comply with mission and vision... it is improper if the system does not show characteristics in line with objectives of this agency" (Respondent E1).

Cultural characteristics reflect the personality to a structure of shared customs, views, and assumptions that grasp people together [36]. According to Kryloza et al. [37], it was mentioned that positive cultural characteristics (trust, openness) in an organization benefit knowledge practice among employees while negative values (silo) lead to knowledge hoarding. Cultural characteristics in MPS can be created and maintained by establishing 'common culture and common nationality'. Besides, Human Resource Management (HRM) within an organization can shape knowledge communication such as staff work rotation, training engagement, and proactively promoting social interaction.

3.1.3 Relations

As for the relations element, the study found the essential collaboration between experts and decision-makers while performing KC. All the participants agreed that interpersonal and team characteristics are important to improve the relationship between the sharers during KC. In terms of the relations element, it focuses on the corporation between the sharer and other-sharer. The team characteristics and processes influence knowledge communication among team members [17, 20]. Persistent cooperation, trustworthiness, and accurate communication between teammates are adequate to smooth out the process of ICT project management. Clearly, in this study, good teamwork and relationship is the key point to reduce problems in ICT projects development. The view was described by the respondent as follow:

> *"I have to be prepared for each meeting because decision-makers have different knowledge in IT... some may need layman language, some may not... thus sometimes technical people need to be in the room with me if I couldn't answer... here is the reason why the good relationship is needed among teammates" (Respondent D3).*

3.1.4   Knowledge

Knowledge is created when the flow of information interrelates with the experience, values, experts' insights, beliefs, and commitment of humans [12, 16, 38, 39]. The KC among IT experts and decision-makers comprises complex and tough activities such as decision-making, strategic forecasting, sensibility-making, and logical reasoning. This kind of activity involves higher-level thinking, and instead of memorizing, perceptive, and applying the value of knowledge; it also involves analyzing, synthesising, creating, and assessing the knowledge. Nevertheless, tacit knowledge can be effectively transferred through extensive personal interaction, regular communication, good and trustable relationships. Wise decisions taken may avoid failure in managing ICT projects as well as minimize unnecessary burdens like a waste of time, finances, and resources. As responded by D1;

> *"I have seen where the middle-man wrongly advised the chairman (decision maker)... the decision-maker didn't get the right picture of the issue and likely mislead the decision... the project took a long way to finish"* (Respondent D1)

The analysis with the experts also verified that the nature of knowledge sub element influences the communicating knowledge process between decision makers and IT experts. This is because knowledge is known as the most important resource and is widely used to deliver daily tasks. Decision makers' nature of task requires cognitive background to see the big picture of design thinking to the related issues. In contrast, IT experts' nature of the task, by contrast, is different from decision-makers in which to carry out technical tasks from the simplest to the most complex. The experts also agreed that sketching and analogy (as mentioned earlier during case studies) supports the cognitive process in generating and disclosing new ideas. These approaches are aligned with tacit knowledge concepts. Tacit knowledge cannot be communicated or practised without the knowledge owner's assistance/inputs. However, explicit knowledge, on the other hand, comprises the knowledge that is easily understood, codified and transferred, such as reports and email. E2 commented that;

"type of knowledge is depending on a certain project... if the project is easy, then I guess explicit knowledge is enough... however, if we have a complex project, at least one or two team members must be experienced personnel... their experience is built up over a long period; hence it is far above average and specialized" (Respondent E2)

In the above statement, it was agreed by all the experts that the knowledge element and its nature of knowledge sub-element influence KC. In addition to that, the experts highlighted the type of knowledge, particularly tacit knowledge, as the most important part of communication. Hence, by integrating the experience, new knowledge and high-level thinking skills, the communication to construct a reliable decision would be straightforward. Subsequently, all the statements relating to the knowledge element support the earlier findings of the case studies that knowledge is a significant element in KC of ICT project management for MPS.

3.1.5 Technology

Technology is a new element found during an interview in Agency C. Due to the potential benefits, many organizations use technology to ease knowledge communication [6]. A study by Yu et al. [40] revealed that the flexibility of technology brings many advantages to organizations and becomes embedded in the organization's activity. Obviously, in some organizations, knowledge is communicated at any time using various mediums such as emails, WhatsApp, Messenger, and Skype, where such kinds of interactions are widely put into practice today. It provides prospect, flexibility, and ease situation between the teammates to converse applicable topics that could be responded to during non-office hours. In MPS, the primary reason for the expansion in technology usage is because the policy has been carried out for IT development to be prioritized as the main tool to achieve efficient knowledge communication. Respondent C2 mentioned that:

"in MPS, we have our digital communication platform... I think we should fully utilize this platform to communicate and interact with team members on the projects... if the discussion is involved with external parties, we may use an external channel (digital communication platform) to communicate because technology is helping much on this". (Respondent C2)

Across all five cases with 15 respondents, it is interesting to note that the five key elements and nine sub-elements can influence the process of KC during the ICT project initial phase in MPS. Hence the Enhanced Model of Knowledge Communication (Fig. 2) ilustrates an enhanced KC model in MPS which provides enough flexibility to integrate an extensive range of elements and basic concepts discovered earlier during the literature review. The model suggests that the five elements covered in the model have different concepts that can be pertinent beyond the findings from this study.

4 Conclusions

This paper presents the findings from the identified factors that proposed to be the enhanced model of KC. The findings indicate that five key elements start with building on the ideas in the literature review and data collection from agencies' documents and interviews. The enhanced KC model presented above is hoped to offer an avenue for other researchers to indicate areas for more research. Additional exploration of tacit knowledge is extremely suggested since it is significant to gain common ground and interpretation among different parties for a consistent process of making decisions. The findings revealed that this new anticipated KC model is expected to be further inclusive because it covers additional significant features of the KC process. It would be interesting to assess the developed KC model in other contexts and carry out studies at different levels of methodologies and analysis to enhance the KM and PM areas. In conclusion, these findings of the innovative study area on KC have provided an enhanced judgment and interpretation on deciding the early stage of ICT projects in the MPS. Furthermore, these discoveries in this study suggest an exciting investigation of other fields of business, like engineering, nursing, and journalism.

References

1. Ya'acob, S., Mohamad Ali, N., Mat Nayan, N.S., Liang, H.-N.: Visualization principles for facilitating knowledge communication in the strategy development process. In: Zaman, H.B., et al. (eds.) Advances in Visual Informatics. IVIC 2017, vol. 10645, pp. 31–42. Springer, Cham (2017). https://doi.org/10.1007/978-3-319-70010-6_3
2. Uden, L., He, W.: How the internet of things can help knowledge management: a case study from the automotive domain. J. Knowl. Manag. **21**(1), 57–70 (2017)
3. Rogers, P.S., Ross, S.M., Pawlik, L., Shwom, B.L., Rogers, P.S.: Working paper what do formal communications contribute to knowledge-intensive project work ? What Do Formal Communications Contribute to Knowledge-Intensive Project Work ? (2016)
4. Abubakar, M.A., Elrehail, H., Alatailat, M.A., Elci, A.: Knowledge management, decision-making style and organizational performance. J. Innov. Knowl. **4**(2), 104–114 (2018)
5. Storey, M.A., Zagalsky, A., Filho, F.F., Singer, L., German, D.M.: How social and communication channels shape and challenge a participatory culture in software development. IEEE Trans. Softw. Eng. **43**(2), 185–204 (2017)
6. Hidayat, B.: The Role of Knowledge Communication in The Effective Management of Post-Disaster Reconstruction Projects in Indonesia (2014)
7. Witarsyah, D., Fudzee, M.F.M.D., Salamat, M.A.: A conceptual study on generic end users adoption of e-government services. Int. J. Adv. Sci. Eng. Inf. Technol. **7**(3), 1000 (2017)
8. Veerankutty, F., Ramayah, T., Ali, N.: Information technology governance on audit technology performance among malaysian public sector auditors. Soc. Sci. **7**(8), 124 (2018)
9. Patanakul, P., Kwak, Y.H., Zwikael, O., Liu, M.: What impacts the performance of large-scale government projects? Int. J. Proj. Manag. **34**(3), 452–466 (2016)
10. Abubakar, M.A., Ravishankar, M.N., Coombs, C.R.: The role of formal controls in facilitating information system diffusion. Inf. Manag. **52**(5), 599–609 (2015)
11. Williams, P., Ashill, N.J., Naumann, E., Jackson, E.: Relationship quality and satisfaction: customer-perceived success factors for on-time projects. Int. J. Proj. Manag. **33**(8), 1836–1850 (2015)
12. Eppler, M.J.: 10 Years of Knowledge- Communication.org Results, Insights, Perspectives (2012)
13. Reinhardt, R., Stattkus, B.: Fostering knowledge communication: concept and implementation. J. Univers. Comput. Sci. **8**(5), 536–545 (2002)

14. Waller, D.S., Polonsky, M.J.: Multiple senders and receivers: a business communication model. Corp. Commun. An Int. J. **3**(3), 83–91 (1998)
15. Dusek, G.A., Yurova, Y.V., Ruppel, C.P.: Using social media and targeted snowball sampling to survey a hard-to-reach population: a case study. Int. J. Dr Stud. **10**, 279–299 (2015)
16. Ipe, M.: Human resource development review. Hum. Resour. Manag. Rev. **2**(4), 337–359 (2003)
17. Noe, R.A., Wang, S.: Knowledge sharing: a review and directions for future research. Hum. Resour. Manag. Rev. **20**(2), 115–131 (2010)
18. Aslani, F., Mousakhani, M., Aslani, A.: Knowledge sharing: a survey, assessment and directions for future research: individual behavior perspective. Int. J. Soc. Behav. Educ. Econ. Bus. Ind. Eng. **6**(8), 2025–2029 (2012)
19. Chen, W.-J., Cheng, H.-Y.: Factors affecting the knowledge sharing attitude of hotel service personnel. Int. J. Hosp. Manag. **31**(2), 468–476 (2012)
20. Schauer, A., Vasconcelos, A.C., Sen, B.: The ShaRInk framework: a holistic perspective on key categories of influences shaping individual perceptions of knowledge sharing. J. Knowl. Manag. **19**(4), 770–790 (2015)
21. Goh, S.C.: Managing effective knowledge transfer: an integrative framework and some practise implications. J. Knowl. Manag. **6**(1), 23 (2002)
22. Bhagat, R.S., Kedia, B.L., Harveston, P.D., Triandis, H.C.: Cultural variations in the cross-border transfer of organizational knowledge: an integrative framework. Acad. Manag. Rev. **27**(2), 204–221 (2002)
23. Ward, V., House, A., Hamer, S.: Developing a framework for transferring knowledge into action: a thematic analysis of the literature. J. Heal. Serv. Res Policy **14**(3), 1–8 (2010)
24. Liyanage, C., Elhag, T., Ballal, T., Li, Q.: Knowledge communication and translation – a knowledge transfer model. J. Knowl. Manag. **13**(3), 1–23 (2009)
25. Van Waveren, C.C., Oerlemans, L.A.G., Pretorius, M.W.: Knowledge transfer in project - e ased organizations. A conceptual model for investigating knowledge type, transfer mechanisms and transfer success, pp. 1176–1181. IEEE (2014)
26. Nonaka, I.: A dynamic theory of organizational knowledge creation. Organ. Sci. **5**(1), 14–37 (1994)
27. Patton, M.Q.: Qualitative Research & Evaluation Methods, 3rd edn. Publications, Sage (2002)
28. Yin, R.K.: Qualitative Research from Start to Finish, vol. 136, no. 1 (2011)
29. Milewski, S.: Managing technological open process innovation (2015)
30. Palinkas, L.A., Horwitz, S.M., Green, C.A., Wisdom, J.P., Duan, N., Hoagwood, K.: Purposeful sampling for qualitative data collection and analysis in mixed method implementation research. Adm. Policy Mental Health Ment. Health Serv. Res. **42**(5), 533–544 (2013)
31. Flake, J.K., Pek, J., Hehman, E.: Construct validation in social and personality research: current practice and recommendations. Soc. Psychol. Personal. Sci. **8**(4), 370–378 (2017)
32. Jones, S., Irani, Z., Sivarajah, U., Love, P.E.D.: Risks and rewards of cloud computing in the UK public sector: a reflection on three organisational case studies. Inf. Syst. Front. **21**(2), 359–382 (2017)
33. Javadi, M., Zarea, K.: Understanding thematic analysis and its pitfall. J. Client Care **1**(1) (2016)
34. Hernández, J., Hernández, Y., Collado-ruiz, D., Cebrián-tarrasón, D.: Knowledge-creating and sharing corporate culture framework. Soc. Behav. Sci. **74**, 388–397 (2013)
35. Greve, L.: Knowledge sharing in knowledge creation: an action research study of metaphors for knowledge. J. Organ. Knowl. Commun. **2**(1), 66–87 (2015)
36. Gray, C.F., Larson, E.W.: Project Management The Managerial Process. McGraw-Hill, New York (2015)

37. Krylova, K.O., Vera, D., Crossan, M.: Knowledge transfer in knowledge-intensive organizations: the crucial role of improvisation in transferring and protecting knowledge. J. Knowl. Manag. **20**(5), 1045–1064 (2016)
38. Omotayo, F.O.: Knowledge Management as an important tool in organisational management: a review of literature. Libr. Philosophy Pract. **1238**, 1–23 (2015)
39. Clark, D.: Nonaka & Hirotaka Takauk - The Knowledge Spiral. A Big Dog, Little Dog and Knowledge Jump Production (2011). http://www.nwlink.com/~donclark/history_knowledge/nonaka.html. Accessed 20 May 2017
40. Yu, T.-K., Lin, M.-L., Liao, Y.-K.: Understanding factors influencing information communication technology adoption behavior: the moderators of information literacy and digital skills. Comput. Hum. Behav. **71**, 196–208 (2017)
41. Mengis, J.: Integrating knowledge through communication-the case of experts and decision makers. In: Proceedings OKLC 2007, the International Conference on Organizational Knowledge, Learning and Capabilities, vol. 44, pp. 699–720 (2007)
42. Foong, M.Y.: Effective Communication: A Challenge To Project Managers. PMtimes, April 2014. https://www.projecttimes.com/articles/effectivecommunication-a-challenge-to-project-managers.html. Accessed 28 Apr 2019
43. Taherdoost, H., Keshavarzsaleh, A., Wang, C.: A retrospective critic re-debate on stakeholders' resistance checklist in software project management within multi-cultural, multi-ethnical and cosmopolitan society context: the Malaysian experience. Cogent Bus. Manag. **3**(1), 1151116 (2016)
44. Al-fedaghi, S.: Modeling communication: one more piece falling into place. In: Poceeding of the 26th Annual Intenational Conferrence on Design of Communication, SIGDOC 2008, Lisbon, Portugal, 22–24 September 2008 (2008)

How Digital Literacy, Could Impact Environmental Scanning, Business Intelligence and Knowledge Management?

Souad Kamoun-Chouk[✉]

Univ. Manouba, ESCT, LIGUE, Campus Universitaire Manouba, 2010 Manouba, Tunisia
Souad.kamoun@esct.uma.tn

Abstract. To answer the question: How could digital literacy (DL) have an impact on Environmental Scanning (ES), Business Intelligence (BI) and knowledge management (KM)? We have designed a model adapted from our previous research built on the commonality between the three fields of Big Data (BD), BI & KM and arguing in favor of their bridging to help managers make an informed strategic decision. Empirical studies carried out in the Tunisian context have shown the limits of the initial model confronted in particular with the problem of the lack of transversal skills in digital literacy within Tunisian organizations.

The improved model aims to go beyond this limit and push managers to consider the skills of DL as a critical success factor and the cement allowing better "urbanization" of the different blocks of the strategic information system.

Keywords: Digital literacy · Environmental scanning · Business intelligence · Knowledge management

1 Introduction

Since the 1960s, data have been increasing exponentially. Inveighed by this amount of flux, organizations realized progressively that more attention is needed to face and let avoid irrelevant data. A urgent need of Information Literacy (IL), emergent as a crucial core competency to have access and to exploit available data intelligently. The abundance of data, as an exponential phenomenon, encouraged data-driven scientific research, opening the door to new emerging disciplines such as data science. Like computer science emerged from Mathematics, Data Science was driven by the tsunami of data flow. The "Data scientist", proclaimed the job of 2016 in the USA, would, in fact, only be an extension of that of Library Information Scientist of the 1970s who founded the first structured databases and information retrievals. More data and information from more and more sources, with greater volume is what characterizes our era. This reinforces the need of skills that allow converting data into knowledge for informed decision. As a mix of Information Literacy (IL) and Computer Literacy (CL), DL is the transversal competence required to be competitive in the digital era.

Our conceptual framework is based on the concepts of Digital Literacy (DL) as a driver of data seeking and sources monitoring. From the lens of the Resource Based

© Springer Nature Switzerland AG 2022
L. Uden et al. (Eds.): KMO 2022, CCIS 1593, pp. 91–102, 2022.
https://doi.org/10.1007/978-3-031-07920-7_8

View these tasks require Intangible resources embedded in organizational routines or practices such as an organization's reputation, culture, knowledge or know-how, [6]. Intangible resources are particularly valuable because they give companies competitive advantages. Environmental Scanning with external information focus, Business Intelligence (BI) as internal information orientation and Knowledge Management (KM) as capturing, storing and protecting organization, are supposed to rely on these intangible resources. [10], think that, the KM and CI are "starting to melt in the same melting pot". They proposed a list of critical success factors for their integration. Certain factors such as technological infrastructure, sharing of culture, evolution and cost of production, accessibility to knowledge, correspond to skills linked to DL. They are necessary both for the KM and the CI.

The proposed conceptual framework is designated to appraise the impact of DL competency on the technologies and practices related to data processing for strategic intelligence.

More accurately, we ought to answer the following question:

How Digital Literacy, could impact Environmental Scanning, Business Intelligence and Knowledge Management?

Big Data is considered here, as source of information feeding environmental scanning, BI and KM information systems that support strategic decision-making and stimulate innovation for stay competitive.

To address this issue, a model is needed as a representation of the processing of the data and its transformation into knowledge. The model will show of the link between theory with experiment (practice), and serve to guide research by presenting a simplified illustration of an imagined reality.

The lack of academic research on the use of data in decision-making processes and the cross-cutting treatment of technological aspects are the key issues highlighted by authors such as [22, 32] whose literature review illustrates that the telecommunication sector is the most concerned with the drastic growth of data.

To give an overview on this impact, we will come back to our previous researches in the Tunisian context, to gather some elements of response. The purpose of this work is to capitalize the results of research in favor of a path of progress towards more mastery of knowledge and better support for strategic decision-making.

2 Conceptual Framework of Literacy

The Cambridge dictionary defines Literacy as "the ability to read and write and to know a particular subject or a particular type of knowledge". Learning is the process through which people become literate.

[23] draw two distinctions between literacy understood as 'the generic capacity to encode and decode alphabetic print', and literacy seen as competent handling of texts that are meaningful to 'insiders' of particular sociocultural practices and discourse communities (cf. Gee, 1996; [14]. The second distinction is between literacy seen essentially in terms of printed texts, and the notion of multi-modal literacies involving texts of different modes [16]. With these distinctions, [23], see themselves allowed to "think in

terms of a continuum extending between literacy as encoding/decoding and literacy as 'discursive prowess'.

[34] defined Literacy as an "appropriate information behaviour" and [26] suggests that literacy means engaging with information in all of its modalities. His point of view is consistent with [15] definition of Literacy: "the concept of literacy goes beyond simply being able to read; it has always meant the ability to read with meaning, and to understand. It is the fundamental act of cognition". As argued by, [9], "this understanding of literacy draws on theoretical positions that include the notions of social construction of meaning, semiotic and hermeneutic interpretation, and criticality", these notions are in all the forms of literacy as information is the common resource.

2.1 Digital Literacy (DL) as a Mix of Information Literacy (IL) and Computer Literacy (CL)

While the business community is in a heightened state of awareness about the value of information and knowledge, it seems that, at the micro level "workers are floundering with too much information readily available, too little relevant and timely information when they need it, and with few tools or skills to deal with information effectively" [27]. This paradox, alerts on the danger of the ignorance of IL in the workplace.

What the business community needs nowadays, is more and more literate persons among their managers. As described by [35], a literate person is someone who possesses *"Learned techniques and skills for utilizing the wide range of information tools as well as primary sources in molding information solutions to [one's] problems"*.

The multiplicity of communication channels and applications for accessing, processing and distributing information, a *"numerically literate person" rather than "literate person"* is needed to feet with the digital era background. [3], defined, a "numerically literate person" as someone who: (1) Has the technical and cognitive skills, allowing him to: (2) locate, assesses, evaluate, create and communicate digital information in different formats, (3) Mobilizes available technologies appropriately and effectively to extract information, interpret results and judge the quality of this information and also to communicate and collaborate with peers, colleagues, family and possibly larger communities (4) capture what connects technology, lifelong learning, confidentiality and information management and become an active citizen in civil society. Two other competencies, safety and problem solving, as further steps of the learning and reflection process, were added by UNESCO (2018). Safety is concerned with protecting devices, personal data and privacy, health and well-being and the environment. The problem solving era is about technical problems, Identifying needs and technological responses, identifying digital competence gaps and creatively using digital technologies. The map below summarizes the main competencies of DL.

Highlighting the crucial role of the connection between DL as a perquisite for mastering information processing and Knowledge generation, DL appear in the literature as a critical success factor for the creation of an enabling environment for mastering the technology and the skills allowing searching, filtering and interpreting information. As a mix of Information Literacy (IL) and Computer Literacy (CL), DL integrates the competences gathered in the conceptual map below.

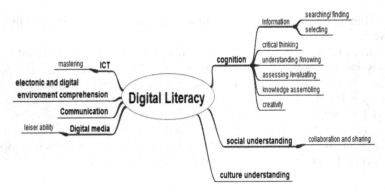

Fig. 1. Conceptual map of digital literacy competences [21]

2.2 Environmental Scanning (ES) Need of DL

This field is dedicated to capturing, analyzing, and driving action related to a company's competitive landscape. CI data includes anything and everything about a company's competitors - their businesses, their movements, and their strategies".[1]

CI focus is the external environment; it includes practices of benchmarking, Environmental Scanning (ES) as the main orientations. ES is the acquisition and use of information about events and trends in the environment external to an organization. It is a *'fractionalized'* process that includes several progressive stages that result, in knowledge that may assist management in planning the organization's future course of action [2]. ES as knowledge generator activity is supposed to be assigned to "information trackers" having skills in information literacy: *"Information literacy is a way of knowing the many environments that constitute an individual being in the world"* [24] (Fig. 2).

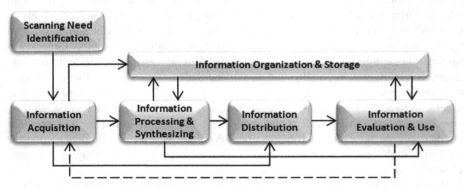

Fig. 2. Environmental scanning process [26] Adapted from [12]

---

[1] https://www.crayon.co/hubfs/Ebooks/Crayon-State-of-Competitive-Intelligence-2019.pdf? hsCtaTracking=a97bc346-a753-4e71-ae5d-053947b950ac%7C7e9e1578-d08a-4541-98ad-59b0a542b6de.

As detailed above, ES seems to be a typical application of information literacy skills in the workplace. Each step requires one of the skills of the cognitive and communicational levels detailed in the mind map of the Fig. 1. The ICT mastering and Digital environment comprehension skills are more and more needed to accompany the current advancement of information and telecommunication technology. More sophisticated infrastructures are emerging, and Big Data with its increasing Volume, Variety, Velocity, Veracity and Value is changing the way of dealing with information on the workplace and organizations have to become more and more Digital Literate. As argued by [1], intelligence is not acquiring relevant information but less irrelevant information. In his pyramid IDKW (Information, data, knowledge, wisdom). The higher levels are knowledge then wisdom. Sensemaking is needed to move from the data level to the information level, experiences sharing is needed to move from information level to knowledge level. The wisdom level is reached when informed decision is made. The ability to make informed decision on the basis of timely actionable intelligence needs more signals and less noise. Collective sensemaking of "weak signals" [7] by experienced collaborators, is needed to generate knowledge. Unstructured information such as "weak signals" known to be ambiguous and uncertain, are considered the most relevant, for strategic decision making. Social and cultural understanding are needed for collaboration and sharing as Digital literacy competencies understanding (see Fig. 1 mind map). They allow organizations to broaden the scope of their BI traditional parameters [11], based on structured internal information.

2.3 Business Intelligence (BI) Need of DL

What we call BI is an evolution of the early 1980s, concept of executive information systems (EIS), designated to support upper-level managers and executives in their decision making. The reporting and analyzing capabilities of EIS have evolved from static systems to dynamic multidimensional reporting systems, trend analysis, drill-down capabilities, and artificial intelligence analysis. These features are included in many BI tools.

[29], defines BI as *"the compendium of techniques and tools that allow the transformation of large amount of data coming from different sources into meaningful information, in order to make decision that improve organizational performance"*. Meaningful information generated through the sensemaking step of internal (BI) and external (CI) data and information, is captured, shared and protected (KM). Data mining, SWOT analysis, balanced scorecards, dashboards and visualization software, used by CI as well as BI, make it possible bringing the two technologies together; BI with capacity to transform the large amount of flow of Big Data and CI&ES with its capacity to broaden the scope of monitoring by the organization and reducing the perceived environmental uncertainty. BI as Information system based on technology is concerned with protecting devices, technical problems solving, Identifying needs and technological responses, identifying digital competence gaps and creatively using digital technologies. These are the latest DL skills of [33] Business intelligence, appears in [4] as a good example of information system for which Digital literacy is a critical success factor. Authors propose Key commentary and models along with best practices and recommendations for implementing successful digital literacy in the context of Business Intelligence.

2.4 Knowledge Management Need of DL

As noticed by [17], KM is characterized by its capacity to turn a company into a learning organization, which consists of transforming the information provided by CI and BI (explicit) and the information that each individual has (Tacit) into functional knowledge supporting informed decision. KM helps organizations to acquire and share Intellectual Capital. SECI model [25] is used for creating and sharing knowledge using four modes known as Socialization, Internalization, Combination and Externalization. Through this learning loop, analysts and stakeholders apply personal and organizational knowledge to evaluate data and information. Structuring IT tools, are used to help categorizing, retrieving, sharing and protecting the Intellectual capital. As argued by [8], these skills allowed digital content creation, and new opportunities for providing wider access through digitization. In accordance with [28], a recent study of information sciences students DL learning in Thailand, revealed that "*to develop an information specialist's digital literacy, s/he has to practice three skills: information management skills, digital tools usage and the creation of new content and the consolidation of information..*" These findings support the shared opinion about the change in the role of information specialist who have to integrate competencies of Knowledge manager who is able to determine what information is worth sharing. "A deep understanding of the business, along with IT expertise, is strong prerequisites for successful knowledge managers. Having an entrepreneurial spirit, is also important, since many knowledge managers have to develop their own vision and mandate" [13, 31].

3   Case Studies from the Tunisian Context

3.1 Overview of the Studies' Results

To fill the gap of digital development, developing countries and Tunisia, for instance, need a strong willingness from the policy makers to overcome the organizational and structural barriers to a rational and efficient appropriation of the digital competencies. Prior studies [18] showed that the main failures of Environmental Scanning (ES) in the Tunisian industry SMEs, is a result of the lack of DL skills among the employees of the organizations. Employees of these organizations were unable to identify the required information, to know where to obtain the information and evaluate the obtained information to be used to sort problems effectively. This lack of Digital Literacy skills has created barriers for Tunisian organizations to introduce and institutionalize CI&ES practices, to be innovative and competitive.

We choose these 4 recent works insofar as we find them a coherent link with the question that we addressed above.

1. Tunisian High Independent Elections Authority (ISIE), Library Information Science (LIS) experts first experience of implementation of a transparent electoral culture [30];
2. Telecommunication operators case study implementation of Big Data solution [5] master thesis supervised by Kamoun Chouk,S.);
3. Information literacy is a key to a competitive world in developing countries [20];

4. Study of entrepreneurial students' perceptions of the impact of digital literacy skills on their future career: evidence from Tunisian higher education, [21],

Through these researches, we could show successively:

- How Library Information Science experts' competency could help implementing a transparent electoral culture supported with ICT.
- The benefits of a marriage between BD BI KM for a rational use of technics and tools and informed strategic decision;
- The drawback of disjointed BD, BI, KM information system within the Tunisian telecommunication operators (empirical study) because of the competencies in DL;
- The lack of a national Information Literacy policy for an enabling environment to integrate the digital era;
- The high perceived uncertainty toward the business environment by entrepreneurship students and their strong need of an early education (college) in Digital Literacy.

3.2 The Competences Considered as Priorities

According to the participants, DL as a concept wider than Information Literacy is an essential skill to possess as future entrepreneurs. They consider that the acquisition of skills that constitute it by future entrepreneurs is a guarantee of success.

They classify these competences in this descending order:

1. Technological competencies: As future entrepreneurs they see that they are forced to master navigation on the Internet and to use computer technologies skillfully.
2. Competence in seeking information through digital tools: It is considered a priority, and should begin to be taught at the secondary school level. This is where, according to them, the institutionalization of digital culture should begin.
3. Competence in interpretation and understanding of information: It requires early training in critical-thinking. This skill is perceived as part of a lifelong learning process. Participants think that this skill should start very early in the life learning cycle (ie at the primary school level) and continue in the workplace.
4. The institutionalization of a digital culture: The students think that it is a national policy choice that consists in creating an enabling environment allowing the creation of structural conditions favoring access to education and learning in DL. It is considered crucial to create an environment conducive to entrepreneurship. Participants are calling for more active learning pedagogies based on the use of digital technology.

Highlighting the crucial role of the connection between DL as a perquisite for mastering information processing and Knowledge generation, the results of the studies presented above, support the founding of the literature review about the crucial role of education public policy in the creation of an enabling environment for DL. To fill the gap of Digital development, countries like Tunisia, need a strong willingness from the policy makers to overcome the organizational and structural barriers to a rational and efficient appropriation of the digital competencies. It is important that DL should be introduced in the school curriculum. DL skills provide organizations with the capacity to perpetuate and institutionalize ES practices of searching, finding and selecting Digital data as the fundamental step of Competitive Intelligence. A continuous flow of structured, semi-structures and unstructured data ensures an on-going process of analysis and sensemaking as business intelligence practices that generates the Knowledge needed for innovation and competitiveness. From this integrative perspective, ES BI KM marriage is necessary for the sake of efficiency and effectiveness. The redundancies and the separate functioning of each of the systems can only break the innovative impetus and prevent it from achieving the performance and competitiveness objectives.

4   The Designated Model of ES BI KM and DL Related Competences

While developed countries, such as USA and GB has already experienced national Information Literacy (IL), the concept seems to be ignored in Tunisia and limited to ICT literacy, which is part of DL [20]. Taking into account the commonality between CI and BI and the role of KM as a trigger of innovative strategic informed decision, we, [19] designated a model integrating named BDBIKM which is largely inspired from the SECI model of [25] for creating and sharing knowledge.

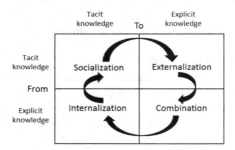

Fig. 3. SECI model

The first three processes of SECI model, socialization, externationalization and combination are applied as KM components of the proposed integrated Big Data (BD), Business intelligence (BI) and Knowledge Management (KM) model (Fig. 4).

The prior BDBIKM model was designated to enable businesses to convert structured, semi-structured and unstructured data into innovate knowledge to provide unique competitive advantage. More specifically it will help BI to move from its traditional parameters, through the enrichment of its flux with unstructured data collected from the Web. Rich and relevant customer opinion and behavioral information need to be tracked through the social media. BD solutions offer to BI the opportunity to move to a unique system based on internal and external data and offering a unique output to the decision makers.

Given the impact of digital literacy on the performance of information systems for decision support, and its integrating power, we propose in the figure below an adaptation of the BDBIKM, with three folds:

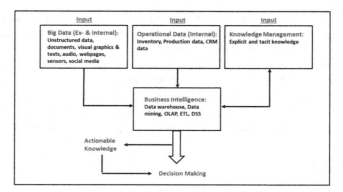

Fig. 4. The prior BDBIKM model

- The integration of ES related to searching finding and selecting skills.
- The association of data analysis and sensemaking DL skills with the BI layer of the model.
- Critical thinking, understanding, knowing sharing collaborating, safety and problem solving as DL are associated to the KM layer as the upper step supporting the strategic decision making.

Through this incremental process, we could integrate the 4th stage of the knowledge creation process, namely intermatlization. DL skills needed for each layer of the model are acquired through the Internalization process for developing skills and experience by learning from existing explicit knowledge; i.e. transforming explicit into tacit knowledge (Fig. 5).

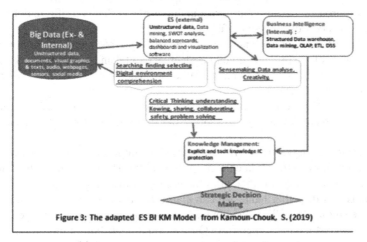

Fig. 5. The ES-BI-KM model & DL related competences adapted from [21]

This model defends a unified vision of the strategic decision support system, connecting the main gradation subsystems of the Ackoff pyramid: data, information, knowledge, wisdom. DL is presented as the prior and crucial skill for moving from one level of the pyramid to the next level. These skills are framed in yellow in the above Fig. 5.

The different digital literacies associated with each capsule of our model play the role of an unifying cement leading to the stage of internalization of Nonaka's model. The relevance of this model lies in its perceived capacity for homogenization and coherence which should lead, on the managerial level, to reducing decision-making uncertainty.

5 Conclusion

To answer this question: **How Digital Literacy, could impact Environmental Scanning, Business Intelligence and Knowledge Management?**
We presented the results of 4 case studies arguing in favor of a DL education policy, one case showing the inconvenient of a disconnection between ES, BI and KM. Based on these results, we suggest the following:

1. A National Information literacy policy exploiting digital inclusion agenda and preparing an enabling environment for the appropriation of a digital culture by the citizens;
2. An awareness of the importance of Information literacy as the major skill in the modern knowledge society
3. Bridging the LIS competencies with "research data literacy" as data librarians and data scientists are information specialists;
4. Encouraging autonomous creation of knowledge among university students and employers in the workplace;
5. Developing awareness of entrepreneurship from an early age through a cross curriculum approach "because entrepreneurship is a skill that is useful in both personal and social aspects of everyday life"
6. Having a unified organizational view of the strategic intelligence based on DL core competencies of the organizational intellectual capital and combining ES-BI-KM in such a way as to achieve a rational use of technics and tools that allows effective and appropriate investment.
7. Applying ES-BI-KM according to the company actual internal and external needs of information and knowledge to achieve the strategic intelligence targets.

The cases to which we are referred were used to support our conceptual choices but they, in no way, allow us to validate the proposed model. The inherent limits of any theoretical model can only be identified after the multiplication and replication of empirical investigations. On the other hand, we can claim that the design of our research based on prior case studies from Tunisian context, allowed us to contextualize the theoretical references gathered from the literature. Our essential contribution therefore, lies in the fact of having constructed and proposed a contextualized model for future research. Our future research will try to test the ES-BI-KM model in a particular context. A feasibility study is envisaged in order to identify the obstacles and or the organizational levers which would prevent or favor this integrative vision of an Information Management System and the role of the common DL skills in bridging ES-BI-KM.

References

1. Ackoff, R.: From data to wisdom. J. Appl. Syst. Anal. **16**, 3–9 (1989)
2. Aguilar, F.: Scanning the Business Environment. Macmillan, New York (1967)
3. ALA Digital Literacy Task Force (2011). http://hdl.handle.net/11213/16260
4. Alexander, B., Adams Becker, S., Cummins, M., Hall Giesinger, C.: Digital Literacy in Higher Education, Part II: An NMC Horizon Project Strategic Brief. The New Media Consortium, Austin, Texas. (Volume 3.4, August 2017) (2017). https://www.learntechlib.org/p/182086/. Accessed 12 Apr 2022
5. Amri, A.: Telecommunication operators case study implementation of Big Data solution master thesis, ESCT, Tunisia, supervised by Kamoun Chouk, S (2018)
6. Andriessen, D.: Making Sense of Intellectual Capital: Designing a Method for the Valuation of Intangibles. Elsevier Butterworth-Heinemann, Burlington (2004)
7. Ansoff, H.: Strategic Management. Palgrave Macmillan, New York (1987)
8. Chawner, B.: How to use web 2.0 in your library. Electron. Libr. **26**, 427–428 (2008)
9. Barnett, R.: Higher Education: A Critical Business. Open University Press, Buckingham (1997)
10. Ghannay, J.C., Zeineb, B.A.M.: Synergy Between Competitive Intelligence and Knowledge Management - a key for Competitive Advantage, Journal of Intelligence Studies in Business (2012). file:///C:/Users/Actinuance/Desktop/bureau%202020/ECIL%202020/38–120–1-PB.pdf. Accessed 27 Jan 2020
11. Chinu, Er., Kanika, Er., Ekta, Er.: Engineering business intelligence in big data. Int. J. Mod. Eng. Res. (IJMER) **6**(5), 10–14 (2016)
12. Choo, C.W.: Information Management for the Intelligent Organization: The Art of Scanning the Environment, 3rd edn. Information Today, Inc., Medford (2002)
13. Cole-Gomolski, B.: Knowledge Managers Need Business Savy. ComputerWorld, January 25, 1999b, 40 (1999)
14. Gee, J.P., Hull, G., Lankshear, C.: The New Work Order: Behind the Language of the New Capitalism. Boulder, Co.: Westview (1996)
15. Gilster, P.: Digital Literacy. Wiley Computer Publications, New York (1997)
16. Jewitt, C., Kress, G. (eds.): Multimodal Literacy. Peter Lang, New York (2003)
17. Fuentes, B.: La gestión del conocimiento en las relaciones académico-empresariales. Un nuevo enfoque para analizar el impacto del conocimiento académico. Tesis Phd. Universidad Politécnica de Valencia, España (2009)
18. Kamoun Chouk, S.: Veille anticipative stratégique: processus d'attention à l'environnement: application à des PMI tunisiennes/Thèse Grenoble 2 (2005)
19. Kamoun-Chouk, S., Berger, H., Sie, B.H.: Towards integrated model of big data (BD), business intelligence (BI) and knowledge management (KM). In: Uden, L., Lu, W., Ting, I.-H. (eds.) KMO 2017. CCIS, vol. 731, pp. 482–493. Springer, Cham (2017). https://doi.org/10.1007/978-3-319-62698-7_40
20. Kamoun-Chouk, S.: Information literacy is a key to a competitive world in developing countries. In: Uden, L., Hadzima, B., Ting, I.-H. (eds.) KMO 2018. CCIS, vol. 877, pp. 401–410. Springer, Cham (2018). https://doi.org/10.1007/978-3-319-95204-8_34
21. Kamoun-Chouk, S.: Study of entrepreneurial students' perceptions of the impact of digital literacy skills on their future career: evidence from Tunisian higher education. In: Uden, L., Ting, I.-H., Corchado, J.M. (eds.) KMO 2019. CCIS, vol. 1027, pp. 392–402. Springer, Cham (2019). https://doi.org/10.1007/978-3-030-21451-7_34

22. Kowalczyk and Buxmann, Pospiech and Felden, Arnott and Pervan, and Shollo and Kautz [30, 44, 6, 50]
23. Lankshear, C., Knobel, M.: New Literacies: Changing Knowledge and Classroom Learning. Open University Press, Buckingham (2003)
24. Lloyd, A.: Information Literacy Landscapes: Information Literacy in Education, Workplace and Everyday Contexts. Chandos, Oxford (2010)
25. Nonaka, I., Takeuchi, H.: The Knowledge-Creating Company: How Japanese Companies Create the Dynamics of Innovation. Oxford University Press, New York (1995)
26. O'Farrill, R.T.: Information Literacy and Knowledge Management: Preparations for an Arranged Marriage. Libri, 2008, vol. 58, pp. 155–171 (2008). Printed in Germany All rights reserved Copyright Saur, Libri, ISSN 0024-2667. https://doi.org/10.1515/libr.2008.017 155
27. O'Sullivan, C.: Is information literacy relevant in the real world? Ref. Serv. Rev. **30**(1), 7–14 (2002)
28. Owen, S. Hagel, P., Lingham, B., Tyson, D.: Development of the digital literacies teaching resource (2013). http://www.deakin.edu.au/__data/assets/pdf_file/0017/38006/digital-lit eracy.pdf
29. Ramakrishnan, T., Jones, M.C., Sidrova, A.: Factors influencing business intelligence (BI) data collection strategies: an empirical investigation. Decis. Support Syst. **52**, 486–496 (2012). https://doi.org/10.1016/j.dss.2011.10.009
30. Seghir, Y., Chouk, S.K.: How could library information science skills enhance information literacy in the Tunisian high independent elections authority (ISIE). In: Kurbanoğlu, S., Grassian, E., Mizrachi, D., Catts, R., Špiranec, S. (eds.) ECIL 2013. CCIS, vol. 397, pp. 162–169. Springer, Cham (2013). https://doi.org/10.1007/978-3-319-03919-0_20
31. TFPL Ltd.: Skills for Knowledge Management. TFPL Briefing Paper, July 1999. http://www.tfpl.com
32. Ularu, E.G., Puican, F.C., Apostu, A., Velicanu, M.: Perspectives on big data and big data analytics. Database Syst. J. **3**, 3–14 (2012)
33. UNESCO: A Global Framework of Reference on Digital Literacy Skills for Indicator 4.4.2, Information Paper No. 51 June 2018 UIS/2018/ICT/IP/51 (2018). http://uis.unesco.org/sites/default/files/documents/ip51-global-framework-reference-digital-literacy-skills-2018-en.pdf
34. Webber, S., Boon, S., Johnston, B.: A comparison of UK academics' conceptions of information literacy in two disciplines: English and marketing. Libr. Inf. Res. **29**(93), 4–15 (2005)
35. Zurkowski, P.G.: The Information Service Environment Relationships and Priorities, Related Paper No. 5., National Commission on Libraries and Information Science, Washington, DC., National Program for Library and Information Services (1974). http://eric.ed.gov/PDFS/ED1 00391.pdf. Accessed Jan 2019

The Competency-Based Business Process Management-Employee-Centered Process Improvement for Digital Transformation

Annika Nowak[✉], Jan Pawlowski[✉], and Michael Schellenbach[✉]

Department of Computer Science, Hochschule Ruhr West, Bottrop, Germany
{annika.nowak,jan.pawlowski,michael.schellenbach}@hs-ruhrwest.de

Abstract. Competencies play an important role for successfully mastering tasks in organizations. However, when designing processes as part of Business Process Management projects, tasks and roles are modelled but not the required competencies for mastering certain processes or tasks. Particularly in the age of Digital Transformation, this leads to insecurities and fears of employees in the change process as it is not clear what is needed to stay employed. In our approach, we extend current modeling practices by introducing competencies into business process models. For this purpose, we propose a specific modeling object as this improves readability and visibility of competencies. Additionally, we provide a data model and a competency model to ease the modeling process. The approach was successfully validated in expert interviews with academics and practitioners.

Keywords: Co-digitalization · Digital transformation · Business processes · Digital competencies

1 Introduction

The current wave of Digital Transformation (DT) leads to significant changes on different levels of organizations (Vial 2019). Changes and transformations occur regarding strategy development (Matt et al. 2015; Kane et al. 2015; Hess et al. 2016), introduction of new business models (Blaschke et al. 2017; Loebecke and Picot 2015; Weill and Woerner 2013), adoption of new technologies (Andriole et al. 2017), digital innovation processes (Barrett et al. 2015; Yoo et al. 2010) as well as organizational changes (Wu et al. 2016; Pagani and Pardo 2017). All of those changes lead to new/transformed business processes (Lederer et al. 2017; vom Brocke and Mendling 2018). Besides, business processes as such are changed towards automated (Lederer et al. 2017) or autonomous processes (Hofmann and Rüsch 2017). Thus, conceptualizing, elaborating and adopting transformed business processes is one of the core activities of Digital Transformation (Lederer et al. 2017; Vial 2019). As a second key issue we can state that there are many barriers and challenges towards Digital Transformation: Vogelsang et al. (2019a, b) and Wolf et al. (2018) describe barriers towards digital transformation, amongst them organizational (e.g., resistance to change, lack of resources) and individual barriers (e.g., fear of job loss) as well as missing skills. To realize successful DT projects, it is thus essential to overcome those barriers. It can furthermore be stated that main barriers

© Springer Nature Switzerland AG 2022
L. Uden et al. (Eds.): KMO 2022, CCIS 1593, pp. 103–117, 2022.
https://doi.org/10.1007/978-3-031-07920-7_9

address individual skills and attitudes regarding DT - thus the initial question is how to identify, represent and train competencies which are required to overcome barriers (such as fears, negative attitudes) and work successfully after the transformation process is done. Revised business processes and related change processes are in the core of Digital Transformation (Lederer et al. 2017) as they represent how firms operate in the future. Skills and individual motivational aspects have a strong influence on organizational performance (Burke and Litwin 1992). Even though it is clear that human aspects (such as process skills, learning and training) is essential to successful Business Process Management (BPM) projects (Rosemann and vom Brocke 2015), this aspect is normally addressed only at later stages of the change process as process experts propose new improved business processes and corresponding roles, change strategies and related learning and training measures (cf. Adesola and Baines 2005; Kettinger et al. 1997; Becker et al. 2013). For a successful adoption, human aspects need to be addressed already at earlier stages - as Kerremans (2008) emphasizes: "Employees should be able to anticipate the impact of change beyond the processes they participate in and the constituents affected by the processes". Employees are only represented during the process in steering committees or late in the process as change agents (de Waal and Batenburg 2014). However, intense participation increases the chance of successful transformation process improvement projects (Lines 2004; Bhatti and Qureshi 2007; Hansen et al. 2011). The following research question will be encountered:

- How can be competencies integrated in digital transformation processes?

Therefore, it is our aim to provide a procedural model for competency-based BPM projects to show how competencies can be integrated in digital transformation processes. We believe that the main barriers can only be overcome when employees continuously participate in the process redesign of DT. The main changes are represented as business processes and competencies needed to successfully master these. The paper is structured as following: In the background section, we discuss the concept of competencies and their integration in BPM projects. The problem identification was based on current studies on barriers and challenges of Digital Transformation as well as a thorough literature review regarding BPM and competencies. The resulting built artefacts are threefold: the participatory process as a reference process/method for transformation processes (Winter and Schelp 2006; Offermann et al. 2010) and the extension of BPMN together with the competency description as IT-related meta-artefacts (Iivari 2015). Using an Design Science Research approach (Baskerville et al. 2018), we develop an extension to current BP Modeling methodologies incorporating competencies. We describe the intended participation process and modeling elements followed by an evaluation in expert interviews. We conclude with a summary of limitations and future research needs.

2   Background

In the following section, we briefly describe the conceptual background as well as the basis for our analysis. We discuss the concept of competencies and their use in BPM approaches.

2.1 Competencies

Competencies denote a set of knowledge, skills, abilities, and attitudes to solve a problem in a given context (cf. Holtkamp et al. 2015). Competencies are addressed in different domains: in the education as part of curricula such as the Information Systems Model Curriculum (Topi et al. 2010; Topi et al. 2017); in the Human Resource Development domain as tools to recruit, assess, and develop staff (Swanson et al. 2001). In the organizational context, competencies play a role for the competitiveness of an organization in different theories such as the resource-based (Wernerfelt 1984; Wernerfelt 1995) or the competency-based view of the firm (Freiling 2004; Freiling et al. 2008). On the individual level, competencies are needed to perform certain job tasks successfully (Motowildo et al. 1997). In the age of Digital Transformation, many studies have researched which competencies are necessary for certain job profiles such as a Chief Digital Officer (Singh and Hess 2017), for certain domains such as industry 4.0/manufacturing industry (Prifti et al. 2017) or on a generic level (Hoberg et al. 2017; Ehlers and Kellermann 2019). As part of our research work, we have analyzed ten frameworks regarding Digital Transformation competencies using the concept matrix approach of Webster and Watson (2002). The following matrix (Table 1) shows the variety of competencies divided in six competency areas (bold). The six competency areas (social

Table 1. Digital competency matrix

	1	2	3	4	5	6	7	8	9	10		1	2	3	4	5	6	7	8	9	10
Social competency	√	√	√	√	√	√	√	√	√	√	**Thematic / Method competency**	√	√	√	√	√	√	√	√	√	√
(Open) communication		√		√	√	√					Evaluation of information & activities	√		√			√		√	√	
Intercultural competence		√									Interdisciplinary thinking & acting										√
Netiquette		√	√	√		√					Media analysis			√	√						
Digital collaboration	√	√	√	√	√	√	√	√			Customer analysis			√							
Digital interaction		√	√	√		√	√				Copyright / Licenses					√					
Conflict resolution		√									Agility			√				√			
Presenting applications		√									Understanding digital transformation and digitalization			√						√	
Participation in the digital culture									√		Protection of personal data and devices				√	√					
Networking										√	IT-Security						√				√
Information Literacy		√	√	√	√	√	√	√	√		Security awareness / data protection	√	√	√	√	√					√
Access to information		√		√	√	√	√	√			Customer focus	√									
Information										√	Diversity							√			

(*continued*)

Table 1. (*continued*)

Literacy								
Information retrieval	√		√	√	√		√	
Knowledge building	√		√		√		√	
Data analysis		√		√	√	√	√	√
Content creation	√	√	√	√			√	√
Data visualization					√			
Information management	√			√	√		√	
Data storage		√	√		√			
Media selection		√			√			
Knowledge sharing		√	√					
Self-competency	√	√	√	√	√	√		√
Willingness to learn / Participation	√	√			√		√	
Critical reflected thinking				√	√			
Making decisions	√							
Digital learning & coaching	√							
Creativity			√					
Delegation	√							
Visionary thinking and acting				√				
Willingness to change / flexibility				√				
Ethics / Responsibility	√		√	√		√		

Problem solving	√	√		√		√				√	√
Social Media											√
Management competency	√	√	√	√	√	√	√	√	√	√	√
Agile Management								√			
Change-Management		√									√
Strategic planning		√					√				
Risk Management		√				√					
Project Management							√				
Identity Management						√	√				
Process Management						√					
Customer Relationship Management											√
Stakeholder Management		√						√			√
Technical competency	√		√	√		√				√	√
Use of technique and software	√			√		√				√	√
Software development					√						
Innovation					√	√					
Evaluation of technical solutions					√						
Network					√						
Big Data											√
Mobile technologies											√
In-memory database											√
Internet of Things											√

competency, thematic/methodological competency, information literacy, management competency, technological and self-competency) form the digital competency.

Overview of the Sources: 1 (Ferrari 2012), 2 (Forty second Information systems research seminar in Scandinavia [IRIS 2019], 2019), 3 (Center for Digital Dannelses 2019), 4 (Ferrari 2013), 5 (Sousa and Wilks 2018), 6 (Ala-Mutka 2008), 7 (Shahlaei et al. 2017), 8 (Calvani et al. 2008), 9 (Ilomäki et al. 2016), 10 (Hoberg et al. 2017).

Summarizing our analysis, we can state that existing competency models provide a good basis for predicting needed knowledge, skills and attitudes in general. It is necessary though, to build specific profiles for specific job roles.

2.2 Business Process Management and Digital Transformation

Processes are one crucial core element of digital transformation (DT) and there are different factors driving the process of DT in business (Verina and Titko 2019). Obviously, Business Process Management is in the core of Digital Transformation (Lederer et al. 2017; vom Brocke and Mendling 2018) and business processes can be optimized by the introduction of digital technologies to modernize organizational cultures (Trushkina et al. 2020). With the emergence of new technologies, also processes are undergoing dramatic changes. BPM in relation to Digital Transformation can be seen from three perspectives: Digital Transformation Process (cf. Vial 2019), Changing Business Process (Lederer et al. 2017) and Change Process (Harmon 2019). Obviously, there is a strong need to involve employees in this process. Approaches like social (Kocbek et al. 2015) or collaborative (Niehaves and Plattfaut 2011) BPM take the need of participation (Pasmore and Fagans 1992) into account in order to overcome resistance and fears and improve acceptance (de Waal and Batenburg 2014; Pflanzl and Vossen 2014). Barriers and fears in DT as well as BPM projects are manifold (da Silva et al. 2012). The lack of knowledge and skills, fear of job loss and resistance to change are amongst the most important barriers (da Silva et al. 2012). However, training new competencies or recruiting new employees with adequate competencies is usually only done at a late stage of DT/BPM projects. Therefore, there is the need to identify competency gaps in an earlier stage. Incorporating competencies into BPM projects are one possibility (Vladova et al. 2017). On the operational level, competencies cannot be modelled directly in modeling languages, in particular BPMN (Allweyer 2016) as the de facto standard allow modeling of roles. The more specific approach of subject oriented BPM (Fleischmann et al. 2012) focuses on the specification of roles and corresponding agents. Competencies would be modelled as descriptions to the roles but not as a specific modeling element (Vladova et al. 2017; Bavendiek et al. 2018). To fill these research gaps, we analyze options of incorporating competency modeling into BPM projects and business process models.

In the following, we outline how competency models can be incorporated in business process models in a participatory process. Our concept consists of three parts: 1) A participatory process of employee-centered process optimization (extending the concept of collaborative/social BPM) (Kocbek et al. 2015; Niehaves and Plattfaut 2011), 2) Extension of BPMN to allow competency modeling (extending the work of Vladova et al. (2017) and Bavendiek et al. (2018)), and 3) a competency toolbox to ease the specification of competencies in the Digital Transformation.

3   Research Method

We follow a Design Science Research approach (Baskerville et al. 2018). In our paper, we focus on the development of the meta-artefacts but also reflect our results towards contributing to theory building (Baskerville et al. 2018). As a contribution towards theory building, we contribute towards the refinement of participatory processes in social/collaborative BPM as well as refining related theories, in particular the competency-based view of the firm (Freiling et al. 2008) and the theory of organizational change and performance (Burke and Litwin 1992). Regarding the practical contribution, we aim at providing guidance for DT projects and individuals by suggestion a reference process and modeling language extensions. The main goal of the evaluation was to validate the appropriateness of the process and the modeling extension. Overall, we used a naturalistic multi-method evaluation (cf. Venable et al. 2016). For the evaluation, we used expert interviews/reviews (Myers and Avison 2002) with academics and practitioners using selected factors from Frank (2007).

3.1   Competency-Based BPM Procedure Model

The first part of our concept describes the overall procedure of BPM projects - we base our model on the work of Becker et al. (2013) and models as described in the background chapter. Our model extends the preparation phase particularly regarding preparation of a competency approach to modeling. The following phases set the frame of our procedure model and include specific reference to competencies (Fig. 1):

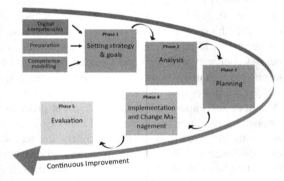

Fig. 1. Procedural model of the competency-orientated approach

Preparation Phase: This phase consists of the initiation of the BPM/DT project and requirements for the BPM project are gathered but also barriers and possible obstacles are identified amongst employees. In addition to these typical preparation processes, we suggest preparing the competency modeling part, i.e., allowing to model competencies in BPMN and creating an initial model of (digital) competencies as a starting point for competency modeling.

Goal Setting Phase: The strategic positioning of the BPM project and the definition of the operational goals take place in this phase. To allow competency-based BPM, it is necessary to anchor specific strategic goals (e.g., allowing employee participation, improving employee wellbeing/job satisfaction; creating perspectives for employees whose work is lost due to digitalization). Regarding organizational culture, it is important to create an atmosphere/mindset which are 1) open for digital solutions, 2) willing to change, and 3) collaborative and participatory.

Analysis Phase: Here, the current situation is analyzed and modeled. First, typical elements of BPM are modeled (processes/activities and their relations, results, IT systems, and roles including gaps and weaknesses). In addition to these elements, we propose to model competencies for each process or for a certain role. This describes the as-is situation which is in many cases also known and described in the Human Resource department.

Planning Phase: The planning phase consists of the process optimization and the planning of future (to-be) business processes as well as planning the implementation as a change concept. For each process or role, competencies should be modeled to understand which competencies are needed in the future. By this, a competency gap analysis provides insights how employees need to be trained to master future processes and to remain employable.

Implementation and Change Phase: In this phase, new processes are implemented and changed usually in a staged procedure (e.g., process by process, department by department). Learning and training must be an essential part of this phase. Clear training requirements are provided by the identification of competency gaps.

Evaluation Phase: Here, the results of the BPM project are measured - it includes measuring process performance but also employee performance. We understand performance not just as a measure regarding efficiency/effectiveness but also incorporating employees' satisfaction and well-being.

Continuous Improvement: The phases are continuously repeated to allow continuous process (and competency) improvement.

Figure 2 summarizes the steps described above. "Petrol-coloured" processes show competency-related processes to illustrate the key changes. "Turquoise" ones show modifications to and additional processes incorporated in the competency-based approach. "Light blue" ones show "traditional" BPMN activities. Processes with black border have an impact on the continuous improvement process. The procedure model for competency-based BPM (cBPM) describes extensions to traditional BPM. We have identified key activities and guidelines to allow employee participation and development.

3.2 BPMN Extensions

The second step is the integration of competencies into existing modeling languages. In principle every modeling language can be extended freely by adding new attributes to existing modeling objects. Further modeling options are adding competencies as comments or data element. In this way competencies could just be added to processes or roles. However, we propose a specific modeling object as this improves readability and visibility of competencies.

We chose the Business Process Modeling Notation (BPMN) (Allweyer 2016) as modeling language as this is the most used process modeling language internationally.

As the standard elements/attributes for a modeling object competency, we see a competency ID, a competency description (using prescribing terminologies/taxonomies

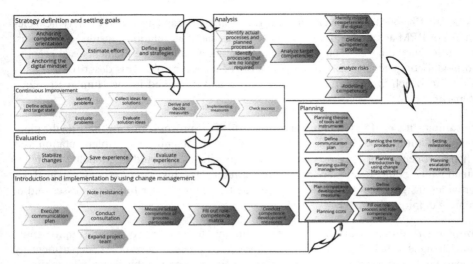

Fig. 2. Process map of competency-orientated process management

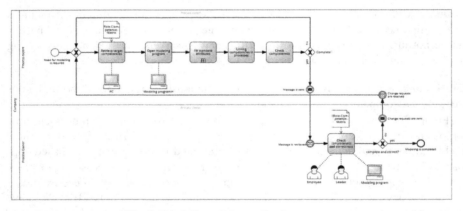

Fig. 3. Modeling competencies in processes

(Paquette 2007)), a proficiency level which describes the level of a competency (a level name and a corresponding description what is necessary to attain this level), a parent/sub competency relation and additional information or links to a curriculum or an enterprise-specific taxonomy/ontology. The illustrated process (Fig. 3) shows an example of the competency element in a BPMN 2.0 process model and at the same time the process of defining competencies. The use of competency objects will enrich process models and can increase the understanding of requirements for employees to master certain processes and tasks. The described data model also provides the link to Human Resource Management or ERP systems in order to create seamless processes between processes and HR development.

3.3 Competency Models as Supplementary Element

Modeling competencies are an additional element to existing models, requiring additional modeling effort (even though this is done in HR practice anyway). However, to reduce effort of modeling specific competencies required in the Digital Transformation/Digitalization, we have developed a competency framework which provides a blueprint for modeling competencies for different hierarchy levels. Each competency is pre-defined using the competency description described in the last paragraph. This type of competency description needs to be adapted for specific contexts and processes or actors/roles. For each process and role, competencies should describe requirements for the involved actors. The competencies are described in the following steps:

1. Describe the future process: In the first step, the envisioned process is elaborated. This needs to include roles/actors, systems and activities.
2. Describe/choose competencies to master the tasks/activities of the process: Competencies are usually described by skills/abilities/attitudes and the problem to be solved. Here, a new description or a pre-defined description from our competency framework can be used.
3. Describe/choose technical competencies to utilize systems involved: technical competencies usually concern specific technologies which are modelled as information systems in BPMN.
4. Describe competency proficiency levels: For each competency, the level needs to be specified (e.g. using vs. adapting/developing systems).
5. Check completeness: A consistency check should be done to ensure that all activities and technologies are also covered by corresponding competencies.
6. Add competencies to the competency framework/glossary: Competencies would be added to the competency framework - in our implementation, the entry would be in a glossary which can also be transferred/used in HR systems.

As shown, the digital competency set (Fig. 4) which consists of six columns can be used as a basis to ease the competency modeling process which resolves from the previous literature analysis (Table 1).

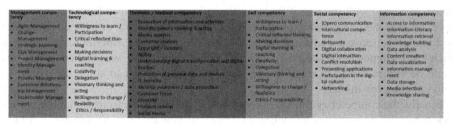

Fig. 4. Digital competency set

4   Evaluation

The approach was evaluated by 12 experts from Germany consisting of a mix of enterprise representatives (n1 = 7) with a strong background in process management and digital transformation as well as academic experts (n2 = 5). We performed the evaluation in expert interviews (duration: 30 min) and one focus group (duration: 2 h). The evaluation criteria based on Frank (2007) looked at complexity, understandability, completeness and adaptability/transferability as well as impact and changes of BPM projects. The following interview parts were discussed: complexity of the process model and the change process, completeness of modeling approach, understandability of the process and competency model, changes caused by the new process, importance of competencies in the competency framework, expected business/performance impact and expected impact on organizational culture. The interviews were classified, in all categories a total of 129 key statements were extracted from the original data. These were compared and systematically ordered for each question category.

As a starting point, all interviewees found the approach clearly understandable and useful. As expert 4 mentioned "For me, the competency-oriented approach is a useful extension of classic process management." Also, the model was seen as generic enough to be adapted to companies needs but specific enough to ease the process of implementing a competency-based approach. All interviews had a strong focus how to implement the approach. This was seen controversially: in companies where HR and process/quality management already work closely together, required changes seem rather small. As expert 1 mentioned: "It corresponds more or less to the competency matrix that I currently use. [...] I have the processes on the left side and the competences on the upper side". Depending on existing collaboration (or the lack of it), the change process might be more complex as expert 9 mentioned: "I find the change process difficult for organizational reasons. A process manager normally does not work with the competency experts." Also, it might depend on the sector as interviewee 2 emphasized: "This can be implemented very well in consulting or IT. It might not be suitable for large manufacturing companies because for each process competencies are mapped." Regarding the use of a process modeling language, the interviewees saw in most cases the approach as feasible. The way of modeling was discussed as well. Most interviewees were in favour of a new object type as expert 4:" I would definitely separate it semantically in some form. There will be problems with the use of the data object in practical tests". It was also seen as important that the competency objects are clearly described and structured, expert 4: "So I think it is necessary to define standard attributes." It was furthermore discussed at which level competencies should be included. The main opinion was that competencies should be either related to roles or to complete processes (not to single activities) to avoid too complex models.

Finally, the competency framework was discussed. It was consensus that the framework eases the competency modeling process and that these competencies can help process managers. It was discussed whether there should be a generic framework or predefined competency profiles for specific roles as expert 2 said: "you need different competency sets. [...] Usually there is not only one level of management, but also departmental staff and divisional managers or a CIO." We suggest developing pre-defined competency sets for specific roles as a preparatory activity. Furthermore, proficiency levels were discussed. Here, expert 9 said:" The general classification from beginner to expert or high to low should be sufficient." We decided to use a standard classification (beginner to expert) but also allow to include proficiency taxonomies (such as the standard levels of language proficiency). The last part of the interviews discussed the potential outcomes and impact of the approach. It was consensus that the overall approach can lead to improved collaboration and participation when teams are involved from the beginning. However, the approach does not solve all acceptance problems and barriers. Expert 7 focused on older employees: "When you have employees in their late 50s, early 60s, it is a challenge to take them with you, because sometimes they don't want to." In many interviews, it was emphasized that the organizational culture of change, trust between hierarchy level and individual mindsets are the most important parts of the overall process and these need to be addressed continuously. As a summary, our expert interviews have shown that the approach is feasible and potentially helpful for BPM project in the DT. The improvement suggestions were already included in the model presented in this paper. Also, new topics of research emerged, e.g. comparing the model in a global context.

5 Discussion

Our approach of competency-based BPM (cBPM) is threefold, consisting of 1) a detailed procedure model of cBPM projects, 2) competency objects for modeling languages, 3) pre-defined competency framework and descriptions. As theoretical contributions, we have extended procedural models such as Becker et al. (2013) by adding competency-related processes and activities. This can help to better understand processes and efforts in BPM projects. Furthermore, we have operationalized employee participation and the social/collaborative BPM perspective (Vladova et al. 2017; Bavendiek et al. 2018) to gain a better understanding of employees and their engagement. This operationalization can also contribute to refine the competency-based view of the firm as an organizational theory as well as the influence of competencies of task performance (Motowildo et al. 1997). Of course, the inclusion of our findings into a competency-oriented theory will require additional research work which cannot be addressed in this paper. The main aspect of following research will be the influence of participation on employee well-being, performance and employability. As practical contributions, our approach contributes towards more employee-orientation in BPM projects. By providing detailed processes and activities, this approach can - as shown in the evaluation - be easily integrated in Digital Transformation projects focusing on business process redesign. We also extended state-of-the-art modeling tools for immediate usage by process managers. We also provide guidance how and which collaborations need to be initiated. This is in particular the case for process/quality management and HR development responsible person. All in all, the approach was seen as useful with the limitation that the competency matrix is quite similar to the competency matrix that uses one expert at work. Furthermore, the experts noted that difficulties regarding the implementation of this approach (expert 9). Additionally, the approach will be extended with standard attributes in the future and the competencies will not be related to single activities anymore, but they will be related to roles or complete processes. As a next step - also showing the limitations of our study - we will run multiple cases of the approach in different types of enterprises as Digital Transformation is in different stages in different industries/sectors. Here, we will study the impact of our approach on the workforce analysing the characteristics of competencies and range of competency changes.

6 Conclusion

In this work the approach of competency-based Business Process Management was outlined. Up to now, competencies have not yet been modelled in business processes, and the competency-oriented process model enables greater transparency of the competency requirements in digitized and partially digitized processes. Our approach consists of three types of artefacts, 1) a detailed procedure model of cBPM projects, 2) competency objects for modeling languages, 3) pre-defined competency framework and descriptions. The approach has been successfully evaluated with experts from industry and academia. The added value of the approach is that competencies and business processes are not viewed separately from each other in the context of digitization but are combined as a holistic view. Some experts think that the framework could be good to use and could improve employee participation in Digital Transformation projects. In the future, the approach should be tested for practical suitability in a company.

References

Adesola, S., Baines, T.: Developing and evaluating a methodology for business process improvement. Bus. Process Manag. J. (2005)

Ala-Mutka, K., Punie, Y., Redecker, C.: Digital competence for lifelong learning. Inst. Prospect. Technol. Stud. (IPTS) Eur. Commission Joint Res. Centre. Tech. Note: JRC **48708**, 271–282 (2008)

Allweyer, T.: BPMN 2.0: introduction to the standard for business process modeling. BoD–Books on Demand (2016)

Andriole, S.J., Cox, T., Khin, K.M.: The Innovator's Imperative: Rapid Technology Adoption for Digital Transformation. Auerbach Publications (2017)

Barrett, M., Davidson, E., Prabhu, J., Vargo, S.L.: Service innovation in the digital age: key contributions and future directions. MIS Q. **39**(1), 135–154 (2015)

Baskerville, R., Baiyere, A., Gregor, S., Hevner, A., Rossi, M.: Design science research contributions: finding a balance between artifact and theory. J. Assoc. Inf. Syst. **19**(5), 3 (2018)

Bavendiek, A.K., Huth, T., Inkermann, D., Paulsen, H., Vietor, T., Kauffeld, S.: Collaborative design: linking methods, communication tools and competencies to processes. In DS 92: Proceedings of the DESIGN 2018 15th International Design Conference, pp. 149–160 (2018)

Becker, J., Kugeler, M., Rosemann, M. (eds.): Process Management: A Guide for the Design of Business Processes. Springer, Heidelberg (2013)

Bhatti, K.K., Qureshi, T.M.: Impact of employee participation on job satisfaction, employee commitment and employee productivity. Int. Rev. Bus. Res. Pap. **3**(2), 54–68 (2007)

Blaschke, M., Cigaina, M., Riss, U.V., Shoshan, I.: Designing business models for the digital economy. In: Oswald, G., Kleinemeier, M. (eds.) Shaping the Digital Enterprise, pp. 121–136. Springer, Cham (2017). https://doi.org/10.1007/978-3-319-40967-2_6

Burke, W.W., Litwin, G.H.: A causal model of organizational performance and change. J. Manag. **18**(3), 523–545 (1992)

Calvani, A., Cartelli, A., Fini, A., Ranieri, M.: Models and instruments for assessing digital competence at school. J. E-Learn. Knowl. Soc. **4**(3), 183–193 (2008)

Center for Digital Dannelses: Digital Competence Wheel (2019). https://digcomp.digital-compet ence.eu/

da Silva, L.A., Damian, I.P.M., de Pádua, S.I.D.: Process management tasks and barriers: functional to processes approach. Bus. Process Manag. J. (2012)

De Waal, B.M., Batenburg, R.: The process and structure of user participation: a BPM system implementation case study. Bus. Process Manag. J. (2014)

Ehlers, U.D., Kellermann, S.A.: Future Skills: the future of learning and higher education, pp. 2–69. Karlsruhe (2019)

Ferrari, A.: Digital competence in practice: an analysis of frameworks: Luxembourg: Publication office of the EU. Research Report by the Joint Research Centre of the European Commission, Eville, Spain (2012)

Ferrari, A.: DIGCOMP: a framework for developing and understanding digital competence in Europe: Publications Office of the European Union Luxembourg (2013)

Fleischmann, A., Schmidt, W., Stary, C.: A primer to subject-oriented business process modeling. In: Stary, C. (ed.) S-BPM ONE 2012. LNBIP, vol. 104, pp. 218–240. Springer, Heidelberg (2012). https://doi.org/10.1007/978-3-642-29133-3_14

Frank, U.: Evaluation of reference models. In: Reference Modeling for Business Systems Analysis, pp. 118–140. IGI Global (2007)

Freiling, J.: A competence-based theory of the firm. Manag. Revue 27–52 (2004)

Freiling, J., Gersch, M., Goeke, C.: On the path towards a competence-based theory of the firm. Organ. Stud. **29**(8–9), 1143–1164 (2008)

Hansen, A.M., Kraemmergaard, P., Mathiassen, L.: Rapid adaptation in digital transformation: a participatory process for engaging IS and business leaders. MIS Q. Executive **10**(4) (2011)

Harmon, P.: Business Process Change: A Business Process Management Guide for Managers and Process Professionals. Morgan Kaufmann, Burlington (2019)

Hess, T., Matt, C., Benlian, A., Wiesböck, F.: Options for formulating a digital transformation strategy. MIS Q. Executive **15**(2) (2016)

Hoberg, P., Krcmar, H., Oswald, G., Welz, B.: Skills for digital transformation (2017). http://idt. in.tum.de/wp-content/uploads/2018/01/IDT_Skill_Report_2017.pdf. Accessed 05 Feb 2019

Hofmann, E., Rüsch, M.: Industry 4.0 and the current status as well as future prospects on logistics. Comput. Ind. **89**, 23–34 (2017)

Holtkamp, P., Jokinen, J.P., Pawlowski, J.M.: Soft competency requirements in requirements engineering, software design, implementation, and testing. J. Syst. Softw. **101**, 136–146 (2015)

Iivari, J.: Distinguishing and contrasting two strategies for design science research. Eur. J. Inf. Syst. **24**(1), 107–115 (2015)

Ilomäki, L., Paavola, S., Lakkala, M., Kantosalo, A.: Digital competence-an emergent boundary concept for policy and educational research. Educ. Inf. Technol. **21**(3), 655–679 (2016)

Kane, G.C., Palmer, D., Phillips, A.N., Kiron, D., Buckley, N.: Strategy, not technology, drives digital transformation. MIT Sloan Manag. Rev. Deloitte Univ. Press **14**, 1–25 (2015)

Kettinger, W.J., Teng, J.T., Guha, S.: Business process change: a study of methodologies, techniques, and tools. MIS Q. 55–80 (1997)

Kerremans, M.: Maturity assessment for business process improvement leaders: six phases for successful BPM adoption. Gartner, Stamford, pp. 7–15 (2008)

Kocbek, M., Jošt, G., Polančič, G.: Introduction to social business process management. In: Uden, L., Heričko, M., Ting, I.-H. (eds.) KMO 2015. LNBIP, vol. 224, pp. 425–437. Springer, Cham (2015). https://doi.org/10.1007/978-3-319-21009-4_33

Lederer, M., Knapp, J., Schott, P.: The digital future has many names—how business process management drives the digital transformation. In: 2017 6th International Conference on Industrial Technology and Management (ICITM), pp. 22–26. IEEE (2017)

Lines, R.: Influence of participation in strategic change: resistance, organizational commitment and change goal achievement. J. Chang. Manag. **4**(3), 193–215 (2004)

Loebecke, C., Picot, A.: Reflections on societal and business model transformation arising from digitization and big data analytics: a research agenda. J. Strateg. Inf. Syst. **24**(3), 149–157 (2015)

Matt, C., Hess, T., Benlian, A.: Digital transformation strategies. Bus. Inf. Syst. Eng. **57**(5), 339–343 (2015)

Motowildo, S.J., Borman, W.C., Schmit, M.J.: A theory of individual differences in task and contextual performance. Hum. Perform. **10**(2), 71–83 (1997)

Myers, M.D., Avison, D. (eds.): Qualitative Research in Information Systems: A Reader. Sage, Thousand Oaks (2002)

Niehaves, B., Plattfaut, R.: Collaborative business process management: status quo and quo vadis. Bus. Process Manag. J. (2011)

Offermann, P., Blom, S., Schönherr, M., Bub, U.: Artifact types in information systems design science – a literature review. In: Winter, R., Zhao, J.L., Aier, S. (eds.) DESRIST 2010. LNCS, vol. 6105, pp. 77–92. Springer, Heidelberg (2010). https://doi.org/10.1007/978-3-642-13335-0_6

Pagani, M., Pardo, C.: The impact of digital technology on relationships in a business network. Ind. Mark. Manag. **67**, 185–192 (2017)

Paquette, G.: An ontology and a software framework for competency modeling and management. J. Educ. Technol. Soc. **10**(3), 1–21 (2007)

Pasmore, W.A., Fagans, M.R.: Participation, individual development, and organizational change: a review and synthesis. J. Manag. **18**(2), 375–397 (1992)

Pflanzl, N., Vossen, G.: Challenges of social business process management. In: 2014 47th Hawaii International Conference on System Sciences, pp. 3868–3877. IEEE, January 2014

Prifti, L., Knigge, M., Kienegger, H., Krcmar, H.: A competency model for "Industrie 4.0" employees. In: International Conference Wirtschaftsinformatik 2017 (2017)

Rosemann, M., vom Brocke, J.: The six core elements of business process management. In: vom Brocke, J., Rosemann, M. (eds.) Handbook on Business Process Management 1. IHIS, pp. 105–122. Springer, Heidelberg (2015). https://doi.org/10.1007/978-3-642-45100-3_5

Shahlaei, C.A., Rangraz, M., Stenmark, D.: Transformation of competence–the effects of digitalization on communicators' work. In: European Conference on Informations Systems. Association For Information System (AIS) (2017)

Singh, A., Hess, T.: How chief digital officers promote the digital transformation of their companies. MIS Q. Executive **16**(1) (2017)

Sousa, M.J., Wilks, D.: Sustainable skills for the world of work in the digital age. Syst. Res. Behav. Sci. **35**(4), 399–405 (2018)

Swanson, R.A., Holton, E., Holton, E.F.: Foundations of Human Resource Development. Berrett-Koehler Publishers (2001)

Topi, H., Karsten, H., Brown, S.A., et al.: MSIS 2016 global competency model for graduate degree programs in information systems. Commun. Assoc. Inf. Syst. **40**(18) (2017)

Topi, H., et al.: Curriculum guidelines for undergraduate degree programs in information systems. ACM/AIS task force (2010)

Trushkina, N., Abazov, R., Rynkevych, N., Bakhautdinova, G.: Digital transformation of organizational culture under conditions of the information economy. Virtual Econ. **3**(1), 7–38 (2020)

Venable, J., Pries-Heje, J., Baskerville, R.: FEDS: a framework for evaluation in design science research. Eur. J. Inf. Syst. **25**(1), 77–89 (2016)

Verina, N., Titko, J.: Digital transformation: conceptual framework. In: Proceedings of the International Scientific Conference "Contemporary Issues in Business, Management and Economics Engineering' 2019", Vilnius, Lithuania, pp. 9–10 (2019)

Vial, G.: Understanding digital transformation: a review and a research agenda. J. Strategic Inf. Syst. (2019)

Vladova, G., Ullrich, A., Sultanow, E.: Demand-oriented competency development in a manufacturing context: the relevance of process and knowledge modeling. In: Proceedings of the 50th Hawaii International Conference on System Sciences, January 2017

Vogelsang, K., Liere-Netheler, K., Packmohr, S., Hoppe, U.: Barriers to digital transformation in manufacturing: development of a research agenda. In: Proceedings of the 52nd Hawaii International Conference on System Sciences (2019a)

Vogelsang, K., Liere-Netheler, K., Packmohr, S., Hoppe, U.: A taxonomy of barriers to digital transformation. In: 14th International Conference on Wirtschaftsinformatik. Universität Siegen (2019b)

Vom Brocke, J., Mendling, J.: Business Process Management Cases. Digital Innovation and Business Transformation in Practice. Springer, Cham (2018). https://doi.org/10.1007/978-3-319-58307-5

Voss, P.M.: A Competency Framework for Digital Transformation - a literature review. In: Forty Second Information Systems Research Seminar in Scandinavia (IRIS2019)

Weill, P., Woerner, S.L.: Optimizing your digital business model. MIT Sloan Manag. Rev. 54(3), 71 (2013)

Wernerfelt, B.: A resource-based view of the firm. Strateg. Manag. J. 5(2), 171–180 (1984)

Wernerfelt, B.: The resource-based view of the firm: ten years after. Strateg. Manag. J. 16(3), 171–174 (1995)

Winter, R., Schelp, J.: Reference modeling and method construction: a design science perspective. In: Proceedings of the 2006 ACM Symposium on Applied Computing, pp. 1561–1562 (2006)

Wolf, M., Semm, A., Erfurth, C.: Digital transformation in companies – challenges and success factors. In: Hodoň, M., Eichler, G., Erfurth, C., Fahrnberger, G. (eds.) I4CS 2018. CCIS, vol. 863, pp. 178–193. Springer, Cham (2018). https://doi.org/10.1007/978-3-319-93408-2_13

Wu, L., Yue, X., Jin, A., Yen, D.C.: Smart supply chain management: a review and implications for future research. Int. J. Logist. Manag. 27(2), 395–417 (2016)

Yoo, Y., Henfridsson, O., Lyytinen, K.: Research commentary—the new organizing logic of digital innovation: an agenda for information systems research. Inf. Syst. Res. 21(4), 724–735 (2010)

Manufacturing Industry's Servitization and Its Future-Case Analysis of the Japanese Electric Company

Akira Kamoshida[1]([⊠]) and Toru Fujii[2]

[1] Hosei University, Tokyo, Japan
akira.kamoshida.34@hosei.ac.jp
[2] Kitami Institute of Technology, Kitami, Japan

Abstract. In this paper, we will take up Sharp Co., Ltd., a Japanese electric appliance maker, and consider the factors that caused the High technology maker, which has dominated the market in the technology driven market, to sharply deteriorate its business performance in the face of globalization and commoditization of the market. We concluded, as a result, a company that has been able to demonstrate its abilities in a technology driven market such as Sharp cannot necessarily demonstrate sufficient results in a non-technology driven market. It was founded that it was due to lack of core competence in the on-technology driven market and insufficient performance. Strategic scenarios in such cases are as follows: first, corporate transformation and promotion of servitization in order to acquire organizational capabilities adaptable to non-technology driven market, or secondly, technology driven markets where the company's core competencies can be adaptable. I summarized the possible strategic scenarios to find and find a win. This could also give implications for servitization strategies and their future in many manufacturing industries in developed countries.

Keywords: Servitization · Manufacturing the future · Sharp corporation · Competitive advantage · Dynamic capability

1 Introduction

Services account for approximately 70% of the GDP (gross domestic product) of advanced countries such as the United States and Europe and Japan.

It is not necessary to look at the term "service-economy", but now the time has come when we cannot talk about the economy without services.

The manufacturing industry is no exception.

Speaking of manufacturing, it is the leading player who has driven the prosperity and growth of Japan today. However, according to the statistics of the Japanese Cabinet Office, Japan's manufacturing industry accounted for 30% of GDP (gross domestic product) in the 1970s during the high-growth period, but in 2000 it was in the 20% range. Has dropped to. Nevertheless, the manufacturing industry has undergone major evolution while overcoming the wave of economic service and globalization, and the transformation of Japanese society itself, and has continued to play an important role as a driving force of the Japanese economy.

L. Uden et al. (Eds.): KMO 2022, CCIS 1593, pp. 118–128, 2022.
https://doi.org/10.1007/978-3-031-07920-7_10

This paper takes Sharp Corporation as an example of the Japanese electric industry, which rapidly lost its competitive advantage in the global market for the first 10 years of the 21st century and analyzes Sharp's strategy in the global market where globalization and commoditization are progressing. The purpose is to do. Based on Sharp's strategic analysis, we will give a perspective on the future of the manufacturing industry, which has undergone major changes from the 20th century and the 21st century.

2   Overview of Sharp Corporation

Sharp Corporation was founded in 1912 by Mr. Tokuji Hayakawa. Initially founded in Tokyo, Japan, it was later relocated to Osaka in 1924 and changed to its current name, Sharp Corporation, in 1970. In Japan in the late 1940s, Matsushita Electric Industrial Co., Ltd. (currently Panasonic) and Sony emerged, and many electrical equipment manufacturers that have grown into global companies are developing during this period. Sharp also launched the microwave oven for the first time as a Japanese electric appliance manufacturer in 1962, and in 1964 developed the world's first all-transistor electronic desk calculator.

In the 1970s, Sharp entered the home appliance market such as refrigerators, CRT TVs, and video recorders one after another, and steadily solidified its position as a home appliance maker. Sharp has also entered the market for personal computers and video cameras, and has grown significantly.

Sharp's sales for the fiscal year ended March 2022 were 2.52 trillion yen ($ 25.2 billion, converted to 100 yen per dollar), ordinary income was 110 billion yen ($ 1.1 billion), and sales for the fiscal year 2008 were 3,417.7 billion yen. Although the yen ($ 34.2 billion) did not reach the record high of 170.6 billion yen ($ 1.7 billion) in 2007, it is gradually recovering after the crisis of bankruptcy that has continued for several years since 2010 (Table 1).

Table 1.   Sharp corporation: corporate overview as of 31 December 2021

Head office	1 Takumi-cho, Sakai-ku, Sakai City, Osaka 590–8522, Japan
Management representatives	Jeng-Wu Tai, Chairman & CEO Katsuaki Nomura, President & COO
Business activities (Current)	Mainly manufacturing and sales of telecommunications equipment, electric and electronic application equipment, and electronic components
Capital stock	5 billion yen (as of December 31, 2021)
Sales	2,425,910 million yen (consolidated) 1,179,143 million yen (unconsolidated) (Fiscal 2020 Financial Results)
Employees	Consolidated: 48,064 Japan: 18,101 (Sharp Corporation 5,763/other Consolidated 12,338) Overseas: 29,963 (Consolidated)

Source: https://global.sharp/corporate/info/outline/ (26 February, 2022)

3   Success and Failure of Sharp's LCD Business

Sharp is an electrical equipment manufacturer that has been working from an early stage on the technological development of LCD panels that have had an innovative impact on various electrical products. Sharp has been a world leader in the development of high technology for many sensor devices such as plasma cluster technology, organic EL technology, photocatalyst technology, sensor technology, and solar cell technology, in addition to liquid crystal technology.

Among them, the development of LCD device technology started from the earliest in the world and has led the development of LCD devices in the world.

The Kameyama model used to be synonymous with the high quality of Sharp LCD TVs.

"Sharp when it comes to LCDs" and "LCD when it comes to sharps" fits in Japan and with the world's leading LCD brands. However, Sharp, which had the momentum to drop flying birds until the mid-2000s, suddenly fell into the red after 2010. It was announced that the current account deficit could not be completely removed even in the fiscal year ended March 31, 2015, and that the final deficit amount would greatly exceed the expected amount of 30 billion yen in the consolidated financial statements for the same period [1].

What happened to Sharp, who is suffering from business difficulties?

Chart 1 Trends in LCD TV share in the global market is a comparison of the market share of liquid TVs in 2001 and 2012. Looking at this, the cause of the predicament of our national electric appliance maker today can be seen through.

As of 2001, Sharp had the overwhelming market share of LCD TVs at 80.5%. However, 11 years later, in 2012, Samsung has the top share in the world market with 20.1%, followed by LG Electronics with 13.5%. And when it comes to Sharp in 2012, it has a 5.1% share. This is also overtaken by the same Japanese Sony (8.5%).

4   Transition from a Technology-Driven Market to a Non-technology-Driven Market

What happened in the market during this time?

When discussing this, let's confirm the history of the spread of LCD TV products. The liquid crystal material, which became the flower shape of the Japanese industry as a display material, was studied by the Austrian botanist Friedrich-Reinitzer in 1889, and then in 1962, RCA (Radio Corporation of America) in the United States developed a display using liquid crystal [2].

Focusing on this technology, it was Tohoku University and Sharp in Japan that started to work on the practical development of liquid crystal technology [3]. sps:id::fig1||locator::gr1||MediaObject::0

In 1995, Sharp launched a 3-inch LCD color TV in 1987, a 10.4 inch LCD TV for general households in 1995, and an LCD TV under the AQUOS brand in 2001. It became known to the world as the sharpness of the liquid crystal display.

According to Chart 1 Trends in LCD TV share in the global market, the total number of LCD TVs shipped worldwide in 2001 was 810,000, and Sharp's global market share

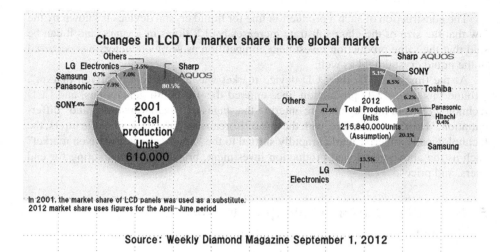

Chart 1. Trends in LCD TV share in the global market

was 80.5%. It can be said that Sharp, which possesses the cutting-edge technology of liquid crystal technology, was at the forefront of the global market and was the only place where other companies could not get close.

However, in 2012, LCD TV technology approached the maturity level, and multiple competitors other than Sharp have emerged in the global market. In particular, Koreans such as Samsung and LG Electronics swept the market in a blink of an eye, and as of 2012, the two companies together accounted for 33.6% of the global market. Looking at it in this way, the changes in the global LCD TV market from 2001 to 2012 are dramatic. As of 2001, the total number of LCD TVs shipped worldwide was 610,000. In 2012, it reached 215.84 million units, an explosive expansion of 354 times. On the other hand, Sharp could not maintain its absolute advantage in the global market as of 2001 until 2012, and its market share dropped sharply from 80.1% to 5.1%.

Here, in the 11 years since 2001, the global market for LCD TVs has dramatically changed that aspect. At the time of 2001, the world's LCD device technology was monopolized by a small number of companies such as Sharp. However, the number of players in the market has increased, with South Korea entering the LCD business three years after Japan and Taiwan in 2002 [2].

Among the product groups using LCD device technology, TVs have become a driving force in the entire market since around 2005, and the screens are heading toward larger size competition.

According to Nakata (2017) [2] (Reference: Japan's Competitiveness in the LCD Industry), increasing the size of glass substrates is the most important factor in building LCD production lines, and it is an electrical equipment manufacturer in both cost competition and competition for larger TV screens. It was an unavoidable point for each company. In fact, the 1st generation production line that started in 1991 is around 300 mm × 350 mm, and the 6th generation production line in January 2004 is a 1470 mm × 1770 mm production line, and its glass area is actually 25 times larger.

The construction of such a production line for liquid crystal devices is known by the law that the size of the glass substrate increases by 1.8 times in 3 years, and it can be said that the same production investment competition as semiconductors has occurred in the liquid crystal field as well.

At the time of 2001, the LCD device market was a "technology driven market". Around this time, LCD production lines entered the 4th to 5th generations, and LCD technology was in the stage before entering the stages of "standardization" and "differentiation." However, after that, with the rise of Korean and Taiwanese manufacturers, the technologically superior market rapidly shifted to the "non- technology driven market" such as the above-mentioned production investment, branding and marketing for end users, and prices.

5   Key Failure Factors of Sharp in the Non-technology Driven Market

Sharp Corporation was acquired by Hon Hai Precision Industry Co., Ltd. of Taiwan on April 2, 2016. At this point, the company may be more famous as a company belonging to the Foxconn Technology Group, which boasts group sales of over $ 150 billion (converted to 100 yen per dollar). Hon Hai is the world's largest EMS (Electronics Manufacturing Service) company that manufactures electronic devices such as smartphones and flat-screen TVs on a contract basis, and has a long-standing partnership with Sharp Corporation. The aim of Hon Hai's acquisition of Sharp is firstly to acquire LCD technology and secondly to acquire the Sharp brand. However, considering that the company is an EMS format and the Sharp brand has already fallen, it must be said that the second aim is more certain.

That is to say that the main purpose is to acquire liquid crystal technology, which is the first aim, but it is thought that "organic EL display technology" was the biggest target. Organic EL displays consume less power than conventional display panels and have flexibility. Hon Hai has major customers such as Apple Inc., Nokia, Samsung, and Sony, and LCD technology incorporated into smartphones and personal computers is an important component positioned at the core of its business.

In other words, it is no exaggeration to say that Hon Hai's intention to acquire Sharp lies in the LCD technology owned by Sharp.

On the other hand, there is a view that Sharp has pointed out strategic mistakes in the LCD market where the technology driven market collapsed at once in about 10 years from the beginning of the 21st century, but the authors consider as follows as to the factors behind the decline in Sharp's LCD market share.

The first factor is the commoditization of LCD device technology.

The misreading at Sharp is that the market has become a commodity at once in a way that far exceeded expectations during this period. In other words, the product technology of LCD TVs, which the company was seen as having an absolute advantage, can hardly be differentiated, at least at the level of commercialization and consumer purchasing. As mentioned above, South Korea has entered the market three years after Japan's entry into LCD technology, and Taiwan has entered the market in 2001. Such development is due to the progress of technology transfer, such as Japan establishing a joint venture with a company such as Taiwan. In addition, technology transfer to South Korea and Taiwan has accelerated through technology licensing and OEM, and the production bases for liquid crystal technology have expanded at once, which can be said to have promoted the commoditization of liquid crystal technology.

Generally, when the market becomes commoditized, it tends toward "price competition". In this case, the competition for price reduction of products will occur, and the companies involved in this will be exhausted. On the other hand, companies aiming for "non-price competition" other than price will select "value-added strategy". Of course, it is desirable for any company to be able to compete with added value without reducing prices, but only a few companies, such as Apple Inc. in the United States, have succeeded in these value-added strategies and have recorded high rates of return.

Then, what was the difference between Sharp and Samsung and LG Electronics?

In the 2010s, the global market for liquid TVs became difficult to make a big difference in product functions and technologies, and as a result, in marketing such as advertising and sales promotion, designs and casters tailored to the local market, and product functions and technologies. It became difficult to make a big difference, and as a result, marketing such as advertising and sales promotion, design for the local market and customer care became more important. Sharp was unable to cope with the demand for faster decision-making in line with the speed of market changes and the international division of labor due to the increase in global suppliers. Meanwhile, both Samsung and LG were able to successfully adapt to the new competition rules as the market became commoditized and transformed.

In other words, while the global LCD market has expanded rapidly in about 10 years from the beginning of the 21st century, Sharp has not been able to respond to a new stage despite the significant transformation from a technology driven market to a non-technology driven market [13].

It can be said that the major factor was the lack of organizational response to the end user market.

So to speak, it lacked the ability and strategy to respond to the next stage beyond what Geoffrey Moore calls "chasm." [4].

The second factor is the transformation of the LCD business into a power play business.

The direct reason why Sharp's LCD business began to tilt after 2010 was that the products produced at the Sakai Plant (started in 2009), which was built with a huge investment of 400 billion yen (about 40 billion dollars), rapidly became obsolete. However, competitors such as LG Korea and AUO Taiwan, which have entered the production of LCDs, have continued to invest more than Sharp [5].

Similar to semiconductor production, LCD production requires a generational change of factory equipment in line with the ever-increasing technological progress. In particular, increasing the size of the liquid crystal glass substrate is essential to meet market demand. Under these circumstances, the interval between generations was about three years, and the size of the glass substrate increased 1.8 times in three years in the 2010s, creating a business environment where huge production investment was forced on a daily basis.

In such a business environment, business owners are required to make swift and decisive management decisions regarding huge investments. The author calls this power play, but when comparing Sharp with competitors such as Samsung and LG, Sharp was far inferior in the speed of its management decision-making. The first reason is that the top management was not the owner-manager who was the founder, but the so-called hired manager. Second, there was conflict among top management, and management leadership was confused. Thirdly, the business performance has already deteriorated (2005–2010), and it was difficult to obtain funds.

6   End of Competitive Advantage and Strategic Flexibility Required for Manufacturing Industry

In recent years, the focus of the world's manufacturing industry has shifted from advanced countries such as Europe, the United States and Japan to later industrialized countries such as South Korea and Taiwan, and countries such as Eastern Europe, Southeast Asia and South America.

It is partly due to the fact that the state of a country that has an advantage as a production base and labor costs has changed due to the acceleration of globalization and commoditization.

As a matter of fact, if we take a look at the Japanese home appliance manufacturing industry, Sanyo Electric was acquired by Chinese home appliance maker Haier in 2011. In 2016, Toshiba transferred its home appliances division to Midea Group in China, and in 2018, it transferred its TV business division to Hisense in China.

In the home appliance market, price competition broke out due to commoditization of product technology, and emerging manufacturers around the world have taken the market share of existing home appliance manufacturers.

On the other hand, such a home appliance market is separated from the commodity home appliance market called generic home appliances, and a high value-added home appliance market that makes full use of AI and other advanced technologies has also started up. Cleaning robots from iRobot in the US and high-performance vacuum cleaners from Dyson in the UK are emerging in this market. Traditional Japanese home appliance makers have advanced into fields such as rice cookers and vacuum cleaners that make full use of AI and advanced technology, and have gained a certain presence.

What is more distinctive is the entry into the home appliance market from different industries, rather than the traditional home appliance manufacturers. For example, companies with characteristics different from the conventional manufacturing model in Japan, such as Iris Ohyama, which has achieved rapid growth in plastic everyday products, and Balmuda, which is growing in design-oriented high-performance home appliances with a fabless business model. It is that the entry of is one after another.

The rise and fall of these manufacturing companies largely depends on their competitive advantage.

As shown in (Chart 1), Sharp's competitive advantage is greatly damaged by shifting from the technology driven market in 2001 to the non- technology driven market in 2012, 11 years later.

In markets where globalization and commoditization are advancing, manufacturers are forced to compete in price or non-price competition other than price.

Sharp has taken various approaches to maintain its competitive advantage in the LCD market, but has gradually lost its competitive advantage as the above market changes progress. There is a stereotype here that the competitive advantage once established as the common sense of corporate management will continue, and it can be said that Sharp was also stuck in that curse.

However, as Rita McGrath states in her book, The End of Competitive Advantage (2013), business owners confront the concept of "sustainable competitive advantage" [6]. It is necessary to abandon the based strategic theory. And Rita emphasizes the importance of looking at strategies based on "temporary competitive advantage". In today's rapidly changing market environment, the manufacturing industry is stopped by "Strategic Flexibility" [7], which continues to build its strategic advantage in response to changes in the business environment. Sector.

7   Organizational Capability of the Manufacturers Required for Servitization

As mentioned earlier, the strategies that the manufacturers should take in these markets are either to realize a business model that wins through price competition, or to differentiate itself from other competitors through non-price competition, that is, value-added competition, and to win. It will be an alternative.

Sharp's core competencies so far have been realized by dominate the market with technological capabilities in the technology driven market, but it is difficult to demonstrate Sharp's competitive advantage in the non-technology driven market.

In such a market, it is the royal road to carry out the value-added strategy by making it a service as seen by Apple Inc. in the United States. However, it is not always easy for Sharp to make it a service.

Here, let us consider the meaning of "manufacturer's servitization". In the first place, services are defined as "Value Co-Creation". So to speak, servitization refers to activities that create customer value. Professor Andy Neely of the University of Cambridge, UK, describes "servitization of the manufacturers" as a system that integrates products and peripheral services from a company that simply produces and sells products, and provides higher value to customers. It is said that it will be transformed into a company that can do it.

The important point here is that even if a company that manufactures and sells products adds a service like a burning blade, it will not be the original service, but will eventually fail. (cf. Chart 2) hereunder summarizes the purpose of the manufacturer's servitization. According to this, the reasons for the purpose of servitization are classified into economic, strategic, and business environment rationality.

Take, for example, the case of Mitsubishi Electric's elevator business. The company has the world's highest level elevator technology such as variable speed elevators and the world's fastest elevators. At the same time, it succeeded in commercializing a remote monitoring service for elevators for the first time in the world, and started a maintenance service for elevators sold by the company.

Economic Rationale	1. Manufacturing firms in developed economies cannot compete on the basis of cost (technological developments are enabling them to add innovative services)...
	2. The installed base argument (e.g. for every new car sold there are already 13 in operation, 15 to 1 for civil aircraft and 22 to 1 for trains)...
	3. Stability of revenues – services vs. products...
Strategic Rationale	1. Lock in customers (sell the original equipment at cost, make money on spares & suppliers - razor, printers)...
	2. Lock out competitors...
	3. Increase the level of differentiation (e.g. equipment provider offers to take customer's risk and give predictable maintenance costs)...
	4. Customers demand it (e.g. contracting for capability)...
Environmental Rationale	1. Environmental rationale (change notions of ownership and resource use – e.g. Mobility cars)...

Source: Anderson et al. 1997, Cusumano 2004, Cohen et al. 2006, Ovans 1997,
Sawhney et al. 2004, Reinartz et al. 2008, Van Looy et al 2003, Wise et al. 1999, etc.

Chart 2. Why is manufacturing servitizing?

As a result, the profit margin on sales of the company's elevator business exceeded 8% (FY2011), resulting in a synergistic effect that exceeds the level of the manufacturing industry in general.

The maintenance service is handled by the subsidiary Mitsubishi Electric Techno Service, and the company's performance is also strong. Looking at the company's servitization (cf. Chart 2), they will steadily increase sales by the cumulative number of elevator sales to the elevator sales business, which sells to newly built buildings that are directly affected by economic fluctuations. The maintenance service business that can be done is suitable for the economic rationality of seizing growth opportunities, stabilizing sales, and improving profit margins. In addition, the fact that customers are locked in and differentiated through services fulfills strategic reason.

However, it is a major US IT company that superficially imitating business models is not enough to bring about such success.

We can also learn from the IBM case. IBM has succeeded in transforming a hardware sales-centric business model (Box Selling) into a solution-centric business model (so-called service) such as software, services, and consulting, and is now half of the company's sales. The above is occupied by the consulting and outsourcing businesses. However, on the sidelines of the company's success, competitors cannot easily follow it, but rather suffer great losses because they cannot imitate it.

According to Gary Hamel, CK Prahalad, the way a company gains a competitive advantage in the market is its internal organizational capabilities: R & D, marketing, or funding. Determine if you can demonstrate your advantage in the target market. And it is to plan and execute market selection and strategy that can demonstrate its capability [8, 11].

Traditionally, in business administration research, the idea of positioning represented by Michael Porter has been common. In other words, after analyzing the market and grasping the competitive situation, the company searches for a market where it can demonstrate its strengths and formulates a strategy (positioning). If this is a theory that focuses on the external environment of corporate management, in recent years, the resource-based view by Jay B. Barney and Gary Hamel mentioned above have been attracting attention. This is a discussion focusing on the internal environment of a company represented by these core competence theories.

Of course, it is not an alternative discussion of external or internal, but in recent years, there is a trend of "servitization" as a background to paying attention to the internal environment such as organizational capability and management resources of such companies... Organizational capability is important for successful servitization. Dr. David J. Teece presented the concept of "Dynamic Capabilities" [9] in his book, but Sharp lacked it.

8 Conclusion: Manufacturing the Future Lessons Learnt from Sharp's Case Studies

Sharp is a high-tech company that boasts technological capabilities and dominated the LCD market during the nascent period. However, Sharp, which has dominated the market in the technology driven market, has sharply deteriorated its business performance in the face of market globalization and commoditization. There are two possible factors, the external environmental factors surrounding the market and the internal environmental factors that are sharply inherent. Sharp was good at ordinary capabilities (Teece 2011), but lacked dynamic capabilities.

What should Sharp have done in this case?

The first possible strategic scenario is to acquire organizational capabilities (dynamic capabilities) that can be applied in the non-technology driven market, transform the company, and promote servitization.

The second scenario is to find a technology driven market where their core competencies can be demonstrated, and take a strategy to find a win there. In other words, this is a scenario in which they can demonstrate their own ordinary capabilities and win the competition [14].

The second scenario is a scenario in which a new battlefield is found and business development is planned, away from the main battlefield so far.

Until the latter half of the 20th century, many manufacturers in the Japanese manufacturing industry were shining brightly.

However, with the spread and development of IT and the progress of globalization, the speed of market change has accelerated far beyond imagination. The manufacturing industry in the 21st century may be divided into an area where technology seeds are sown and slowly grown, and an area where products and services continue to be born while the market rapidly approaches and changes at a tremendous speed.

As you can see in "Makers" by Chris Anderson [10], the personal manufacturing industry makes full use of digital tools such as small printers. A manufacturing industry called (Personal Fabrication), which is developing close to the former IT venture, is also being born.

In addition, we have our own core competencies such as Tesla, an electric car maker born in the United States, Dyson, a British vacuum cleaner maker, Iris Ohyama, which recently entered the home appliance market in Japan, and Balmuda, a home appliance venture that is attracting attention due to its unconventional ideas. Based on this, unique manufacturing industries have also been born all over the world.

Sharp is also aiming to revitalize by focusing on the B2B market from the B2C market, with an eye on its corporate culture, technological base, and management style.

"Manufacturing the future" in the 21st century is expected to evolve from the concept of manufacturing up to the 20th century into more diverse forms. Manufacturing the future may transform into a new industry rooted in customer value.

References

1. Keizai, N.: Newspaper, March 5, 2015
2. Yukihiko, N.: Japan's competitiveness in the LCD industry-analysis of the cause of the decline and proposal of "core national management"-RIETI Discussion Paper Series, 07-J-017 Research Institute of Economy, Trade & Industry-Japan (2017)
3. Dammer, D., Slackin, T., et al.: History of LCD. Asahi Selection Book (2011)
4. HarperCollins: Crossing the Chasm: Marketing and Selling High-Tech Products to Mainstream Customers (Collins Business Essentials) (English Edition) e-books; Revised Edition, 17 March 2019
5. PRESIDENT: "I found out the real cause of Sharp's decline" President Company, May 30, 2016
6. McGrath, R.G.: The End of Competitive Advantage: How to Keep Your Strategy Moving as Fast as Your Business (English Edition) Kindle Version (2013)
7. Deloitte Research: Strategic Flexibility in the Energy Sector (2010)
8. Gary Hamel, Prahalad, C.K.: The core competence of the corporation. Harvard Business Review (1990)
9. Teece, D.J.: Dynamic Capabilities and Strategic Management: Organizing for Innovation and Growth (2011)
10. Anderson, C.: Makers: The New Industrial Revolution (English Edition) (2012)
11. Prahalad, C.K.: Competing for the Future, Harvard Business School Press, April 1996. ISBN 978-0-87584-716-0
12. Baldwin, C.Y., Clark, K.B.: Design Rules: The Power of Modularity. MIT Press, Cambridge (2000)
13. Kamoshida, A.: Textbooks on Practical MBA Business Administration. Paru Publishing Co. (2015)
14. Kamoshida, A.: Servitization and value creation of manufacturing industry: thinking about the future of manufacturing in the 21st century. Suruga Institute Report, Institute of Corporate Management, vol. 130, pp. 8–11 (2015)

The Business Model Transformation Framework Using Design Science Approach

Aravind Kumaresan[1]([✉]) and Dario Liberona[2]

[1] University of Vaasa, Vaasa, Finland
Aravind.kumaresan@gmail.com
[2] Seinajoki University of Applied Sciences, Seinäjoki, Finland
Dario.Liberona@seamk.fi

Abstract. A good business model is a core component of any business to be successful whether it's a startup or an established company. However, it is realized that most of the businesses do not give enough consideration to re-invent their business model in line with the ever-changing environment. This led them to be an unsustainable business and in turn they become a failure over time. Business model should be considered equal to that of scientific methods, which needs to be constantly tested against the given hypothesis and revised according to the changing needs. Also, there is a strong need and the responsibility of the business owners to clearly communicate their business model to their employees. It is often proved that employees who are valued and made felt like being part of a bigger purpose have contributed massively to their business success. Thus, it is very important to draft and communicate an easily understandable business model to all of the company's employees. This study is aimed at creating a business model transformation framework using design science approach. This study was inspired by the various existing work around developing variants of business model canvas using design science approach. For the purpose of this study the employees from a reputed UK based asset management firm have participated in a focused workshop to create, develop and evaluate the research artefact.

Keywords: Business model framework · Business model canvas · Dynamic business model · Design science

1 Introduction

The former British Prime Minister Benjamin Disraeli once quoted 'change is inevitable, change is constant'. This message is very appropriate for businesses operating in today's world (Wheelen et al. 2000). The influences of changes in STEEPLE (Social, Technological, Economic, Environmental, Political, Legal, Ethical) are having an immediate impact on today's businesses. The businesses that do not understand or willing to react for these changes will fail miserably.

We have witnessed these failures in many businesses as in case of Blockbuster (An American movie and video game rental business), Kodak (An American technology company that produces camera-related products), Nokia (A Finnish multinational

© Springer Nature Switzerland AG 2022
L. Uden et al. (Eds.): KMO 2022, CCIS 1593, pp. 129–142, 2022.
https://doi.org/10.1007/978-3-031-07920-7_11

tele-communications firm), Borders (An American booksellers), Lehman Brothers (An American investment bank). The innovative models will accelerate the economic growth, contribute to the quality of our communities and our lives. Late after the dotcom bubble in 2000 there were numerous calls and proposals for new modelling methods in the business model domain from various authors like Rent Meister and Klein (Rentmeister and Klein 2003). Inspired by the designed science research framework and ontology models the author Alexander Osterwalder proposed the business model ontology and business model canvas in an attempt to simplify the business model design so that it can be easily created and communicated among various stake holders (Osterwalder 2004). After the release of the Business Model Generation book in 2010, the BMC has become a worldwide phenomenon. Ash Maurya further extended the BMC model into The Lean Canvas especially targeting the entrepreneurs to focus particularly on problems, solutions, key metrics and competitive advantages. However recently there are numerous approaches attempting to add the dynamic capability to the business model designs. Authors like Boris Fritscher and Yves Pigneur proposed a dynamic perspective to the BMC (Teece 2007). They suggest the business model method should consider the external/internal changes and adapt to it. Hence, the business model should consider the dynamic nature of transformation and evolution of the model. Raphael Amit and Christoph Zott proposed a business model design with dynamic capability Inspired from Teece. Dynamic capability model. The results from the work the limits of the business model canvas as a dynamic framework by Vivian Candido Rodrigues and Humberto Eliad Garcia Lopes indicates the strong need for integration tools, methodologies, indicators to the BMC to make it dynamic to further help the businesses to innovate their business models. The above all sums up a strong need for research in a business model transformation framework with dynamic capability and monitoring/alerting concepts as threat indicators. Therefore, it's of paramount importance not just to come up with a clear business model but also to have a relevant monitoring and alerting systems around this model to understand the impacts from the various STEEPLE factors and change the business model accordingly for business sustainability employing a suitable methodology like design science.

2   Business Model Literature

Business model is a tool for outlining and capturing the ultimate value of the business. It may be used in various aspects such as how to design a product/service, how to advertise, pricing, distribution etc. According to Joan Magretta a business model has two parts: part one is all about the product/service: designing, purchasing raw materials, manufacturing etc. part two is all about selling that product/service: finding and reaching the targeted customers, supporting the sales transaction, distributing or delivering the service (Magretta 2013). The business model indicates how the firm will convert the cost of capital into a valuable outputs such as a higher return of investment etc. Any business model should be designed considering the various assumptions in the ever-changing business environment otherwise the company is likely to go out of business. Traditionally a business will draft their business model and try and operate using that model for numerous years. Due to the constant change in market environment conditions or other changing factors these models have become outdated over a period of time.

Today the businesses have to constantly innovate their business model according to the change in assumptions and this has opened a new concept called business model innovation. They have to do this to stay competitive or to add a new revenue stream. Today the business models are mostly driven by emerging technologies and using these technologies the businesses now can reach more customers with minimal costs. Also, the rise of globalization has meant the modern business models includes outsourcing as a strategic option to create or sell their products or services. With the recent advancements in technology the business models have become much more sophisticated.

In early years the innovative business models are used extensively by McDonald's restaurants. McDonald's was the first major international fast-food chain in the world. What we might have not realized is how we have as a customers adopted to these innovative models introduced by them. Some of these innovations are well advertised, but others are designed so that customers will never notice such as outsourcing order taking at the drive thru, expanding the dollar menu to breakfast, specialty coffee etc. Through its innovative business model approach McDonald's has managed to generate higher sales and more profits. Then in 1960's Wall-Mart and supermarkets have dominated the super market industries with innovative business models. From 2000 onwards until now due to the technological advancements the companies are now innovating more business models with platform structure and generating huge profits. According to Sangeet Paul Choudary there are two broad types of business models, Its pipes and platforms. In pipes model, businesses create goods or services then push them out and sell it to customers (Choudary 2015). In this case the value is created by the business and then consumed by the consumers. This is linear model very similar to water flowing through the pipes. In the platform model the users co-create the value and also consume the thus created value. World's most valuable companies like Apple, Amazon, Microsoft, Alphabet etc. have created some of the high revenue generating products around the platform-based business model. In case of Alphabet, which is a parent company of Google Inc. have created its flagship product Google search employing the platform business model. Google search indexes the user created websites using their flagship page rank algorithm and it displays these websites as a very relevant search results for users searching for service or products using their search engine. Thus, one persona of users generates the content to attract the customers and other persona of users seek for the relevant content for their use. Google search just facilitate the connecting service between these personas and thus generates huge revenue from its Google search product.

3   Need for Business Model Innovation

Companies however good in producing innovation products or services using emerging technologies could fail miserably if they do not innovate their business models. Kodak is a good example for failure to innovate their business model and go down miserably. Kodak did partnered with Microsoft on digital imaging but predicted a slow growth for digital camera. However, the digital cameras growth was tremendous and in the year 2009 only 5% of the market remained for analog camera and 95% moved to digital cameras. Kodak was unable to adopt to this market change on time and in 2012 they eventually filed bankruptcy protection. According to BCG companies innovating business models post on average 6% more profits than the companies that are not (IBM 2010). Over 90% of the CEO's surveyed in a study conducted by IBM plan to innovate their company's business model over the coming years. However, it's easier said than done and very top CEO's manage to innovate their business models successfully and transform their business accordingly. In order to simplify the understanding of the business model the St. Gallans University have defined them in four dimensions: the who, the what, the how, and the value. As shown in the Fig. 1.

Who: Who is the customer? The companies have to understand clearly and define their target customers. Constantly they have to re-evaluate their target customers.
What: What is offered to the customers. It's commonly referred to customer value proposition. How: How the companies are going to deliver the value to the customers. What process and resources will be utilized to achieve this delivery of value for the customers? Value: The final dimension explains why the business model is financially viable. How your business makes money.

We have been highly influenced for generations focusing on Porters's five forces of industry analysis and try and stay ahead of the competitors by positioning strongly in the market. On the other hand, Kim and Mauborgne advises to beat the competitors without trying to beat them but re-inventing a new market and innovate and exhale in that- new market. Like how Apple re-invented the industry boundary (Kim 2005).

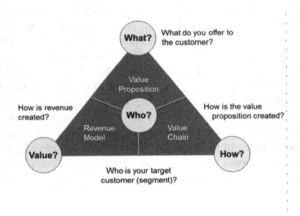

Fig. 1. Business model definition – the magic triangle

4   Nespresso's Business Model Innovation

Nespresso, subsidiary of the Nestle Group has successfully diffused an innovative business model to sell premium coffee's directly to the end customers. They have developed a stylish coffee machine which prepares the coffee's using the capsules. The capsules are stylishly packed coffee powders in aluminum casings and colored with different shades based on the variety of coffee it contains. They offer about 22 varieties of capsules packed with coffee from various countries like Colombia, Ethiopia, India or Brazil etc. to emphasize the uniqueness of capsule's origin. With this variety of capsules, Nespresso could address the large profile of customers coffee drinking taste. Nespresso business model is very similar to that of 'Bait and Hook' model where they sell the coffee making machines at a very affordable prices to the penetrate the customer base and in turn sell the capsules at premium prices. The coffee machines will only work with the Nespresso capsules and not with any other capsules produced by third parties. Also, Nespresso have registered various patents to stop the competitors from imitating its coffee machine and capsules designs. The customers who bought the Nespresso coffee machines will eventually keep buying the capsules and thus hooked into buying the capsules, which generates huge revenue and profits for Nespresso. Nespresso's success is not just with their bait and hook model in selling their products. Nespresso charges between $0.60 to $1 per capsule, which contains roughly about five grams of espresso, which equates to about $200 per kg of coffee. The other premium coffee providers in the market like Lavazza and Costa charges roughly about $19 and $24 per kg of coffee. This premium pricing means Nespresso is charging roughly about 833% more than their immediate premium coffee providers (Markides and Oyon 2000, p. 297). How could Nespresso charge this high pricing for their coffee's and further successfully establish a sustainable business? the answer to the successful business is all down to their innovative business model. They have shown tremendous innovations in various aspect of their business this includes products, supply chain, customer engagement innovation etc.

4.1 Life Style Product Innovation

(Alich 2013) With the help of simple and yet powerful advert they have managed to place their coffee machines and capsules as a luxury lifestyle product for the customers. They have appropriately partnered with Hollywood celebrities, George Clooney and Penelope Cruz as their brand ambassadors to endorse their product. They have also conveyed the message to the customers that by having a Nespresso machine they are able to drink a tasty and high-quality coffee with a press of a button at home. Nespresso have carefully designed their machines and capsules to exhibit this luxury.

4.2 Supply Chain Innovation

Nespresso have shown innovation in the upstream coffee buying process as well. Due to the popularity of the taste and the demand for the premium coffee they are pushed into sourcing the premium and high-quality coffees around the world. Nespresso claims that only 1–2% of coffee produced in the world qualifies their strict quality guidance. Thus, the demand of the high-quality standards has pushed Nespresso to have a much closer relations with farmers in order to produce more quality coffee's. The sourcing model they have used is called Nespresso AAA sustainable quality program (Matzler et al. 2013), which focuses mainly on three aspects i.e., quality (maintaining highest quality), sustainability (respecting people and environment), productivity (farm management) to obtain sustainable value creation. This program is targeted more towards a farmer's club in a region than specific individual farmer. This program is operationalized by a consortium of several partners like ECOM (the commodity trader), Rainforest Alliance (the environmental NGO), International Finance Corporation (the financier). This program is a good example for co-creation value. With the right partnership all the participants in this program are benefited. Through this program Nespresso claims in 2013 that it could be able to source a high-quality coffee of up to 1.3 million bags (60 kg per bag) i.e., almost 80% of Nespresso's requirements. Also, an impact assessment report by the IFC has shown that the farmers clubs participating in this program has earned on average 27% more than the clusters of farmers which are outside of this program in countries like Mexico, Guatemala. It's clearly a win-win strategy for both the farmers and Nespresso. This program gives clear traceability for Nespresso from farm to cup.

4.3 Manufacturing and Distribution Channels

Nespresso have outsourced the manufacturing of their coffee machine at cost technology licensing. The manufacturers could act as a distribution channel as well for selling the machines and they do sell the machines in the luxury life style products in high end retail shops.

4.4 Nespresso Club

(IIBD 2015; Nespresso 2013) Nespresso's strategy of selling the capsules directly to the end customers is very essential part of their success. The customers are able to buy the capsules in online, telephone or via one of their boutique shops. The boutique shops are launched specifically in order to achieve an exclusive customer relationship. In the year 2000, the first boutique was opened in Paris and today they have over 700 boutique shops around the world at the end of 2017. They are located in the immediate vicinity of well-known luxury and designer brands. Nespresso encourages highly their customers to register as a Nespresso club member for a seamless coffee buying experience.

They currently have around ten million registered members. This allows the company to build up a customer profile and target its customers appropriately. To support the customers personal connections with the brand, Nespresso continually organizes special sports and lifestyle events for club members. This direct connection with the end customers means they know everything about their customers, and they have the emotional connect with the end customers.

4.5 Nespresso Capsule Patent Rights

Nespresso was able to launch this successful business by registering required patents for their coffee machines and capsules technology. This has kept their competitors a way from duplicating its core product innovation. But with many of the patents are already expired this has opened up a load of Nespresso compatible capsule makers in the market recently. Nespresso strongly believes they could stay ahead of this competition with the help of the connection with the Nespresso customers via club membership and through the strong brand quality programs.

5 Business Model Canvas

Business model canvas is a simple way of expressing the business model as shown in Fig. 2. It was first proposed by Alexander Osterwalder (2010) as part of his PhD work on Business Model Ontology. The various components of the business model canvas are:

Customer Segments: Who are the targeted customers?
Value Propositions: What is the value you are adding for your customers?
Channels: How the products/services will be sold to customers?
Customer Relationships: How do we engage and interact with the customers?
Revenue Streams: How the business makes revenue from the value propositions offerings?
Key Activities: hat strategic things does the business do to deliver the value propositions
Key Resources: What strategic resources the company needs to compete?
Key Partnerships: What activities can the company offload to the partners to add more value to their core business? Cost Structure: What are the business's major cost drivers?

The idea of designing the whole business in one single page gives a clarity in understanding and also communicating about the business to others. Below is the business model canvas template.

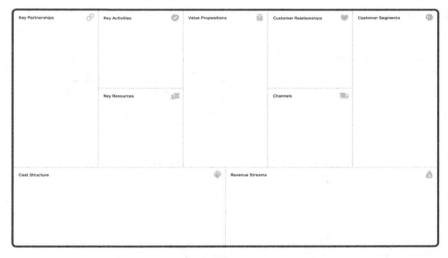

Fig. 2. Business model canvas template

Coffee machine manufacturers
Ecom
IFA
Rainforest Alliance
Procurement and production
Marketing and club maintenance
Key Resources
Distribution networks
Patents
Cup factory
Premium expresso with a press of a button
Nespresso club
Channels
Boutiques
Nespresso.com
Stand in shops
machines sold everywhere
Upper segment home
Upper segment offices
Cost Structure
Coffee procrument
manufacturing
Distribution
Marketing
Revenue Streams
Small revenue on machines
Big revenue on capsules

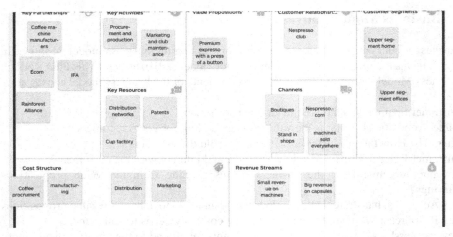

Fig. 3. Nespresso business model canvas

If we map the Nespresso's business model canvas based on the idea proposed by Alexander Osterwalder (2010) and his team it would look very much like the above proposed model in Fig. 3.

5.1 Lean Canvas

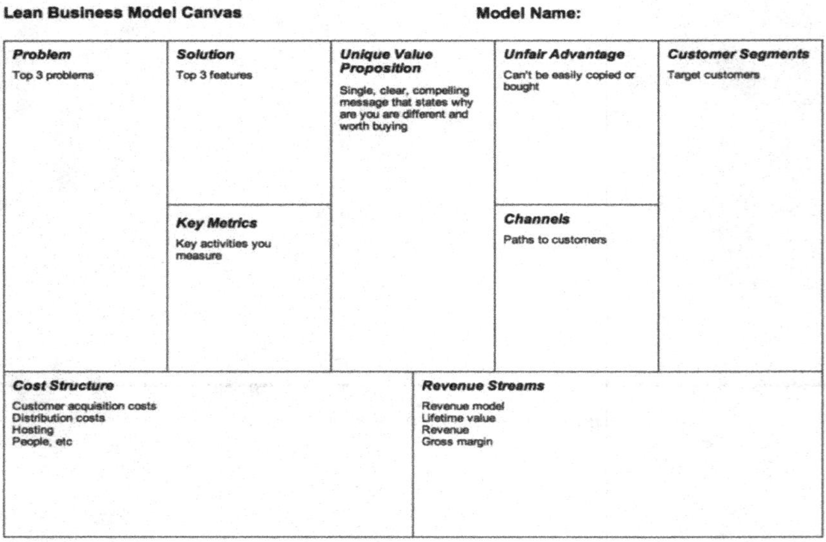

Lean Business Model Canvas
Model Name:
Problem
Top 3 problems
Solution
Top 3 features
Unique Value Proposition
Single, clear, compelling message that states why are you are different and worth buying
Unfair Advantage
Can't be easily copied or bought
Customer Segments
Target customers
Key Metrics
Key activities you measure
Channels
Paths to customers
Cost Structure
Customer acquisition costs
Distribution costs
Hosting
People, etc
Revenue Streams
Revenue model
Lifetime value
Revenue
Gross margin

Fig. 4. Lean business model canvas

Various authors have been inspired by Alexander Osterwalder's business model canvas, and they have extended the model further. One such inspirational work is the Lean canvas from Ash Maurya as shown in Fig. 4. This model is specially targeted for startup entrepreneurs. It replaces the key partnerships, key activities, customer relationship, key resources from the proposed Osterwalder's business model ontology with problem, solution, key metrics and unfair advantage (Maurya 2012).

Problem: The whole need for a business to exist is trying to solve a problem. This component is for listing the core problems the business is trying to solve.
Solution: Finding a solution of the problem is the biggest challenge. The more interaction and- feedback with the customer segment will lead to finding a better and appropriate solution. This solution component is about listing out the possible solutions and then following the principles of lean startup to continually optimize it through build, measure and learn cycle.
Key metrics: key metrics to monitor the business performance.
Unfair advantage: The advantages over the competitors which cannot be bought or copied.

5.2 Social Business Model Canvas

The Social innovation lab created the social business model canvas as in Fig. 5 inspired by the business model canvas especially for social innovators. In comparison with business model canvas the social business model canvas takes the following components into equation.

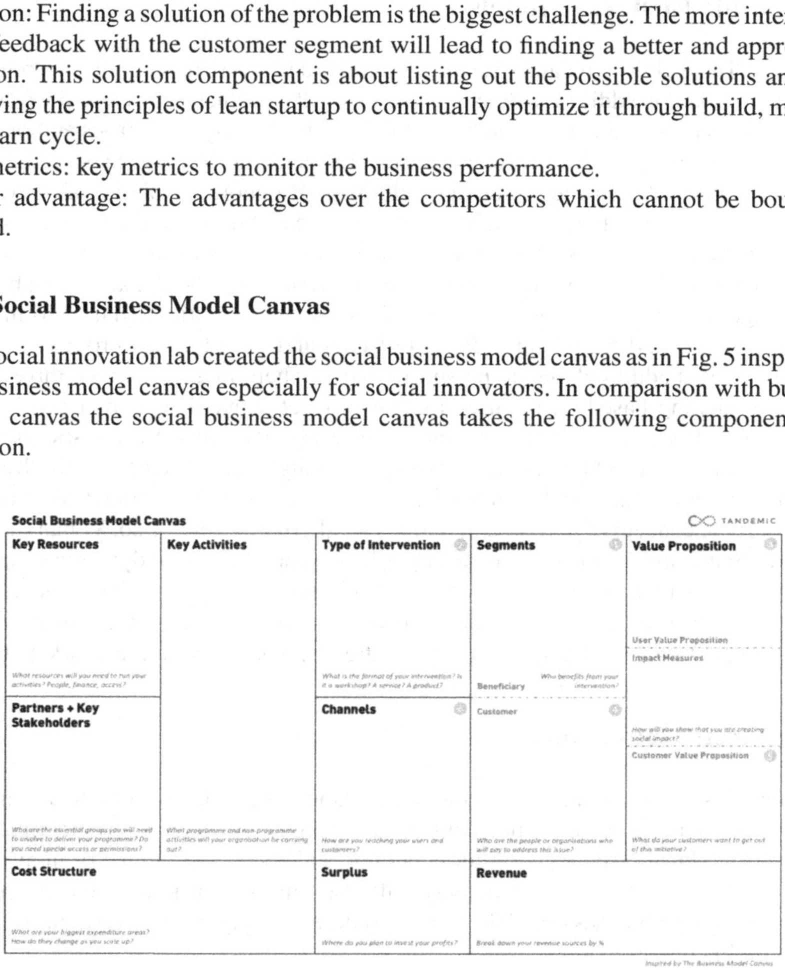

Fig. 5. Social business model canvas.

Beneficiary and customer segments: The segments are split into beneficiary and customer segments. It helps to detail the list of beneficiaries and customers. Although the beneficiaries might not directly contribute to the revenue, but they are critical for a business model.

Three split of value proposition: The value propositions are split into three social value proposition, customer value proposition and impact measures.

The type of intervention: This describes the type of product that will deliver the value.

Stake holders: The stakeholders are clearly listed.

Surplus: This is for add-on investment of profits.

6 Dynamic Business Models

(Afuah and Tucci 2003) Dynamic business model is a new and upcoming research area. This area focusses on adding the dynamic features to the business model, so the transformation process is embedded with in the business model directly. Numerous authors have published their work on this area. According to Afuahand Tuccihave suggests that adding dynamic nature to the business models could play an important role in value creation process. To understand how to enable the dynamic capabilities in the business model various scholars have begun to analyse the micro foundations of dynamic capabilities. Major contributions are from Teece (2007) in understanding the dynamic capabilities. Teece categories them into sense opportunities, seize opportunities and transform (i.e.., enhance, combine and reconfigure). Boris Fritscher and Yves Pigneur proposes extending the BMC and adding dynamic perspective to it. Their idea is to create three levels of BMC modelling based on the user's maturity level as Novice, Expert and Master. The Novice will work with the static model. The experts will get a holistic vision to understand and target a business models sustainability. The master's use the BMC in the global strategy, which evolves and adapts to the changing environment constantly. It will support the concept of iteration, mutation and alternatives etc. Also, Vivian Candido Rodrigues and Humberto Elias Garcia Lopes have proposed a new dynamic capability framework as an alternative to the BMC due to its static nature. They have also applied the SWOT analysis on the various components in the BMC to show the impacts due to the changing external forces like industry, top trends, macro-economic, market etc.

7 Research Significance

This research study is aimed at contributing a framework to design a more sustainable and dynamic business model, which could help the businesses to stay relevant in today's market. Strong businesses are vital for economic and social aspirations from any individual perspective. The part of the study will also aim at contributing the concept of threat indicators in business models, which could be of importance for other research scholars in this research domain.

Today's business are heavily impacted by the STEEPLE changes and yet there are only few approaches and concepts exists in business model transformation framework. This research contributions could be used by the businesses as a tool to transform their failing business models on time.

8   Research Question

The research question of this study is: Cana dynamic business model save a failing business and turn it into a sustainable and a successful business?

To tackle the above question, I would firstly propose to extend an existing widely adapted business model design by adding appropriate threat indicators for alerting with credible reasons to trigger the business model transformation process. The threat indicators are a very commonly used concept in the cyber security domain. According to the white paper published by MITRE Corporation in association with U.S. Department of Homeland Security. "A cyber threat indicator is a set of cyber observables combined with contextual information intended to represent artefacts and/or behaviors of interest within a cyber security context. The threat indicators are used slightly in a different way as monitoring and alerting in the ICT's context for notifying any system warnings or failures.

9   Research Methodology

The Alexander Osterwalder's business model canvas template will be used for designing the static model first and then the threat indicators will be added to the model for introducing the dynamic property. The study uses the design science methodology to design and evaluate the artefact for the problem. It uses the specific process steps of awareness of problem, suggestion, development, evaluation and conclusion as proposed by Vaishnavi et al. Workshop based qualitative method will be used for performing the process steps. It is essential for having a high degree of engagement with the focused group of contributors hence the workshop-based method is adopted. The participants are from a UK based asset management firm. There were totally 5 participants in the workshop representing various business units.

The workshop was designed into 3 one-hour sessions. The sessions were divided based on the design science method approach. First session if for understanding the problems, followed by suggestions/development and finally finishing it with evaluation process (Kuechler and Vaishnavi 2012).

10   Scope and Limitations

Following are the scope and limitations of this research study:

- This research is only intended to research the popular and widely adapted business model design and extend it accordingly to the research requirements. There is no intention to propose a completely new business model design approach.
- The scope of the case study application of the transformation framework will be conducted only in UK targeting UK based firm. This knowledge contribution could be extended by further research in other countries by researchers.
- The derived business model will be validated. However, the other factors influencing the successful business outcome like implementation strategy, resources skills etc. are not part of this study.

11 Results

Workshop session 1 - Understand the problems:
The first workshop session was aimed at understanding the problems. In our research context it is to find out if the majority of participants feel a need for drafting the business model of the company in a simplified business canvas template format. We used a voting approach to come to a conclusion and all the participants have agreed a need for simplified business model design for the company. This session was focused primarily on listing out the various components in the business model canvas and the session participants have decided collectively to use the lean canvas template to draft the components of the business model. The session time is not enough to come up with a full and clear component in the business model canvas. Below is the final draft outcome out of the workshop session 1.

Workshop session 2 - Suggestions/Development:
The next workshop was to further focus on developing the model and listing out the main threats in each component. Each listed threats were voted in priority order and top 3 threats for each component are selected and attached to the model along- with the various threat's properties like person in-charge, threat level, next validation date etc.

Workshop session 3 - Evaluation:
The final session was to evaluate the outcome of a dynamic business model. Majority of the participants proposed an idea of presenting the drafted business model to wider audiences in their business units to collect more feedbacks.

Hence the artefacts were circulated to wider audiences for their feedbacks. It's an open-ended feedback format and the audiences was allowed to give a general comment about the artefact. Totally the study received about 32 feedbacks from various business units, and they mostly followed a general common pattern about the artefact produced. Below are the summarized listings of the received feedbacks.

- Overall, it was positive feedback for the approach taken to present the business model in simple easily understandable template.
- Some of the components and the threat indicators were questioned for the correctness and also majority of the respondents wants more involvement in drafting and maintaining of the model.
- There were few comments to clearly explain the components in a detailed separate document to understand it better.
- Few comments expressed their disinterest in this holistic view of the business and the sustainability of the dynamic nature of the model itself.
- Few comments were around the senior management commitment for the transparency to draft a more accurate model.

Problem Top 3 problems	Solution Top 3 features	Unique Value Proposition Single, clear, compelling messages that states why you are different and worth buying	Unfair Advantage Can't be easily copied or bought	Customer Segments Target customers
Brexit - Trade deal negotiations. (Regs & Control - 01/03/2020) Resourcing - IR35 compliance. (HR partners /Chapter Leads - 31/03/2020) Product Innovations. (Senior leaders - 20/01/2020)	Fund Migrations / Increase the perm head count / New location strategy / Product workshops (show and tell)	Best savings outcome / Innovative products	Investment barrier.	Pension savings / Life insurances / Retail savings
Existing Alternatives	Key metrics Key activities you measure	High-Level Concept	Channels Path to customers	Early Adopters
	Fund Nav (Performances - Fund managers - monthly) / Resource Costing (HR & Finance - monthly)/ New Product Roll out (Sales - monthly).		Direct investment channel / New distribution partners	

12   Recommendations

It is very evident from the study that the senior management have not effectively communicated the business model across the business and there was lot of confusions and contradictions while developing the dynamic model framework in the workshop sessions. Drafting and managing the dynamic business model requires a change in strategy, culture and operations. It will be a time-consuming exercise to manage the dynamic business model but yet it is a valuable process for the business in a long run. It needs a strong cultural change in the organization and it should be initiated by the senior management. Also, the workshop-based methodology definitely worked very well in cases requiring heavy engagement with the participants in drafting the business model development.

13   Conclusions

Even today many senior executives still make their key decisions based on the provided fragmented facts. They often do not clearly understand the wider impacts as a result of their change process. The proposed dynamic business model will not only tackle this problem but also will help the business leaders to stay on top of their business. It is evident from this study that there are bigger challenges that needs to be addressed by the senior leaders in the business to achieve this transparency in developing the dynamic business model. This study clearly illustrates the usefulness of the design science approach in solving the current problem statement. The workshop conducted was considered to be short and also there were criticism around the evaluation feedback process, which needs to be improved. Due to the time and scope limitation this study was only aimed at small groups of employees and thus there is a plenty of scope for further extension of this model with wider audience participation. Also, only drafting a business model with dynamic property is just a first step and it needs commitment from group of senior leaders and other valuable employees in keeping it up to date.

References

Wheelen, T., et al.: Concepts: Strategic Management and Business Policy. Addison Wesley (2000)

Rentmeister, J., Klein, S.: Geschäftsmodelle – ein Modebegriff auf der Waagschale. Z. Betriebswirt. **73**, 17–30 (2003)

Osterwalder, A.: The business model ontology: a proposition in a design science approach. Ph.D. thesis. Universite de Lausanne – Ecole des Hautes Etudes Commerciales (2004)

Teece, D.J.: Explicating dynamic capabilities: the nature and micro foundations of (sustainable) enterprise performance. Strat. Manag. J. **28**(13), 1319–1350 (2004)

Magretta, J.: What Management Is: How It Works And Why It's Everyone's Business. Profile Books Ltd. (2013)

Choudary, S.P.: Platform scale: how an emerging business model helps startups build large empires with minimum investment (Platform Thinking Labs) (2015)

IBM: CEO survey 2010: capitalizing on complexity (2004)

Kim, W.: Chanand Mauborgne, Renee, Blue Ocean strategy: from theory to practice. Calif. Manage. Rev. **47**(3), 105–121 (2005)

Markides, C., Oyon, D.: Changing the strategy at Nespresso: an interview with former CEO Jean-Paul Gaillard. Eur. Manag. J. **18**(3), 296–301 (2000)

Alich, H.: Nestlé contra Mondelez: Nespressoplays a trump in the quarrelover capsules. Handelsblatt (2013)

Matzler, K., Bailom, F., von den Eichen, S.F., Kohler, T.: Business model innovation: coffee triumphs for Nespresso. J. Bus. Strat. **34**(2), 30–37 (2013)

IIBD: Strategy newsletter: differentiating a commodity. Volume 12, Letter 8 (2013). www.iibd.com/news/?action¼viewone&newsid¼160. Accessed 20 Dec 2019

Maurya, A.: Running Lean: Iterate From Plan A to A Plan That Works (lean Series). O'reilly Media, Sebastopol (2012)

Afuah, A., Tucci, C.L.: Internet Business Models and Strategies: Text and Cases, 2nd edn. McGraw-Hill/Irwin, New York (2003)

Kuechler, W., Vaishnavi, V.: A framework for theory development in design science research: multiple perspectives. J. Assoc. Inf. Syst. **13**(6), 395–423 (2012)

Social Innovation Lab: Social Business Model Canvas (2013). http://www.socialbusinessmodelcanvas.com/. Accessed 20 Jan 2020

Knowledge and Service Innovation

Creativity and Innovation in Polish Universities: The Knowledge Triangle Approach

Magdalena Marczewska[1]([⊠]) and Marzenna Anna Weresa[2]

[1] University of Warsaw, Warsaw, Poland
mmarczewska@wz.uw.edu.pl
[2] Warsaw School of Economics, Warsaw, Poland
mweres@sgh.waw.pl

Abstract. Recently, the role of universities is gradually shifting from academic focus towards more entrepreneurial and innovation-oriented. This requires creativity and interaction, in terms of innovation, research and educational activities of universities. The challenge of developing creativity is crucial particularly for countries like Poland, which still do not belong to the leaders in innovation. The aim of this paper is to identify the position of Polish universities in terms of creativity in comparison to other EU countries from Central and Eastern Europe (CEE). The analysis is carried out using the "knowledge triangle" concept, encompassing involvement of universities in education, research, innovation and entrepreneurship. The analysis covers selected indicators characterizing each of the vertices of the knowledge triangle considered in the context of activities undertaken by universities. It is based on data obtained from Eurostat and OECD databases for the period of 2010–2016.

A comparative analysis of these indicators showed that Poland stands out in the CEE region in terms of the relatively high share of the higher education sector in conducting scientific research and the availability of scientific staff resources. However, this does not translate into the leading position of Polish universities when it comes to creativity measured by citations or the number of patents. Poland's advantages in terms of creativity are only visible in industrial design. Therefore, the effects of the interactions within the "knowledge triangle" in Poland are insufficient to stimulate creativity and broaden the involvement of national actors in global research and innovation networks.

Keywords: Creativity · Knowledge triangle · Innovation · Poland · CEE

1 Introduction

The creation and use of knowledge have become one of the key focuses of entrepreneurs and scientists. The value and importance of knowledge is also highly appreciated by policymakers and the entire society. Dynamic development of information and communication technologies (ICT) reinforced the importance of knowledge-based economy, which is accompanied by the growing internationalization of businesses, research and development and innovation. Such change is also visible in the higher education sector

© Springer Nature Switzerland AG 2022
L. Uden et al. (Eds.): KMO 2022, CCIS 1593, pp. 145–159, 2022.
https://doi.org/10.1007/978-3-031-07920-7_12

and its key players – universities. Recently, the role of univer ities is gradually shifting from academic focus towards more entrepreneurial. Currently the broader dimension of innovation is gaining importance, such as innovations in the public sector focused on new quality of services provided to society [1], as well as social innovations - new products, models, institutional solutions, etc. bringing a change in social relations [2]. However, innovation relies, among others, on creativity and interaction, which is described by the concept of the "knowledge triangle" referring to innovation, research and educational activities of universities [3, 4]. Universities should focus not only on teaching and knowledge creation, but also on its commercialization [5]. This challenge is crucial particularly for countries such as Poland, which still do not belong to the leaders in innovation [6].

The aim of this article is to identify the position of Polish universities in terms of creativity in comparison to universities' performance of other countries from Central and Eastern Europe. The analysis is based on the data from the pre-pandemic period (2010–2016).

The article consists of five following sections: introduction, literature review, research methodology, research results and discussion with conclusions. The introductory remarks outlined above present the objectives and scope of this study. The following section, literature review, presents the theoretical framework that allows to link innovation with creativity. The next part of the paper aims at identifying the position of Polish universities among other EU Member States in terms of creating new knowledge, its dissemination and protection. The analysis is based on data obtained from Eurostat [7] and OECD [8] databases and covers the period of 2010–2015. The paper conclusions present a summary of research results and recommendations on the possible paths for developing creativity in Polish universities.

2   Theoretical Framework: Creativity and Innovation How They Are Connected?

Creativity is a multi-faceted notion that may be explained from various points of view, including psychological, sociological, philosophical, and economical. Considering the latter one, numerous research studies on creativity and its dimensions stress the relevance of creative thinking in the creation of innovation. In fact, Joseph Schumpeter used the term "creative destruction", which means destruction of existing structures and solutions and replacing them with new ones, which may result in a new product, discovery of new resources, emergence of new markets, changes in production methods or organization of production [9]. According to Schumpeter there is a distinction between invention (creativity) and innovation because the latter arises only when the novelty is brought to the market, followed by its distribution and imitation. Thus, entrepreneurship is also essential to develop something previously unknown (creative) and distinct from existing alternatives (innovation). Innovation is crucial because it allows for the development of individuals, organizations and societies [10–13].

Researchers examine the relationship between creativity and innovation from various perspectives, including organizations [14, 15], human talent development [16], education [17, 18] and science [19]. All of these analyses reach the same conclusion and emphasize the interdependence of creativity and innovation. Creativity refers to people's ability to generate new ideas, whereas innovation refers to the transformation of these ideas into new economic solutions. For this reason, it is crucial to educate and encourage young entrepreneurs and scientists to develop creativity and skills to transform it into innovation [20]. The rapid development of new technologies and modernization of work professions, make innovativeness, entrepreneurship, and soft skills increasingly important for professional success [21]. These skills are often treated on a par with technical and scientific skills and determine employment opportunities along with corresponding wages [22, 23]. Many studies show that technological skills are important to start a business, but to succeed in business, they must be supplemented with flexibility, creativity, perseverance and social skills necessary to create teams, manage teamwork, and deal with clients and other stakeholders [24]. This allows to conclude that innovativeness and entrepreneurship require a combination of different types of creativity. This is also indicated by Richard Florida in the concept of the creative class emphasizing its internal diversity [25, 26]. Florida identifies two main groups of creative people: a super-creative core and creative professionals. The first group is made up of scientists, engineers, artists, designers and people shaping the views of society, whereas the second one consists of professionals seeking to solve the problems identified by the creative core. These include managers and employees employed in knowledge-intensive industries, such high-tech sectors, the legal and healthcare professions, financial services and business management [26]. Florida identifies three components that determine creativity: technology, talent and tolerance. They constitute, so called, "3T approach" showing that creativity is diverse geographically, which is reflected in the unequal innovativeness of economies [26]. The social and location dimension of creativity and innovation cause the need to compete for talents. That is why contemporary universities should not only teach and do research, but also focus on shaping talents [27].

The concept of the "knowledge triangle" describing the new role of universities focuses on stimulating creativity and innovation seems to be an extension of Florida's thesis. This "knowledge triangle" has three vertices that describe the activities of a contemporary university: education/learning, research/discovery, and innovation/engagement [28]. The linkages between these three aspects encourage multidirectional knowledge flows, which can boost economic growth dynamics [29].

Functional model of interactions between the three vertices of the "knowledge triangle" includes:

1) Interactions between scientific research and education, which take place, among others, through geographical and sectoral mobility of graduates, post-graduate studies, using the results of basic and applied research as the basis for teaching in order to improve the alignment of graduates' skills with the needs of enterprises.
2) Interactions between research and innovation, aimed at supporting and intensifying knowledge transfer by, e.g.:

   - public-private partnership (e.g. clusters, science parks),
   - commercialization of publicly funded research (intellectual property rights),
   - research and development services provided by universities for business,
   - spin-off companies and academic start-ups,
   - knowledge and technology transfer offices,

- business incubators,
- open science platforms.

3) Interactions between education and innovations implemented through: cooperation for the development of entrepreneurial culture (e.g. industry-oriented doctoral programs) and support for the development of business-related competences (trainings on business plan creation, management, etc.) [30].

According to empirical studies on universities' role in the knowledge triangle, there is no one widely cited model that describes the above-mentioned interactions. The reason for this is that education systems are usually country-specific, thus universities differ a lot looking at their characteristic, functions they perform and goals they serve in terms of education, knowledge creation and innovation development [31].

Summing up, the theories described above show that regional specificity should be considered while conducting research on creativity and innovation. Changes in country's position related to its innovativeness can be described using various indicators (e.g. expenditures on R&D, number of patents) and they are associated with other elements of the "knowledge triangle", such as level of education and scientific research potential. Human resources are particularly important because, as indicated above, creativity that determines innovation is an attribute of a human being.

3   Research Objective, Methodology and Data

The literature review presented above leads to the conclusion that innovation is associated with creativity, which is affected by, among others, quality of research and education, especially at the university level. Therefore, several questions arise about the role of Polish universities in creating new knowledge.

- How creative are universities in Poland compared to other EU countries, especially those from Central and Eastern Europe?
- What is the contribution of Polish universities to increasing knowledge resources and its dissemination in the form of scientific publications, or - if justified - its protection through patents?
- To what extent does the direction and pace of changes in the creativity of Polish universities give a chance to improve the innovativeness of the economy?

This article aims to present answers to the research questions listed above.

This study presents Poland with comparison to other Central and Eastern European countries that joined the European Union as a result of enlargements in 2004, 2007 and 2013. Thus, the EU countries to which Poland's position is compared are the Czech Republic, Hungary, Slovakia, Estonia, Latvia, Lithuania, Slovenia, Romania, Bulgaria and Croatia. The analysis is carried out using the framework the "knowledge triangle" concept discussed above, encompassing involvement of universities in education, research, innovation and entrepreneurship. The analysis will cover selected indicators characterizing each of the vertices of the "knowledge triangle" considered in the context of activities undertaken by universities. The indicators are synthetically presented in Table 1. The data used in this study comes primarily from the Eurostat and OECD databases.

Table 1. Indicators of university innovativeness and creativity corresponding to the "knowledge triangle" concept. Source: own elaboration

Type of university activities according to the concept of the knowledge triangle	Indicators
Research	Expenditures on research and development (R&D) carried out by the higher education in relation to GDP
	Participation of scientists and engineers in the 25–64 age group as % of the working population
	Percentage of scientific publications among 10% of the most cited publications worldwide as a % of all scientific publications of the country
	Patents, trademarks, utility models in relation to GDP
	Patents filed at the same time for 5 key patent offices of the world (patent families) by universities and research institutions
Education	Public expenditures on higher education (% of GDP)
	The percentage of people aged 25–34 who have completed tertiary education (ISCED 5–8) (%)
	Foreign doctoral students (as a percentage of all doctoral students)
	Population aged 25–64 completing supplementary programs (lifelong learning) as % of the total population
Innovation (and entrepreneurship)	Research and development activities carried out by higher education and financed by private entities (enterprises and private non-profit organizations) (% of GDP)
	Share of employees aged 25–64 with higher education (%)
	Share of enterprises cooperating with universities or other higher education institutions (%)
	Synthetic indicator of the countries' potential to be part of global education, innovation and research networks

4 Research Results and Discussion

4.1 Creativity as the Result of Scientific Research

Knowledge creation requires the expenditure on research and development, which is also considered as one of the factors of determining innovativeness of economies (cf. e.g. [31, 32]). What is the level of the expenditures on R&D in the higher education sector? Is there a systematic increase of the expenditures on R&D in relation to GDP that would enable permanent support for creativity and innovation in universities? Table 2 presents Poland's position with comparison to other EU Member States from Central and Eastern Europe (CEE) in terms of expenditures on research and development (R&D) carried out by higher education sector in relation to GDP in 2010–2016.

Table 2. Expenditures on research and development (R&D) carried out by higher education (as a percentage of GDP) in 2010–2016. Source: own elaboration based on [7, 8]

	2010	2011	2012	2013	2014	2015	2016
EU28	0.47	0.46	0.47	0.47	0.47	0.46	0.47
Bulgaria	0.07	0.05	0.05	0.05	0.07	0.05	0.04
Croatia	0.21	0.21	0.20	0.20	0.20	0.20	0.28
Czech Republic	0.27	0.38	0.49	0.52	0.50	0.48	0.34
Estonia	0.60	0.64	0.68	0.73	0.64	0.62	0.46
Hungary	0.23	0.24	0.23	0.20	0.18	0.17	0.13
Latvia	0.24	0.34	0.33	0.26	0.28	0.31	0.19
Lithuania	0.42	0.49	0.48	0.52	0.54	0.58	0.33
Poland	**0.27**	**0.26**	**0.30**	**0.25**	**0.27**	**0.29**	**0.30**
Romania	0.11	0.11	0.10	0.08	0.06	0.09	0.05
Slovakia	0.17	0.23	0.27	0.27	0.30	0.51	0.22
Slovenia	0.29	0.29	0.29	0.27	0.25	0.22	0.22

Poland spends a relatively small percentage of GDP on R&D (0.97% in 2016), by half less than the EU average (2.03% in 2016). From the group of EU countries from Central and Eastern Europe, Poland is ahead of Slovenia, the Czech Republic, Estonia and Hungary (Eurostat, 2018). However, when it comes to expenditures on R&D activities conducted by universities, Poland's position in the CEE is slightly better. In 2016, Poland allocated 0.3% of GDP to R&D to research conducted by higher education. This is still below the EU28 average (0.47%), but only three countries from the analyzed group achieved better results in this respect than Poland, i.e.: Estonia, the Czech Republic and Lithuania.

In contrast, Slovenia and Hungary, which on the one hand, have higher R&D expenditures than Poland, on the other hand, allocate relatively less funding to research conducted by the higher education sector. In Hungary, R&D expenditures are higher than in Poland in relation to GDP (1.21% in 2016), but the share of funding for R&D activity conducted by universities is relatively low and has been gradually decreasing (from 0.23% of GDP in 2010 to 0.13% of GDP in 2016). There are similar trends also in Slovenia. In both countries, the enterprise sector plays a dominant role in conducting R&D and its share has been systematically increasing, weakening importance of the higher education sector (Fig. 1). In the Czech Republic and Estonia, which are also ahead of Poland in terms of expenditure on R&D in relation to GDP, the importance of the enterprise sector is also increasing, but the role of higher education in conducting research has been also strengthening, with the decreasing share of the government sector. In Poland, the share of the higher education sector in R&D was rather stable in the period 2010–2016 standing at around 0.3% of GDP, whereas the share of the enterprise sector gradually increased with the weakening importance of the government sector.

Conducting scientific research requires not only financial resources, but also people – talented scientists and researchers. In the period of 2010–2016, the number of scientists and engineers as a percentage of the economically active population aged 25–64 has been increasing gradually from 5.7% in 2010 to 7.0% in 2016. Nevertheless, the indicator was in 2016 still below the EU average (7.4%), but above the results achieved by most EU countries in the CEE region. This demonstrates the relatively large potential for creativity in Poland compared to most EU countries from the CEE (at least when it comes to the quantitative side of this phenomenon), however, one should remember that creativity is a human attribute, and the number of researchers is only a proxy. Slovenia is the leader in this respect in the CEE region.

The results of scientific activities include scientific publications, patents, trademarks and utility models. Available statistical data capture these on as an aggregate for the whole country, which gives only a rough picture of the activity of universities. However, these aggregate indicators can be compared for individual countries in order to capture Poland's position in terms of results of scientific activities. All countries of the CEE significantly deviate from the average UE28 terms of the proportion of scientific publications among the 10% most cited publications worldwide. Poland, with a score lower than half the EU average, is ahead of only four CEE countries (i.e. Bulgaria, Lithuania, Latvia, Croatia) in this category [7, 8].

Comparative analysis of creativity based on patent statistics confirms this conclusion. All CEE countries present relatively low patenting activity in the international procedure (PCT). In 2011–2016 the number of patent applications per 1 billion of GDP (in PPS) was significantly lower in the CEE than the EU average. For example, the average EU indicator in 2016 was more than six times higher than this indicator for Poland, two and a half times higher than in Hungary and more than fifteen times higher than in Romania [6].

Some of the CEE countries achieved slightly better results in terms of trademark applications and utility models. Estonia, Slovenia and Bulgaria stand out in the first of these categories. Bulgaria and Poland are the leaders in the CEE group in terms of utility model applications [6]. These results show that Poland's creativity is revealed in the area of design, rather than creating new solutions that can be patented on a global scale.

These general data for the whole economy can be supplemented by indicating universities, which in recent years have filed the most PCT patent applications. According to the World Intellectual Property Organization (WIPO), in 2015–2017 the most active universities in Poland in terms of patenting were: Jagiellonian University, Rzeszów University of Technology, University of Warsaw and Wrocław University of Technology [33].

A picture of the universities' creativity can be obtained by analyzing the data published by the Innovation Policy Platform on patent applications filed at 5 key patent offices (so called patent families) in the world, i.e. the European Patent Office (EPO), the Japan Patent Office (JPO), the Korean Intellectual Property Office (KIPO), the National Intellectual Property Administration of the People's Republic of China (CNIPA) and the United States Patent and Trademark Office (USPTO) [34]. Although the data is incomplete, it presents a very positive picture of patent activities by Polish universities and thus confirming creativity of Polish inventors. The percentage of patent applications from universities and research institutions is the highest in Poland among the CEE countries, and since 2003 it has more than doubled (from 18% to 41% of all applications). It can therefore be assumed that Polish scientists are more creative and willing to patent their ideas than researchers from other CEE countries. However, due to the limited availability of detailed data, this hypothesis requires further study.

Reflections on the position of Polish universities in terms of scientific research can be summarized by indicating the location of the best universities in the EU. Research of 1,337 universities from around the world, based on indicators such as: the number of scientific publications, the number of citations, average values of the Hirsch index of scientific employees, commitment to international scientific cooperation, show that 273 European universities successfully compete internationally. Most of these universities are in the United Kingdom (53 universities), Germany (43), Spain (30), Italy (29) and France (26) [35]. Only 8 universities from the CEE region reached the top of the ranking - three from Poland, two from the Czech Republic and one from Estonia, Romania and Slovenia. Polish universities can compete effectively only in two fields of science, whereas the Czech Republic, although they have two universities ranked among the top 30% in Europe, is able to compete effectively in three fields of science. The United Kingdom is the European leader in terms of tertiary education and scientific research excellence. 53 British universities competitive in 171 fields of science are included in 30% of the best universities in the world.

The analysis of indicators describing the creativity of Polish universities in comparison to other CEE countries presented above shows that Poland stands out in the CEE region in terms of scientific staff resources and a relatively high and stable share of the higher education sector in conducting R&D activities. However, this does not mirror the position of Polish universities when it comes to creativity measured by the number of citations of Polish authors or the number of patents. Some Poland's advantages with regards to creativity can be seen in industrial design.

4.2 Creativity and Education

The second area of universities activities closely related to creativity according to the concept of the "knowledge triangle" is education. What are the public expenditures on higher education? Is there a systematic increase in relation to GDP, which could suggest increasing support of the higher education sector? What percentage of the population has a university degree? Can the Polish education system be considered open and friendly to students and doctoral students from abroad? Do Poles care about developing creativity and innovative by completing further training programs (lifelong learning)?

Poland stands out among other analyzed CEE countries by the highest and relatively stable public expenditure on higher education, reaching about 1.5% of GDP during the period considered. The EU28 average in the same period was by half lower (0.8% in the years 2010–2015, 0.7% in 2015). In the group of EU countries from Central and Eastern Europe, expenditure at a similar level to Poland can be observed in Estonia, but in this country a downward trend is visible, which was not recorded in Poland. Other analyzed countries have relatively stable public expenditure on higher education, in general higher than the EU28 average but lower than Poland.

The results of the scientific activities of the universities can be analyzed considering, among others, number and quality of scientific publications, research commercialization and educational activities, i.e. successful talents training. In order to measure educational activities of universities it is worth considering the percentage of people who completed tertiary education. Poland's position in this area is relatively good compared to other EU countries from the CEE and also compared to the EU28 average. In 2010–2016 in Poland, the percentage of people aged 25–34 who completed university studies gradually increased from 37.1% in 2010 to 43.5% in 2016. Only Lithuania achieved a better result than Poland. Since 2013 this ratio in Lithuania has been over 50%. Countries that rank similarly to Poland include Slovenia (43% in 2016), Latvia (42.1% in 2016) and Estonia (41.2% in 2016). In all of the above-mentioned countries, the percentage of people aged 25–34 who completed higher education exceeded the EU28 average in 2016 by several percentage points (e.g. Poland by 5.3 p.p. and Estonia by 3.0 p.p.) [7, 8].

A way to improve creativity is to promote openness of the education system and attract talented students and PhD students from abroad. The research show that less successful countries in attracting international students and scientists may weaken their competitiveness in the long run [36]. One of the indicators of the countries' position in attracting talent from abroad is the share of foreign doctoral students in the total number of doctoral students in a given country. In 2010–2016, on average the percentage of foreign PhD students in EU28 remained stable (in 2010 it was 21.2% and in 2016 it was 21.0%). The EU Member States from the CEE that are the most attractive for foreign PhD students include: the Czech Republic, Estonia, Hungary, Latvia, Slovenia and Slovakia. In Poland, the percentage of foreign PhD students is very low (2.0% in 2016) and, moreover, it decreased compared to 2010.

The low degree of internationalization of higher education in Poland is also indicated by data on the share of foreign students at the graduate level in the total number of students. In 2014, they accounted for only 3% of all students, while on average in the OECD it was 12% [36].

Many countries have introduced in higher education new management methods, as well as marketing strategies adopted from business in order to increase the inflow of international students. Lithuania is a good example in this respect. An analysis of the case of Mykolas Romeris University has shown that such management innovations brought a steady flow of incoming international exchange students [37].

The relatively high percentage of people in Poland who have completed university studies does not translate into their willingness to continuous development of knowledge and skills and further education. Compared to the CEE countries, Poland is quite weak considering the population aged 25–64 competing training programs (lifelong learning). The percentage of such people in Poland amounted to 4.3% in 2010–2013, and from 2014 gradually decreased to a value of 3.7% in 2016. Out of the eleven countries surveyed, only four have a worse position in this respect than Poland (i.e. Croatia, Slovakia, Bulgaria and Romania). In the period of 2010–2016, the percentage of the population aged 25–64 competing training programs in EU28 was stable (10.7–10.8%) and almost three times higher than in Poland. Among the CEE countries, Estonia and Slovenia occupy a leading position, where this indicator in 2016 was 15.7% and 11.6% respectively.

The above presented analysis of indicators regarding the importance and attractiveness of higher education in the CEE countries shows that this region, and in particular Poland, stands out in terms of relatively high public expenditures on higher education in relation to GDP and the percentage of people aged 25–34 who completed tertiary education however, unlike EU28 citizens, a significant proportion of well-educated Poles is not interested in post-university development, in particular in participation in further training programs (lifelong learning). Nevertheless, Polish universities and scholars offer many interesting learning opportunities for people at different levels of education (e.g. [38]). Despite relatively high public expenditure on higher education, Poland is not very attractive to talented students and PhD students from abroad. Almost every fourth doctoral student in the EU is a foreigner, while in Poland only less than two out of hundred. The results presented above may suggest that actions taken in Poland aimed at stimulating higher education and creativity of universities in shaping educational programs tailored to societal and industrial needs are insufficient.

4.3 Interactions Between Research, Education and Innovation

The concept of the "knowledge triangle" indicates that interactions between research, education and innovation take place at the universities. They are implemented through cooperation of higher education institutions with enterprises with regards to scientific research, development of entrepreneurship and shaping competences in business [29]. How is this cooperation carried out in Poland? Is it sufficient to create talents and drive innovation? The level of funding for R&D activities of universities by private entities is one of its measures. In Poland, such funding has been very low for many years. Funds allocated by the private sector to finance research conducted by higher education institutions constitute only 0.01% of GDP, while the average indicator in EU28 is five times higher (two times higher in Hungary and Czech Republic, and in Lithuania up to seven times higher) [7].

The interaction of universities with business in the field of education can be measured by the percentage of employees with a university diploma. Poland has a relatively good position in this area compared to other EU countries from the CEE. In the period of 2010–2016, the share of employees aged 25–64 with higher education in the total number of employees systematically increased from 31.6% to 37.2% and exceeded in 2016 the EU28 average by almost 2 percentage points. Only three CEE countries, Estonia, Latvia and Slovenia, achieved a better result than Poland [7]. Educating future employees (and employers) is undoubtedly one of the ways of knowledge transfer between universities and enterprises and Poland has the potential to affect such transfer and diffusion of knowledge.

However, one of the most effective channels of knowledge transfer between science and business are joint projects related to research and education. Statistical data showing the scale of this phenomenon come from surveys conducted under the Community Innovation Survey (CIS). It is a study on innovative activities in enterprises, taking into account the size of enterprises and their structure by industry, various types of innovations and many aspects of implementing innovations, such as goals, sources of innovation, public financing or R&D expenditure. The survey is carried out every two years throughout the European Union, EFTA countries and EU candidate countries [7].

In order to compare the involvement of universities and other higher education institutions in cooperation with enterprises and its changes in 2010–2016, data from the last four surveys within the Community Innovation Survey, i.e. CIS2010, CIS2012, CIS2014 and CIS2016 were compiled (Table 3). The data shows that in Poland the share of enterprises cooperating in innovation activities with universities or other higher education institutions was stable in 2010–2014 and oscillated around 10%. At the same time, the average indicator in the EU28 increased by 3 percentage points, reaching 13.2% in 2014. In 2016, almost all analyzed countries from the CEE region reported a decrease in cooperation between enterprises and universities or other higher education institutions. The reverse trend is only observed in Bulgaria, Latvia and Lithuania. Comparing Poland with other countries of the CEE region, it can be seen that in 2016 the activity of universities and enterprises in cooperating for innovation is not very high. Only Romania had weaker results than Poland (Table 3).

Table 3. Share of enterprises cooperating in innovation activities with universities or other higher education institutions (%). Source: own elaboration based on [7]

	2010	2012	2014	2016
EU28	10.8	13.0	13.2	9
Bulgaria	6.7	4.5	3.9	6
Croatia	12.0	14.7	8.0	5.8
Czech Republic	14.6	14.6	12.2	5.4
Estonia	8.8	10.8	14.6	11.5
Hungary	21.4	18.1	12.3	5.7
Latvia	9.8	7.7	7.3	7.9
Lithuania	11.3	18.9	8.0	10
Poland	**10.8**	**10.5**	**10.6**	**5.2**
Romania	6.4	4.9	12.2	3.4
Slovenia	22.0	25.4	19.9	13.6
Slovakia	13.6	12.7	12.8	11.8

Conclusions from the above analysis of creativity as an effect of interactions between research, education and innovation can be supplemented with a comparison of a synthetic indicator of countries' potential to be part of global education, innovation and research network, which consists of the following three components [36]:

- funding incentives for international co-operation,
- foreign/international students and high-skilled workers,
- international co-operation in research.

Scientific research co-operation between institutions from different countries in terms of joint publications or patent cooperation, streamlines networking and increases the likelihood that research will be applied by the enterprise sector [39]. Global educational networks are just as important as collaboration in innovation and research. Increasing competition is visible when it comes to talent acquisition, as the influx of foreign students increases the possibilities of knowledge diffusion. Knowledge can spread faster, because interpersonal relationships create new learning opportunities that go beyond the exchange of codified information [36]. For this reason, financial incentives for higher education institutions aimed at encouraging research and teaching internationalization are increasingly important.

Comparison of a synthetic indicator of countries' potential to be part of global education, innovation and research network among analyzed CEE countries reveals relatively small potential of Poland [35]. All components of this synthetic indicator (i.e. international cooperation in research, foreign/international students and high-skilled workers, funding incentives for international cooperation) have the lowest values for Poland among the analyzed group of countries. The leaders in the CEE region are Hungary and the Czech Republic, with indicators higher than the OECD average [35].

This result may indicate that the effects of interactions between research, education and innovative entrepreneurship in Poland are insufficient to stimulate the creativity of innovation system actors. To improve the efficiency of the knowledge triangle, support of this type of interactions within universities and between universities and enterprises is required.

5   Conclusion

The review of scientific literature presented in this study confirms that innovation is the result of human creative activity, while creativity is influenced by, among others quality of research and education, and mainly university-level education. This empirical observation has set the objective of this study, which is to identify the position of Polish universities in terms of creativity compared to other EU countries, in particular those from CEE.

A comparative analysis of a number of indicators characterizing the potential of Polish universities in the field of creativity showed that Poland stands out in the CEE region in terms of the relatively high share of the higher education sector in conducting scientific research and the availability of scientific staff resources. However, this does not translate into the leading position of Polish universities in the CEE region when it comes to creativity measured by citations of Polish authors' publications, or the number of patents filed by inventors. Poland's advantages in terms of creativity over analyzed CEE countries are only visible in industrial design - this is confirmed, among others, by higher than average in the EU and one of the highest in the region number of applied utility models in relation to GDP. However, this does not change the fact that the effects of the interaction within the "knowledge triangle" in Poland between research, education and innovative entrepreneurship are insufficient to stimulate creativity and broaden the involvement of national actors in global research and innovation networks.

Chances to change Poland's position described above are seen in the OECD research results on readiness to learn and creative thinking. The synthetic indicator constructed by the OECD is based on six factors related to openness to new experiences and creative thinking. Source data for calculating the indicator of readiness to learn and creative thinking were collected in the Survey of Adult Skills (PIAAC) questionnaire in June 2017, which covered 23 countries, including 6 EU countries from Central and Eastern Europe. OECD research shows that Poles are a creative nation compared to other CEE countries. Unfortunately, the OECD study did not cover all the CEE countries analyzed in this article (the index for Hungary, Latvia, Romania, Bulgaria, Croatia was not calculated). Thus, broader comparison of Poland's position with all the countries of the CEE region is not possible. However, among the six CEE countries covered by the OECD survey, Poland was ranked second (behind Slovakia) in terms of readiness to learn and creativity. Interestingly, the Czech Republic, which is in general performing better than Poland in terms of innovativeness of the economy and is ranked higher than Poland in the European Innovation Scoreboard [6], is in the light of OECD research a less creative nation [36].

Activation of the creativity potential of Polish universities requires stronger support for strengthening interactions within the "knowledge triangle", both locally and internationally. When developing an innovation policy, keep in mind that research, education, and innovation activities have all become more globalized as a result of the globalization of production processes. Nowadays, countries compete not only for physical capital, but also for talents. However, talent development is not possible without wider international cooperation in research, science, education and production processes. Cooperation in all of its forms (national, international, intersectoral) is a source of inspiration for creativity and a means of better utilizing local resources to generate new ideas. Polish universities should work towards strengthening this cooperation.

Last, but not least, there are research limitations that should be taken into account. Main limitations concern the dataset – its small size, data availability and completeness as well as sample, which encompasses only entire countries, neither regions nor individual universities. Moreover, while interpreting the research results the selection of indications should be also considered.

References

1. OECD: Innovation in Public Services: Context, Solutions and Challenges. OECD, Paris (2012)
2. Murray, R., Caulier-Grice, J., Mulgan, G.: The Open Book of Social Innovation. National Endowment for Science, Technology and the Arts, London (2010)

3. Soriano, F., Mulatero, F.: Knowledge policy in the EU: from the Lisbon strategy to Europe 2020. J. Knowl. Econ. **1**, 289–302 (2010)
4. Turcinovic, P.: EU knowledge triangle: renaissance or ocean of papers? Donald Sch. J. Ultra-sound Obstet. Gynecol. **7**(3), 272–277 (2013). https://doi.org/10.5005/jp-journals-10009-1293
5. Veugelers, R., Cassiman, B.: R&D Cooperation between firms and universities, some empirical evidence from Belgian manufacturing. Int. J. Ind. Organ. **23**, 355–379 (2005)
6. European Commission: European Innovation Scoreboard 2019 (2019) . https://ec.europa.eu/docsroom/documents/36062
7. Eurostat: Database. http://ec.europa.eu/eurostat/data/database
8. OECD: Statistics. https://www.oecd-ilibrary.org/statistics
9. Schumpeter, J.: Teoria wzrostu gospodarczego. PWN, Warszawa (1960)
10. Freeman, C., Soete, L.: The Economics of Industrial Innovation. Continuum, London (1997)
11. Filion, L.J.: Empreendedorismo: Empreendedores e proprietários-gerentes de pequenos negócios. Revista de Administração [RAUSP] **34**(2), 5–28 (1999)
12. Howkins, J.: The Creative Economy. How People Make Money from Ideas. Penguin Press, London (2002)
13. Govindarajan, V.: The Three-Box Solution: A Strategy for Leading Innovation. Harvard Business Review, Cambridge (2016)
14. Amabile, T.M.: A model of creativity and innovation in organizations. In: Cummings, B.S. (ed.) Research in Organizational Behavior 1988, pp. 123–167. JAI Press, Greenwich (1988)
15. Amabile, T.M., Pratt, M.: The dynamic componential model of creativity and innovation in organizations: making progress, making meaning. Res. Organ. Behav. **36**, 167–183 (2016). https://doi.org/10.1016/j.riob.2016.10.001
16. Haefele, J.W.: Creativity and Innovation. Reinhold Publishing Corporation, New York (1962)
17. Stojanova, B.: Development of creativity as a basic task of the modern educational system. Procedia Soc. Behav. Sci. **2**, 3395–3400 (2010). https://doi.org/10.1016/j.sbspro.2010.03.522
18. Hossieni, A., Khalili, S.: Explanation of creativity in postmodern educational ideas. Procedia Soc. Behav. Sci. **15**, 1307–1313 (2011). https://doi.org/10.1016/j.sbspro.2011.03.283
19. Demetrikopoulos, M.K., Pecore, J.L. (eds.): Interplay of Creativity and Giftedness in Science. Sense Publishers, Rotterdam (2016)
20. Leite, Y.V.P., de Moraes, W.F.A.: The ability to innovate in international entrepreneurship. Revista de Administração [RAUSP] **50**(4), 447–459 (2015)
21. Balcar, J.: Soft skills and their wage returns: overview of empirical literature. Rev Econ Persp **14**(1), 3–15 (2014). https://doi.org/10.2478/revecp-2014-0001
22. Kautz, T.D., Heckman, J., Diris, R., ter Weel, B., Borghans, L.: Fostering and Measuring Skills: Improving Cognitive and Non-cognitive Skills to Promote Lifetime Success. National Bureau of Economic Research, Cambridge (2014)
23. Holmberg-Wright, K., Hribar, T.: Soft skills – the missing piece for entrepreneurs to grow a business. Am. J. Manag. Dev. **16**(1), 11–18 (2016)
24. Florida, R.: The Rise of the Creative Class: And How It's Transforming Work, Leisure, Community, and Everyday Life. Basic Books, New York (2002)
25. Florida, R.: The Rise of the Creative Class: Revisited. Basic Books, New York (2012)
26. Florida, R.: The flight of the creative class: the new global competition for talent. Lib. Educ. **92**(3), 22–29 (2006)
27. Sjoer, E., Nørgaard, B., Goossens, M.: From concept to reality in implementing the knowledge triangle. Eur. J. Eng. Educ. **41**(3), 353–368 (2015). https://doi.org/10.1080/03043797.2015.1079812
28. Maassen, P., Stensaker, B.: The knowledge triangle, European higher education policy logics and policy implications. High Educ. **61**(6), 757–769 (2011). https://doi.org/10.1007/s10734-010-9360-4

29. Unger, M., Polt, W.: The knowledge triangle between research, education and innovation –
    a conceptual discussion. Foresight STI Gov. **11**(2), 10–26 (2017). https://doi.org/10.17323/
    2500-2597.2017.2.10.26
30. Cervantes, M.: Higher education institutions in the knowledge triangle. Foresight STI Gov.
    11(2), 27–42 (2017). https://doi.org/10.17323/2500-2597.2017.2.27.42
31. Furman, J.L., Porter, M.E., Stern, S.: The determinants of national innovative capacity. Res.
    Policy **31**, 899–933 (2002). https://doi.org/10.1016/S0048-7333(01)00152-4
32. Ulku, H.: R&D, innovation and output: evidence from OECD and nonOECD countries. Appl.
    Econ. **39**(3), 291–307 (2007). https://doi.org/10.1080/00036840500439002
33. WIPO: Statistical Country Profiles (2018). http://www.wipo.int/ipstats/en/statistics/cou
    ntry_profile/profile.jsp?code=PL
34. Innovation Policy Platform: Patent data - The role of universities in technological devel-
    opment (2018). https://www.innovationpolicyplatform.org/content/patent-data-role-universit
    ies-technological-development
35. Bonaccorsi, A., Cicero, T., Secondi, L., Setteducati, E.: Are European universi-
    ties facing the Asian challenge in excellent S&T research? Innov. Growth Policy
    Brief **10** (2013). https://ec.europa.eu/research/innovation-union/pdf/expert-groups/i4g-rep
    orts/i4g_policy_brief__10_-_excellence_eu_universities.pdf
36. OECD: OECD Skills Outlook 2017: Skills and Global Value Chains. OECD Publishing, Paris
    (2017). https://doi.org/10.1787/9789264273351-en
37. Bileviciute, E., Draksas, R., Nevera, A., Vainiute, M.: Competitiveness in higher education:
    the case of university management. J. Compet. **11**(4), 5–21 (2019). https://doi.org/10.7441/
    joc.2019.04.01
38. Kostrzewski, M.: One design issue – many solutions. different perspectives of design think-
    ing – case study. In: Uden, L., Hadzima, B., Ting, I.-H. (eds.) KMO 2018. CCIS, vol. 877,
    pp. 179–190. Springer, Cham (2018). https://doi.org/10.1007/978-3-319-95204-8_16
39. OECD: OECD Science, Technology and Industry Scoreboard 2015: Innovation for Growth
    and Society. OECD Publishing, Paris (2015). https://doi.org/10.1787/sti_scoreboard-2015-en

Value in Digital Technologies and Services

Uwe V. Riss[1]([✉])(iD), Michael Ziegler[1](iD), and Lindsay J. Smith[2]

[1] Eastern Switzerland University of Applied Sciences, Rosenbergstr. 59, 9001, 08544 St. Gallen, Switzerland
{uwe.riss,michael.ziegler}@ost.ch
[2] University of Hertfordshire, College Lane, Hatfield AL10 9AB, UK
l.l.smith@herts.ac.uk

Abstract. Developing innovative digital services and applications is determined by the value of digital technologies. The value of technologies is difficult to grasp because it ultimately manifests itself only in customers' active use. Therefore, the assessment of value of technologies must start with the study of customer activities. We synthesize service-dominant logic (SDL) and activity theory (AT) to provide an integrative approach to understand customer activities and their use of digital services. We demonstrate that both theories complement each other due to the focus on the individual and communal aspects of creating value. SDL concentrates on the social side of creating value, but this value is determined by the service beneficiary. AT has a focus on individual actors but also includes the social dimension of action in the division of labor. To this end, value creation theory (VCT) is taken as the common perspective and means to perform a theory synthesis of AT and SDL. Such synthesis allows for a comprehensive view of technology-enabled digital services. It is the aim to identify dimensions of technological development and investigate the value they provide to customers. Dimensions are the following four: dematerialization, virtualization, servitization and platformization. We show how they increase the customer value.

Keywords: Service-dominant logic · Activity theory · Digital technologies and services · Value creation theory · Conceptual paper

1 Introduction

The question of the value of digital technologies in customer services is crucial for digital business and service innovation [1,16,23]. While digital technologies are extensively used and extremely successful, research on value of digital technologies has made progress shifting from a firm-centric to a service system perspective [7]. Less of the focus of the mentioned research is the value perceived by users of customer services in relation to their value-creating activities. However, the fact how

Supported by the Swiss National Science Foundation (SNF) project VA-PEPR, ref. no. CRSII5_189955.

L. Uden et al. (Eds.): KMO 2022, CCIS 1593, pp. 160–173, 2022.
https://doi.org/10.1007/978-3-031-07920-7_13

well a digital application supports customers in conducting their activities determines the value of the underlying technologies. Investigations have focused on the concept of value-in-use and customer experience of service [27] and although the influence of the customer activity has been recognized [26], research in the role of activities in value creation can still be expanded. Progress towards a deeper investigation in the role of customer activity required a suitable theory. Mickelsson [39] used Activity Theory (AT) [8,11] as an appropriate instrument to understand customer activities. However, his study did not include a detailed investigation of how digital technologies influence their value in activities.

Another very prominent line of research that focus on the network nature of service systems and places value at the center of its interest is service-dominant logic (SDL) [53–55]. Value plays a crucial role with a focus on co-creation of value in networks of service providers. Value co-creation and value creation show different characteristics which has initiated a debate on the nature of value itself [17–19,21,55]. SDL has been used for the analysis of digital technologies [35] but has not thoroughly included AT. An exception is a recent investigation of mobility services using SDL and AT [46].

Beyond the tension between SDL and AT, which might be caused by the unclear connection of value creation and co-creation, we will show that there is a deep complementarity between the two theories. The paper is organized as follows. In Sect. 2 we will explain our methodology that aims at a theory synthesis [29] with SDL and AT as domain theories and value creation theory (VCT) [21,59] as method theory. In Sect. 3 we present the three used theories: SDL, AT, and VCT. We than perform the proper theory synthesis in Sect. 4. In Sect. 5 we give an outlook how the joint theories can be used to explain certain value dimensions of digital technologies (including concrete examples) and finalize the investigation in Sect. 6 with a discussion.

2 Research Methodology

Conceptual research methodology is an evolving field that is attracting growing interest and requires systematic consideration. Therefore we have chosen it as a firt step in our research design; more precisely we apply theory synthesis as research methodology [29]. The goal of theory synthesis is to bring together different theoretical perspectives into a new view, to combine previously unrelated or incompatible ways of looking at things in a novel way. The second step in the research design consists in choosing 4 dimensions of technology-enabled value creation and corresponding examples of digital technologies to demonstrate that the synthesized theory of AT and SDL helps interpret the contribution of technology-based services innovation to users' value creation.

In this conceptual paper, we consider the value of digital technologies as an embodiment of value creation. So far value creation appears in the light of two theories. On the one hand, we have SDL, which views value from the perspective of resource integration and value co-creation and thus reflects the interconnectedness of digital technologies. On the other hand, there is activity theory, which looks at value from the perspective of an individual actor or user of such technology. So far, both disciplines have only been dealt with in a piecemeal fashion, although both views are necessary for a complete systematization. To address this issue, we use theory synthesis.

To conduct the theory synthesis, we use VCT as method theory and apply it to AT and SDL as domain theories. Here, we follow the idea that the two domain theories are complementary with respect to value creation as AT can be connected to actor (customer) value creation while SDL has its main focus on value co-creation. Since VCT is used as method theory it is not necessary to give a complete account of the VCT, but we concentrate on those parts necessary to synthesize AT and SDL.

The aim of the current theory synthesis is to close the gap between the individual consideration of value creation as a result of action in connection to AT [39] and value co-creation as basic concept in SDL. The objective is to develop a "big picture" that helps us to better understand the economic role of digital technologies, that show both sides as tools and resources in service systems. As [52] described it, the development of new theoretical frameworks goes hand-in-hand with empirical studies, which require a theoretical lens to interpret results beyond their own methodological soundness.

At the core of the current theory synthesis, we place activities and refer to their illustrative descriptions in activity systems [8]. These activity systems form the pictorial core of AT. Moreover, they describe the interplay of individual and communal activities. Interpreting these communal activities as resource integration, we find the link to SDL. Although activities of individual actors are not always without conflict to their role in service systems [38], most individual activities go hand-in-hand with cooperative resource integration. The link between AT and SDL is the concept of value, which is individually created or co-created, respectively. This connection was taken as a motivation to interpret activity systems in terms of SDL. Indeed, scholars have already realized the necessity to integrate value creation and co-creation, which has led to the paradigm of customer-dominant logic [21,27]. Mickelsson [38] made an earlier attempt to bring AT and SDL closer together, which we will discuss in more detail below.

3   Theory

3.1   Service-Dominant Logic

Since marketing research has developed a new paradigm that has shifted the focus to service as the basis of digital economy [53–55], the resulting service-dominant logic (SDL) has led to a reorientation in the understanding of economic value and its creation. Thus, SDL provides key insights into the functioning of the evolving service economy [37]. This reflects the fact that in the digital transformation, services have gradually emancipated themselves from the dominance of the production of goods, which has made them a focus of significant interest and academic research [37,57]. SDL places services at the center and subordinates goods to them as resources; services replace products as the central economic concept. In its latest version SDL is based on fundamental premises (FP1–FP11), four of which are regarded as axioms [55].

In the current paper we will only consider those FPs that we consider to be relevant for the value analysis of digital technologies. SDL suggests that digital technologies are regarded as means to realize a service (FP1). In some settings, digital technologies may enable a dematerialization and resource liquefaction [41], which refers to the decoupling of information from an underlying object.

In addition, SDL distinguishes between operant and operand resources; operant resources can act on other resources while operand resources must be acted on by other resources. Although digital technologies represent operant resources [1] and FP4 states that operant resources provide strategic benefits, we must clarify how they contribute to creating value.

Moreover, SDL emphasizes the role of networks for services and that their value is always co-created (FP6). Since this also holds for the service provided by digital technologies, we have to ask how they support services in networks and value co-creation. Another insight of SDL is that value creation is always based on resource integration (FP9), which digital technologies can support or even enable.

In addition to the focus on value co-creation, SDL points to the coordination of value co-creation through institutions and institutional arrangements (FP11) [55]. In this context, Vargo and Lusch refer to the observed "restricted cognitive abilities and bounded rationality" of economic actors, which entails a need for heuristics given by institutions and institutional arrangements (e.g., norms, meaning, symbols, etc. to facilitate coordination and cooperation).

SDL makes a significant contribution to explaining the role of digital technologies in value co-creation by identifying opportunities for innovation through opening up physical devices to digital service infrastructures. However, SDL tends to hide the value contribution of actor's agency focusing on resources as means of service delivery [39]. Here, Activity Theory plays an essential complementary role that we will investigate next.

3.2 Activity Theory

Activity theory (AT) is a theoretical approach that is used as a framework for the study of different forms of human practices [8]. AT has a long application history in human computer interaction [33] and beyond, for example, in the study of work activities [12], service design [45] or digital applications [32,50]. AT is concerned with processes in their social development and takes into account that activities are influenced by their social and cultural embeddedness. In this context, conflicts of social practice receive particular attention; they are regarded as driving forces of development and offer starting points for changes [30].

Its fundamental premise is that the interaction between an actor (**subject**) and an **object** (directed by the actor's objective) is generally mediated by material tools or signs, **tools** for short. Also, the object must not be simply identified with a material object but represents rather the focus and limiting horizon of the action [10]. This object orientedness means that we look at the object of activity in the double sense, namely oriented to a perceived (real) object and to a goal. The object also determines how the performed action creates value for the actor [31]. The mediation by tools always comes with a trade-off because tools require specific skills and can also limit the range of action. For example, a car can run faster than a human being but not everywhere and requires driving skills. This obviously affects the value of a tool (in both directions).

In addition to the interaction of subject and object, AT also considers the social dimension of activities, which means that most activities are carried out in cooperation with a **community**, organized according to a certain **division of labor** and governed by certain **rules** (cf. Fig. 1). In contrast to SDL, where all actors are in some way equal, AT focus on the actor as the focal service beneficiary. The connections between these different components are described in activity systems [8].

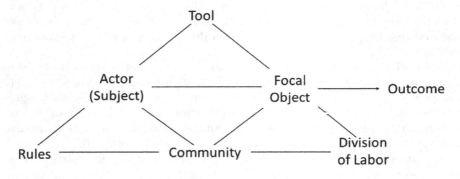

Fig. 1. Basic acitivty system.

The final principle of AT that we will use is that of the hierarchy of activity, that is, AT distinguishes three levels of activities: (1) **activity** (in general), which is driven by motives, (2) **action**, which aims at specific goals to be achieved and (3) **operations**, which consist in routines, which depend on given conditions such as the availability of resources. An example for the activity level is the motivation to improve the capabilities of a production site. Which activities serves this goal is quite open. It might even include the dismantling of old machines or implementing completely new business models. Operations are those routines that are conducted by human actor but also those that are executed by automated services and only require the actor to trigger them.

3.3   Value Creation Theory

The theory of value creation has become the focus of increasing attention among researchers [21,22,59,60]. The strands of research show that the topic is broad and multifaceted. For the current purpose it is only necessary to focus on the way technologies as tools help actors to create value n application. Turning to the literature review provided in [22], we find three fundamental streams of value creation: firm value creation, value co-creation, and customer value creation. Since we are here only interested in the actor's perspective we restrict our consideration to the two latter streams, where value co-creation is mainly in the focus of SDL [53] while customer value creation is more closely related to AT [39].

In the current context we use the term **value co-creation** as an expression for the value creation of a number of actors, which only become meaningful by their interrelation. For example, the production of a tool may be the result of an individual actor's work but the value created in this activity can only be understood if a user applies this tool in another value creating activity. This separation is the reason why the result of the toolmaker's activity is only considered potential value (to the user) [17–21]: because the tool might never been used. Nevertheless, the toolmaker will consider it as value creation. We regard this as the dialectics of value creation but will not go further into this topic. For the current purpose it is sufficient that actors regard their activities as value creating and take part in a system of communal activities.

Starting from the actors' focus on their actions, we see that this is the locus of value creation. According to AT, actors strive to master their situation through appropriate courses of action. The value of the outcomes reflects on the extent to which the situation has changed positively for them. This also includes which effort has been necessary to achieve this. Value is not only created in business activities but in all kinds of human activities if the final states appear to be desirable; this does not only concern acts of production but also performances, where value emerges retrospectively after the action [34].

We can now refer to AT and see how value appears at the different levels of the activity hierarchy: **activity**, **action** and **operation**. At the operation level focus is on routines that are more or less automatically performed and where the limiting factor is often the availability of resources. Value is mostly perceived in freeing oneself from limiting conditions. The outcome of an operation is mostly not deliberately chosen but implicitly assumed. We only become aware of this if an operation fails. In that case the expected outcome does not occur and alternative actions are required. In operations we regard the ease with which an operation can be performed as the determining factor for value. This includes the amount of **operand resources** that is required; the value can be increased if the number of required resources is reduced. It might also refer to required **operant resource** such as the intellectual capacity requirements for actors to run the operations. Central ways to operationalize activities consists in providing already integrated resources as products or automated services that autonomously perform resource integration.

At the **action** level, we mainly refer to the effects that Normann [41] has described as **resource density**, which roughly describes how easily the resources for an action are accessible. Performing an action requires the actor to choose an object, which might not be material but always materially based—even if the actor only thinks this requires a brain. Action requires more mental capacity, but the value can be increased by making all required resources easily available. Making resources easily available for the respective action simplifies the requirements for the actor in terms of location, time, or skills. At the **activity** level, agency is driven by motivation instead of objects and objectives. Value is added if the actors are supported in choosing the most suitable action in line with their motivation. This might depend on the resources available and corresponds to value constellation as the suitable combination of resources [41]. In this way AT already shows where value can be created (from the actor's perspective). If we proceed from AT to SDL the major difference is that value is no longer related to one actor's activity but the result of the collaboration of different actors, described as value co-creation. The focus of SDL is resource integration provided by multiple actors and the way integration is enabled.

Although value co-creation is a central concept in SDL, it is not only important *that* digital technologies contribute to value co-creation but also *how* they do this and how the role of individual actors manifest in there; value co-creation is always based on the consent of all involved parties, which means that each party must also perceive the co-creation as individual value creation. This becomes clear in SDL's FP10 that says that "value is always uniquely and phenomenologically determined by the beneficiary" [54], that is the respective actor.

4   Synthesis of Activity Theory and Service-Dominant Logic

Starting point for the theory synthesis is the reinterpretation of the activity system in terms of SDL, which is inspired by [5], the major difference to which is that we shift the focus from business models to services and value (co-)creation.

One of the central questions concerns the relationship of the object in AT und value co-creation in SDL. Roughly we can say that the intention in acting on the object is creating value, which is based on communal value co-creation. Therefore, we use the expression value (co-)creation in the dual sense of value creation by the individual actor associated with value co-creation through the cooperation of all service providers. One of the aims is to show that these are only two perspectives of the same thing. In this picture the actor becomes the service beneficiary of the cooperation. As we already mentioned before tools are represented by operant resources in SDL.

Both AT and SDL start from the actor as the central protagonist. The only difference is that in AT the actor is individually related to the activity while in SDL the actor appears as value co-creator in an actor-to-actor-network among other co-creators [35]. In both cases, the common factor is that the actors want to achieve their respective goals. The second parallel is in the tools they use for this, namely tools in AT and operant resources in SDL. Turning to the community of actors in AT, which we can recognize as service providers in SDL, the apparent parallel is to understand this community as the **service ecosystem**, in which the respective action is embedded. This is a generalization of the interpretation of the community as marketplace in [5], which is just a special technical configuration.

Regarding the rules that govern the community we agree with [5] that it is mainly a cost/benefit architecture, however, there might be rules such as regulations so that the term **economic rules** appears to be more appropriate. In SDL the major role of actors is to provide services for the ecosystem with the focus on the services; in AT services enable actors' intended activities with the focus on the actors. In analogy to the division of labor in traditional activity systems, we now focus on the network of connected services that contribute to the respective activity. Such networks have been described as value networks [2,4], which are reinterpreted as service value network in the current setting as an expression of the interplay of services. The general logic behind it, however, remains the same. The service value network is balanced by the economic rules that ensure the viability of the cooperation [3].

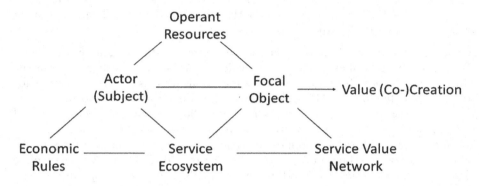

Fig. 2. Service-oriented activity system.

With the reinterpretation of the activity system (Fig. 2) we have achieved the largest part of the synthesis. The most challenging aspect, however, is the object in AT, for which we do not see an obvious parallel in SDL because services are general and not related to actors' individual objectives. To close this gap, we must better understand the connection between object and value. It is important that the object should not be misinterpreted as a material object but considered that it can also be an intangible object such as an idea or a hybrid object such as a plan [42]. It is only important that it can be shared and used by the service providing actor of the respective activity. Moreover, if we look at the value related to the activity, we find that it is depends on the outcome of the activities or the fulfilment of the need associated with this outcome [24,44,46]. Referring to [34] again, value stands for a retrospective view, as we explained before. Therefore, it seems to be appropriate to place value at the end of the activity.

The problematic relationship of value creation in AT and value co-creation in SDL has been mentioned before. The only point that is important in the current context is that both are closely entwined. Individual value creation is mostly based on a value co-creating service systems. Even if we assume that some activity, such as the production of a tool, which is never used, is hard to understand as value creation without a user of this tool according to the understanding of SDL.

5   Dimensions of Value Increase

As SDL describes it, the decisive perspective for determining the value of a service is that of the actor as service beneficiary. The question is how technology contributes to this value via service. Therefore, we must analyze the effect of digital technologies on the actors' activities to understand its value. In the following we refer to various value dimensions that we have mainly taken from service-related studies (dematerialization [41]; modular service systems, platforms [35]; virtuality [40]). We have taken these service dimensions as lenses to examine how they affect individual actors and their perceived value. The selection of dimensions must be regarded as provisional.

Value in Dematerialization: The term dematerialization originates from Normann [41] and describes the degree to which information is decoupled from the object that carries the information. Dematerialization is the precondition for resource liquefaction [35,41], which means the translocation of information via digital infrastructure [6,28]. Although resource liquefaction has been connected to SDL [35], it is mainly related to the increase in resource density, which is better understood with respect to individual actors. Resource density addresses the way how actions (resource integration) are performed. From an AT perspective this concerns the action level and, if automation is included, the operation level. Dematerialization and resource liquefaction also form the basis for the cooperative use of digital technology since it allows to deal with an object simultaneously from different locations. Such flexibilization of interfaces does not only increase the actor's value creation but contributes to value co-creation of the service system, too.

Example technologies for dematerialization include sensors and sensor-based devices, such as digital thermometers. They transform information from the focal object into data of which actors make use. They can take advantage of such transformed information to control an action (action level) or to automate certain operations (operation level). Another example is simulation technologies. They generate information that would otherwise only be obtained through physical experimentation. They help actors to explore possible courses of action (activity level), while they can support actors' decision between alternatives (action level). Voice assistants make spoken language digitally available facilitating actors' routine (operation level).

Value in Servitization: The term servitization has been used to describe the transition from products to services that satisfy customer needs in a comparable way [51]. In the current context we use the term servitization to refer to the way services increase value through their connectivity, modularity and generativity [6,35]. These value-creating forces depend on dematerialization that gives services access to data. Thus, it allows actors to involve services in their activities, to which we refer as servitization of action. Such servitization gives actors remote access to a multitude of resources. The access to such services can significantly change the skills that are required to conduct an action. The result is an increase of resource density. For example, online maps with geolocation services do not make maps remotely accessible but help users in finding their location on the provided map. Lusch and Nambisan [35] looked at servitization from the perspective of service ecosystems pointing at the opportunities of service-based resource integration. Such servitization is often directly integrated in actors' tools. In servitization, we also aim at the action and operational level from an AT perspective.

As an example of servitization, we can consider voice assistants whose essential task is to simplify a service call with the help of an additional speech recognition service, i.e., at the action level. A similar provision of additional services is offered by recommender systems, which help actors to select certain goals (activity level) or to decide between certain alternatives (action level) by means of additional data-based services.

Value in Virtualization: From AT we can learn that the object of activity is essential for actors to form a focus for action. In contrast, objects only appear as resources in SDL. Whereas dematerialization primarily leads to a dispersion of data and information, virtualization means their combination in single objects used as unique reference point for actors. Indeed, there is a growing interest in digital objects [14,15]. Such reference points are not only relevant for individual actors but also serve collaboration and have been used to refer to different kinds of artefacts [13]. Recently, researchers have pointed to the proximity between objects of activity and intermediary objects [58] drawing a connecting line to Engeström [9] saying that an "object is both something given and something projected or anticipated" in an action. The central value contribution of virtualization to actors appears at the activity level, where objects provide a focus for sensemaking as starting point for various activities—providing horizon and scope for possible action—but also at action level, where objects bundle information and ease the access to various object-related resources.

Augmented reality supports the perception of real world objects by providing additional information. The object under consideration retains its richness of information, but is supplemented by digital services that simplify actions (action level). Video conferencing technologies also aim to present the participants as real as possible (operation level).

Value in Platformization: SDL has already contributed to the discussion of platforms in terms of their relevance for service ecosystems [35]. In addition to that it is important to understand how they increase actors' value: service ecosystems provide "an organizing structure for the actors" while service platforms "provide an organizing structure for the resources". Access to this target includes two aspects: **transparency**—to know about actors and resources—and availability to bring actors and resources within easy reach. However, we can go further when we delve deeper into the analysis. For example, [48] have distinguished between integrative platforms that provide already integrated resources for required services and aggregative platforms that only provide access to resources whereas integration is due to the actors. Both types of platforms create value but serve actors in different ways.

The relevance of platforms is also given from the perspective of individual actors. It is to be seen in the actors' challenges to find the right service for their particular action. Partially, service providers assume this task, but this limits the generativity of service integration. The generativity can be significantly increased if actors select services to be used, but this requires them to find suitable services. Digital platforms can be seen as essential enablers that give actors transparent access to services [35, 43]. Platforms can support actors at the activity level where they provide a variety of services that can inspire activities following a motivation. For example, search platforms give access to wide range of information which invites users to further exploration. Platforms also work at the action level help users to find specific foreknown objects in a repository.

Blockchain is an example of an emerging platform-enabling technology. It can be used by governments for public notary services to residents, where it enbales transactional services within a multi-party business network. In addition, blockchain enables governments to offer services, such as voting or identity management [25]. This means that blockchain will enable governments to build platforms that can offer a variety of digital services on a trusted architecture (activity and action level). A second example of platform-enabling technologies are voice assistants. They allow a user to select and activate services via simple voice commands (often operation level).

6   Discussion

The fundamental assumption of the perspective chosen in this thesis is that the value of digital technologies must be considered primarily from the perspective of the acting users, but that the essential properties and mechanisms of service systems must be included. The complementarity of AT and SDL provides the ideal basis for this. The dimensions of digitization, such as dematerialization, servitization, virtualization and platformization, are already widely known, but the investigation of the concrete impact of these dimensions on users usually does not go down to the individual action.

Starting from AT and SDL being complementary, the four presented dimensions can only be seen as a starting point for following investigations. The perspective in this paper mainly refers to the user as a service consumer. Further investigation is required on the relationship between individual value creation and communal value co-creation. This includes users' contributions towards the service providers and other users (social dimension) and leads to the changing role of users towards prosumers [49]. This might lead to another dimension.

More insights can be gained form further investigations in specific digital technologies. At the same time, additional research in the theoretical foundations and a more detailed elaboration of technoloigcal dimensions is required and will follow in future research.

References

1. Akaka, M.A., Vargo, S.L.: Technology as an operant resource in service (eco)systems. Inf. Syst. e-Bus. Manag. **12**(3), 367–384 (2014). https://doi.org/10.1007/s10257-021-00524-5
2. Allee, V.: Reconfiguring the value network. J. Bus. Strateg. **21**(4), 36–39 (2000). https://doi.org/10.1108/eb040103
3. Allee, V.: Value network analysis and value conversion of tangible and intangible assets. J. Intellect. Cap. **9**(1), 5–24 (2008). https://doi.org/10.1108/14691930810845777
4. Basole, R.C., Rouse, W.B.: Complexity of service value networks: conceptualization and empirical investigation. IBM Syst. J. **47**(1), 53–70 (2008). https://doi.org/10.1147/sj.471.0053
5. Beckett, R.C., Dalrymple, J.: Business model value capture: an activity theory perspective. In: Huizingh, E., Kokshagina, O., Bitran, I., Conn, S., Torkkeli, M., Tynnhammar, M. (eds.) ISPIM Conference Proceedings, pp. 1–13. ISPIM (2017)
6. Blaschke, M., Haki, M.K., Riss, U.V., Winter, R., Aier, S.: Digital infrastructure —a service-dominant Logic Perspective. In: Ågerfalk, P.J., Levina, N., Kien, S.S. (eds.) Proceedings of ICIS 2016, Dublin (2016)
7. Brust, L., Breidbach, C.F., Antons, D., Salge, T.-O.: Service-dominant logic and information systems research. In: Kim, Y.J., Agarwal, R., Lee, J.K. (eds.) Proceedings of ICIS 2017, Seoul (2017)
8. Engeström, Y.: Learning by Expanding, 1st edn. Orienta-Konsultit Oy, Helsinki (1987)
9. Engeström, Y.: Objects, contradictions and collaboration in medical cognition an activity-theoretical perspective. Artif. Intell. Med. **7**(5), 395–412 (1995)
10. Engeström, Y.: Innovative learning in work teams. In: Engeström, Y., Miettinen, R., Punamöki, R. (eds.) Perspectives on Activity Theory, pp. 377–404, Cambridge University Press, London (1999)
11. Engeström, Y.: Expansive learning at work toward an activity theoretical reconceptualization. J. Educ. Work. **14**(1), 133–156 (2001)
12. Engeström, Y.: Developmental Work Research. Lehmanns Media, Berlin (2005)
13. Ewenstein, B., Whyte, J.: Knowledge practices in design the role of visual representations as "Epistemic Objects". Organ. Stud. **30**(1), 7–30 (2009). https://doi.org/10.1177/0170840608083014
14. Faulkner, P., Runde, J.: Technological objects, social positions, and the transformational model of social activity. MIS Q. **37**(3), 803–818 (2013)
15. Faulkner, P., Runde, J.: Theorizing the Digital Object. MIS Q. **43**(4), 1279–1302 (2019). https://doi.org/10.25300/MISQ/2019/13136
16. Frey, A., Trenz, M., Veit, D.: A service-dominant logic perspective on the roles of technology in service innovation. J. Bus. Econ. **89**(8–9), 1149–1189 (2019). https://doi.org/10.1007/s11573-019-00948-z
17. Grönroos, C.: Service logic revisited who creates value? And who co-creates? Eur. Bus. Rev. **20**(4), 298–314 (2008)

18. Grönroos, C.: A service perspective on business relationships. Ind. Mark. Manage. **40**(2), 240–247 (2011). https://doi.org/10.1016/j.indmarman.2010.06.036
19. Grönroos, C., Gummerus, J.: The service revolution and its marketing implications service logic vs service-dominant logic. Manag. Serv. Qual. **24**(3), 206–229 (2014)
20. Grönroos, C., Ravald, A.: Service as business logic implications for value creation and marketing. J. Serv. Manag. **22**(1), 5–22 (2011)
21. Grönroos, C., Voima, P.: Critical service logic: making sense of value creation and co-creation. J. Acad. Mark. Sci. **41**(2), 133–150 (2013)
22. Gummerus, J.: Value creation processes and value outcomes in marketing theory. Mark. Theory **13**(1), 19–46 (2013). https://doi.org/10.1177/1470593112467267
23. Häikiö, J., Koivumäki, T.: Exploring digital service innovation process through value creation. J. Innov. Manag. **4**(2), 96–124 (2016). https://doi.org/10.24840/2183-0606_004.002_0006
24. Haksever, C., Chaganti, R., Cook, R.G.: A model of value creation. J. Bus. Ethics **49**(3), 295–307 (2004). https://doi.org/10.1023/b:busi.0000017968.21563.05
25. Hassanein, A.A., El-Tazi, N., Mohy, N.N.: Blockchain, smart contracts, and decentralized applications: an introduction. In: Rawal, B.S., Manogaran, G., Poongodi, M. (eds.) Implementing and Leveraging Blockchain Programming. BT, pp. 97–114. Springer, Singapore (2022). https://doi.org/10.1007/978-981-16-3412-3_6
26. Heinonen, K.: The influence of customer activity on e-service value-in-use. Int. J. Electron. Bus. **7**(2), 190–214 (2009). https://doi.org/10.1504/ijeb.2009.024627
27. Heinonen, K., Strandvik, T., Mickelsson, K.-J., Edvardsson, B., Sundstrom, E., Andersson, P.: A customer-dominant logic of service. J. Serv. Manag. **21**(4), 531–548 (2010). https://doi.org/10.1108/09564231011066088
28. Henfridsson, O., Bygstad, B.: The generative mechanisms of digital infrastructure evolution. MIS Q. **37**(3), 907–932 (2013)
29. Jaakkola, E.: Designing conceptual articles four approaches. AMS Rev. **10**, 18–26 (2020). https://doi.org/10.1007/s13162-020-00161-0
30. Kaptelinin, V., Nardi, B.A., Macaulay, C.: The activity checklist: a tool for representing the space of context. Interacti. Maga. **6**(4), 27–39 (1999)
31. Kaptelinin, V., Uden, L.: Understanding delegated actions. In: Tossavainen, P.J., Harjula, M. Holmlid, S. (eds.) Proceedings of ServDes. 2012, Nordic Conference on Service Design and Service, pp. 101–109. Linköping University Electronic Press (2012)
32. Karanasios, S., Nardi, B., Spinuzzi, C., Malaurent, J.: Moving forward with activity theory in a digital world. Mind Cult. Act. **28**(3), 1–20 (2021). https://doi.org/10.1080/10749039.2021.191466
33. Kuutti, K.: Activity theory as a potential framework for human-computer interaction research. In: Nardi, B.A. (ed.) Context and Consciousness: Activity Theory and Human-Computer Interaction, pp. 17–44. MIT Press, Cambridge (1996)
34. Lambek, M.: The value of (performative) acts. HAU: J. Ethnogr. Theory **3**(2), 141–160 (2013). https://doi.org/10.14318/hau3.2.009
35. Lusch, R.F., Nambisan, S.: Service innovation. MIS Q. **39**(1), 155–175 (2015). https://doi.org/10.25300/MISQ/2015/39.1.07
36. Mele, C., et al.: Shaping service ecosystems: exploring the dark side of agency. J. Serv. Manag. **29**(4), 521–545 (2018)
37. Maglio, P.P., Vargo, S.L., Caswell, N., Spohrer, J.: The service system is the basic abstraction of service science. Inf. Syst. e-Bus. Manag. **7**, 395–406 (2009). https://doi.org/10.1007/s10257-008-0105-1
38. Maglio, P.P., Spohrer, J.: Fundamentals of service science. J. Acad. Mark. Sci. **36**, 18–20 (2008). https://doi.org/10.1007/s11747-007-0058-9

39. Mickelsson, K.-J.: Customer activity in service. J. Serv. Manag. **24**(5), 534–552 (2013). https://doi.org/10.1108/josm-04-2013-0095
40. Nardi, B.: Virtuality. Annu. Rev. Anthropol. **44**, 15–31 (2015). https://doi.org/10.1146/annurev-anthro-102214-014226
41. Normann, R.: Reframing Business. Wiley, Chichester (2001)
42. Naaranoja, M., Uden, L.: Why co-creation of value may not work? In: Uden, L., Oshee, D. F., Ting. I-H., Liberona, D. (eds.) Proceedings of KMO 2014, pp. 362–372 (2014). https://doi.org/10.1007/978-3-319-08618-7_35
43. Parker, G., Van Alstyne, M.W., Jiang, X.: Platform ecosystems: how developers invert the firm. MIS Q. **41**(1), 255–266 (2017). https://doi.org/10.25300/MISQ/2017/41.1.13
44. Ravald, A.: The Customer's Process of Value Creation. Mercati & Competitivitá **1**(1), 41–54 (2010). https://doi.org/10.3280/mc2010-001005
45. Sangiorgi, D., Clark, B.: Toward a participatory design approach to service design. In: Proceedings of the Eighth Conference on Participatory Design, Toronto, Canada. pp. 148–151. ACM Press, Toronto (2004)
46. Schulz, T., Gewald, H., Böhm, M., Krcmar, H.: Smart mobility contradictions in value co-creation. Inf. Syst. Front. pp. 1–21 (2020). https://doi.org/10.1007/s10796-020-10055-y
47. Setia, P., Venkatesh, V., Joglekar, S.: Leveraging digital technologies. MIS Q. **37**(2), 565–590 (2013). https://doi.org/10.25300/misq/2013/37.2.11
48. Tapscott, D., Lowy, A., Ticoll, D.: Digital Capital. Harvard Business Review Press, Boston, MA (2000)
49. Toffler, A.: The Third Wave. William Morrow, New York, NY (1980)
50. Uden, L., Valderas, P., Pastor, O.: An activity-theory-based model to analyse Web application requirements. Inf. Res. **13**(2), 2–13 (2008)
51. Vandermerwe, S., Rada, J.: Servitization of business: adding value by adding services. Eur. Manag. J. **6**(4), 314–324 (1988). https://doi.org/10.1016/0263-2373(88)90033-3
52. Vargo, S.L., Koskela-Huotar, K.: Advancing conceptual-only articles in marketing. AMS Rev. **10**, 1–5 (2020). https://doi.org/10.1007/s13162-020-00173-w
53. Vargo, S.L., Lusch, R.F.: Evolving to a new dominant logic for marketing. J. Mark. **68**(1), 1–17 (2004). https://doi.org/10.1509/jmkg.68.1.1.24036
54. Vargo, S.L., Lusch, R.F.: Service-dominant logic: continuing the evolution. J. Acad. Mark. Sci. **36**, 1–10 (2008)
55. Vargo, S.L., Lusch, R.F.: Institutions and axioms: an extension and update of service-dominant logic. J. Acad. Mark. Sci. **44**(1), 5–23 (2015). https://doi.org/10.1007/s11747-015-0456-3
56. Vargo, S.L., Maglio, P.P., Akaka, M.A.: On value and value co-creation: a service systems and service logic perspective. Eur. Manag. J. **26**(3), 145–152 (2008). https://doi.org/10.1016/j.emj.2008.04.003
57. Vargo, S.L., Morgan, F.W.: Services in society and academic thought. J. Macromark. **25**(1), 42–53 (2005). https://doi.org/10.1177/0276146705275294
58. Vetoshkina, L., Paavola, S.: From the abstract to the concrete and outlines. Crit. Pract. Stud. **22**(1), 125–168 (2021)
59. Voima, P., Heinonen, K., Strandvik, T.: Exploring customer value formation-a customer dominant logic perspective. Working paper, No. 552, Publications of Hanken School of Economics, Helsinki, Finland (2010)
60. Windsor, D.: Value creation theory. In: Wasielewski, D.M., Weber, J. (eds.) Stakeholder Management, Series. Business and Society 360, vol. 1, pp. 75–100. Emerald (2017). https://doi.org/10.1108/S2514-175920170000004

Teachers' Readiness of Information and Communication Technology Integration in Higher Education Innovation

Ju-Chuan Wu[1,2]([⊠]) and Jui-Chi Wang[1,2]

[1] Department of Business Administration, Feng Chia University, Taichung, Taiwan, R.O.C.
katejcwu@mail.fcu.edu.tw
[2] Institute of Information Management, National Taiwan University of Science and Technology, Taipei, Taiwan, R.O.C.
d10909203@mail.ntust.edu.tw

Abstract. This study aims to identify the elements involved in Information and Communication Technology (ICT) integration in higher education innovation and examine its adoption effects and the support received from the institute and teachers. This study adopted the Activity Theory framework to collect related factors and examined them using stages involved in the diffusion process. The data were collected from teachers who has implemented ICT integrated innovative teaching and from the responses of 250 questionnaires from the universities in Taiwan and analyzed by AMOS. The study had three main findings: (1) Information-based Readiness has positive effect on User Readiness, (2) User Readiness has positive effect on Actual use, and (3) Actual use has positive effect on Satisfaction. The findings could enrich the research of ICT integrated education with different perspectives and would be helpful in extending the long-term development in academics and practical ICT application.

Keywords: ICT integrated in higher education innovation · Activity theory · Diffusion of innovation

1 Introduction

With advancing digital technology, teaching methods in higher education have extended to ICT integration into the classrooms, which is viewed as an important educational innovation to enhance teaching and learning processes [1]. It is expected to prepare proficient learners to cope with unfamiliar problems and varying situations in response industry [2].

Previous studies show that ICT integrated teaching is a commonly adopted teaching method nowadays. It invokes the student to participate in a digital society. Teachers' adoption of educational technologies using resources like hardware or software applications to implement specific teaching processes helps students in the learning process [3–5]. Teachers have a key role in innovative teaching that enables students to share knowledge [6]. "Profiling teachers' readiness for online teaching and learning in higher

© Springer Nature Switzerland AG 2022
L. Uden et al. (Eds.): KMO 2022, CCIS 1593, pp. 174–189, 2022.
https://doi.org/10.1007/978-3-031-07920-7_14

education: Who's ready?" as the research topic that evaluated whether teachers have enough readiness to implement online teaching [7].

However, this study revealed the following. First, most studies have shown that ICT tools effectively support the teaching and learning process and also guide teachers in their usage [8, 9]. Second, several studies focus on students' learning, including their readiness, expectations, identity, and participation but rarely cover both the perspectives of learning and teaching [10]. The role of teachers' motivation is seen as a critical prerequisite for the success of ICT integrated innovative education in the early phases [1]. It has been shown that barriers in ICT integrated innovative teaching are multifaceted [7].

Few studies have examined teaching behavior, specifically, the influencing factors and teaching effects on such behavior [6]. It is necessary to survey ICT integrated teaching activity factors related to teachers' adoption, such as the use of ICT tools to support teaching [11] and how teachers' attitude affects its adoption. Fourth, few studies surveyed higher education teachers as a sample [12]. Higher education is expected to provide high-quality talent for the industry. It is difficult to know the ground reality of ICT integrated innovative teaching in higher education, its implementation outcome, and if it is satisfactory as per industry needs. There are many challenges and obstacles in implementing innovative teaching involving various elements.

This study aims to survey technical competence, behavior, influencing factors, and process in technology integration into classrooms from teachers' perspectives. Students' information-based readiness, user readiness, and actual use factor have a positive relationship with students' satisfaction [13]. It showed that user-oriented readiness and actual use are essential factors in technology integrated innovative teaching. This study adopted the Activity Theory framework to collect related factors from the teacher's perspective and examined them using stages involved in the diffusion process.

2 Theoretical Background

2.1 ICT Integrated in Higher Education Innovation

With the increase in the importance of educational technology, schools have increased ICT-related resources of teaching tools, equipment, software, and Internet integrated teaching [14]. Integrating ICT into higher education courses can promote digital literacy and self-efficacy, collaborative learning, perceptual understanding, and advanced thinking skills [15, 16]. There is no doubt that the use of ICT in digital learning as sustainability is well known and widely used, especially among students who are already familiar with the technology [17]. Since ICT integration is an ongoing process and has a positive impact on students' academic performance, schools should strive to invest in the development of ICT infrastructure [18].

Following [19], course activity from a constructivism perspective is demonstrated in Fig. 1. The framework highlighted course activity consisted of learners, personalized/adaptive technologies, and environments; it formed three interactions of generation (learning outcomes), learning support, and parameters of learning (user-oriented) [19] and showed that readiness and spiral organization generation affected course activity. The study surveyed innovative teaching situations from a constructivism perspective which is shown in Table 1. It provides a better understanding of teachers' readiness as an important step toward understanding ICT resources to support them in ICT integrated innovation education [7]. It views key factors in innovative teaching activities from a wider perspective.

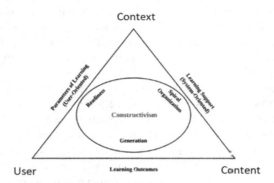

Fig. 1. Course activity can be from a constructivist perspective

Table 1. Innovative teaching situation from a constructivist perspective

Issues	Research content	Source
Learner	Expectations, ICT Readiness, User Readiness, Identity, Participation	[11]
Personalized/Adaptive Technologies	MOOC, Mobile, Game, Mobile, Simulations, Cloud-based Learning	[20–24]
Parameters of Learning (User-Oriented)	Teaching styles, Instructional strategies, Time, Content Development	[11]
Learning Outcome	Satisfaction, Performance	[25]
Learning Support (System-Oriented)	Transition from face-to-face to online	[11]
Environment	Extend learning of teachers and schools, Internship ICT integration into the teaching environment, Technical and multimedia support	[11, 13, 26]

2.2 Activity Theory

Human activities consist of four sub-activity systems: Production, Consumption, Exchange, and Distribution. Therefore, projects such as community, the division of labor, and rules are added to form the framework of the second-generation activity theory. In this theory, the contradiction has become the core of activity theory analysis, and expanded activity theory has three main intermediary paths: (1) The subject and object will be affected by the intermediary of the tool unit, (2) The community and the subject will also be subject to rules, and (3) The community unit and the object unit will be affected by the division of labor. Other additional lines may have secondary mediating relationships [27]; Therefore, in multiple and complex mediational structures of activities, the triangular analysis framework is used to highlight the "contradictions" of activities, which is also the basis for the development and transformation of the activity system. Three generations of activity theory were developed in response to the need to develop conceptual tools to understand dialogue, multiple perspectives, and the interaction of two or more activity system networks with common objects and practices [28–30] that promote the continuous change of the activity system and interaction with other activities. Therefore, it also pays attention to the contextual view. It describes the analysis of the activity from the perspective of element performance and communication process, and the activity involves the object, the activity goal, the applied tools, and language-related projects set in the framework [31]. The dynamic knowledge view of activity theory echoes the knowledge view based on practice [32]. Activity analysis helps in multiple fields in understanding complex work and social activities [33] that used to explore the complex process relationships in activities and has now become the founding theory of understanding the changes and development of work and social activities [34], activities theory-related framework, and analysis unit.

The complexity of ICT integration process is increasing, as surveys and discussions on educational technology are integrated into the classroom Bower [35]. Previous studies have shown that ICT integrated innovative education depends on several connected factors related to teachers' characteristics, institutions, and educational system [36]. Hence, this study adopted the eight-step model to summarize the activity factor of ICT Innovative education in Table 2. It has continued to discover the factors influencing the integration process. Teachers' preparation, belief, motivation, and readiness are important factors in ICT integrated innovative teaching activities. Teacher's readiness is viewed as state of teacher's preparedness [37]. Readiness can be divided into three factors: technical, organizational, and social readiness [38]. Previous studies have only focused on teachers' and organizational readiness. With the development of ICT, the technologies are no longer the primary object but become a tool that enables schools to provide equal education to students [39]. Technical readiness such as teachers' ICT readiness and the school's ICT-support environment are important factors. It is necessary to explore how these factors affect teachers' adoption of ICT integrated innovative teaching and their teaching performance. Hence, this study deduced important factors, including ICT readiness, user readiness, ICT-support, actual use, and satisfaction to understand how teachers implement ICT integrated education.

2.3 Diffusion of Innovation

Roger's "Diffusion of Innovations" published in (1962) integrated the past innovation research into Diffusion of Theory [41]. Innovations often find it difficult to gain widespread recognition, thus Roger defined it as "a new idea, practice, or object deemed by an individual or other adopters." He defined diffusion as "the process of spreading innovation through communication channels among members of the social system over

Table 2. Eight-step model summarizes the activities of ICT in innovative teaching

Analysis steps and units	Open-ended question	Components of the activity	Related factors	Sources
Activity of interest	What sort of activity am I interested in?	The integration of higher education in ICT into innovative teaching activities		
Objective of activity	Why is this activity taking place?	The advancement of information technology has changed the current teaching environment. The purpose is to understand the actual use of teachers in ICT integration into innovative teaching or learning	Satisfaction	[25]
Subjects in this activity	Who is involved in carrying out this activity?	Teacher	Instructor preparation, Belief, Motivation, Readiness	[7]
Tools mediating the activity	By what means are the subjects carrying out this activity?	MOOC, Mobile, Game, Mobile, Simulations, Cloud-based Learning		
Rules and regulations	Are there any cultural norms, rules, or regulations governing the performance of this activity?	School's ICT policy, ICT-based resources, infrastructure, and standards	School-based ICT policy	[40]
Division of labor	Who is responsible for what, when carrying out this activity and how are the roles organized?	School ICT support and support for innovative teaching courses The roles, functions, and tasks that teachers play in activities The tasks teachers should perform during the activity Teachers course design	Organizational innovation climate	[6]
Community	What is the environment in which this activity is carried out?	School units, teachers, and students have a variety of ICT channels for interaction		
Outcome	What is the desired Outcome of carrying out this activity?	Teachers have enough ICT skills, knowledge, and problem-solving ability that enable them to fit industry needs	Satisfaction	[25]

time" [42] in trying to explain the diffusion of innovation in society from the perspective of innovation diffusion. Its essence and connotation include innovation (Innovation), communication channels (Communication Channels), time (Time), social system (Social System), and innovation-decision process (Innovation-Decision Process). Innovation diffusion is an activity of seeking information and processing information, which encourages individuals to reduce the uncertainty about the advantages and disadvantages of innovation. It can be divided into Knowledge, Persuasion, Decision, Implementation, and Confirmation, which are the other five stages to decide whether to adopt new technologies/products/services [42]. Assuming that people's social system is a social structure with social norms, influential individuals, and groups, innovation will spread through two communication channels, mass media and interpersonal communication in the social system, forming innovative effects and imitations. The effect of time is used to measure the rate of adoption of innovation by members of the social system. According to the adoption rate, it is divided into Innovators, Early Adopters, Early Majority, Late Majority, Laggards and exposes the differences in adoption between the adopter categories [43, 44].

With different application requirements, many quantitative models have been developed for innovation diffusion analysis. Among them, Bass's innovation diffusion model is the most representative, which is different from Roger's (1976), which integrates. The most famous application examples are the marketing of new products and in society are the proliferation of changes and the penetration of public policies, discussing diverse and wide-ranging topics, mainly based on the individual or organizational point of view of the innovation decision-making process, the characteristics of innovation, the types of adopters, and the attitudes before and after adoption, such as the late adoption impact of digital innovation factors [45], use of mobile social networking sites by the elderly [46], cloud computing to explore the impact of transformational leadership on the spread of corporate innovation [47], low-carbon policies, for the impact of green diffusion among Chinese alliance companies [48], understanding the multi-stage diffusion process with potential market losses and related pricing policies [49], the diffusion effect of chain technology [50], the exploratory research on the diffusion of digital technology in the retail industry [51], and the rethinking of the innovation diffusion process from the perspective of service ecosystems and systems [52].

With the development of technology and industry trends, the application of innovation diffusion theory has been upgraded from new technology, products, and services to industrial standards and service innovation, and its discussion level has also expanded from individuals, organizations, and service ecosystems [52]. We have explored the process of research objects from potential adopters, early adopters to late adopters, the evolution of phased factors in the time dimension, and whether to persuade organizations to accept emerging technologies and service innovations. Although there is a wealth of innovation research literature for reference in the past, there is still a lack of empirical research on information system process innovation. The lack of relevant knowledge on the late adoption phenomenon of innovation and the driving factors of digital innovation diffusion may lead to innovation. Proliferation is slow and allows competitors to seize market opportunities, which ultimately leads to losses [45].

2.4 Relationship Between User's Behavior, Contextual, Content Factors, and Satisfaction in ICT Integrated Innovation Teaching Process

This study investigated how teachers get ready to implement ICT integrated innovative teaching and operation process, whether schools support enough ICT resources, and how its actual use affects teacher satisfaction.

(1) Information-based readiness and user readiness

Students' information-based readiness has a positive relationship with users' readiness Huang, Wu [13]. Teachers play an important role in students' learning activity. ICT capabilities have been transformed from knowledge based on technical skills to an overall concept of building pedagogical knowledge about technology, including instructional and cognitive tools to promote student learning [53]. All teaching materials and ICT-support tools are prepared by the teacher. The degree to which teachers use ICT tools is related to their readiness to implement ICT integrated innovation education [1].

Based on the above discussion, this study proposes the following hypothesis:

H₁: Teacher's information-based readiness will have a positive relationship with user's readiness.

(2) Information-based readiness and the actual use of ICT integrated innovative teaching

Teachers' attitudes and beliefs significantly influence their actions and practices in the classroom. For ICT-based courses, their attitudes and beliefs along with ICT skills and knowledge affect their course implementation. Previous findings have shown that teachers' positive perceptions are critical factors for increasing levels of ICT integration, they tend to be more confident in implementing technology into the course [54, 55].

Based on the above discussion, this study proposes the following hypothesis:

H2: Teacher's information-based readiness will have a positive relationship with actual ICT use.

(3) User readiness and the actual use of ICT integrated innovative teaching

Previous research has shown that teachers who believe that ICT meets their educational goals, teaching goals, and practices may regard ICT as an alternative and adopt it [10, 12, 56]. Students' user readiness has a positive relationship with actual use of ICT integrated innovative learning Huang, Wu [13]. The teacher has the main role in ICT integrated innovative teaching activity, their readiness is more important than the students'. In addition to teachers' knowledge, their beliefs are another factor that impacts ICT integrated innovative teaching [12]. The teacher must have enough skills and competence to implement ICT integrated innovative teaching [1].

Based on the above discussion, this study proposes the following hypothesis:

H3: User readiness will have a positive relationship with actual ICT use.

(4)   ICT support from school and the actual use of ICT integrated innovative teaching

In ICT integrated innovative teaching courses, building an ICT-support environment is necessary for teachers and students. Hence, institutional support is an important factor in readiness for online teaching and learning [7, 57]. Support helps teachers overcome ICT barriers [58]. This is closely related to the implementation of ICT in school-related learning environments [59].

Based on the above discussion, this study proposes the following hypothesis:

H4: ICT support from schools will have a positive relationship with actual ICT use.

(5)   The actual use of ICT integrated innovative teaching and satisfaction

Satisfaction is an important factor that presents a teacher's outcome and performance. It is viewed as the success of ICT integrated innovative teaching. Teachers' actual ICT use has a positive relationship with user satisfaction Unal and Unal [60]. Therefore, this study believes that the degree of perceived satisfaction of teachers should also be considered after their actual adoption as a feedback mechanism from the innovation decision process to the adoption.

Based on the above discussion, this study proposes the following hypothesis:

H5: The actual ICT use will have a positive relationship with satisfaction.

3   Research Methods

3.1   Research Framework

The following hypotheses explore the adoption of ICT integrated innovative teaching and combined with a readiness to investigate the impacts of the actual use of ICT integrated innovative teaching and satisfaction. Hence, the hypotheses are illustrated as shown in Fig. 2.

3.2   Measures

The measures used in this study were obtained from the literature review and then used to develop a questionnaire for this study. The research objective of this study focuses on teachers who have adopted ICT integrated innovative teaching in higher education. The seven-point Likert-type scale was employed for evaluating the constructs with anchors ranging from strongly disagree (1) to strongly agree [61]. This study examines the relationship between contextual factors and teachers' satisfaction by quantification of questionnaire data.

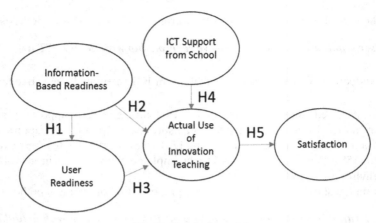

Fig. 2. Research model

3.3   Research Method

This study has two-stage analytical procedures to analyze the data from the question-naires. In the first stage, this study adopted SPSS to examine data to analyze descriptive statistics and reliability and validity. It can help us understand the structure of the sample and attributes and then examine its credibility and convergence. In the second stage, this study adopted Amos to test the hypothesis, and then examine relationships between contextual factors, and teacher satisfaction (Table 3).

Table 3. Measures

Measure dimension	Operational definition	Reference
Information-based readiness	The degree to which the teacher is ready to use ICT	[62–67]
User readiness	The degree to which the teacher is ready to use ICT to integrate into innovative teaching	[68–71]
Actual use	The degree to which the teacher's experience of using or making good use of ICT in innovative teaching is different from the traditional face-to-face teaching method in the past	[72, 73]
ICT support	The degree to which the school can integrate ICT into innovative teaching and learning and can provide the teacher with technical and information related support in the use of ICT	[74]
Satisfaction	The degree of satisfaction of the teacher's perception of knowledge acquisition, experience, sharing, and achievements in using ICT to integrate into innovative teaching	[75, 76]

4 Data Collection and Analysis

The questionnaire survey was distributed through Google forms. The period of distribution was from April 1, 2016, to June 30, 2021. The effective sample was 250. After the research data was processed, the sample analysis was executed by SPSS and AMOS, including descriptive statistical analysis, reliability analysis, validity analysis, and hypothesis testing.

4.1 Sample Characteristics

This descriptive statistical information was shown. Gender: male (69.9%) and female (30.1%); age: under 29 (0.5%), 30–34 (6.3%), 35–39 (13.6%), 40–44 (21.4%), 45–49 (17.5%), 50–54 (16.5%), 55–59 (16.5%), 60–64 (6.3%), and over 65 (1.5%); grade: Professor (26%), Associate Professor (35%), Assistant Professor (35%), and Lecturer (3%).

The high average (5.1–5.53) and low standard deviation (1.07–1.4) of experience show that the new generation is familiar with ICT since the ICT tools exist in their daily lives. The highest factor loading in the questions is ICT Support: When we integrate ICT in schools, we can get technical support (.92); When we integrate ICT in schools, we can get teaching support (.91); Information-Based Readiness: When using ICT to integrate innovative teaching, I know what resources are available (.88); I know what preparation is required to use ICT to integrate into innovative teaching (.86).

4.2 Reliability and Validity

To check reliability and validity of the questionnaire's measure, different sets of test were required. Cronbach's α and composite reliability test were used for the internal consistency. All the Cronbach's α values (.85–.96) exceed 0.7 which reflected that the variables in each construct are highly relevant.

The model analysis results are divided into two parts, including model adaptation degree and convergent validity and discriminant validity. Among them, the convergent validity is used to measure the observation variables of the same construct to confirm whether they are highly correlated with each other. In the standard value of the evaluation measurement model, the standardization residual value is too high or factor measurements with too low a load should be deleted and the standard factor load (SFL) value after normalization is retained above 0.78. Finally, the remaining 16 questions were for constructs' confirmatory factor analysis, and each question reached a significant level (P < .05). Convergent validity was evaluated using Average Variance Extracted (AVE). All the AVE values exceeded the threshold of 0.5 which reflected reasonable values.

The degree of correlation between the items of different facets should be low for discriminant validity. The square root of the AVE value of each construct correlation coefficient matrix is between 0.66 and 0.89, and the total number is greater than the correlation coefficient between the constructs. The analysis results meet the criterion; therefore, the research scale has discriminant validity. After the above model-related appraisal, the internal and external quality of the model is consistent and suitable for structural model analysis in the next phase to verify the causal relationship between potential variables.

4.3 Hypothesis Testing

This study used AMOS-SEM to examine relationship among parameters of research model and whether they fall in the rejection region (T > 1.645) of 90% confidence interval ($\alpha = .01$). The results show this model to be structurally good, based on the user readiness ($R^2 = 0.83$), actual ICT use ($R^2 = 0.72$), and satisfaction ($R^2 = 0.68$). SEM model fits are good ($x^2/df = 2.103$; GFI $= 0.909$; AGFI $= 0.868$; NFI $= 0.955$; CFI $= 0.975$; RMR $= 0.061$; RMSEA $= 0.067$).

After hypothesis testing, the following results are derived (1) Information-based Readiness has a positive effect on User Readiness. (2) Information-based Readiness has a positive effect on Actual use. (3) User Readiness has a positive effect on Actual use [61]. Actual use has a positive effect on satisfaction. Other hypotheses were not supported.

Result of hypothesis testing shown in Table 4.

Table 4. Summary results (*P < 0.1; **P < 0.05; ***P < 0.001)

	Path	Path coefficient (*p-value*)	Result
H_1	Information-based Readiness -> User Readiness	2.377(***)	Supported
H_2	Information-based Readiness -> Actual use	−0.646(0.576)	Not supported
H_3	User Readiness -> Actual use	1.061(0.026**)	Supported
H_4	ICT support -> Actual use	0.062(0.184)	Not supported
H_5	Actual use -> Satisfaction	0.898(***)	Supported

5 Findings and Discussion

Discussion of this study can be divided into three parts.

First, teachers' Information-based readiness has a positive effect on their readiness (H1) but not on actual use (H2). Past research indicated that the beliefs and attitudes of teachers towards ICT in teaching and learning have always been regarded as central criterion for successful implementation of new technologies [77]. However, with Information Communication Technology becoming more widespread, people have enough ICT skills and knowledge. That reason may cause H2 to tend to reject. The result indicated that teacher's Information-based readiness affects their attitude (H1) and usage in innovative teaching (H3). This study has shown the same results as [1], teacher's readiness and motivation will affect ICT integrated innovation teaching success and then to figure out how it forms sequential route. The result is congruent with the findings of previous research. It has shown that teachers' attitudes towards technology affect their acceptance of the usefulness of technology and its integration into teaching. Second, ICT support does not have a positive effect on actual use, this finding is incongruent with the findings of [58], and [59] that teachers do not need support for innovative teaching.

This study finds out that ICT school-related learning environment is full. Another reason is teachers do not need ICT support. They can use mobile and computer to implement innovative teaching. Hence, H4 is not supported. Third, actual use has a positive effect on satisfaction. The result is consistent with the finding of [60].

6 Conclusion

When implementation of ICT integrated innovative education becomes essential, teachers must know how to prepare and implement them. Teachers' ICT readiness, belief, and knowledge are seen as critical factors for ICT integrated innovation education success. Result has shown that if the teacher has enough ICT readiness and a high-degree of perceived usefulness, it makes them more confident in implementing ICT integrated innovative teaching in knowledge stage of innovative process [6]. When teachers have well-prepared knowledge and abilities, it will directly have positive effects on their actual use of ICT integrated innovative teaching in the persuasion stage of innovative process and satisfaction. Teacher's information-based readiness state directly affects the actual ICT use through the user's readiness state, but it has no direct effect. This shows that the more teachers are prepared to implement ICT integrated innovative teaching after they understand and know how to use these ICT-related tools, the more confidence and motivation they invoke to use ICT in innovative teaching and are satisfied with their teaching outcome. Teacher's readiness and motivation will affect ICT integrated innovation teaching success and allow students to have enough skills and knowledge to participate in the digital society.

Additionally, this study finds that ICT support-base indirectly affects teachers using ICT integrated innovative teaching, it has shown that implementing it is essential whether teachers have enough ICT-based resource or not. There is another possibility that ICT-support environment is full-resource that is enough to enable teachers to implement ICT integrated innovative teaching. There is a specific need for empirical work examining technologically-related practices in different subject areas, the role of digital technologies, external factors.

Acknowledgements. This work was supported by Ministry of Science and Technology, Taiwan, ROC, under Grant MOST105-2410-H-035-027.

References

1. Backfisch, I., et al.: Variability of teachers' technology integration in the classroom: a matter of utility! Comput. Educ. **166**, 104159 (2021)
2. Ioannou, A., Brown, S.W., Artino, A.R.: Wikis and forums for collaborative problem-based activity: a systematic comparison of learners' interactions. Internet High. Educ. **24**, 35–45 (2015)
3. Danniels, E., Pyle, A., DeLuca, C.: The role of technology in supporting classroom assessment in play-based kindergarten. Teach. Teach. Educ. **88**, 102966 (2020)
4. Dukuzumuremyi, S., Siklander, P.: Interactions between pupils and their teacher in collaborative and technology-enhanced learning settings in the inclusive classroom. Teach. Teach. Educ. **76**, 165–174 (2018)

5. Paratore, J.R., et al.: Engaging preservice teachers in integrated study and use of educational media and technology in teaching reading. Teach. Teach. Educ. **59**, 247–260 (2016)
6. Chou, C.-M., et al.: Factors influencing teachers' innovative teaching behaviour with information and communication technology (ICT): the mediator role of organisational innovation climate. Educ. Psychol. **39**(1), 65–85 (2019)
7. Scherer, R., et al.: Profiling teachers' readiness for online teaching and learning in higher education: Who's ready? Comput. Hum. Behav. **118**, 106675 (2021)
8. Chauhan, S.: A meta-analysis of the impact of technology on learning effectiveness of elementary students. Comput. Educ. **105**, 14–30 (2017)
9. Tamim, R.M., et al.: What forty years of research says about the impact of technology on learning: a second-order meta-analysis and validation study. Rev. Educ. Res. **81**(1), 4–28 (2011)
10. McCulloch, A.W., et al.: Factors that influence secondary mathematics teachers' integration of technology in mathematics lessons. Comput. Educ. **123**, 26–40 (2018)
11. Kebritchi, M., Lipschuetz, A., Santiague, L.: Issues and challenges for teaching successful online courses in higher education: a literature review. J. Educ. Technol. Syst. **46**(1), 4–29 (2017)
12. Taimalu, M., Luik, P.: The impact of beliefs and knowledge on the integration of technology among teacher educators: a path analysis. Teach. Teach. Educ. **79**, 101–110 (2019)
13. Huang, C.-Y., Wu, J.-C., Lee, S.-M.: ICT integrated in higher education: the activities, context and effects. In: PACIS (2019)
14. Hsu, S.: Developing and validating a scale for measuring changes in teachers' ICT integration proficiency over time. Comput. Educ. **111**, 18–30 (2017)
15. Zheng, L., Huang, R.: The effects of sentiments and co-regulation on group performance in computer supported collaborative learning. Internet High. Educ. **28**, 59–67 (2016)
16. Barak, M.: Closing the gap between attitudes and perceptions about ICT-enhanced learning among pre-service STEM teachers. J. Sci. Educ. Technol. **23**(1), 1–14 (2014)
17. Sayaf, A.M., et al.: Information and communications technology used in higher education: an empirical study on digital learning as sustainability. Sustainability **13**(13), 7074 (2021)
18. Kimuya, C.M., Kimani, G., Mwaura, J.: Relationship between teachers' perceptions of principals' enhancement of ICT in teaching and learning strategy and students' academic performance in public secondary schools in Nairobi City County, Kenya. Eur. J. Educ. Stud. **8**(6) (2021)
19. Chang, C.-Y., et al.: Effect sizes and research directions of peer assessments: from an integrated perspective of meta-analysis and co-citation network. Comput. Educ. **164**, 104123 (2021)
20. Larsen, D.P., et al.: Tying knots: an activity theory analysis of student learning goals in clinical education. Med. Educ. **51**(7), 687–698 (2017)
21. Westberry, N., Franken, M.: Pedagogical distance: explaining misalignment in student-driven online learning activities using activity theory. Teach. High. Educ. **20**(3), 300–312 (2015)
22. Ajjawi, R., Rees, C., Monrouxe, L.V.: Learning clinical skills during bedside teaching encounters in general practice. J. Workplace Learn. (2015)
23. Barhoumi, C.: The effectiveness of whatsapp mobile learning activities guided by activity theory on students' knowledge management. Contemp. Educ. Technol. **6**(3), 221–238 (2015)
24. Park, S., et al.: Comparing team learning approaches through the lens of activity theory. Eur. J. Train. Dev. (2013)
25. Han, J., et al.: Faculty stressors and their relations to teacher efficacy, engagement and teaching satisfaction. High. Educ. Res. Dev. 1–16 (2020)
26. Thanh Pham, T.H., Renshaw, P.: Formative assessment in Confucian heritage culture classrooms: activity theory analysis of tensions, contradictions and hybrid practices. Assess. Eval. High. Educ. **40**(1), 45–59 (2015)

27. Georg, G., et al.: Synergy between activity theory and goal/scenario modeling for requirements elicitation, analysis, and evolution. Inf. Softw. Technol. **59**, 109–135 (2015)
28. Engeström, Y.: Activity theory and individual and social transformation. Perspect. Activity Theory **19**(38), 19–30 (1999)
29. Engeström, Y.: Expansive learning at work: toward an activity theoretical reconceptualization. J. Educ. Work. **14**(1), 133–156 (2001)
30. Allen, D.K., et al.: How should technology-mediated organizational change be explained? A comparison of the contributions of critical realism and activity theory. MIS Q. 835–854 (2013)
31. White, L., Burger, K., Yearworth, M.: Understanding behaviour in problem structuring methods interventions with activity theory. Eur. J. Oper. Res. **249**(3), 983–1004 (2016)
32. Simeonova, B.: Transactive memory systems and web 2.0 in knowledge sharing: a conceptual model based on activity theory and critical realism. Inf. Syst. J. **28**(4), 592–611 (2018)
33. Karanasios, S., Allen, D.: ICT for development in the context of the closure of Chernobyl nuclear power plant: an activity theory perspective. Inf. Syst. J. **23**(4), 287–306 (2013)
34. Karanasios, S., Allen, D.K., Finnegan, P.: Activity theory in information systems research. Inf. Syst. J. **28**(3), 439–441 (2018)
35. Bower, M.: Technology-mediated learning theory. Br. J. Edu. Technol. **50**(3), 1035–1048 (2019)
36. Fehintola, J.: Teachers' characteristics as correlates of students' academic performance among secondary school students in Saki-west local government area of Oyo state. J. Educ. Soc. Res. **4**(6), 459 (2014)
37. Martin, F., Budhrani, K., Wang, C.: Examining faculty perception of their readiness to teach online. Online Learn. **23**(3), 97–119 (2019)
38. Keramati, A., Afshari-Mofrad, M., Kamrani, A.: The role of readiness factors in e-learning outcomes: an empirical study. Comput. Educ. **57**(3), 1919–1929 (2011)
39. Pettersson, F.: Understanding digitalization and educational change in school by means of activity theory and the levels of learning concept. Educ. Inf. Technol. **26**(1), 187–204 (2020). https://doi.org/10.1007/s10639-020-10239-8
40. Vanderlinde, R., Dexter, S., van Braak, J.: School-based ICT policy plans in primary education: elements, typologies and underlying processes. Br. J. Edu. Technol. **43**(3), 505–519 (2012)
41. Rogers, E.M., et al.: Complex adaptive systems and the diffusion of innovations. Innov. J. Public Sector Innov. J. **10**(3), 1–26 (2005)
42. Rogers, E.M.: Diffusion of innovations. Simon and Schuster (2003)
43. Kapoor, K.K., Dwivedi, Y.K., Williams, M.D.: Rogers' innovation adoption attributes: a systematic review and synthesis of existing research. Inf. Syst. Manag. **31**(1), 74–91 (2014)
44. Min, C., et al.: Innovation or imitation: the diffusion of citations. J. Am. Soc. Inf. Sci. **69**(10), 1271–1282 (2018)
45. Jahanmir, S.F., Cavadas, J.: Factors affecting late adoption of digital innovations. J. Bus. Res. **88**, 337–343 (2018)
46. Kim, M.J., Lee, C.-K., Contractor, N.S.: Seniors' usage of mobile social network sites: applying theories of innovation diffusion and uses and gratifications. Comput. Hum. Behav. **90**, 60–73 (2019)
47. Carreiro, H., Oliveira, T.: Impact of transformational leadership on the diffusion of innovation in firms: application to mobile cloud computing. Comput. Ind. **107**, 104–113 (2019)
48. Zhang, L., Xue, L., Zhou, Y.: How do low-carbon policies promote green diffusion among alliance-based firms in China? An evolutionary-game model of complex networks. J. Clean. Prod. **210**, 518–529 (2019)
49. Singhal, S., Anand, A., Singh, O.: Understanding multi-stage diffusion process in presence of attrition of potential market and related pricing policy. Yugoslav J. Oper. Res. **29**(3), 393–413 (2019)

50. Grover, P., Kar, A.K., Janssen, M.: Diffusion of blockchair technology: insights from academic literature and social media analytics. J. Enterp. Inf. Manag. **32**(5), 735–757 (2019)
51. Pantano, E., Vannucci, V.: Who is innovating? An exploratory research of digital technologies diffusion in retail industry. J. Retail. Consum. Serv. **49**, 297–304 (2019)
52. Vargo, S.L., Akaka, M.A., Wieland, H.: Rethinking the process of diffusion in innovation: a service-ecosystems and institutional perspective. J. Bus. Res. **116**, 526–534 (2020)
53. Margaryan, A., Littlejohn, A., Vojt, G.: Are digital natives a myth or reality? University students' use of digital technologies. Comput. Educ. **56**(2), 429–440 (2011)
54. Miranda, H.P., Russell, M.: Understanding factors associated with teacher-directed student use of technology in elementary classrooms: a structural equation modeling approach. Br. J. Edu. Technol. **43**(4), 652–666 (2012)
55. Claro, M., et al.: Teaching in a digital environment (TIDE): defining and measuring teachers' capacity to develop students' digital information and communication skills. Comput. Educ. **121**, 162–174 (2018)
56. Hamari, J., Nousiainen, T.: Why do teachers use game-based learning technologies? The role of individual and institutional ICT readiness. In: 2015 48th Hawaii International Conference on System Sciences. IEEE (2015)
57. Naylor, D., Nyanjom, J.: Educators' emotions involved in the transition to online teaching in higher education. High. Educ. Res. Dev. 1–15 (2020)
58. Uluyol, Ç., Şahin, S.: Elementary school teachers' ICT use in the classroom and their motivators for using ICT. Br. J. Edu. Technol. **47**(1), 65–75 (2016)
59. Hatlevik, O.E.: Examining the relationship between teachers' self-efficacy, their digital competence, strategies to evaluate information, and use of ICT at school. Scand. J. Educ. Res. **61**(5), 555–567 (2017)
60. Unal, Z., Unal, A.: Comparison of student performance, student perception, and teacher satisfaction with traditional versus flipped classroom models. Int. J. Instr. **10**(4), 145–164 (2017)
61. Fugate, B.S., Stank, T.P., Mentzer, J.T.: Linking improved knowledge management to operational and organizational performance. J. Oper. Manag. **27**(3), 247–264 (2009)
62. Laforet, S., Li, X.: Consumers' attitudes towards online and mobile banking in China. Int. J. Bank Mark. (2005)
63. Karjaluoto, H., Mattila, M., Pento, T.: Factors underlying attitude formation towards online banking in Finland. Int. J. Bank Mark. (2002)
64. Gardner, C., Amoroso, D.L.: Development of an instrument to measure the acceptance of internet technology by consumers. In: Proceedings of the 37th Annual Hawaii International Conference on System Sciences. IEEE (2004)
65. Hall, G.E.: Measuring stages of concern about the innovation: a manual for the use of the SoC Questionnaire (1977)
66. Khalifa, M., Cheng, S.K.: Adoption of mobile commerce: role of exposure. In: Proceedings of the Annual Hawaii International Conference on System Sciences (2002)
67. Chang, Y., Thorson, E.: Television and web advertising synergies. J. Advert. **33**(2), 75–84 (2004)
68. Rizzo, J.R., House, R.J., Lirtzman, S.I.: Role conflict and ambiguity in complex organizations. Adm. Sci. Q. 150–163 (1970)
69. Joosten, T., Cusatis, R.: Online learning readiness. Am. J. Distance Educ. **34**(3), 180–193 (2020)
70. De Freitas, S., Oliver, M.: Does E-learning policy drive change in higher education?: a case study relating models of organisational change to e-learning implementation. J. High. Educ. Policy Manag. **27**(1), 81–96 (2005)
71. Tyagi, P.K.: Relative importance of key job dimensions and leadership behaviors in motivating salesperson work performance. J. Mark. **49**(3), 76–86 (1985)

72. Liao, H.-L., Lu, H.-P.: The role of experience and innovation characteristics in the adoption and continued use of e-learning websites. Comput. Educ. **51**(4), 1405–1416 (2008)
73. Hernandez, B., et al.: The role of social motivations in e-learning: how do they affect usage and success of ICT interactive tools? Comput. Hum. Behav. **27**(6), 2224–2232 (2011)
74. Vanderlinde, R., van Braak, J.: A new ICT curriculum for primary education in Flanders: defining and predicting teachers' perceptions of innovation attributes. J. Educ. Technol. Soc. **14**(2), 124–135 (2011)
75. Lin, W.-S.: Perceived fit and satisfaction on web learning performance: IS continuance intention and task-technology fit perspectives. Int. J. Hum. Comput. Stud. **70**(7), 498–507 (2012)
76. Dağhan, G., Akkoyunlu, B.: Modeling the continuance usage intention of online learning environments. Comput. Hum. Behav. **60**, 198–211 (2016)
77. Eickelmann, B., Vennemann, M.: Teachers 'attitudes and beliefs regarding ICT in teaching and learning in European countries. Eur. Educ. Res. J. **16**(6), 733–761 (2017)

Industry 4.0

Google Big Data Trend Index Analysis of Industry 4.0 Technologies: Technology and Key Concept Trends of Global Landscape in 2004–2021

Jari Kaivo-oja[1,2]([✉]), Teemu Santonen[3], Theresa Lauraëus[1],
and Mikkel Stein Knudsen[1]

[1] Finland Futures Research Centre, Turku School of Economics, University of Turku, Turku, Finland
{jari.kaivo-oja,mikkel.knudsen}@utu.fi,
theresa.lauraeus@aalto.fi
[2] Kazimieras Simonavičius University (KSU), Vilnius, Lithuania
[3] Laurea University of Applied Sciences, Espoo, Finland
teemu.santonen@laurea.fi

Abstract. In this article, we analyse Google trends of Industry 4.0 technologies and key concepts. This study provides global landscape analysis of Industry 4.0 technologies and two key concepts, digital transformation and business transformation in years 2004–2021. The study reports key trends of Google Trends database. To understand (1) the importance of key technology trends and (2) interactions of key Industry 4.0 trends, empirical Big Data study reports correlation analysis and ranking analyses of Industry 4.0 technologies for years 2005, 2010, 2015 and 2021. The study covers nine technology domains of Industry 4.0 technologies: Big Data and AI analytics, Horizontal and Vertical Integration, Cloud computing, Augmented and Virtual Reality (AR-VR), Industrial Internet of Things (IIoT), (6) Additive manufacturing/3D/4D printing, Robotics, Autonomous robots or/and collaborative robots, Simulation/digital twins, Cybersecurity and Blockchain technology.

Keywords: Industry 4.0 · Google trends · Big Data · Trend analysis · Global landscape · Pyramid method of trend and foresight analyses

1 Introduction

In this study, we examine the global interest of Industry 4.0 technologies based on Big Data of Google Trends database. A historical turning point in Industry 4.0 discussions was year 2011, when the concept of Industry 4.0 ("Industrial Internet") was presented to the public at Hannover Messe, Germany. The concept of Industry 4.0 has become one of the key topics in intelligent manufacturing and digital transformation process. Within the industry, digitization of production processes is on everyone's lips. In Fig. 1 there are basic variants of data analytics of quantitative and qualitative methods. This study

© Springer Nature Switzerland AG 2022
L. Uden et al. (Eds.): KMO 2022, CCIS 1593, pp. 193–206, 2022.
https://doi.org/10.1007/978-3-031-07920-7_15

can be classified as a qualitative study based on mass data. In the field of technology foresight both quantitative and qualitative methods are widely applied [1].

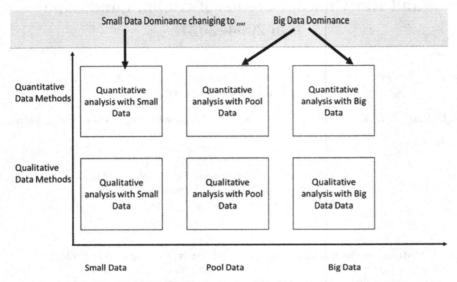

Fig. 1. Big Data and quantitative and qualitative scientific methods [2].

2   Google Trends of Industry 4.0 Technologies and Digitalization Concepts

Industry 4.0 technologies can be listed by following different criteria often leading on nine to twelve technology pillars [3–7] including (1) Big Data and AI analytics, (2) Horizontal and Vertical Integration, (3) Cloud computing, (4) Augmented and Virtual Reality (AR-VR), (5) Industrial Internet of Things (IIoT), (6) Additive manufacturing/3D/4D printing, (7) Robotics, Autonomous robots or/and collaborative robots, (8) Simulation/digital twins, (9) Cybersecurity and (10) Blockhain technology. In this study we analyse these Industry 4.0 technology trends as well as the two key concepts of digitalization: digital transformation and business transformation. We also separate the analysis of industrial internet of things (IIoT) IIoT to Internet of Things (IoT) and Internet of Services (IoS) (see Fig. 2). Google Trends data is utilized as a data source [8]. As a result, this study can be seen as a study about innovation system foresight [9, 10] or future-oriented technology analysis [11, 12], but this study is also an industrial history research [13].

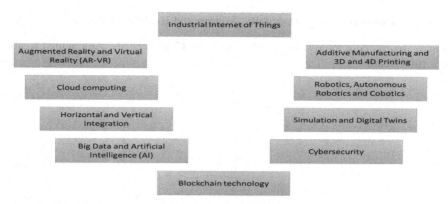

Fig. 2. Ten key Industry 4.0 trends and two key concepts of transformation.

2.1 Digital Transformation and Business Transformation

In Fig. 3 we report Google Trends for Big Data, Artificial Intelligence, Industrial Horizontal Integration and Industrial Vertical Integration. Figure 3 shows us how global interest in Big Data has boomed strongly after 2013 and how interest in Artificial Intelligence (AI) started to boom in 2016. Interest in AI was strong already in 2004–2005, but it decreased in 2006. Interest in AI increased again in 2017. Global interest in Industrial Horizontal and Vertical integration has been on a lower level excluding few spikes at the early years.

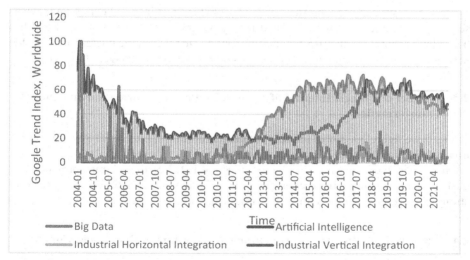

Fig. 3. Global interest in Big Data, Artificial Intelligence, Industrial Horizontal Integration and Industrial Vertical Integration [8].

2.2 Cloud Computing, Cybersecurity, Augmented Reality, Virtual Reality

In Fig. 4 we compare interest in Cloud computing, Cybersecurity, Augmented Reality and Virtual Reality.

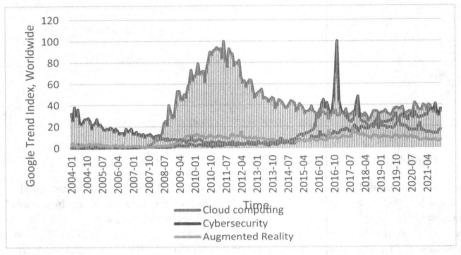

Fig. 4. Global interest in Cloud computing, Cybersecurity, Augmented Reality and Virtual Reality [8].

In Fig. 4. we can see long-run trends of global interest in cloud computing, cyber-security, augmented reality and virtual reality. In 2004–2021 the strongest trend has been cloud computing. In 2015 cybersecurity started to raise public interest in the global networks. Interest in augmented and virtual reality have been stronger after 2016.

2.3 Internet of Things, Internet of Service, Digital Transformation and Digital Transformation

In Fig. 5 we figure out global interest in Internet of Things, Internet of Service, Digital transformation and Digital transformation.

In Fig. 5 we can observe key Google trends of IoT, IoS, digital transformation and business transformation. Internet of Things and digital transformation are together very strong trends compared to Internet of Services and business transformation.

2.4 Additive Manufacturing, 3D Printing, 4D Printing, Robotics and Cobotics

In Fig. 6 we report Google Trends for Additive Manufacturing, 3D Printing, 4D Printing, Robotics and Cobotics (collaborative robotics).

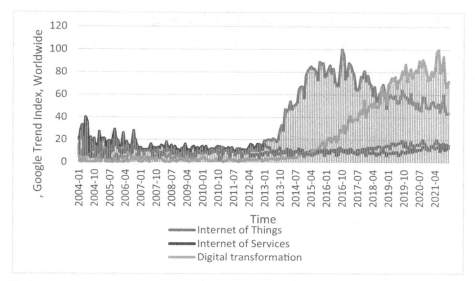

Fig. 5. Global interest in Internet of Things, Internet of Service, Digital transformation and Digital transformation [8]

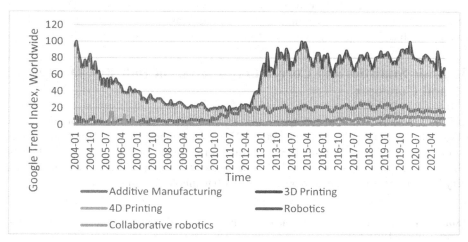

Fig. 6. Global interest Additive Manufacturing, 3D Printing, 4D Printing, Robotics and Cobotics [8]

In Fig. 6 we have reported global trends in interest to Additive Manufacturing, 3D Printing, 4D Printing, Robotics and Cobotics. We can observe that Google Trend of 3D Printing is the strongest trend in Fig. 6. Robotics has been a strong trend in 2004–2010 but now it is quite stable trend. 4D Printing and Collaborative robotics are quite weak trends, but have potential to be stronger trends in the future.

2.5 Digital Twin, Simulation and Blockchain Technology

In Fig. 7 we report Google Trends for Digital Twin, Simulation and Blockchain technology.

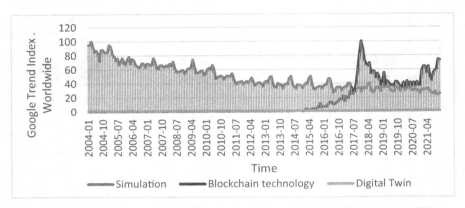

Fig. 7. Global interest in Digital Twin, Simulation and Blockchain technology [8]

In Fig. 7 we can observe three Industry 4.0 trends of Simulation, Digital Twin and Blockchain. Interest in simulation has been decreasing, but interest in Blockchain technology has dramatically increased since 2015 reaching peak level in Dec 2017.

3 Basic Statistics and Correlation Analysis of Industry 4.0 Trends and Concepts

In Table 1 we have reported average, minimum, maximum, range and standard deviation of Google Trend index numbers in 2004–2021. The strongest Google Trends are Simulation (mean 48.5), 3D Printing (43.2), Artificial Intelligence (37.6), Internet of Things (33.5) Cloud computing (average 34.7) and Big Data (average 31.2). There have been very big variances of interest in the Industry 4.0 technologies and concepts.

Table 1. Mean, minimum, maximum, range and standard deviation of Google Trend index numbers in 2004–2021 [8]

Name	Mean	Min	Max	Range	Std. Dev.
1. Simulation	48.5	24.0	100.0	76.0	18.1
2. 3D Printing	43.2	1.0	100.0	99.0	36.0
3. Artificial Intelligence	37.6	15.0	100.0	85.0	17.5
4. Cloud computing	34.7	0.0	100.0	100.0	25.4
5. Internet of Things	33.5	0.0	100.0	100.0	29.5

(continued)

Table 1. (*continued*)

Name	Mean	Min	Max	Range	Std. Dev.
6. Big Data	31.2	1.0	73.0	72.0	26.7
7. Robotics	27.8	15.0	100.0	85.0	16.1
8. Digital transformation	21.9	0.0	100.0	100.0	29.9
9. Virtual Reality	16.1	4.0	100.0	96.0	12.1
10. Blockchain technology	14.1	0.0	100.0	100.0	22.9
11. Internet of Services	11.5	4.0	40.0	36.0	4.5
12. Business Transformation	11.1	2.0	33.0	31.0	4.7
13. Cybersecurity	9.4	0.0	40.0	40.0	10.6
14. Augmented Reality	7.3	0.8	18.0	17.3	3.7
15. Industrial Vertical Integration,	5.6	0.0	100.0	100.0	11.1
16. Additive manufacturing	3.8	0.0	12.0	12.0	3.7
17. Industrial Horizontal Integ,	2.9	0.0	32.0	32.0	4.4
18. Collaborative robotics	1.0	0.0	15.0	15.0	2.0
19. Digital Twin	0.8	0.8	1.0	0.3	0.1
20. 4D Printing	0.6	0.0	2.0	2.0	0.5

In Table 2 we have reported median statistics of Industry 4.0 statistics in 2004–2020 and 2011–2021. This table clearly shows the power of Industry 4.0 trends before experts started to talk about Industry 4.0 revolution in 2011. There was clear change in key trends and in power of trends. Table 2 verifies this kind of interesting finding.

Table 2. Median Google Trend Index (GTI) in 2004–2010 and in 2011–2021 ranked based on change

Name	2004–2010	2011–2021	Change
3D Printing	5.0	76.0	71.0
Big Data	4.0	56.0	52.0
Internet of Things	6.0	54.0	48.0
Cloud computing	0.9	36.0	35.1
Digital transformation	1.0	22.0	21.0
Blockchain technology	0.0	12.0	12.0
Cybersecurity	1.0	11.5	10.5
Augmented Reality	2.5	9.0	6.5

(*continued*)

Table 2. (*continued*)

Name	2004–2010	2011–2021	Change
Additive manufacturing	0.0	6.0	6.0
Industrial Vertical Integration	0.0	4.5	4.5
Virtual Reality	12.0	16.0	4.0
Artificial Intelligence	28.0	31.0	3.0
Industrial Horizontal Integration	0.0	3.0	3.0
4D printing	0.0	1.0	1.0
Collaborative robotics	0.0	1.0	1.0
Digital Twin	0.8	0.8	0.0
Business transformation	10.0	10.0	0.0
Internet of Services	11.5	10.0	−1.5
Robotics	31.5	20.0	−11.5
Simulation	66.0	35.0	−31.0

How Industry 4.0 and key concepts are correlated and ranked? In Appendix 1 Tables 4 and 5 we report the Kendall rank correlation coefficients, commonly referred to as Kendall's τ coefficient (after the Greek letter τ, tau). Furthermore, in Table 4, Industry 4.0 technologies correlation with running quarter is presented to evaluate Industry 4.0 developments in 2004–2021. Kendall coefficients are statistics used to measure the ordinal association between two measured quantities [14, 15]. A τ test is a non-parametric hypothesis test for statistical dependence based on the τ coefficient. The Kendall rank coefficient is normally used as a test statistic in a statistical hypothesis test to establish whether two variables may be regarded as statistically dependent. This test is non-parametric, as it does not rely on any assumptions on the distributions of X or Y or the distribution of (X,Y). This is a reason why we apply this methodological choice.

Table 3. Kendall's tau b and running quarter

Industry 4.0 technology	Mean
1. Simulation	−0.896**
2. 3D Printing	0.671**
3. Artificial Intelligence	
4. Cloud computing	
5. Internet of Things	0.612**
6. Big Data	0.631**
7. Robotics	−0.509**

(*continued*)

Table 3. (*continued*)

Industry 4.0 technology	Mean
8. Digital transformation	0.727**
9. Virtual Reality	
10. Blockchain technology	0.757**
11. Internet of Services	−0.424**
12. Business transformation	
13. Cybersecurity	0.879**
14. Augmented Reality	0.321**
15. Industrial Vertical Integ,	0.210*
16. Additive manufacturing	0.826**
17. Industrial Horizontal Integ,	0.409**
18. Collaborative Robotics	0.429**
19. Digital Twin	
20. 4D Printing	0.569**

**Correlation is significant at the 0.01 level (2-tailed).
*Correlation is significant at the 0.05 level (2-tailed).

Key findings of Kendall correlation analyses are:

1. Industry 4.0 technologies are both negatively and positively correlated and the results can now be seen in detail in this paper. Key result is that there is are not clear Win-Win setup between all the Industry 4.0 technologies and concepts, at least when we study Google Trend index data. Because of both positive and negative correlations, we can expect that some kind of complex technological disruption can be assumed to be final outcome in the global economy.
2. Digital transformation is strongly correlated relative to many Industry4.0 technologies, while business transformation is statistically significantly correlated only with two variables (Digital Twin and Cobotics). Big Data indicates that digital transformation is stronger than business transformation.
3. Artificial Intelligence (AI) is positively correlated for many 4.0 variables but not for cloud computing, which is quite a surprising result.
4. Blockchain correlations are very interesting and raise a lot of further research needs, because both strong negative and positive correlation occur simultaneously. We can note that Blockchain technology is a very disruptive technology.
5. Internet of Services is mainly negatively correlated with most 4.0 technologies, only Digital Twin has a positive correlation. This finding is one of the most interesting results.

6. The correlations of Cybersecurity are really interesting and positive correlations occur with Augmented Reality, Industrial Vertical Integration, Industrial Horizontal Integration, Additive Manufacturing, Collaborative Robotics and 4D Printing.

7. Digital Twin is a disruptive technology because both strong positive and negative correlation coefficients occur. Highest positive statistically significant correlation coefficient for business transformation, which may predict a big turnaround, if Digital Twin Web will be developed in the future.

8. We can note that simulation has strong negative correlations with Blockchain technology and Additive Manufacturing. 3D Printing has strong positive correlation with Big Data, Artificial Intelligence has quite strong positive correlations with Business transformation and Virtual Reality, but negative correlation with Cloud computing, Cloud computing is negatively corrected with many variables, only positive correlations is with Augmented reality and Industrial horizontal integration, Internet of Things is very strongly positively correlated with Big Data, Big Data is positively correlated with Blockchain technology, Cybersecurity, Additive Manufacturing, 4D Printing and Digital transformation, Robotics is quite negatively correlated with Cybersecurity, Digital transformation is very strongly positively correlated with Blockchain technology, Cybersecurity and Additive Manufacturing. Virtual reality have two slightly positively correlated with Blockchain Technology and Business transformation, Blockchain technology is very strongly positively correlated with Cybersecurity and Additive Manufacturing, Internet of services have many negative correlations and only one positive correlation with Digital Twin, Business transformation have two positive correlations, with Collaborative robotics and Digital Twin, Cybersecurity has very strong correlation with Additive Manufacturing and weaker correlation with 4D Printing, Augmented reality is not very strongly positively correlated with other Industry 4.0 technologies and concepts, but middle-range positive correlation was found with Industrial Horizontal integration, Industrial vertical integration is not having strong positive or negative correlations, but middle-range positive correlation was found with Industrial horizontal integration, Collaborative robotics has very low positive correlation with 4D Printing, Digital Twin has weak positive correlation with 4D Printing.

In Fig. 8 we report the key results concerning Google Trend index results in yearly time points of 2005, 2010, 2015, 2020 and 2021 [8].

New technologies do never emerge from vacuum [16–20]. This empirical study with Big Data, confirms the general perception that the use of technologies is directly and indirectly linked to each other. This study confirms this kind of basic strong hypothesis of interlinked and complex technological development.

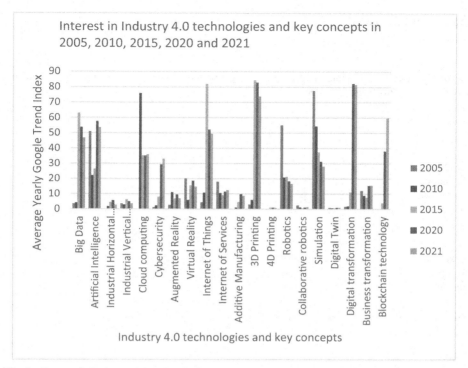

Fig. 8. Interest in Industry 4.0 technologies and key concepts in 2005, 2010, 2015, 2020 and 2021 [8]

4   Conclusions

Based on the Jan2004-Dec 2021 statistics [8] this article presents a variety of trend analyses of concepts and Industry 4.0 technologies. In this article we do not repeat details of previous Google trend analyses. Results are reported in the chapter 3. A general result of this explorative empirical study is that Industry 4.0 transformation is not a linear process. Industry 4.0 development process seems to be complex or partly complicated process where technology developments and global interest levels in technologies are counter-cyclical. Both statistically significant positive and negative correlations can be found. Interest in Industry 4.0 technologies has fluctuated sharply over the period under review in years 2004–2021. Some kind of historical turning point was year 2011, when the concept of Industry 4.0 ("Industrial Internet") was presented to the public at in Hannover Messe, Germany. We can state that with regard to the future assessment of the industrial Internet and the development of the industry 4.0 technology waves, it is necessary to continue a more detailed analysis of the trends in Industry 4.0.

Acknowledgments. Authors gratefully acknowledge new technologies financial support from the Research Council of Lithuania (LMTLT) and the European Regional Development Fund implementing the project "Platforms of Big Data Foresight (PLATBIDAFO)" (project No 01.2.2-LMT-K-718-02-0019).

Appendix 1: Table 3

Table 4. Kendall correlation analysis of Industry 4.0 technologies and key concepts. (Source: Google Trends 2021, Jan 2004-Dec 2021).

Industry 4.0 technology	1	2	3	4	5	6	7	8	9	10
1. Simulation										
2. 3D Printing	−.61**									
3. Artificial Intelligence										
4. Cloud computing		.19*	−.43**							
5. Internet of Things	−.61**	.69**								
6. Big Data	−.61**	.72**			.83**					
7. Robotics	.54**	−.29**	.30**	−.51**	−.31**	−.22*				
8. Digital transformation	−.65**	.57**	.36**		.47**	.50**	−.25**			
9. Virtual Reality			.66**	−.50**	.23*	.26**	.29**	.29**		
10. Blockchain technology	−.72**	.56**	.43**		.56**	.61**	−.26*	.74**	.42**	
11. Internet of Services	.42**	−.38**			−.43**	−.47**	.23*	−.29**		−.40**
12. Business transformation			.61**	−.40**			.24*	.28**	.43**	.30**
13. Cybersecurity	−.80**	.65**	.22*		.62**	.62**	−.41**	.73**		.75**
14. Augmented Reality	−.32**	.30**		.42**	.38**	.37**	−.24*	.24*		.32**
15. Industrial Vertical Integ,	−.20*	.34**			.35**	.36**				.24*
16. Additive Manufacturing	−.75**	.69**	.27**		.63**	.65**	−.36**	.72**		.73**
17. Industrial Horizontal Integ,	−.41**	.43**		.24*	.42**	.42**		.26**		.37**
18. Collaborative robotics	−.39**	.35**	.26**		.38**	.43**		.36**	.24*	.50**
19. Digital Twin			.49**	−.36**	−.30**	−.24*	.27*		.26*	
20. 4D Printing	−.57**	.62**			.64**	.60**	−.35**	.42**		.52**

** Correlation is significant at the 0.01 level (2-tailed)
* Correlation is significant at the 0.05 level (2-tailed)

Table 5. Kendall correlation analysis of Industry 4.0 technologies and key concepts. (Source: Google Trends 2021, Jan 2004-Dec 2021).

Industry 4.0 technology	11	12	13	14	15	16	17	18	19
13. Cybersecurity	−.36**								
14. Augmented Reality	−.31**		.39**						
15. Industrial Vertical Integ,			.21*	.25*					
16. Additive Manufacturing	−.40**		.81**	.35**	.27**				
17. Industrial Horizontal Integ,	−.21*		.40**	.40**	.50**	.41**			
18. Collaborative robotics	−.34**	.25*	.44**	.36**		.45**			
19. Digital Twin	.40**	.55**		−.30**					
20. 4D Printing	−.41**		.56**	.30**	.30**	.55**	.37**	.26*	−.31**

**Correlation is significant at the 0.01 level (2-tailed)
*Correlation is significant at the 0.05 level (2-tailed)

References

1. Haegeman, K., Marinelli, E., Scapolo, F., Ricci, A., Sokolov, A.: Quantitative and qualitative approaches in future-oriented technology analysis (FTA): from combination to integration? Technol. Forecast. Soc. Change Future-Orient. Technol. Anal. **80**, 386–397 (2013). https://doi.org/10.1016/j.techfore.2012.10.002
2. Kaivo-oja, J.: Big Data Classification for Foresight Research. Finland Futures Research Centre. Turku School of Economics. University of Turku, Turku (2021)
3. Strange, R., Zucchella, A.: Industry 4.0, global value chains and international business. Multinatl. Bus. Rev. **25**(3), 174–184 (2017). https://doi.org/10.1108/MBR-05-2017-0028
4. Dachs, B., Kinkel, S., Jäger, A.: Bringing it all back home? Backshoring of manufacturing activities and the adoption of Industry 4.0 technologies. J. World Bus. **54**(6), 101017 (2019). https://doi.org/10.1016/j.jwb.2019.101017
5. Daim, T., Lai, K.K., Yalcin, H., Alsoubie, F., Kumar, V.: Forecasting technological positioning through technology knowledge redundancy: patent citation analysis of IoT, cybersecurity, and blockchain. Technol. Forecast. Soc. Change. **161**, 120329 (2020). https://doi.org/10.1016/j.techfore.2020.120329
6. De Reuver, M., Sørensen, C., Basole, R.C.: The digital platform: a research agenda. J. Inf. Technol. **33**(2), 124–135 (2018). https://doi.org/10.1057/s41265-016-0033-3
7. Duman, M.C., Akdemir, B.: A study to determine the effects of industry 4.0 technology components on organizational performance. Technol. Forecast. Soc. Change. **167**(June), 120615 (2021). https://doi.org/10.1016/j.techfore.2021.120615
8. Google: Google Trends 2021 Data. Data from Jan 2004-Dec 2021 (2021). https://trends.google.com. Accessed 17 Apr 2022

9. Andersen, A.D., Andersen, P.D.: Innovation system foresight. Technol. Forecast. Soc. Change **88**, 276–286 (2014). https://doi.org/10.1016/j.techfore.2014.06.016

10. Culot, G., Orzes, G., Sartor, M., Nassimbeni, G.: The future of manufacturing: a Delphi-based scenario analysis on Industry 4.0. Technol. Forecast. Soc. Change. **157**, 120092 (2020). https://doi.org/10.1016/j.techfore.2020.120092

11. Cagnin, C., Havas, A., Saritas, O.: Future-oriented technology analysis: its potential to address disruptive transformations. Technol. Forecast. Soc. Change. **80**, 379–385 (2013). https://doi.org/10.1016/j.techfore.2012.10.001

12. Ramos, J., Mansfield, T., Priday, G.: Foresight in a Network Era: Peer-Producing Alternative. Futures. Journal of Future Studies **17**(1), 71–90 (2012)

13. Büchi, G., Cugno, M., Castagnoli, R.: Smart factory performance and Industry 4.0. Technol. Forecast. Soc. Change. **150**, 119790 (2020). https://doi.org/10.1016/j.techfore.2019.119790

14. Kendall, M.: A new measure of rank correlation. Biometrika **30**(1–2), 81–89 (1938)

15. Daniel, W.W.: Kendall's tau. Applied Nonparametric Statistics (2nd edn.), pp. 365–377. PWS-Kent, Boston (1990)

16. Pickover, C.A.: From Medieval Robots to Neural Networks. Artificial Intelligence. An Illustrated History. Sterling, New York (2019)

17. Parker, G., Van Alstyne, M.W.: Innovation, openness, and platform control. Manage. Sci. **64**(7), 3015–3032 (2018)

18. Nath, S.V., Dunkin, A., Chowdhary, M., Patel, N.: Industrial Digital Transformation. Accelerate Digital Transformation with Business Optimization, AI, and Industry 4.0. Pact, Birmingham and Mumbai (2020)

19. Jaskó, S., Skrop, A., Holczinger, T., Chovan, T., Abonyi, J.: Development of manufacturing execution systems in accordance with Industry 4.0 requirements: a review of standard- and ontology-based methodologies and tools. Comput. Indust. **123**, 103300 (2020)

20. Varghese, A., Tandur, D.: "Wireless requirements and challenges in Industry 4.0". In: 2014 International Conference on Contemporary Computing and Informatics (IC3I), pp. 634–638 (2014)

Key Variables for the Implementation of Industry 4.0 in the Colombian Service Sector

Cristhian Naranjo and Luz Rodríguez[✉]

Faculty of Engineering, Industrial Engineering Program, Universidad Distrital Francisco José de Caldas, Bogotá D.C, Colombia
crdnaranjom@correo.udistrital.edu.co,
larodriguezr@udistrital.edu.co

Abstract. This document presents a review of variables that affect the implementation of Industry 4.0 in Colombian service SMEs. This through review of related scientific articles and the collection of first-hand information through surveys applied to service companies. A total of 12 key variables were proposed, which cover implementation strategies, investment, used technologies, leadership, and culture, among others. Then, through the application of the surveys, 100 responses were obtained from local companies, which made it possible to visualize an approximate behavior of these variables, not only for SMEs, but large companies also participated in these surveys. This allowed a comparison between SMEs and large companies (LC), for example, the leadership and culture necessary to implement industry 4.0 in these companies is stronger in smaller companies. Also, the investment levels in proportion to their net profits are similar between both types of companies. In general, great potential is seen in the implementation of industry 4.0 in Colombian service SMEs.

Keywords: Industry 4.0 · Readiness · Key variables · Implementation · SMEs

1 Introduction

The fourth industrial revolution, also known as Industry 4.0 (I4.0), includes technologies such as Artificial Intelligence, Big Data, Cloud Computing, Internet of Things, among others, that increase automation and connectivity in production processes [1]. The use of these new tools requires, in the first instance, that companies carry out a digital transformation of information and procedures, too, for example, have inventory data in the cloud and allow the internet of things to start with production batches. This implies an understanding of the characteristics of new technologies and how to coordinate them with existing activities within the company. In general, it represents a challenge due to the acquisition cost and the sufficient knowledge to do it properly [2].

For micro, small, and medium enterprises (SMEs), venturing into I4.0 represents a higher level of complexity, given the lack of knowledge to implement these new technologies and ensure that the investment is profitable [3]. It is important to highlight that SMEs have a great weight in the Colombian economy, since they represent more

© Springer Nature Switzerland AG 2022
L. Uden et al. (Eds.): KMO 2022, CCIS 1593, pp. 207–218, 2022.
https://doi.org/10.1007/978-3-031-07920-7_16

than 90% of the companies [4], they generate around 35% of the GDP and 80% of the country's employment [5]. Specifically, the services industry, according to the Annual Survey of Services (EAS), carried out by the National Administrative Department of Statistics (DANE) in 2019, generated approximately COP 105.470 billion [5]. This same report highlights the increase in the operating income of the subsectors of services such as Call Centers, Production, distribution, and exhibition of cinematographic films, Development of computer systems and data processing, and Messaging services, which were 22%, 12 0.4%, 12.2%, and 9.7% respectively [5]. Considering the weight of SMEs and the growth of the service industry in the local economy, it was thought to study the conditions and opportunities to implement I4.0 in Colombian companies, considering the different adversities they face in this process. This through a review of related scientific articles and the search for first-hand information through surveys applied to companies in the service sector. This is intended to achieve an approximation of the status of these variables in the Colombian service industry, which could serve as a point of reference for further studies.

2   Methodology

The collection of information on key aspects for the development of Industry 4.0 was carried out through a systematic search in articles, conferences, books, and reports. The databases selected were Scopus, Web of Science, ScienceDirect and Google Scholar. To find relevant publications on I4.0 implementation, search equations were developed with the following terms: Industry 4.0 readiness; Industry 4.0 AND readiness OR assessment OR key indicators; and Industry 4.0 implementation. Table 1 shows the search results:

Table 1. Search results

Database	Found	Relevant	Not repeated
Scopus	55	15	4
Web of Science	63	14	2
Science Direct	37	6	1
Google Scholar	29	6	3

As a criterion to define relevant articles, those that were specific to a single type of industry or did not make a proposal of key variables were discarded. Some articles had occurrences in two or more databases and were therefore only counted once. In total, 10 reference articles were selected for the construction of the key variables.

With this, a comparison of the common variables established by the different authors was made. The proposed variables and the authors who reference them in their research are shown below:

Table 2. Key variables mentioned in papers.

Variable	Reder & Klünder [6]	Pérez et al. [7]	Leyh et al. [8]	Rojko [9]	Gökalp et al. [10]	Klötzer & Pflauml [11]	Erol, et al. [12]	Charbonneau & Gamache [13]	Brozzi et al. [14]	Angreani et al. [15]
Use of 4.0 technologies in service provision	x	x	x	x	x	x	x	x	x	x
Knowledge of collaborators	x			x	x	x	x	x	x	x
Customer data analysis		x		x		x		x		x
Cohesion between areas of the company	x	x	x		x	x	x			
Investment in I4.0	x						x	x		
Strategy	x	x		x	x		x		x	x
Leadership and culture	x	x		x	x	x	x	x		x
Cybersecurity		x	x					x	x	
Information exchange within the value chain	x	x	x	x		x	x	x		

In addition to the variables shown in Table 2, additional ones are proposed to de-scribe the relevant aspects in consideration of the effects of COVID-19 and the limitations of the territory. The pandemic potentiated e-commerce due to restrictions on face-to-face activities. In this sense, digital sales and customer service are considered key due to the growing demand for services from connected platforms on the web [16]. The new reality requires dynamic, fast, and functional sales models at any time of the day [17]. In relation to I4.0, not having web platforms for sales and customer service would limit the potential use of technologies such as AI, IoT and Big data to achieve greater personalization of the service provided, reducing the ability to satisfy the customer.

The second to consider is the quality of the ICT connection, this corresponds to the deficiencies of the speed, regularity, and coverage of the Internet connection in the territory [18]. The intermittent network connection can affect the workflow in SMEs, generating limitations in the use of new technologies. Finally, the third variable to consider is the Governance of the information, this satisfies the regulatory requirements of the state in terms of data protection of service consumers. Its ignorance or non-compliance could generate pecuniary sanctions and stoppage of activities [19]. Table 3 shows the 9 variables identified in the scientific articles and the 3 additional variables mentioned above. The order of these variables does not correspond to a specific weighting or valuation, only the variables are shown to facilitate their identification in the subsequent analysis.

Table 3. Key variables description.

No	Variable
V1	Use of 4.0 technologies in service provision
V2	Knowledge of collaborators
V3	Customer data analysis
V4	Cohesion between areas of the company
V5	Investment in I4.0
V6	Strategy
V7	Leadership and culture
V8	Cybersecurity
V9	Information exchange within the value chain
V10	Digital sales and customer service
V11	ICT connection quality
V12	Information governance

As shown in Table 2, V1 is the most cited variable in the publications. This is due to the importance of considering which are the 4.0 technologies that have a greater im-pact on the operation of companies [13]. Next, the importance of promoting digital thinking is shown, encompassing the use of ICT and knowledge of new technologies (V2), all supported by the leadership and culture (V7) that the company develops to make the implementation effective. from I4.0 [10]. Likewise, the need to start the innovation process through a roadmap and internal architecture that allows techno-logical development (V4 and V6) is highlighted, which subsequently generates better participation in the value chain (V9), resulting in an increase in the competitiveness of the company. The other variables shown in Table 3 will be analyzed in the results section.

To approximate the state of the key variables in Colombian companies, a digital survey of 19 questions was designed and sent. The collection of information was carried out in 2021, where responses were obtained from 100 companies in the ser-vice sector. In this sense, what is offered in this paper approximates what the behavior of the variables identified in service SMEs in Colombia could be, approximately 6,610 service companies in total.

3 Results

The first variable, V1, shows which are the 4.0 technologies most used by SMEs and LC. As Table 4 shows, cloud computing is the most popular technology for SMEs. In the case of LC, the IoT has participation close to 100% indicating greater automation in these companies. A big difference is the use of Big Data, in SMEs it only corresponds to 55%, while for LC it represents 83%.

Table 4. Key variable V1.

Technology	SMEs	LC
IoT	85%	96%
Big Data	55%	83%
Collaborative robots (drones, robotic arms, mobile robots)	30%	25%
Machine maintenance prediction using artificial intelligence	6%	6%
Virtual agents (chatbots)	36%	40%
A Visual image or video recognition	60%	68%
Voice recognition	28%	60%
Word processing (NPL)	11%	15%
cloud computing	89%	83%
Object design using CAD/CAM/3D design applications	26%	25%
ERP systems	72%	85%
None	4%	0%

Regarding the knowledge of employees for the use of technologies (V2), as shown in Table 5, at least 96% of them can use ICT, both in SMEs and in LC. However, the knowledge required for the use of 4.0 technologies decreased to 51% and 32% respectively. On the other hand, the analysis of demand and consumption trends (V3) differs by 7 percentage points between SMEs and LC. The third variant in this table indicates that high cooperation between the different areas of the company (V4) occurs in 57% of SMEs and 19% in LC. An important requirement is evidenced by LC in the development of strategies to optimize collaboration between areas of the company.

Table 5. Key variable V2-V4.

Variables		SMEs	LC
V2	More than half of the employees in the company have the necessary knowledge for the use of ICT and use of 4.0 technologies	51%	32%
	Less than half of the company's employees have the necessary knowledge to use ICT and some systems for data processing	45%	68%
	No presence of employees with the necessary knowledge to handle ICT	4%	0%
V3	Analysis of demand and consumption trends is carried out in the company	57%	64%
V4	High cooperation between the areas of the company for the provision of the service	53%	19%
	The company is developing strategies regarding the improvement of communication and cooperation between its areas	45%	75%
	In the company, there is constant conflict between several of its areas, which has made it difficult to provide the service	2%	6%

In Table 6, 45% and 47% of SMEs and LC have made an investment in I4.0 (V5), higher than 20% of the net profits of the last year of the companies. Although most companies, 59% of SMEs and 66% of LC, are in a strategic planning phase or in an early phase of implementation of I4.0 (V6).

Most SMEs and LC, in Table 7, report acceptable leadership and culture (V7), 45% and 36% respectively. Next, 34% of SMEs have a regular or scarce leadership and culture, while for LC these categories represent 44%. It is important to highlight that this variable considers the level of impact and leading knowledge of this process.

As protection strategies against cyber-attacks (V8), Table 8, the use of antivirus and periodic maintenance of equipment are the most used in companies in general. On the other hand, 42% of LC conduct research on new cyber-attack models while only 28% of SMEs do so.

Table 6. Key variable V5-V6.

Variables		SMEs	LC
V5	Investment in I4.0 of more than 20% of the net profits resulting from the financial year in the last year	45%	47%
	Investment in I4.0 from 5% to 20% of the net profits resulting from the financial year in the last year	28%	34%
	Investment in I4.0 of less than 5% of net profits resulting from the financial year in the last year	28%	19%
V6	I4.0 implementation strategy developed almost entirely, and results are closely monitored	9%	4%
	Strategy under development, several of the activities planned for the implementation of I4.0 have been carried out and the first results have been analyzed	21%	13%
	Early phase, some activities to implement the strategy have been carried out, but the results have not been studied	19%	21%
	Strategy planning, diagnoses were carried out to identify implementation opportunities	40%	45%
	It is not planned to develop any I4.0 implementation strategy	11%	17%

Table 7. Key variable V7.

Leadership and culture	SMEs	LC
Leadership and culture with great impact within the organization, all supported by leaders with deep knowledge in I4.0	13%	8%
Acceptable leadership and culture, delegated to area managers or supervisors with a sufficient knowledge level about technologies and about how to develop the required skills in their collaborators	45%	36%
Regular leadership and culture, delegated to area managers or supervisors who do not have the necessary knowledge to propose and implement an adequate roadmap	15%	23%
Scarce leadership and culture, a process managed by collaborators who do not generate a significant impact	19%	21%
No leadership or culture to implement I4.0	9%	13%

Table 8. Key variable V8.

Cybersecurity option	SMEs	LC
Firewall	79%	85%
Antivirus	100%	98%
Anti-spy	62%	70%
Antimalware	64%	70%
Maintenance of computer equipment	96%	94%
Policies regarding the creation of secure passwords	85%	94%
Security patches	55%	66%
Information access control lists	64%	68%
Train staff on secure methods for using information systems	51%	45%
Ongoing research on new models of cyber attacks	28%	42%

Interactions between companies (V9), Table 9, mostly occur, 74%, through integrated systems that notify customer requirements, in the case of SMEs. Meanwhile, 77% of LC still use manual formats such as forms, letters, paper inventories, physical invoices, etc.

Table 9. Key variable V9.

Interaction in the value chain	SMEs	LC
Coordination between suppliers/customers manually	66%	77%
Use of standardized business language and formats	49%	70%
ERP systems	64%	68%
Use of integrated systems that notify customer requirements automatically	74%	62%
Analysis of consumption trends in the niche market jointly with business alloys	38%	30%

In the last variables, Table 10, it is observed that the use of digital platforms for the management of sales and customer service (V10) does not exceed 60% in SMEs and LC. Internet connection (V11) is stable for 77% of SMEs and 55% of LC. The Information Governance variable (V12) indicates that, in most companies, 83% SMEs and 85% LC, there is adequate data flow and protection.

Finally, as an additional question, the main barriers perceived by the surveyed companies were investigated. As can be seen in Fig. 1, around 70% of the companies indicate that the main problem in entering I4.0 is the high acquisition costs. Next, there is a lack of knowledge about I4.0 and its technologies, with around 30% for SMEs and LC.

Table 10. Key variables V10-V12.

Variables		SMEs	LC
V10	Use of digital platforms for customer management	53%	58%
V11	Stable connection and allows the provision of the service constantly	77%	55%
	Sporadic connection failures, but good technical support in case of problems	19%	42%
	Sporadic failures in connection with low technical support in problem solving	4%	2%
	Low internet speed and tends to constantly crash	0%	2%
V12	All the information reaches the appropriate recipients in an efficient way, there is a control in the protection of data ensuring an adequate treatment of these inside and outside the organization	83%	85%
	The information reaches the appropriate recipients most of the time, however, there is a lack of data protection (leakage of sensitive data, unauthorized copies of data)	15%	15%
	Errors occur in the information flow because, constantly, unnecessary, or improper data is sent to some processes within the company	2%	0%

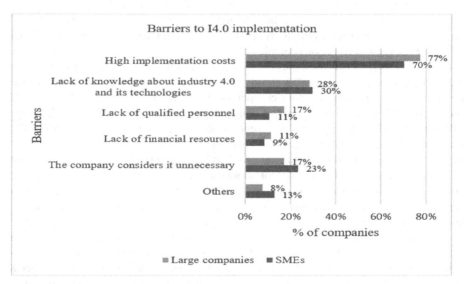

Fig. 1. Barriers to I4.0 implementation.

4 Discussion

According to the variables (12) defined in this study, it was shown that the I4.0 (V6) development strategy is in the process of advanced implementation or fully executed in 30% of SMEs. In contrast, only 17% of CLs are in this stage of development. This would indicate a greater facility in the development of I4.0 strategies, which could be due to the risk tolerance of innovative technologies [4]. SMEs could venture into I4.0 with less rigorous implementation plans compared to the plans made in LC. This could explain why there is a greater number of LC that do not implement or are in the planning and early implementation stage, 83%, compared to SMEs in the same situation, 70%.

Variables V4 and V7 presented similar behaviors, SMEs indicate, to a greater extent, compared to LC, high cooperation between the areas of the company. Also, in terms of leadership and culture, SMEs present better results. This could be associated with the resistance to change manifested by employees, which increases with a greater number of people.

In terms of support for I.40, investment (V5), LC invest between 5% and 20% of their net profits in I4.0, but this proportion is only exceeded by 7% compared to SMEs. In other words, the investment made by companies, in proportion to their net profits, does not differ greatly according to the size of the company. Having more developed implementation strategies by SMEs could be the cause of these levels of investment [13].

On the other hand, the knowledge necessary for the management of 4.0 technologies by employees (V2) is higher in SMEs, exceeding the knowledge in LC by 19%. However, most employees in companies in general, have the knowledge to use ICT. The above represents a base of employees with basic knowledge which serves as pillars to develop skills in the management of 4.0 technologies.

In general, the quality of the ICT connection (V11) is stable for the provision of the service. In other words, there is continuity of activities in both SMEs and LC. However, consumer connectivity is still lagging behind in the territory [18], making the consumer-business connection difficult.

The use of 4.0 (V1) technologies shows that some of these are widely used in Colombian companies. This is the case of cloud computing, due to the high demand for access to information in real-time within companies. Furthermore, its relationship with the Internet of Things (IoT) makes cloud computing necessary for further developments [20]. On the other hand, the 25% difference in the use of Big Data implies that SMEs have a lower capacity to make decisions based on the analysis of large amounts of information. However, V3 indicates that only 64% of LC do demand analytics and customer consumption trends. Added to this, Colombian service companies that have digital platforms for customer service do not exceed 60% in SMEs or LC. This represents a field of action for improvement in the relationship with the client, which is necessary for this new reality [16, 17].

Regarding the protection of business information (V9), the wide use of different strategies for data protection stands out. However, measures such as employee training to avoid falling into cyber traps and the review of new attack models are key to the effective protection of information [21]. In this sense, Colombian companies in general present considerable vulnerabilities in this regard. Likewise, although in terms of information governance (V12) more than 80% of the companies surveyed have expressed adequate management of their client's information, having security problems would lead to the leakage of sensitive data.

Finally, the variable that integrates companies in the value chain (V9) shows a deficiency in the digitization of some information delivery processes between companies. In the case of SMEs, not using standardized business language could mean difficulties in communicating massive information regarding orders for products or supplies. In addition, there is no evidence of collaborative work between the companies for the joint analysis of market trends, which limits the association within the value chain.

5   Conclusion

Understanding the relationships between the key variables allows us to understand and anticipate aspects that occur when implementing Industry 4.0. In the case of employee knowledge, SMEs presented good results in this regard, which may be related to the good level of leadership and culture evidenced in this type of company. The dissemination of knowledge and skills for the management of technologies results in a staff with better qualities to enter I4.0.

Considering the agility of SMEs by having reduced internal areas and less extensive or complex processes, entering I4.0 may be easier than in LC. However, the high costs of these technologies represent a greater risk for them. Although this does not mean that SMEs cannot make considerable investments in I4.0, in fact, the results of the survey affirm that investment levels, in proportion to their profits, are similar for all companies in general.

Colombian services SMEs have the necessary tools to venture into I4.0 in the coming years. In addition, the effects of COVID-19 have accelerated this process at least in its initial phase, the digital transformation of processes. Actions such as increasing their participation in digital platforms for customer management, conducting more consumer trend analytics, and improving cybersecurity will allow them a foray into adequate I4.0.

References

1. Sukhodolov, Y.A.: The notion, essence, and peculiarities of industry 4.0 as a sphere of industry. In: Popkova, E.G., Ragulina, Y.V., Bogoviz, A.V. (eds.) Industry 4.0: Industrial Revolution of the 21st Century. SSDC, vol. 169, pp. 3–10. Springer, Cham (2019). https://doi.org/10.1007/978-3-319-94310-7_1
2. Wiesner, S., Gaiardelli, P., Gritti, N., Oberti, G.: Maturity models for digitalization in manufacturing - applicability for SMEs. In: Moon, I., Lee, G.M., Park, J., Kiritsis, D., vonCieminski, G. (eds.) Advances in Production Management Systems. Smart Manufacturing for Industry 4.0. IAICT, vol. 536, pp. 81–88. Springer, Cham (2018). https://doi.org/10.1007/978-3-319-99707-0_11
3. Asociación Cluster de Industrias de Medio Ambiente de Euskadi: Tecnología e industria 4.0: la sostenibilidad en la cuarta Era industrial. In: Congreso Nacional del Medio Ambiente 2018 (2018)
4. Confederación Colombiana de Cámaras de Comercio: Industria 4.0 tranformación empresarial para la reactivación económica. Red de Cámaras de Comercio, Bogotá D.C., Colombia (2020)

5. Departamento Administrativo Nacional de Estadística: Boletín Técnico Encuesta Anual de Servicios (EAS). Presidencia de la República, Bogotá D.C., Colombia (2019)
6. Reder, L., Klünder, T.: Application of SCOR flexibility metrics to assess the Industry 4.0-readiness of supply chain networks: an empirical study. Bochum, 16 (2017)
7. Pérez Lara, M, Saucedo Martínez, J.A., Salais Fierro, T.E., Marmolejo Saucedo, J.A.: Caracterizacion de modelo de negocio en el marco de industria 4.0. Congr. Int. Logística y Cadena Suminist., October 2017
8. Leyh, C., Schäffer, T., Bley, K., Forstenhäusler, S.: Assessing the IT and software landscapes of industry 4.0-enterprises: the maturity model SIMMI 4.0. Lect. Notes Bus. Inf. Process. **277**, 103–119 (2016)
9. Rojko, A.: Industry 4.0 concept: Background and overview. Int. J. Interact. Mob. Technol. **11**(5), 77–90 (2017)
10. Gökalp, E., Şener, U., Eren, P.E.: Development of an assessment model for industry 4.0: industry 4.0-MM. In: Mas, A., Mesquida, A., O'Connor, R.V., Rout, T., Dorling, A. (eds.) Software Process Improvement and Capability Determination. CCIS, vol. 770, pp. 128–142. Springer, Cham (2017). https://doi.org/10.1007/978-3-319-67383-7_10
11. Klötzer, C., Pflaum, A.: Toward the development of a MM digitalization suppl.pdf. In: Proceedings of 50th Hawaii International Conference System Science, pp. 4210–4219 (2017)
12. Erol, S., Schumacher, A., Sihn, W.: Strategic guidance towards industry 4.0 – a three-stage process model. In: International Conference on Computer Manufacturing, January, pp. 495–501 (2016)
13. Genest, M.C., Gamache, S.: Prerequisites for the implementation of industry 4.0 in manufacturing SMEs. Proc. Manuf. **51**(2019), 1215–1220 (2020)
14. Brozzi, R., Riedl, M., Matta, D.: Key readiness indicators to assess the digital level of manufacturing SMEs. Proc. CIRP **96**, 201–206 (2020)
15. Angreani, L.S., Vijaya, A., Wicaksono, H.: Systematic literature review of industry 4.0 maturity model for manufacturing and logistics sectors. Proc. Manuf. **52**(2019), 337–343 (2020)
16. Comisión Económica para América Latina y el Caribe: Universalizar el acceso a las tecnologías digitales para enfrentar los efectos del COVID-19. Naciones Unidas, Santiago, Chile (2020)
17. Asociación Nacional de Empresarios de Colombia: Balance 2020 y perspectivas 2021. ANDI, Bogotá D.C., Colombia (2020)
18. IMD World Competitiveness Center: IMD World Digital Competitiveness Ranking 2020. IMD World Competitiveness Center, p. 180 (2020)
19. Congreso de la Republica: Ley 1581 de Octubre de 2012. Departamento Administrativo de la Función Pública, Bogotá D.C., Colombia (2012)
20. Pedone, G., Mezgár, I.: Model similarity evidence and interoperability affinity in cloud-ready Industry 4.0 technologies. Comput. Ind. **100**(May), 278–286 (2018)
21. Dimitriadis, A., Ivezic, N., Kulvatunyou, B., Mavridis, I.: D4I - digital forensics framework for reviewing and investigating cyber attacks. Array **5**, 100015 (2020)

Information and Knowledge Systems

Agile Portfolio Management for Hybrid Projects: How to Combine Traditional and Agile Projects in a Project Portfolio

Christian Ploder[✉], Annalena Hüsam, Reinhard Bernsteiner,
and Thomas Dilger

Management Center Innsbruck, Universitätsstrasse 15, 6020 Innsbruck, Austria
christian.ploder@mci.edu

Abstract. In today's dynamically changing environment, projects are conducted increasingly with agile methods. Still, traditional waterfall methods exist which, depending on the requirements, are successfully used to implement projects. Thus, hybrid project environments arise. The management of project portfolios has to deal with this ambivalent project landscape, requiring a system suitable for the mixture of both methods. As little research has addressed this topic so far, the paper identified success factors that empower an agile project portfolio management that is able to deal with hybrid projects. A case study was chosen as the research method, supported by findings of a literature review conducted beforehand. The case study brought to light the complexity of current problems and challenges, while the factors found in the literature provide the first-time compilation of theoretically supported success factors in this context. It was found that all identified dimensions of PPM need to change, i.e. strategy and roadmap; identify and funnel; review, prioritize and balance; allocate and delegate. The results showed that when it comes to strategy, precise strategic goals are to be established, that need to be adapted according to changes in the environment. Clear project scopes, consistent rating methods, and corresponding metrics are identified as success factors as well. Furthermore, empowered individuals knowing their roles and those of other departments are important factors regarding resource allocation and delegation. The paper provides new insights into agile portfolio management for hybrid projects for both practice and academia and thus also can serve as the starting point for further research in this field.

Keywords: Agility · Hybrid projects · Project portfolio management

1 Introduction

Current digital environments change faster from year to year, forcing companies to successfully identify at an early stage which products and services to develop and adapt to satisfy the high market requirements. Simultaneously, companies

L. Uden et al. (Eds.): KMO 2022, CCIS 1593, pp. 221–232, 2022.
https://doi.org/10.1007/978-3-031-07920-7_17

increasingly struggle with complex IT landscapes and tough competitive situations all around the globe. In this environment, agile projects have proven useful especially in departments where software development and e-commerce projects determine the daily work routine [15].

If you take a closer look at the practice, however, this approach alone is not enough. Though agile projects inevitably have benefits, there are still projects that require a more long-term oriented and plan-driven view. These projects are characterized by the fact that the focus is on implementing an initial plan or goal as precisely as possible, resulting in more waterfall-oriented project management techniques [35]. Furthermore, there exist hybrid approaches that neither can be categorized as typically agile nor plan-driven, leading to a diverse mix of methods and project forms within one single organization. Especially when operating in complex organizations and applying project methods at a larger scale, hybrid methods are frequently used. This is done by adopting agile methods and complementing them with practices from traditional methods [6]. The phenomenon can be observed across various industries and results in the so-called Agilefall environment, the in-between state of traditional and agile [5].

It now becomes obvious that choosing the right projects and pushing them into the right direction becomes more relevant in this context, while leading to severe issues if not doing so. Typically, the mix of agile and traditional project management contradicts the way the organization is generally structured, especially if there are rigid workflows and lengthy processes for strategic and portfolio management in place. This situation becomes particularly dangerous with the latter. If processes for Project Portfolio Management (PPM) are not able to deal with the mix of project forms, major challenges arise. If no or no proper PPM is in place, this can lead to having too many projects in the pipeline, shortage of resources, projects that are not linked to strategy, or wrong projects in general as well as slowing project progress [30]. In this context, also project controlling gets difficult and synergy potential between projects can be lost, leading to an overall risk of not being able to achieve long-term operational excellence. As Perez [25] states, interactions between synergistic projects, if taken into account, lead to projects that would not be selected if considered on their own. However, the author further claims that these project choices can end up in increased sales and better distribution of resources. Isolated approaches of agile PPM, which mainly deal with the management of agile projects, are already reaching their limits. As Stettina and Hörz [33] state, newer PPM forms deal with a lack of alignment to existing project management, non-appropriate software as well as contradictions to established business practices. The described gap mentioned can in some cases be attributed to missing knowledge. Gasik [9] therefore presents a model for project knowledge management which is devided into two different types of knowledge: micro-knowledge, supporting the single task performance and the for this paper more important macro-knowledge which focuses on all the knowledge possessed by people from a given organizational level as they are part ot the whole PPM strucutre. Therefore, especially in IT-related fields, new ways of flexible and agile portfolio management need to be analyzed, established and supported by knowledge management systems [8,27] that can deal with agile as well as traditional-oriented projects and thus drive competitiveness and operational excellence forward. Especially in IT environments, current developments put serious pressure on IT PPM, requiring project portfolios to be strategically aligned and efficient yet agile [7,12]. However, little research has addressed the topic so far.

Therefore, the authors compared different approaches of PPM as a starting point: the traditional PPM cycle and the agile portfolio management [33]. Even though portfolios themselves provide an opportunity to make organizations more agile outside of single projects, this opportunity highly depends on the way PPM is implemented. While traditional PPM focuses more on cyclic and ordered project management behavior [33], agile PPM chooses a different direction. Prominent examples of agile PPM include publications of Leffingwell [18,19], Krebs [17] and Vähäniitty et al. [37]. All propose ways of agile PPM while considering different hierarchies like senior management, portfolio management, and project management. Figure 1 shows the agile way of structuring a PPM process by introducing four practice domains: strategize and roadmap; identify and funnel; review, prioritize and balance, allocate and delegate. What changes, compared to a traditional PPM, is how the practices and following activities are done and not the practices themselves [26]. The main areas of the standard PPM process were resumed in agile PPM. Nonetheless, the order and composition of the traditional process steps are changed towards a more intertwined process.

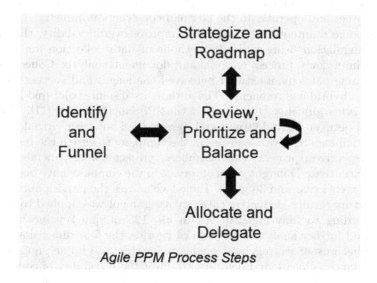

Fig. 1. Agile PPM process (adapted from Stettina & Hörz, 2015)

However, this approach requires full agile project management and is neither designed for hybrid techniques nor tested in hybrid environments. This leads to the following research question:

RQ: Which factors enable agile PPM in hybrid project management settings?

To be able to answer this research question, the methodology used for discovering the topic is explained in Sect. 2 and all the elaborated results are shown in Sect. 3 with discussing them in comparison to current literature. Finally the paper is summarized in Sect. 4 and the limitations and a future outlook is provided in Sect. 5.

2   Methodology

To best address the research question, different methods have been taken into account. As Tallon [34] states, applied research is key to moving the understanding of organizational agility with all its areas and implications forward. Secondly, the chosen topic can be described as a contemporary phenomenon with little available research so far, making a holistic and real-world perspective necessary for further research [39]. These factors are pointing towards a case study, which is additionally reinforced by the fact that specifically, the topic of agility has many facets with no one-size-fits-all concept [15]. The case study is backed up and compared to the results of an initial literature review based on Webster and Watson [38] as well as Snyder [31]. The case study has been carried out in one of the IT departments at a large enterprise that employs more than 5,000 employees and operates in the German construction industry.

To overcome unintentional biases and improve overall validity, the authors applied triangulation using multiple methods of data collection and analysis: qualitative interviews, process analysis and document analysis. Concerning the interviews, nine participants stated perceived challenges and success factors of agile PPM in hybrid environments. The authors used semi-structured interviews with an interview guideline [14], based on the SPSS methodology [11]. The interviews lasted between 25 and 60 min and were carried out with virtual meetings. Chosen participants held various roles in the company to enrich the results from various perspectives: project team members, project leaders, members of the PMO and executives. Different years of service in the company have been chosen, ranging between 1 year and 36 years. Table 1 visualizes the participant overview.

To structure results, deductive category assignment was applied to the transcripts according to Mayring [21]. All in all, 128 unique key messages were extracted and further analyzed. To form categories, the four dimensions of agile PPM have been used: strategy and roadmap; identify and funnel; review, prioritize and balance; allocate and delegate. To limit the possibility of coder biases, intercoder reliability was applied, leading to an overall result of 89.7%.

The following process analysis included a process discovery, process analysis, and process redesign phase according to the Business Process Management (BPM) Lifecycle, intended to also look at the topic from a different angle. The same applied to the document analysis. Three different document types that

Table 1. Participant overview

Participant	Sequence	Position	Company affiliation
A1	Test	-	-
A2	Test	-	-
B	1	Project Lead	5 years
C	2	Executive	2 years
D	3	PMO	12 years
E	4	Project Lead	4 years
F	5	Executive	36 years
G	6	Executive	25 years
H	7	Project Team Member	1 year
I	8	Project Team Member	14 years
J	9	PMO	5 years

were needed to complete the process have been analyzed according to document conformity. In total, the number of analyzed documents was 68, with an overall document conformity of 58.8%. Non-conform documents showed issues in similar areas as in the document analysis and in the interviews, allowing to draw overall conclusions from different angles. To enable comparability and a comprehensible overview, the four dimensions of agile PPM introduced above were used to structure all areas of the case study in the same way. The case study results have been compared to and aligned with current theoretical findings, conducted with a literature review. The procedure is shown in Fig. 2.

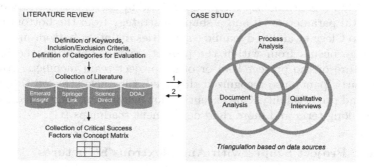

Fig. 2. Applied methodological procedure

3   Results and Discussion

In this section, the results of the case study are presented and set in relation to the literature.

Traditional PPM has been a common approach in the last decades. With the advent of agile methodologies especially in software-related departments and companies, however, traditional PPM needs to be changed to provide value [26]. PPM of modern and innovative projects, as well as the underlying strategy, should have functions of adaptability and flexibility in a dynamically changing environment [36]. This finding was prevailing throughout the initial review of literature. Consequently, agile capabilities present a suitable way of adapting the portfolio to uncertain environments and transforming this uncertainty into a higher success of the portfolio [13,16]. When now turning to the results of the case study, different success factors arise.

3.1   Precise Strategic Goals with the Aim of Constant Adaption

Comparing the findings from theory to the results of the case study, similarities and differences become clear. As Hall [10] states, usually, there are discrepancies between literature and observations, which is why the analyst must make simultaneous judgments about the validity of the observations as well as about the plausibility of the theory. Concerning the first dimension *Strategy and Roadmap*, the case study results confirmed the suggested success factors in the literature. PPM needs to be aligned with strategic goals [1]. To achieve this, mentioned problems in the case study of not knowing how to contribute to the overall goal need to be solved by providing a clear vision and an existing company strategy broken down to measurable targets on different levels [2]. In the interviews, similar results arose (B, C, D, E, F, G, I, & J). Additionally, theory puts a strong focus on a continuously adapted strategy by systematic assessments for environmental parameters [4] and a shape of strategy from the bottom-up [16]. According to Clegg et al. [2], dynamic capabilities maintain bottom-up elements where change occurs from within the project, mainly based on the improvisational nature of the project lead or other project team members. Although interview participants also recognized this need, they also stressed to maintain reliability and predictability. One executive, for instance, strengthened the need for creating long-term and more rigid department roadmaps (G).

3.2   Clear Project Scopes with Ambidextrous Structures

In the second dimension *Identify and Funnel*, the interviews agreed with the literature to the extent that a clear project scope in early project phases is important (D, F, & G). To achieve that, all possible projects of the unit have to be collected [3]. In the interviews, it was suggested to use centralized contact points for this and communicate them company-wide (C, H & J). To increase the number of project ideas in general, creativity is considered important for brainstorming and figuring out ideas, ensured by providing space and time for creative thinking (I & J). In this way, the total number of project ideas increases and people can come up with alternative problem-solution approaches. To be able to implement these innovative ideas in the project environment, ambidextrous structures are often used in the literature [20,23,32,40]. Like this, diverse projects are chosen with low and high risk to be able to strategically conquer new markets but maintain current business at the same time [4].

3.3 Consistent Evaluation Method with the Flexibility for Individual Key Figures

When reviewing, prioritizing, and balancing an agile portfolio, a consistent rating methodology is considered to be crucial both in the interviews as well as in literature. As three participants mentioned, there are too many exceptions to the pre-defined process in the case company (C, F, & I). This leads to a flood of projects being executed simultaneously (C, G & H). Project lead B offers the following for consideration: *"But then what do we have the process for? If everyone does what they want? It is a super fine line between sticking completely to the process and doing everything uniformly and between there being exceptions because it's necessary"* [1] (B, 00:14:26-6).

In this context, key figures play a major role (B). However, there is disagreement about how metrics should be created. While, among other authors, Linhart et al. [20] suggest fixed evaluation criteria that do not differ across projects, this view is not shared by others. The application of consistent metrics throughout the company may hamper innovations, as innovative projects will fail more often than others [22].

Therefore, one approach that needs further analysis can be to create a mix of consistent metrics for the corporate overview as well as individual metrics for each project. This approach also has to be mappable with the technology. However, there is currently no consensus on the use of the technology. Instead, various approaches have been enumerated in the literature. One noticeable difference was the use of mathematical or algorithmic approaches to extract the success factors. While 13 of the analyzed papers used algorithmic models, the remaining 20 did not. Both methods have advantages and disadvantages. Even though mathematical procedures have been frequently used for traditional PPM to determine an optimal portfolio, Hoffmann et al. [12] stated the insufficiency of mere rationality-based planning approaches when it comes to IT PPM. A recommended path, based on the articles and the case study results, may therefore be a mixture of both procedures. The tendency though should be to take the focus away from pure algorithmic models and thus being able to mix consistent and individual metrics.

---

[1] "Aber wofür haben wir dann den Prozess? Wenn jeder tut, was er will? Es ist halt ein super schmaler Grat zwischen wir halten uns komplett an den Prozess und machen alles einheitlich und zwischen es gibt Ausnahmen, weil es nötig ist.".

3.4   Clear Roles and Empowered Individuals Across Departmental Boundaries

Clear roles and empowered individuals are the main success factors for allocating and delegating projects through agile PPM. Nevertheless, different perspectives occurred in theory and practice. In the interviews, it was found that especially the project lead needs more freedom and responsibility to strengthen the interests of customers, the team, and the project itself (B & J). This responsibility should then also be used to communicate more with neighboring departments and to involve them in the process (D, E, & F). As one project team member states, it is crucial that *"people can network well with each other, that they can coordinate quickly, that there are no inhibition thresholds or the like"* [2] (H, 00:23:51-1). In literature, the view is shared that more responsibility should be given to the project team and the individuals within it [28]. As Kaufmann et al. [16] state, due to their operative tasks, project team members are closer to the market and the customer and focus their tasks only on few projects, which is why they have a deeper knowledge of the topic. There are even voices that grant the project manager less formal power to empower the team individuals more [29], which contradicts the statement of the case study mentioned above to some extent.

4   Summary

Agile project methods are gaining ground and are increasingly being mixed with existing approaches in established companies. However, hybrid project models that deal with elements of both agile as well as waterfall projects, and respective portfolio approaches, have so far been neglected in the literature. The paper, therefore, addressed this research gap by identifying critical success factors for agile PPM in hybrid project environments.

To provide profound information in this context, current theoretical models have been analyzed, followed by a case study of an IT department of a German enterprise operating in the Agilefall environment and thus dealing with hybrid projects daily. To improve construct validity and overcome unintentional biases, triangulation has been applied using multiple methods of data collection and analysis for the case study.

Finally, it was found that concerning strategy, precise strategic goals need to be established, but with the aim of constant adaption according to the dynamically changing environment. They need to be broken down to various levels. Furthermore, agile portfolio management needs to focus on clear project scopes to be able to identify and funnel the right projects. Moreover, consistent rating methods to prioritize projects and balance them in a portfolio are seen as crucial throughout academia and practice. Creating appropriate metrics plays a major role in this context, to both provide a possibility to compare projects across the

---

[2] "Dass die Leute sich gut miteinander vernetzen können, sich schnell absprechen können, dass es da halt keine Hemmschwellen gibt oder sonstiges.".

company and be able to steer projects individually in the right direction. Based on the fact that the empowerment of individuals is an important factor as well, bottom-up decision-making and trust in teams have also been found to be critical success factors. This, in turn, increases the need for roles and responsibilities of all involved parties and individuals to be set and clear.

5   Limitations and Potential Future Work

As with all scientific studies, limitations arise that leave room for future research. First, as a single case study has been conducted, only one PPM process in one organization has been analyzed. The department under study is influenced by specific environmental factors that cannot be easily projected onto other departments or companies. It is rather recommended to conduct further research, for instance using multiple case studies, that enrich the achieved results.

Second, Case Studies do not represent samples [39]. Therefore, the paper will contribute to expand and specify theories rather than doing statistical research. The conducted qualitative methods do not replace quantitative research, which is advised to be executed in an additional step.

Third, the outcomes are based upon perceptions of case study participants who may have a biased view on their work in the process [24,33]. It cannot be ruled out that participants may answer differently when asked again, depending on recently experienced situations they may have encountered while implementing projects, current personal situations, relationships with colleagues and managers and other influencing factors. Therefore, it may be reasonable to conduct the study either with other participants or with the same participants at another time again.

Furthermore, the literature review and thus the choice of theoretical models is limited to a selection of current theory. Hence, not all existing and applicable methods are considered in this paper. Here, too, it is recommended to extend the current literature review and also take additional articles into account.

Last, the analysis stops before the actual implementation of the proposed success factors. First recommendations exist on how on implement a PPM process that aim to be agile in the approach [28]. However, there are still multiple open questions regarding the practical implementation of agility and agile concepts [15]. These questions could be tackled by further research projects.

References

1. Alaeddini, M., Mir-Amini, M.: Integrating COBIT with a hybrid group decision-making approach for a business-aligned IT roadmap formulation. Inf. Technol. Manage. 21(2), 63–94 (2019). https://doi.org/10.1007/s10799-019-00305-0
2. Clegg, S., Killen, C.P., Biesenthal, C., Sankaran, S.: Practices, projects and portfolios: current research trends and new directions. Int. J. Project Manage. 36(5), 762–772 (2018). https://doi.org/10.1016/j.ijproman.2018.03.008

3. Şahin Zorluoğlu, Ö., Kabak, Ö.: Weighted cumulative belief degree approach for project portfolio selection. Group Decis. Negot. **29**(4), 679–722 (2020). https://doi.org/10.1007/s10726-020-09673-3

4. Davies, A., Brady, T.: Explicating the dynamics of project capabilities. Int. J. Project Manage. **34**(2), 314–327 (2016). https://doi.org/ 0.1016/j.ijproman.2015.04.006

5. Dilger, T., Ploder, C., Haas, W., Schöttle, P., Bernsteiner, R.: Continuous planning and forecasting framework (CPFF) for agile project management: overcoming the agilefall-budgeting trap. In: SIGITE 2020 (2020)

6. Dingsøyr, T., Moe, N.B., Fægri, T.E., Seim, E.A.: Exploring software development at the very large-scale: a revelatory case study and research agenda for agile method adaptation. Empir. Softw. Eng. **23**(1), 490–520 (2017). https://doi.org/10.1007/s10664-017-9524-2

7. Doz, Y.: Fostering strategic agility: how individual executives and human resource practices contribute. Human Resour. Manage. Rev. **30**(1) 100693 (2020). https://doi.org/10.1016/j.hrmr.2019.100693

8. Fink, K., Ploder, C.: A comparative study of knowledge processes and methods in Austrian and Swiss SMEs. In: ECIS 2007 Proceedings, pp. 704–715 (2007)

9. Gasik, S.: A model of project knowledge management. Project Manage. J. **42**(3), 23–44 (2011). https://doi.org/10.1002/pmj.20239, http://journals.sagepub.com/doi/10.1002/pmj.20239

10. Hall, P.A.: Systematic process analysis: when and how to use it. Eur. Manage. Rev. **3**, 24–31 (2006)

11. Helfferich, C.: Die Qualität qualitativer Daten: Manual für die Durchführung qualitativer Interviews. VS Verlag für Sozialwissenschaften, Wiesbaden, 4 edn. (2011). https://doi.org/10.1007/978-3-531-92076-4

12. Hoffmann, D., Ahlemann, F., Reining, S.: Reconciling alignment, efficiency, and agility in it project portfolio management: recommendations based on a revelatory case study. Int. J. Project Manage. **38**(2), 124–136 (2020). https://doi.org/10.1016/j.ijproman.2020.01.004

13. Huff, A.S.: Project innovation: evidence-informed, open, effectual, and subjective. Project Manage. J. **47**(2), 8–25 (2016). https://doi.org/10.1002/pmj.21576

14. Hüsam, A., Ploder, C.: Interview Guideline to the KMO 2022 Paper - Agile Portfolio Management for hybrid projects: How to combine traditional and agile projects in a project portfolio, April 2022. https://doi.org/10.13110/RG.2.2.12445.38883

15. Jesse, N.: Organizational evolution - how digital disruption enforces organizational agility. IFAC-PapersOnLine **51**(30), 486–491 (2018). https://doi.org/10.1016/j.ifacol.2018.11.310

16. Kaufmann, C., Kock, A., Gemünden, H.G.: Emerging strategy recognition in agile portfolios. Int. J. Project Manage. **38**(7), 429–440 (2020). https://doi.org/10.1016/j.ijproman.2020.01.002

17. Krebs, J.: Agile Portfolio Management. Microsoft Press, Redmond, WA (2008)

18. Leffingwell, D.: Scaling Software Agility: Best Practices fo Large Enterprises. Pearson Education Inc., Boston, MA (2007)

19. Leffingwell, D.: Agile Software Requirements: Lean Requirements Practices for Teams, Programs, and the Enterprise. Pearson Education Inc., Boston, MA (2010)

20. Linhart, A., Röglinger, M., Stelzl, K.: A project portfolio management approach to tackling the exploration/exploitation trade-off. Bus. Inf. Syst. Eng. **62**(2), 103–119 (2018). https://doi.org/10.1007/s12599-018-0564-y

21. Mayring, P.: Qualitative content analysis: theoretical foundation, basic procedures and software solution. In: Social Science Open Access Repository, Klagenfurt (2014). https://nbn-resolving.org/urn:nbn:de:0168-ssoar-395173

22. Moore, S.: Strategic Project Portfolio Management: Enabling A Productive Organization. Microsoft Executive Leadership Series, Wiley, Hoboken, NJ (2010)

23. O'Dwyer, C., Sweeney, B., Cormican, K.: Embracing paradox and conflict: towards a conceptual model to drive project portfolio ambidexterity. Proc. Comput. Sci. **121**, 600–608 (2017). https://doi.org/10.1016/j.procs.2017.11.079

24. Pentland, B.T., Feldman, M.S.: Narrative networks: patterns of technology and organization. Organ. Sci. **18**(5), 781–795 (2007). https://doi.org/10.1287/orsc.1070.0283

25. Perez, F., Gomez, T.: Multiobjective project portfolio selection with fuzzy constraints. Ann. Oper. Res. **245**(1-2), 7–29 (2016). https://doi.org/10.1007/s10479-014-1556-z

26. Pinto, J., Ribeiro, P.: Characterization of an agile coordination office for IST companies. Proc. Comput. Sci. **138**, 859–866 (2018). https://doi.org/10.1016/j.procs.2018.10.112

27. Ploder, C., Fink, K.: An orchestration model for knowledge management tools in SMEs. In: Proceedings of the I-KNOW 2007, J. UCS, pp. 176–184 (2007)

28. Porter, S.: Project management in higher education: a grounded theory case study. Libr. Manage. **40**(5), 338–352 (2019). https://doi.org/10.1108/LM-06-2018-0050

29. Sanchez, O.P., Terlizzi, M.A., de Moraes, H.R.O.C.: Cost and time project management success factors for information systems development projects. Int. J. Project Manage. **35**(8), 1608–1626 (2017). https://doi.org/10.1016/j.ijproman.2017.09.007

30. Sarbazhosseini, H., Banihashemi, S., Adikari, S.: Human-centered framework for managing IT project portfolio. In: Nah, F.F.-H., Siau, K. (eds.) HCII 2019. LNCS, vol. 11589, pp. 432–442. Springer, Cham (2019). https://doi.org/10.1007/978-3-030-22338-0_35

31. Snyder, H.: Literature review as a research methodology: an overview and guidelines. J. Bus. Res. **104**, 333–339 (2019). https://doi.org/10.1016/j.jbusres.2019.07.039

32. Stelzl, K., Röglinger, M., Wyrtki, K.: Building an ambidextrous organization: a maturity model for organizational ambidexterity. Bus. Res. **13**(3), 1203–1230 (2020). https://doi.org/10.1007/s40685-020-00117-x

33. Stettina, C.J., Hörz, J.: Agile portfolio management: an empirical perspective on the practice in use. Int. J. Project Manage. **33**(1), 140–152 (2015). https://doi.org/10.1016/j.ijproman.2014.03.008

34. Tallon, P.P., Queiroz, M., Coltman, T., Sharma, R.: Information technology and the search for organizational agility: a systematic review with future research possibilities. J. Strat. Inf. Syst. **28**(2), 218–237 (2019). https://doi.org/10.1016/j.jsis.2018.12.002

35. Thesing, T., Feldmann, C., Burchardt, M.: Agile versus waterfall project management: decision model for selecting the appropriate approach to a project. Proc. Comput. Sci. **181**, 746–756 (2021). https://doi.org/10.1016/j.procs.2021.01.227

36. Tkachenko, I., Evseeva, M.: Leading approaches to managing organizational portfolio in a dynamically changing environment. In: Strielkowski, W. (ed.) Sustainable Leadership for Entrepreneurs and Academics. SPBE, pp. 191–199. Springer, Cham (2019). https://doi.org/10.1007/978-3-030-15495-0_20

37. Vähäniitty, J.: Towards Agile Product and Portfolio Management. Aalto University, Helsinki (2012)

38. Webster, J., Watson, R.T.: Analyzing the past to prepare for the future: writing a literature review. MIS Q. **26**(2), xiii–xxiii (2002)
39. Yin, R.K.: Case Study Research and Applications: Design and Methods, 6th edn. SAGE Publications, Thousand Oaks, California (2018)
40. Zaman, U., Nadeem, R.D., Nawaz, S.: Cross-country evidence on project portfolio success in the Asia-pacific region: role of CEO transformational leadership, portfolio governance and strategic innovation orientation. Cogent Bus. Manage. **7**(1), 1727681 (2020). https://doi.org/10.1080/23311975.2020.1727681

The Crowdsourcing Delphi: A Method for Combing Expert Judgements and Wisdom of Crowds

Teemu Santonen[1]([✉]) and Jari Kaivo-oja[2]

[1] Laurea University of Applied Sciences, Espoo, Finland
teemu.santonen@laurea.fi
[2] University of Turku, Turku, Finland
jari.kaivo-oja@utu.fi

Abstract. How to combine expert judgment and mass intelligence? This study can be characterized as methodological concept development. We combine the relevant theories and methodological approaches from expert-dominated Delphi methods and layman-dominated crowdsourcing approaches to introduce a novel Crowdsourcing Delphi research approach. The key contributions of this study consist: (1) the definition of Crowdsourcing Delphi term, (2) identification of differences between crowdsourcing and Delphi methodologies, (3) developing a framework for selecting and evaluating Crowdsourcing Delphi research strategies and (4) identifying pros and cons for different research strategy combinations. One notable advantage for knowledge management need is that the Crowdsourcing methodology allows a large variety of different Delphi variants and different Crowdsourcing techniques. The Crowdsourcing Delphi allows also combination of Data pools/Big Data flows of crowds to the methodological practices of various Delphi expert-panel methods (Delphi variants). The Crowdsourcing Delphi is a new knowledge management methodology tool package.

Keywords: Crowdsourcing · Delphi · Hybrid foresight · Expert judgement · Expert opinion · Mixed method approach · Wisdom of crowds

1 Introduction

1.1 Calling Out Greater Variety in Delphi Panels

Delphi technique is a structured communication method to obtain a reliable group opinion from a group of individual experts on a variety of topic such as technology forecasting, policy making, scenario planning and decision making [1]. A pivotal component of the Delphi study is a panel of experts. In simplified terms, an expert is a person having a high level of knowledge or skill relating to a particular subject or activity [2]. Characteristics to define expertise in Delphi studies can consist knowledge, experience and position, but among scholars there is a lack of clarity and limited consensus, who can be an expert in a Delphi study [3]. "Informed individuals", "specialists' in their field", "someone

© Springer Nature Switzerland AG 2022
L. Uden et al. (Eds.): KMO 2022, CCIS 1593, pp. 233–244, 2022.
https://doi.org/10.1007/978-3-031-07920-7_18

having knowledge about a specific subject" have for example been suggested as suitable Delphi panelist [4]. To clarify the expert selection process and to reduce selection bias, a multiple-step iterative approach has been suggested [5, 6].

The success of a Delphi study is mainly depending on the expert panel capability to provide proficient judgment. Using carefully selected experts is grounded on an assumption that using experts will result significantly better and substantially different responses from non-'experts' [7]. However, prior studies challenged this assumption and argued that (1) it is difficult to establish criteria to distinguish experts from layman and (2) there is no clear evidence that expert judgement will more reliable results than layman judgement [3, 8]. In all, layman opinions are rarely utilized in Delphi studies [9].

Using too homogenous expert panel can easily lead to biased and limited outcome, especially when trying to resolve ill-structured problems such as 17 Sustainable Development Goals (SDGs) defined by the United Nations General Assembly (UN-GA). Prior Delphi studies have called out greater participatory democracy and variety in Delphi panels [3]. Non-expert layman judgment can offer viewpoints, which otherwise would be omitted due entrenched positions of homogenous experts [10].

1.2 Objectives of This Study

The main of this study is to conceptualize expert dominated foresight Delphi method [1] and layman dominated crowdsourcing approach [11], and define the Crowdsourcing Delphi research approach [12]. Halicka [13] proposed a classification scheme to systematize the selection of future-oriented research methods. However, her comprehensive list did not include crowdsourcing techniques. Over the years a great number of various Delphi methods have been proposed [14], but none of these approaches have genuinely utilized and clarified the possibilities of crowdsourcing in context of foresight and innovation management research.

2   Crowdsourcing in Brief

2.1 Definition of Crowdsourcing

Howe [15] popularized the crowdsourcing term, which in its simplified form means a process where a task or tasks are delegated (i.e. outsourced) to a large group of people (i.e. crowd) who complete the task (e.g. propose a solution idea how to solve the problem). To provide first unifying definition for crowdsourcing [11] identified the following eight key characteristics to be included in a definition. (1) there is a clearly defined crowd; (2) there exists a task with a clear goal, (3) the recompense received by the crowd is clear, (4) the crowdsourcer is clearly identified, (5) the compensation to be received by the crowdsourcer is clearly defined (6) it is an online assigned process of participative type, (7) it uses an open call of variable extent and (8) it uses the internet. Numerous other definitions have been proposed to define the nature of the task, the crowd characteristics, the type of crowd knowledge, the kind of remuneration, how far can contributors access each other's contributions, how closely solvers work together, the methods used to aggregate the contributions and how the crowdsourcing process actually takes place [16]. In this study crowdsourcing is defined as follows:

"(1) A crowdsourcer" (i.e. a person or a team managing the crowdsourcing process) "(2) defines a task and" "(3) recruit a crowd" "(4) via an open call" "(5) by using the internet". "(6) A participatory process is applied and completed" and "(7, 8) both the crowd and crowdsourcer receives a compensation".

2.2 Classification of Crowdsourcing Approaches

The crowdsourcing archetypes found in prior literature are grounded on similar classification principles, but using varying and mixing names [17, 18]. In Table 1 we have combined the two partially overlapping four-quadrant models into one holistic framework.

Table 1. Key characteristics and classification of crowdsourcing applications

Term	Crowd rating	Micro-tasking	Crowd-creation	Crowd solving
Alternative names	Crowd Opinion	Crowd content, Virtual Labor Marketplaces, Crowdfunding, Crowd-processing	Crowd-collaboration	Solution crowd-sourcing, Crowdcasting
Generic purpose	"Harvesting crowd opinion and preferences	"Using crowd as outsourced labor force to complete predefined task(s)"	"Provide as many different creative contributions as possible"	"Finding first or the best actual solution for a well-defined problem"
Purpose in context of research process	Collecting quantitative and/or qualitative rating or judgment data	Providing additional human resources across all the research process under Delphi-manager or team supervision	Generating diverse qualitative data relating the research question(s)	Generating the best qualitative data relating the research question(s)
Aggregated vs. filtered contributions	*Aggregated:* No prior validation required	*Aggregated* No prior validation required	*Filtered:* Prior validation required	*Filtered:* Prior validation required
Subjective vs. objectives content	*Subjective:* Based on Beliefs and opinions	*Objective:* Based on facts	*Subjective:* Based on beliefs and opinions	*Objective:* Based on facts
Emergent vs. non-emergent	*Emergent:* Value as a combined collection	*Non-emergent:* Value as an individual contribution	*Emergent:* Value as a combined collection	*Non-emergent:* Value as an individual contribution
Homogeneous vs. Heterogeneous	*Homogeneous:* Value emerges due to quantitative properties	*Homogeneous:* Value emerges due to quantitative properties	*Heterogeneous:* Value emerges due to individual qualities	*Heterogeneous:* Value emerges due to individual qualities

The archetypes includes (1) **crowd-rating** focusing on harvesting crowds opinions through voting, (2) **micro-tasking** where a crowdsourcer breaks a large task into a small homogenous and routine type of jobs which are easy and quick to complete, and then re-assembles them to complete the task, (3) **crowd collaboration** grounded on the idea of aggregating various crowd members inventive and creative contributions (e.g. idea) into a larger whole, which in its accumulated form provides collective value and (4) **crowd solving** where a well-defined problem is defined by a crowdsoucer and crowd members are proposing actual solutions instead of ideas.

Prpić et al. [18] model main dimensions are "aggregated vs. filtered" and "subjective vs. objective". In the case of aggregated contributions, individual contributions are combined without any additional processing (e.g. voting results), whereas filtered contributions require prior processing before providing value (e.g. idea suggestions). Subjective contributions are grounded on beliefs and opinions (e.g. selecting the preferred option when voting), whereas in the case of objective contributions only facts matter (e.g. completion of micro-task).

On the other hand, Geiger et al. [17] four-quadrant model is grounded on "emergent vs. non-emergent" and "homogeneous vs. heterogeneous" dimensions. Emergent contributions provide value only as a part of a combined collection (e.g. voting results) whereas, in the case of non-emergent contributions, an individual contribution provides also value in isolation (e.g. problem-solving proposal). Homogenous contributions value all (valid) contributions equally (e.g. voting opinion), while heterogeneous contributions provide value due to their individual qualities (e.g. idea suggestion).

3   Delphi Technique in Brief

3.1   Definition of Delphi

More than 60 years have passed since the first Delphi study took place and more than 50 years since the first scientific article came to light describing the Delphi method and procedure [19]. According to Linstone and Turoff [1] *"Delphi may be characterised as a method for structuring a group communication process so that the process is effective in allowing a group of individuals, as a whole, to deal with a complex problem"*. The Delphi method is probably the most often used in foresight studies, but there are variety of other application areas [20].

The key characteristics of the Delphi technique includes [21]: (1) the use of a panel of 'experts' for obtaining data, (2) participants do not meet in face-to-face discussions, (3) the use of sequential questionnaires and/or interviews, (4) the systematic emergence of a concurrence of judgement/opinion, (5) the guarantee of anonymity for subjects' responses, (6) the use of frequency distributions to identify patterns of agreement and (7) the use of two or more rounds between which a summary of the results of the previous round is communicated to and evaluated by panel members.

For our study purposes Delphi technique is defined by following structure as the previous crowdsourcing term.

"(1) A Delphi-manager" (i.e. a person or a team managing the Delphi process) "(2) defines a question(s) relating complex problem solving or forecasting task, improves

it/them during the research process and" "(3) recruit carefully selected anonymous experts" via "(4) personal request to participate" "(5) by using direct communication methods". "(6) An iterative feedback process having at least two rounds is applied and completed in a way that the previous rounds form the basis for the next and experts are not allowed to directly collaborate. The process ends when the desired level of agreement or stability in experts' responses has been reached". "(7, 8) The completion of the task both experts and crowdsourcer receives a compensation".

3.2 Classification of Delphi Techniques

A great variety of Delphi techniques have been proposed [14, 22]. The most typical Delphi technique variant is *Classical Delphi*, which aim is to serve as a forum for to elicit opinions and seek a consensus among group of experts. *Modified Delphi* consist Classical Delphi technique having combined with another research method [23]. Another popular technique – *the Policy Delphi* – serves as a forum for ideas seeking to generate the strongest possible opposing views among informed advocates [24]. Decision Delphi focuses on preparing and supporting decision making by recruiting experts based on their position in the decision-making hierarchy [25]. *Ranking-Type Delphi* objective is to reach a group consensus about the relative importance of a set of issues [26]. *Argument Delphi* – a policy Delphi variant – develops relevant arguments and expose reason [27]. Scenario and *Disaggregated Policy Delphi* are constructing scenarios [28, 29]. Other Delphi technique variant are e.g. *Electronic Delphi, Real-Time Delphi, EFTE Delphi, Mini Delphi, Online Delphi, Technological Delphi, Conventional Delphi and Historical Delphi* [14, 22]. It is good to aware of different variants of the Delphi methodology.

4 The Differences Between Crowdsourcing and Delphi Technique

4.1 Comparison of Crowdsourcing and Delphi Technique Characteristics

To our knowledge, a study by Flostrand [30] is the only prior study evaluating similarities and differences between crowdsourcing and Delphi technique. In the following these suggestions were critically evaluated by (1) comparing the term definitions and the key characteristics [11, 14] and (2) searching examples of real-life implementations and prior studies to identify fundamental differences thru falsification logic [31]. The differences are justified and discussed from the following viewpoints: (1) participant anonymity, (2) number of rounds and feedback mechanism, (3) participant recruitment and selection logic, (4) range, depth, and controllability of expertise, and (5) sample size [32].

Participant Anonymity: In crowdsourcing non-anonymity is possible and common in some cases, but based on Delphi's definition it is not. In Delphi technique anonymity can range from total to restricted anonymity (i.e. participants' names are known but responses remain anonymous). In crowdsourcing anonymity can range from total to non-anonymity (e.g. in crowdrating services such as Google Maps, participants can be non-anonymous to each other).

The Number of Rounds and Feedback Mechanism: Delphi process requires multiple rounds whereas in crowdsourcing "one round" is a de facto standard. By definition, the Delphi process must include more than one round and have an iterative and controlled feedback process. However, the crowdsourcing process is in most cases conducted in one round. In the case of prize-based crowd-solving competitions, one round is a mandatory requirement [33] whereas in crowdrating services such as Google Maps crowdsourcing is a continuous process.

Participant Recruitment and Selection Logic: In Delphi technique participants are selected via a careful invitation process, while crowdsourcing does not consist of participant selection due to an open call to participate. In Delphi technique, a multistep process is utilized to define relevant participant profiles and to recruit matching persons via the invitation process [5]. In the case of crowdsourcing participants are recruited via open call by using the internet and therefore crowdsourcers cannot directly control who is participating (i.e. anyone willing can participate).

Range, Depth, and Controllability of Expertise: In both methods, participant expertise can vary. However, Delphi studies emphasize expertise as a selection criterion but in crowdsourcing, expertise cannot be directly controlled due to the open call approach. In Delphi studies expertise can range between narrow broad sense. Inboard sense, the position in the decision-making hierarchy or affiliation with an interest group defines the participation, not the expertise. Due to the open call to participate, anybody regardless of expertise or non-expertise can participate in crowdsourcing. In practice, expertise can vary greatly e.g. very limited in microtasking to highly specialist in crowd-solving competitions [33].

Sample Size: In both methods, the number of participants can greatly vary, but only in Delphi maximum sample size is predefined. The method selection in Delphi has a great impact on appropriate sample size, while the success of engaging participants via open call determines the "panel size" in crowdsourcing. Typically, the Delphi panel size is more modest. Delphi panel size is disputed and partially dependent on the Delphi methods variant. Anyhow, panel size is predefined but can become lower due to dropouts. The suggested minimum being four to seven, but usually ranging between 10 to 30 experts. Sample sizes over one hundred are rare and sizes over one thousand are extremely rare. Also, the size of the crowd is disputed and is depending on succeeding in an open call. In prior studies, size has ranged from less than ten to over one hundred thousand [34]. Crowds having over one hundred members are common.

To conclude, in Fig. 1 we have illustrated the key distinct dimensions between Crowdsourcing and Delphi methodologies to highlight the positions of typical crowdsourcing and Delphi projects in the cubic illustration. The three key distinct dimensions and the scales include: (1) the number of contributors, anonymity, and recruitment logic: ranging from a small group of pre-profiled people who have been invited to a large anonymous or non-anonymous crowd recruited via an open call, (2) range, depth, and controllability of expertise: ranging from layman to experts having forefront knowledge on the narrow topic area and (3) iteration and the number of rounds: ranging from one continuous round to iterative feedback process consisting multiple iteration rounds. Crowdsourcing and Delphi methods when implemented traditionally, remain typically at the opposite corners of the cube. Since Crowdsourcing Delphi inherits the characteristics from both methods, it could cover any location in the cube. When methods are implemented individually, certain locations in the cube are extremely rare (i.e. anomaly) or impossible due to definition.

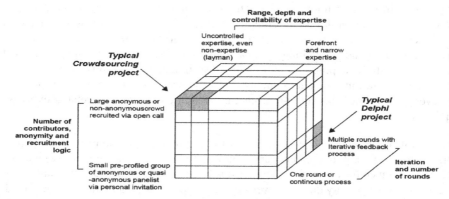

Fig. 1. The key distinct dimensions of the Crowdsourcing and Delphi methods.

4.2 Crowdsourcing Delphi Definition

Grounded on our prior Crowdsourcing and Delphi definitions, the following definition is proposed Crowdsourcing Delphi:

"Crowdsourcing Delphi is a multimethod research approach in which (1) a Delphi manager (or Delphi team) is acting also as a crowdsourcer who (1) by personal request and via rigorous selection process recruits committed expert panel(s) and (2) by open call recruits a diverse voluntary crowd of individuals to undertake a pre-defined targeted task(s). An iterative participatory process having at least two expert rounds and at least one interaction round between experts and crowd is applied and completed in a way that the previous rounds form the basis for the next. During the Delphi, phase participants are not allowed to directly communicate with each other. The process ends when the desired level of agreement or stability in experts' and crowds' responses has been reached" and both experts, crowd, and crowdsourcer has received compensation for their efforts.

5   Advantages and Disadvantages of Crowdsourcing Delphi Method Variants

5.1   Classification of Crowdsourcing Delphi Methodologies

When combining Crowdsourcing Delphi methodologies, we can choose from four different crowdsourcing approaches (Crowd rating, Crowdcreation, Crowd solving and Microtasking) and six main Delphi approaches (Traditional Delphi, Policy Delphi, Argument

Delphi, Decision Delphi, Ranking-type Delphi Rankings and Scenario Delphi or Disaggregated Policy Delphi Scenarios). This results a total of twenty-four different variants such as traditional Delphi – Crowd rating.

Micro-tasking. Applying the micro-tasking-based Crowdsourcing Delphi process is somewhat similar for all Delphi variants since the aim is to conduct a simple routine type of job. In practice micro-tasking can be applied (1) during the initial planning phase to support e.g. desk research/literature review process, participant and/or crowd recruitment or topic setting process, (2) in data collection phase to support data collection, (3) between the rounds by helping in data analysis and next round planning and (4) at the end of the study helping in reporting and disseminating the results. Advantages of applying micro-tasking include reducing costs and speeding up the research process. However, possibilities for micro-tasking can be limited due to task-related expertise requirements.

Crowd Rating. Benefits for applying crowd rating in a Delphi study consist (1) possibilities to compare public and expert opinions, preferences, and support, (2) gaining greater acceptance for the study outcomes due to possibility of participation and influence, (3) increased clarity due to converting language and argumentation for the crowd, (4) crowd becomes informed at the same or nearly at the same time as experts, and (5) enables agenda setting based on crowd priorities. Disadvantages consist (1) difficulties to achieve consensus, (2) possible bias if over emphasizing public opinion over fact-based expert opinions, (3) more work due simplifying and reformatted statements used in the rating process, (4) in some cases crowd has only indirect influence, (5) to avoid bias, a representative sample is required, (6) more vulnerable for biased options and bounded rationality, and (7) greater possibility for manipulation.

Crowdcreation. Advantages for applying crowdcreation in a Delphi study include more (1) diverse, (2) extensive, and (3) out-of-box viewpoints, thus (4) lowering the risk of ignoring relevant issues. Furthermore, the ability for (5) early engagement of those whose life is impacted and (6) comparison of the layman and expert contributions. Weaknesses incorporate (1) spending a lot of efforts for little results, (2) difficulty to focus, interpret or apply due to a high number of contributions, and (3) irrational contributions, lack of long-term vision, and bias are more likely occurring due lack of expertise, knowledge, and experience.

Crowd Solving. Benefits for applying crowd solving comprises (1) better motivation to participate and engaging those who otherwise would not, (2) ensuring crowd contributions and influence via winning proposals, and (3) likely higher quality contributions due to a possibility to receive a reward. Drawbacks include (1) limitations what kind of research questions can be formatted in a competition format, (2) logic is based on the zero-sum game, therefore only winning proposals are notified and many good proposals may be neglected, (3) competition can lead to hidden agenda, narrow mindedness and omit collaborative based solutions.

5.2 Framework for Selecting and Evaluating Crowdsourcing Delphi Research Strategy

In Fig. 2, the different possibilities to combine Crowdsourcing and Delphi methodologies in a single data collection round are presented by adopting a typology of mixed methods designs [35].

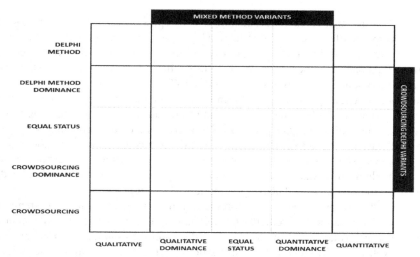

Fig. 2. Possible combinations to utilize Crowdsourcing and Delphi methodologies.

Both horizontal and vertical dimensions include emphasis between the extremes of the continuum. Either Crowdsourcing or Delphi can have dominant status in the research. Equal status is also possible when both approaches receive similar importance. Similar combinations can be identified in the case of qualitative and quantitative data, resulting in fifteen different alternatives for around in the Crowdsourcing Delphi study. Classification of mixed methods consists also of time orientation dimensions indicating that the different method variants can be executed concurrently or sequentially while varying the sequence order [35]. Time orientation can be included in the framework by indicating phases as numbers in the appropriate matrix cell. By accumulating all rounds, "average position" in the framework can be defined to illustrate the overall balance. Finally, Crowdsourcing Delphi study can be partially or fully mixed in the following four components [35]: (1) the research objective, (2) type of data and operations, (4) type of analysis, and (4) type of inference.

Research strategies including qualitative methods can utilize crowd creation, crowd solving and crowdcreation methods, whereas studies utilizing quantitative methods can benefit only on Crowd rating. Qualitative crowdsourcing methods activities consist of discussing, arguing, and reviewing research topics via qualitative contributions as well as giving feedback and reflecting on the prior rounds accumulated results. Quantitative crowdsourcing activities include rating the proposed statements based on various dimensions such as desirability, feasibility, probability, risk, uncertainty, and/or importance.

6 Conclusion

It has been argued that foresight studies need to adopt a mixed-methods approach to combine the cycles of deductive and inductive logic [36]. Furthermore, the triangulation approach where foresight studies use more than one method, more than one source of data, more than one theoretical framework, or more than one research group in the study of social phenomena is also suggested as criteria [37].

One notable advantage is the Crowdsourcing methodology s a large variety of different Delphi variants and different Crowdsourcing techniques. The Crowdsourcing Delphi allows also combinations of Data pools/Big Data flows of crowds to the methodological practices of various methodological Delphi variants. In this way, a new methodological solution reduces shortcomings and weaknesses of both crowdsourcing techniques and expert methods. In this was the Crowdsourcing Delphi is a new promising knowledge management methodology and also a pragmatic KM solution.

We argue that the proposed Crowdsourcing Delphi approach fully meets both mixed-method and triangulation requirements. Crowdsourcing Delphi utilizes different sources of data, both quantitative and qualitative (i.e. data and information from experts and crowd), as well as two different research methodologies (i.e. Crowdsourcing and Delphi). The follow-up case studies should focus on validating the claimed benefits, identifying implementation challenges, and possible performance differences between the various types of Crowdsourcing Delphi studies.

References

1. Linstone, H.A., Turoff, M.: The Delphi Method: Techniques and Applications. Wesley Publishing Company, Reading (1975)
2. Expert in Cambridge Dictionary. https://dictionary.cambridge.org/. Accessed 10 Mar 2022
3. Baker, J., Lovell, K., Harris, N.: How expert are the experts? An exploration of the concept of 'expert' within Delphi panel techniques. Nurse Res. 14(1), 59–70 (2006)
4. Keeney, S., Hasson, F., McKenna, H.P.: A critical review of the Delphi technique as a research methodology for nursing. Int. J. Nurs. Stud. 38(2), 195–200 (2001)
5. Okoli, C., Pawlowski, S.D.: The Delphi method as a research tool: an example, design considerations and applications. Inf. Manag. 42(1), 15–29 (200–)
6. Van Zolingen, S.J., Klaassen, C.A.: Selection processes in a Delphi study about key qualifications in senior secondary vocational education. Technol. Forecast. Soc. Chang. 70(4), 317–340 (2003)
7. Goodman, C.M.: The Delphi technique: a critique. J. Adv. Nurs. 12(6), 729–734 (1987)
8. Sackman, H.: Delphi Critique, Expert Opinion, Forecasting and the Group Process. Lexington Books (1975)
9. McMillan, S.S., King, M., Tully, M.P.: How to use the nominal group and Delphi techniques. Int. J. Clin. Pharm. 38(3), 655–662 (2016). https://doi.org/10.1007/s11096-016-0257-x

10. Hussler, C., Muller, P., Rondé, P.: Is diversity in Delphi panelist groups useful? Evidence from a French forecasting exercise on the future of nuclear energy. Technol. Forecast. Soc. Change **78**(9), 1642–1653 (2011)
11. Estellés-Arolas, E., González-Ladrón-De-Guevara, F.: Towards an integrated crowdsourcing definition. J. Inf. Sci. **38**(2), 189–200 (2012)
12. Kaivo-oja, J., Santonen, T., Myllylä, Y.: The crowdsourcing Delphi: combining the Delphi methodology and crowdsourcing techniques. In: International Society for Professional Innovation Management. ISPIM Conference Proceedings (2013). URN:NBN:fi:amk-2016101015024
13. Halicka, K.: Innovative classification of methods of the Future-oriented Technology Analysis. Technol. Econ. Dev. Econ. **22**(4), 574–597 (2016)
14. Strasser, A.: Delphi method variants in information systems research: taxonomy development and application. Electron. J. Bus. Res. Methods **15**(2), 120–133 (2017)
15. Howe, J.: Crowdsourcing: How the Power of the Crowd is Driving the Future of Business. Business Books, Great Britain (2008)
16. Ghezzi, A., Gabelloni, D., Martini, A., Natalicchio, A.: Crowdsourcing: a review and suggestions for future research. Int. J. Manag. Rev. **20**(2), 343–363 (2018)
17. Geiger, D., Rosemann, M., Fielt, E., Schader, M.: Crowdsourcing information systems-definition typology, and design. In: George, J.F. (ed.) Proceedings of the 33rd Annual International Conference on Information Systems, pp. 1–11. Association for Information Systems/AIS Electronic Library (AISeL) (2012). http://aisel.aisnet.org/
18. Prpić, J., Shukla, P.P., Kietzmann, J.H., McCarthy, I.P.: How to work a crowd: developing crowd capital through crowdsourcing. Bus. Horiz. **58**(1), 77–85 (2015)
19. Dalkey, N., Helmer, O.: An experimental application of the Delphi method to use of experts. Manag. Sci. **9**(3), 458–467 (1963)
20. Turoff, M., Linstone, H.A.: The Delphi method-techniques and applications (2002). https://web.njit.edu/~turoff/pubs/delphibook/delphibook.pdf. Accessed 10 Mar 2022
21. McKenna, H.P.: The Delphi technique: a worthwhile research approach for nursing? J. Adv. Nurs. **19**(6), 1221–1225 (1994)
22. Mullen, P.M.: Delphi: myths and reality. J. Health Organ. Manag. **17**(1), 37–52 (2003)
23. Keeney, S.: The Delphi technique. In: Gerrish, K., Lacey, A. (eds.) The Research Process in Nursing, 6th edn., pp. 227–236. Wiley-Blackwell, London (2010)
24. Turoff, M.: The design of a policy Delphi. Technol. Forecast. Soc. Change **2**(2), 149–171 (1970)
25. Rauch, W.: The decision Delphi. Technol. Forecast. Soc. Change **15**(3), 159–169 (1979)
26. Schmidt, R.C.: Managing Delphi surveys using nonparametric statistical techniques. Decis. Sci. **28**(3), 763–774 (1997)
27. Kuusi, O.: Expertise in the future use of generic technologies. VATT research reports 59. VATT, Helsinki (1999)
28. Nowack, M., Endrikat, J., Guenther, E.: Review of Delphi-based scenario studies: quality and design considerations. Technol. Forecast. Soc. Change **78**(9), 1603–1615 (2011)
29. Tapio, P.: Disaggregative policy Delphi: using cluster analysis as a tool for systematic scenario formation. Technol. Forecast. Soc. Change **70**(1), 83–101 (2003)
30. Flostrand, A.: Finding the future: crowdsourcing versus the Delphi technique. Bus. Horiz. **60**(2), 229–236 (2017)
31. Popper, K.: The Logic of Scientific Discovery. Routledge, London (2005)
32. Marchau, V., van de Linde, E.: The Delphi method. In: van der Duin, P. (ed.) Foresight in Organizations. Methods and Tools, pp. 59–79. Routledge, New York (2016)
33. Brabham, D.C.: Crowdsourcing as a model for problem solving: an introduction and cases. Convergence **14**(1), 75–90 (2008)

34. Ranard, B.L., et al.: Crowdsourcing—harnessing the masses to advance health and medicine, a systematic review. J. Gen. Internal Med. **29**(1), 187–203 (2014). https://doi.org/10.1007/s11606-013-2536-8

35. Leech, N.L., Onwuegbuzie, A.J.: A typology of mixed methods research designs. Qual. Quant. **43**, 265–275 (2009). https://doi.org/10.1007/s11135-007-9105-3

36. Kaivo-oja, J.: Towards better participatory processes in technology foresight: how to link participatory foresight research to the methodological machinery of qualitative research and phenomenology? Futures **86**, 94–106 (2017)

37. Jari, K.-O., Theresa, L.: Knowledge management and triangulation logic in the foresight research and analyses in business process management. In: Uden, L., Lu, W., Ting, I.-H. (eds.) KMO 2017. CCIS, vol. 731, pp. 228–238. Springer, Cham (2017). https://doi.org/10.1007/978-3-319-62698-7_20

Continuous Reporting Through RADAR: The Case Study of Environmental Monitoring

Antonia Azzini[1,3P] ![ID], Nicola Cortesi[1,2(✉)] ![ID], and Giuseppe Psaila[2] ![ID]

[1] Consortium for the Technology Transfer (C2T), Milan, Italy
`antonia.azzini@consorzioc2t.it`
[2] Department of Management, Information and Production Engineering, University of Bergamo, Dalmine, BG, Italy
`{nicola.cortesi,giuseppe.psaila}@unibg.it`
[3] CEFRIEL, Milan, Italy
`antonia.azzini@cefriel.com`

Abstract. Born in the context of the financial market, "continuous reporting" is an activity that many municipalities must perform, to address novel issues such as ecology. In this paper, we study the case of "environmental reporting" by adopting the vision provided by the *RADAR Framework*. The paper shows how the innovative approach provided by the framework for continuous reporting can be beneficial for municipalities, to address the long-lasting activity of environmental monitoring, provided that data and knowledge about data are collected by the framework, which supports design and continued generation of reports.

Keywords: Continuous reporting in environmental monitoring · Integrated management of knowledge and data · Aiding long-term reporting

1 Introduction

Due to the recent consciousness about environmental issues, a series of laws and regulations impose municipalities to gather data about levels of pollution in the administered territory, so as to send (periodically and continuously) specific reports to regional and/or country governments and agencies. Such reports are often defined by laws and regulations.

It appears that this is a problem of knowledge management, but the question is: "what kind of knowledge"? Clearly, it is necessary to collect measurements performed by sensors disseminated on the territory. However, the key knowledge to gather and store is "the meaning of data and how to prepare reports, based on current and past regulations". In other words, it is necessary to accompany raw data with semantic annotations and descriptions of their meaning, modeled and represented in such a way reports can be easily defined and generated. In [1], we presented the *RADAR Framework*, a suite of software tools specifically designed

© Springer Nature Switzerland AG 2022
L. Uden et al. (Eds.): KMO 2022, CCIS 1593, pp. 245–256, 2022.
https://doi.org/10.1007/978-3-031-07920-7_19

to build a long-lasting environment to collect data, possibly coming from multiple data sources, described by means of a unified model that exploits ontologies and semantic annotations to semantically characterize data. Since several users with specific skills are involved over time with possibly-high levels of turnover, the *RADAR Framework* assists the overall process. In [1], we presented a running example related to a financial application, which is the context from which the idea of the *RADAR Framework* has originated. Here, we show how, without any modification, it supports environmental monitoring too, due to its design choices: in fact, environmental reporting is more difficult than financial reporting, due to the heterogeneity of sensors, regulations and bodies involved in the activity: the *RADAR Framework* works as a collector of data and knowledge about data, providing effective support for designing and generating reports.

The contribution of this paper is to investigate the adoption of the *RADAR Framework* by municipalities for performing environmental monitoring through continuous reporting. At the best of our knowledge, this problem has been investigated in a limited way (see Sect. 2). The case we study in this paper directly derives from preliminary analysis we performed for real municipalities. Section 3 briefly introduces the main characteristics of the *RADAR Framework* and of the *RADAR Data Model* (see [1] for an extensive presentation). Section 4 presents a small-sized case study and a *RADAR Schema* for the addressed application context. Finally, Sect. 5 draws conclusions and future work.

2   Related Work

In recent years, environmental and ecological issues have become of particular interest, particularly with regard to the ability to acquire and manage heterogeneous data from sensors (see [8] for a review), for analysis purposes.

Ecology is a multidisciplinary science that involves physical, chemical and biological factors. The need to access such different data sources becomes particularly important in analyses carried out to address ecological studies. Governments increasingly need integrated analyses to make decisions, so as to manage the environment in a sustainable way. However, "a mess" is the current status of environmental data, for many reasons. (i) There are so many aspects that concern environment; thus, many different measurements are made (levels of pollutants, rain, and so on), which are heterogeneous by nature. (ii) The lack of a world-wide standard for representing data describing the same concepts, as well as the lack of common and agreed vocabulary and semantics, are still significant issues. (iii) Data are stored in proprietary systems, for which documentation that explains structure and semantics is often limited or absent.

The lack of formalization of ecological and environmental concepts has led to controversial interpretations. Ecological data are often incomplete, ambiguous and difficult to understand. However, the need to monitor long-term trends in ecological data has led to perform environmental reporting activities.

As reported by the literature, ontologies are useful as they allow for defining concepts and relations, improving the interpretation and integration of information coming from heterogeneous sources (databases). For example, [5] presented the problem caused by the lack of formalized concept definitions for ecological and environmental topics, and provided an interesting review of the positive efforts that could be obtained by developing ontologies for this context.

The paper [6] proposed a formal ontological framework for capturing the semantic information of observational data sets. This work was done within the context of the "Science Environment for Ecological Knowledge" (whose acronym is SEEK) project[1]. In particular, the authors described the "SEEK Extensible Observation Ontology" (whose acronym is OBOE[2]), thought as a framework for semantically annotating observational data. The work also provided an approach for developing domain-specific ecological ontologies.

Another interesting proposal is the ENVO "Environmental Ontology", for which [4] presented some interesting applications in different domains.

Consequently, the discipline called *Ecoinformatics'* [7] provides scientists with innovative tools and approaches for managing, analyzing and visualizing relevant biological, environmental, and socio-economic data and information. Moreover, [7] characterized ecology as a data-intensive science, which needs massive amounts of data collected by environmental-sensor networks.

Consequently, environmental reporting is going to become important; however, with respect to financial reporting, the perception of its importance and the consequent development of technical solutions are still in the very early stages.

3   The RADAR Framework

The *RADAR Framework* [1] has been developed to solve the problem of automatic generation of reports, by collecting data and domain knowledge, by assisting the design of reports. The architecture (see Fig. 1) is structured in two layers: *Design Layer* and *Information-System Layer*.

The *Design Layer* is composed by the following tools.

- *Knowledge-Base Manager*. This tool is responsible for designing the *RADAR Schema* of the data to collect and integrate, on the basis of the *RADAR Data Model*, which provides an integrated view of the data, semantically characterized by an ontology and possibly enriched with semantic annotations. This tool builds the *Knowledge Base* and generates descriptions deployed to the *Information-System Layer*.
- *Report Designer*. This tool assists experts of the application domain, through a user-friendly interface, with the following functionalities: browsing of the knowledge base, definition of aggregations among data, design of reports.

The domain experts that provide the basic domain knowledge can upload a *Source Ontology* to the *Knowledge Base*. On its basis, the *RADAR Schema* can

---

[1] Science Environment for Ecological Knowledge. http://seek.ecoinformatics.org/ [accessed 07 April 2022].

[2] The extensible observation ontology. https://bioportal.bioontology.org/ontologies/ OBOE [accessed on 07 April 2022].

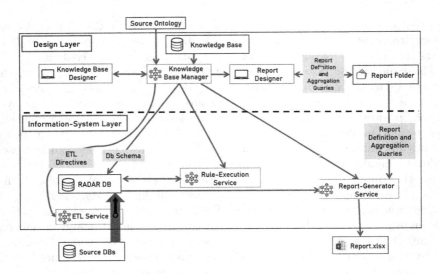

Fig. 1. Architecture of the *RADAR Framework*.

be built. Users devoted to build reports exploit the *Knowledge Base* to design reports, by specifying possibly-complex aggregations on the data.

The *Information-System Layer* encompasses several tools too.

- *RADAR DB*. The core of the *Information-System Layer* is the database that collects and stores the data to aggregate into reports. This database, called *RADAR DB*, is deployed by means of the *DB Schema*, provided by the *Knowledge-Base Manager*, which describes the structure of the database.
- *ETL Service*. This tool actually feeds the *RADAR DB*, by performing classical ETL (Extract, Transform and Load) activities on the *Source DBs*, i.e., the external databases from which data are gathered. This tool operates on the basis of the *ETL Directives*, deployed by the *Knowledge-Base Manager* in the *Design Layer*.
- *Rule-Execution Service*. In Sect. 4.2, we will see that the *RADAR Data Model* encompasses a rule language called *RADAR Rule Language*, whose goal is to automatically complete missing data. The tool called *Rule-Execution Service* actually executes these rules on the *RADAR DB*, when new data are loaded. It acquires rules directly from the *Knowledge Base*.
- *Report-Generator Service*. This tool actually generates reports. It acquires the data contained in the *RADAR DB* by executing the queries contained in the *Report Definition* (deployed by the *Report Designer* tool in the *Design Layer*). It generates reports in the XLSX format.

The RADAR Data Model. The core intuition behind the *RADAR Framework* is to provide a unique data model that describes data at a high (yet operational)

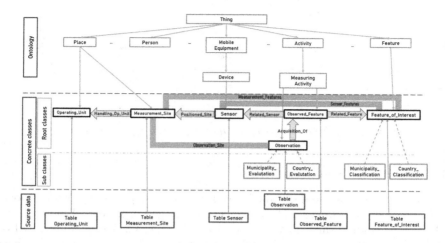

Fig. 2. Complete *RADAR Schema* for the case study.

level, their semantics and their provenance. For this reason, the *RADAR Data Model* is organized in three different layers.

- The *Ontological Layer* describes the *Reference Ontology*, i.e. a graph that contains ontological classes and inheritance relationships between them. The ontology constitutes the basic domain knowledge.
- The *Concrete Layer* provides the actual user model for data. It is an object-oriented model, where classes are called *concrete classes*, because they provide a concrete interpretation of concepts reported in the *Reference Ontology*. The *Concrete Layer* gives a unified view of gathered data.
- The *Mapping Layer* describes how concrete classes in the *Concrete Layer* are mapped to tables in the *Source DBs*, so as the *RADAR DB* can be automatically populated by the *ETL Service*. This way, knowledge about provenance of data is explicitly maintained in the *Knowledge Base*.

By means of the *Knowledge-Base Manager*, various users define the *RADAR Schema* for the application domain. Then, users in charge for designing and generating reports exploit the *Reference Ontology* to identify the proper concrete classes to query, so as to aggregate data and put them into reports.

Figure 2 shows the *RADAR Schema* for the case study; it shows the three layers and the relationships between them. Classes are denoted as rectangles, while relationships are denoted as arrows. In Sect. 4, the notation will be further explained; nevertheless, the reader can find a detailed description in [1].

4   Addressing Environmental Reporting

We now provide the contribution of the paper: we describe the case study and show how the *RADAR Framework* provides an integrated view of the problem.

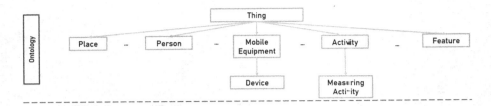

Fig. 3. Excerpt of the *Reference Ontology* in the *RADAR Schema*.

4.1   Introducing the Case Study

Suppose that the municipality called MyCity periodically has to provide reports to the regional government and to agencies in charge for ecological monitoring.

Data are acquired through sensor networks that measure, for example, hydro-morphological, physico-chemical, and micro-biological water features. Furthermore, in the most industrialized areas, the municipality constantly monitors the levels of pollutant emissions into the air in intense-traffic areas and in the town center. Sensor networks are usually run by specialized companies/agencies, which periodically provide data to the municipality.

Employees of the office in charge to gather environmental data may need to customize the reports to generate, in order to satisfy requirements from the organizations that request them. In fact, they periodically receive indications from authorities and agencies regarding the reports to produce, in compliance with regulations. These define, for example, standard measurement ranges within which measurements are considered either good or critical for health; however, these ranges can vary, depending on the specific authority.

To generate reports, a large amount of data must be gathered. Sensor networks are typically organized in a (both geographical and categorical) hierarchical way, so as to allow for defining multi-dimensional aggregations. Furthermore, several sensor networks and managing systems could be involved; consequently, many different sources of information could provide data to aggregate to prepare reports. Of course, many different people with an incredible variety of skills are involved, in order to manage sensor networks, manage systems and databases, interpret regulations and create reports. Each of them provides a specific piece of knowledge, that can be precious for another person involved in the process many years later; in fact, this is a typical case of "continuous reporting", which involves many different competences for a long period with high turnover. The *RADAR Framework* has been designed to assist such a long-lasting activity.

4.2   Modeling Data for Environmental Reporting

This section shows how to obtain the *RADAR Schema* for the case study, shortly explaining it. The schema is completely depicted in Fig. 2.

Choice of the Reference Ontology. The *Ontological Layer* provides the basic semantic framework for data collected in the *RADAR DB*. In the context of

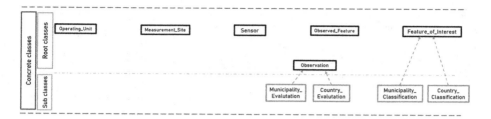

Fig. 4. *Concrete Layer* for the case study.

environmental reporting, the most-widely accepted ontology is the ENVO ontology[3], which defines common concepts in the environmental field. Consequently, we decided to adopt it as *Reference Ontology* in the *RADAR Schema*. The *Ontological Layer* is represented in Fig. 3 (extracted from the upper part of Fig. 2); of course, since it is not possible to depict the overall ontology, Fig. 2 and 3 report only those classes that are referred to by the *Concrete Layer*. Specifically, the ontological classes named "Place", "Device", and "Measuring Activity" are reported. Furthermore, an extra class named "Feature" was added to the ontology, because it is not defined within ENVO; in fact, the reference ontology defined in the *Ontological Layer* can be obtained by extending external ontologies.

Defining Concrete Classes. Once chosen the *Reference Ontology*, it is possible to provide the logical model for data to store into the *RADAR DB*. This is the *Concrete Layer*, whose name denotes the fact that it makes concepts provided by the ontology concrete.

As far as the case study is concerned, it is possible to define six root-level concrete classes; depicted in Fig. 4. The Operating_Unit concrete class describes the position of a district of the municipality, in which a team of technicians manages sensors. The Measurement_Site concrete class describes positions of sensors (typically, sensors are within stations, i.e., containers dedicated to perform environmental measurements).

The Sensor concrete class describes the sensors used for measurements. The Observed_Feature concrete class describes the various features measured by each sensor: each instance associates a sensor to a feature; this latter one is described by an instance of the Feature_of_Interest concrete class.

Finally, the Observation concrete class describes single observations, which are performed by sensors, of a specific feature. The Observation class has two sub-classes. The sub-class, as defined in Definition 4 in [1], is a specialization of the concrete class, where properties are inherited and novel properties are added. Specifically, the Municipality_Evaluation sub-class and the Country_Evaluation sub-class report if constraints posed by the municipality and by the country government (respectively) on (e.g. chemical) features are met or not by observations. Similarly, the Feature_of_Interest class has

---

[3] Environment Ontology (ENVO), http://www.obofoundry.org/ontology/envo.html [accessed on 07 April 2022].

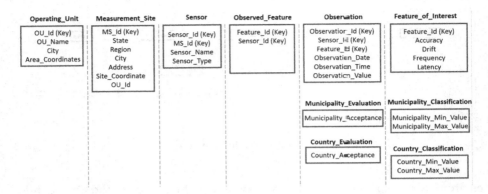

Fig. 5. Properties of concrete classes for the case study.

two sub-classes, named `Municipality_Classification` and `Country_Classification`. For each feature, they define the ranges within which a measurement of the feature is considered acceptable by the Municipality and by the Country, resp.. Figure 5 reports the properties for the concrete classes.

Defining Look-Up Relationships. Once concrete classes are defined, it is necessary to introduce "Look-Up Relationships" between concrete classes: they specify logical relationships between instances of the associated concrete classes, specifically the fact that an instance o_1 in the C_1 concrete class refers to an instance o_2 actually present in the C_2 concrete class. In other words, look-up relationships ensure referential integrity in the data and facilitate the query phase. Figure 6 reports the *Concrete Layer* for the case study extended with relationships; look-up relationships are depicted as labeled thick yellow arrows.

Specifically, five look-up relationships are defined. Through the relationship named `Handling_Operating_Unit`, every instance of the `Measurement_Site` concrete class refers to the `Operating_Unit` whose team is responsible to manage it. The `Positioned_Site` relationship says in which `Measurement_Site` a `Sensor` is installed.

Two look-up relationships originate from the `Observed_Feature class`: the `Related_Sensor` relationship refers to an instance of the `Sensor` concrete class; then, the `Related_Feature` relationship refers to the `Feature_of_Interest` class. This way, the `Observed_Feature` concrete class actually realizes a many-to-many relationship between the `Sensor` and the `Feature_of_Interest` concrete classes.

Finally, the `Acquisition_of` relationship makes an instance of the `Observation` class able to refer to the corresponding instance of the `Observed_Feature` class; in fact, for each instance of this latter class, which denotes a feature measured by a sensor, many instances of the `Observation` class can be stored in the database, each one corresponding to a single measurement of the feature by the sensor.

Defining Virtual Relationships. Look-up relationships implicitly define transitive associations between concrete classes: in fact, by navigating look-up

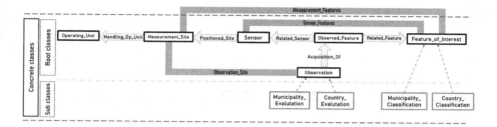

Fig. 6. *Concrete Layer* with look-up and virtual relationships.

relationships, it is possible to discover (possibly many-to-many) indirect relationships; some of them could be precious for analysts, to further explain semantics of data. In the *RADAR Data Model*, "virtual relationships" can be defined as aggregations of look-up relationships; this way, the name of a virtual relationship semantically characterizes indirect relationships. Figure 6 depicts virtual relationships as well; they are depicted as labeled thick light-blue arrows.

Specifically, three virtual relationships are defined for the case study. The first one is named `Sensor_Features` and associates each sensor to the features (the `Feature_Of_Interest` class) measured by the sensor. The second one is named `Measurement_Features` and associates instances of the `Measurement_Site` to features (the `Feature_Of_Interest` class) that are measured by sensors installed within the measurement site. Finally, the third one is named `Observation_Site` and associates an observation (the `Observation` class) to the measurement site (the `Measurement_Site` class) within which the sensor that made the observation is installed. Remember that virtual relationships are obtained by aggregating look-up relationships, to be navigated. Nevertheless, a virtual relationship is not necessarily a many-to-many relationship: in fact, the `Observation_Site` relationship is one-to-many, since the aggregated look-up relationships are all oriented to the same direction.

Associating Concrete Classes to Ontological Classes. The "concretization" of ontological classes is made through *Concreting Relationships*. Figure 7 shows the *Ontological Layer* and the *Concrete Layer* for the case study, by adding the concreting relationships: they are depicted as thin green arrows, oriented from the ontological class to the concrete class. Observe that the same ontological class can be made concrete by many concrete classes, because they represent different facets of the same generic concept.

Specifically, the `Operating_Unit` and `Measurement_Site` classes are concrete interpretations of the "Place" ontological class, because they both describe geographical areas or places. The `Sensor` class is the concretization of the "Device" ontological class, since a sensor can be abstracted as a device. The `Observation` and `Observation_features` classes derives from the "Measuring_Activity" ontological class, because they record the data collected by the sensors. The `Features_Of_Interest` class derives from the "Features" ontological class, because it describes the characteristics of a measurement.

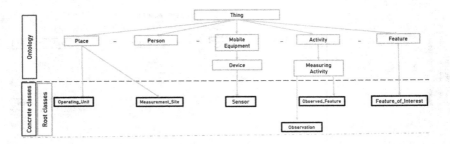

Fig. 7. Concreting Relationships defined for the case study.

Looking at the schema reported in Fig. 5, the reader can observe that some classes share the same properties, as they descend from the same ontological class. An example is the property called "city", which is shared by Operating_Unit and Measurement_Site.

Mapping Source Tables. The *Mapping Layer* (represented in Fig. 8) describes the external tables in the *Source DBs* that provide data to feed the *RADAR DB*. Specifically, five external tables are defined and associated with concrete classes by mapping relationships (depicted as gray thin arrows).

Defining RADAR Rules. The data model is completed by the *RADAR Rule Language*. Since not all the properties specified in a concrete class are necessarily instantiated through the data provided by sensors, rules set the value for missing properties. Listing 1 reports the rule named Accepted_Municipality_Range; its action assigns the value ''Accepted'' to the Municipality_Acceptance property defined in the Municipality_Evaluation concrete sub-class. The condition is true if the value of the Observation_Value property is between the range of the measured feature of interest (reached though the Reach operator by navigating the Acquisition_Of and the Related_Feature relationships.

Notice that *RADAR Rules* are Condition-Action rules; based on the declarative approach, so as to be suitable for analysts without programming skills.

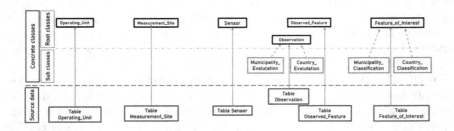

Fig. 8. *Mapping Layer* and Mapping Relationships for the case study.

Listing 1. *RADAR Rule* for the case study.

```
Rule: Accepted_Municipal_Range
Class:Municipality_Evaluation
Condition: Reach(Observed_Feature via Acquisition_Of via Related_Feature)
           .Municipality_Min_Value <= Observation_Value and
           Reach(Observed_Feature via Acquisition_Of via Related_Feature)
           .Municipality_Max_Value >= Observation_Value
Action: Municipality_Acceptance="Accepted"
```

4.3 Life Cycle of the System

The *RADAR Framework* has been designed to assist "continuous reporting" with a "long-term perspective". In fact, in particular in the context of small municipalities, turnover of employees is high, as well as technical and domain-specific competences are provided by external consultants. Hereafter, we illustrate the typical life cycle of a system based on the *RADAR Framework*, highlighting the key role of the *Knowledge Base*.

1. *Installation.* At the beginning of the life cycle, domain experts design the *RADAR Schema*: specifically, they choose the *Reference Ontology* and define concrete classes and relationships. Then, administrators of the sensor networks that provide the data to collect help defining mapping relationships, to feed the *RADAR DB*.
2. *Design of Initial Reports.* Domain experts and employees design the initial reports. While requirements and regulations does not change, reports can be periodically generated by employees by using the dedicated user interface.
3. *Novel Data to Acquire.* Depending on the evolution of sensor networks as well as of regulations, novel data could be acquired: if they fit the current *RADAR Schema*, it is sufficient to change the *Mapping Layer*; otherwise, novel concrete classes (and related relationships) can be defined. Domain experts involved in this activity could be different from those that performed the initial set up.
4. *Novel Reports to Design.* Employees in charge to generate reports every now and then have to design new reports, to accomplish changing requirements and regulations. They exploit the *Knowledge Base* to discover semantics of collected data, by browsing the *Reference Ontology* and the properties (with their semantic annotations) of concrete classes, as well as descriptions of relationships. Due to turnover, these employees might not be the ones that participated to the original set up.

Steps 3 and 4 might be repeated several times along many years. The *Knowledge Base* invaluably helps collect the necessary knowledge that allows for keeping the system alive and effective, so as to collect not only data but their semantics; this way, turnover of domain experts and employees should have limited impact on the efficiency of designing and generating new reports along time.

5 Conclusion

In this paper, we analyzed the adoption of the vision provided by the *RADAR Framework* (that we introduced in [1] for supporting continuous reporting in the financial market) to assist municipalities in the activity of "continuous reporting" for "environmental monitoring". We studied how the integrated vision provided by the *RADAR Data Model* can support the gathering of the environmental data measured by sensors disseminated in the administered territory. We discussed how data can be semantically enriched, by the *Knowledge Base* that stores the *RADAR Schema*. Then, the *RADAR DB* collects all data to aggregate into reports. The ultimate goal is to collect the contributions of many experts throughout the life cycle of the system.

As a future work, we plan to further address the case study, by choosing a pilot municipality, so as to validate the approach. Furthermore, we will identify other practical contexts in which continuous reporting plays a key role in the mission of institutions. Moreover, we will investigate the integration of JSON data [2], possibly obtained by analyzing open data ad social media data [3].

References

1. Azzini, A., Cortesi, N., Psaila, G.: RADAR: resilient application for dependable aided reporting. Information **12**(11), 463 (2021)
2. Bordogna, G., Ciriello, D.E., Psaila, G.: A flexible framework to cross-analyze heterogeneous multi-source geo-referenced information: The J-CO-QL proposal and its implementation. In: Proceedings of Web Intelligence, pp. 499–508 (2017)
3. Bordogna, G., Cuzzocrea, A., Frigerio, L., Psaila, G., Toccu, M.: An interoperable open data framework for discovering popular tours based on geo-tagged tweets. Int. J. Intell. Inf. Database Syst. **10**(3–4), 246–268 (2017)
4. Buttigieg, P.L., Pafilis, E., Lewis, S.E., Schildhauer, M.P., Walls, R.L., Mungall, C.J.: The environment ontology in 2016: bridging domains with increased scope, semantic density, and interoperation. J. Biomed. Semant. **7**(1), 57–57 (2016). https://doi.org/10.1186/s13326-016-0097-6
5. Madin, J.S., Bowers, S., Schildhauer, M., Krivov, S., Pennington, D., Villa, F.: An ontology for describing and synthesizing ecological observation data. Ecol. Inf. **2**(3), 279–296 (2007)
6. Madin, J.S., Bowers, S., Schildhauer, M.P., Jones, M.B.: Advancing ecological research with ontologies. Trends Ecol. Evol. **23**(3), 159–138 (2008)
7. Michener, W.K., Jones, M.B.: Ecoinformatics: supporting ecology as a data-intensive science. Trends Ecol. Evol. **27**(2), 85–93 (2012)
8. Rundel, P.W., Graham, E.A., Allen, M.F., Fisher, J.C., Harmon, T.C.: Environmental sensor networks in ecological res. New Phytol. **182**(3), 589–607 (2009)

Model of Long-Term Preservation of Digital Documents in Institutes of Higher Education

Verónica Judith Paucar-León[1], Fernando Molina-Granja[2(✉)], Raúl Lozada-Yánez[3], and Juan Carlos Santillán-Lima[4]

[1] Unidad Educativa Particular El Despertar, Riobamba, Ecuador
[2] Facultad de Ingeniería, Universidad Nacional de Chimborazo - UNACH, Riobamba, Ecuador
fmolina@unach.edu.ec
[3] Escuela Superior Politécnica del Chimborazo - ESPOCH, Riobamba, Ecuador
raul.lozada@espoch.edu.ec
[4] Universidad Nacional de La Plata, La Plata, Argentina
juancarlos.santillan1@info.unlp.ar

Abstract. The preservation of both physical and digital documents is a legal mandate, but above all a social responsibility to preserve the digital heritage of a public or private institution. This research aims to propose a model of long-term preservation of digital documents in higher education institutes, based on OAIS (Open Archival Information System), adjusted to the needs of the Higher Technological Institute "Juan de Velasco", for an evaluation of the digital preservation processes is carried out with an estimate of the current state and the determination of needs according to the catalog of criteria of safe repositories NESTOR (Nestor Catalogue of Criteria for Trusted Digital Repositories). An analysis of the most used digital preservation models and the strategies, policies, techniques, standards on which they base their management is carried out. A review of regulations, international and local laws of digital preservation is also carried out to support the elaboration of the model so that it is applicable in higher technological institutes of education. Based on the OAIS reference framework, a Long-Term Digital Preservation model called MPDL-ISTJV is proposed with adjustments in its functional entities to guarantee complete adaptability and an improvement in the assurance of the intellectual heritage managed by the Higher Technological Institutes.

Keywords: Digital preservation · OAIS · PREDECI · PREMIS · DAMM · NESTOR · MPDL-ISTJV

1 Introduction

The world has become digitized due to the impact of technologies that have revolutionized writing, printing, speaking, sound, image, accessing, and using data; Thus the theory of access, the dynamic model, complexity, convergence, technology, and representation is reflected in the changes in the management of resources that today are represented and recovered in an informational digital environment, types of documents, standards, technologies, objects, and software [1].

© Springer Nature Switzerland AG 2022
L. Uden et al. (Eds.): KMO 2022, CCIS 1593, pp. 257–269, 2022.
https://doi.org/10.1007/978-3-031-07920-7_20

Likewise, digitalization and automation processes are seen thinking only about the present and not with a focus on the future; it is necessary to raise awareness on the part of planners and stakeholders about the problems of access to the future since it is assumed that technology will solve everything. There is a gap in the legal and institutional framework, in many countries very general, inadequate and/or outdated legislation, as well as a deficient national policy that has not introduced and/or applied international standards.

The limited practical capacity for the management and preservation of digital resources is evident, given that there are few professionals with sufficient experience in the management and preservation of digital objects, digitization initiatives are susceptible to failure due to the lack of adequate preparation and adoption of standards [2].

Due to these circumstances, documentary heritage, especially digital, faces severe threats: looting and dispersal, illicit trade, destruction, as well as the fragile particularity of its support, the obsolescence of storage, and the lack of financing, this situation cause that much of the documentary heritage have disappeared forever and another important part is in danger [3].

Worldwide and mainly in developed countries, organizations and sectors specialized in knowledge and information management have already integrated for some decades the operational awareness and active culture on the importance of establishing protocols, activities, and formal collaborations aimed at the preservation of their memories and digital heritage. Institutes of higher education, governments, and world organizations such as NASA, UNESCO, Massachusetts Institute of Technology (MIT), Harvard, Library of Congress, IBM, Stanford University, National Library of Australia among others, have developed research, systems, and work models aimed at maintaining permanent long-term access to the documentary heritage of digitally born content and digitized materials [4].

Ecuador, like many countries, has few policies, regulations, specific strategies that regulate the long-term preservation of digital documentation, there are laws such as the Law of the National Archive System, the Document Management Standard for Public Administration Entities, and statutes of companies and institutions that do not have a specific regulation or a model that guarantees the Long-Term Preservation of Digit Documents Ales [5]. In the case of Higher Education Institutes, they are governed by regulations of the Council of Higher Education, and in the same way, it is defined in a general way and open to definitions and interpretations, without mechanisms, or specific methodologies of how to treat the preservation of documents and digital data.

For this reason, implement a long-term preservation model of digital data that allows maintaining, protecting, and safeguarding in advance and permanently with specific procedures to ensure the continuation and access of the content of digital documents over time and the technologies independent of their support, format, or system, and that in case of deterioration or damage due to different causes they can be restored. This work focuses on the analysis of digital preservation models and the proposal of a model to guarantee the authenticity and long-term traceability of digital documents in the environment of higher education institutes in Ecuador.

2 Contextualization

Molina, in 2107, in his research "The preservation of digital evidence and its admissibility in the court", analyzes the common models of digital preservation that exist, the elements, the degree of compliance with general guidelines, the use of techniques and compliance with specific requirements, as well as evaluate the need for a solution to the problem, and concludes that the issues ignored by current preservation models are the tool museum, terminology, intake quality control, partial ingest metadata environment evidence to preserve and ensure the integrity of the original, risk assessment, distributed storage, time preservation, strategy certifications, legality of evidence, respect for fundamental rights, the reliability and effectiveness of evidence, respect for the rules of data protection and secrecy of communications, regarding the right to freedom of expression, confidentiality, preservation of roles, management of roles, control of physical evidence, transmission, traceability, and continuity of preservation. It is necessary to demonstrate that no model meets all the parameters, requirements, principles, and minimum standards established to preserve digital evidence in criminal investigation institutions [6].

Alvarez in 2017, in his research "The digital repositories for conservation. An approach to the digital long-term preservation", aims to contribute to the formation of criteria related to long-term digital preservation, to the knowledge of digital repositories, as well as to suggest a set of general measures that allow drawing up a successful strategy for the preservation of digital information. Contributing with the following conclusions:

A critical point for digital information is technological obsolescence, technological fragility, the rapid updating of technologies, the expiration of software and formats, technological dependence, and the loss of functionalities.

There is no universally applicable practical solution to the problem of technological obsolescence of digital materials and it is unlikely that a single solution will be found that offers a means of economic access to all materials, for all purposes and always [1].

Giusti's research in 2014 with the theme "A methodology for evaluating digital repositories to ensure preservation over time and access to content" of the National University of La Plata, aims to improve the quality of repositories, as well as standardize, help interoperability and obtain greater visibility of the productions that an educational institution keeps in a repository, as well as ensuring the preservation of the contents of the repository, so that it is always possible to access them and that they are readable for both human users and machine, determining the compliance of the repository to the constituent elements of the information package of the OAIS model of the ISO 14721 standard [7].

UNESCO, in its report "Guidelines for the Preservation of Digital Heritage," contains general and technical guidelines for the preservation of the growing global digital heritage and permanent access to it and aims to serve as a reference manual on the Draft Charter for the Preservation of Digital Heritage, and proposes some strategies to preserve digital objects [3].

Giménez tries to identify what differences or similarities exist between the activity of preservation or conservation of physical and digital documents, too, on the one hand, contextualize the actions and elements of digital preservation and, on the other, analyze the main proposals made by different ISO standards for organizations to implement a digital preservation program that guarantees the usability of documents throughout the time.

This author mentions that ISO standards propose solutions and actions that must be taken to ensure that digital documents are preserved over time f organizations consider them essential as evidence of their heritage or activities and wish to guarantee their authenticity, integrity, and usability throughout that time [8].

Any organization producing digital documents must des gn a strategy to ensure their conservation and availability, to face the risks of technological obsolescence. It is essential that these documents are organized, classified, described, and dated, to be identified and retrieved in the most relevant way at the time you want.

To ensure the protection of electronic documents and their authenticity, it is recommended that they are not dependent on the software that created them and, in addition, that they are converted to the.pdf format, with the incorporation of metadata.

3   Analysis of Models for File Preservation

3.1   OAIS Reference Model

The OAIS model was proposed for use in the scientific area of space, to digitally preserve data from space missions. It has been adopted by the libraries of countries that have participated in its elaboration and implementation such as the ibraries: Congress of the United States, Great Britain, even Germany.

OAIS has wide application for long-term preservation in any context incorporates technological surveillance, digital preservation, and processes that demand the digital documents of any data center that should not be subjected to changes, transformations, or losses. The OAIS model is a digital objective preservation model that implements a series of data flows that determine the obligations of a long-term preservation system to archive and manage digital objects [9].

PREDECI Model. The PREDECI model is based on the OAIS model; This model is divided into a set of six functional entities, which are Ingest, File Storage, Data Management, Administration, Planning, and Preservation Access. These functional entities retain the information according to the information defined in the model. This model specifies how information should be managed and how information is transmitted from the data of the ingest functional entity to the functional entity. The digital preservation models used PREMIS as a reference that focuses on strategies for the preservation of metadata in Digital Archives [10].

Model PREMIS. Signifies "Preservation Metadata: Implementation Strategies", which is the name of an international working group sponsored by OCLC and RLG from 2003 to 2005. That working group produced a report called the PREMIS Data Dictionary for Preservation Metadata that includes a data record. It defines a central set of semantic units that repositories must know to perform their preservation functions. They will generally include actions to ensure that digital objects can be read from media and can be displayed, reproduced, or otherwise interpreted using the application software, as well as to ensure that digital objects in the repository are not inadvertently altered and that legitimate changes to objects are documented. The Data Dictionary is not intended to define all possible preservation metadata elements, only those that most repositories will need to know most of the time [11].

DAMM Model (Digital Preservation Maturity Model). Is based on the key features of information preservation, such as the identification of file formats and conceptual objects that make up the information ingested. The term Maturity Model is used to imply layers of sophistication in processes, [12, 13].

The evaluation of the study of digital preservation models is seen in Table 1, the results of the previous points are evaluated to determine which model meets a degree of effectiveness in terms of information security and compliance with UNESCO parameters and strategies and techniques proposed by Nestor (Fig. 1).

Table 1. Percentage of compliance with the effectiveness of the models

Feature	AWARDS	OAIS	PREDECI	DAM
UNESCO guidelines	72%	86%	83%	72%
Strategies and preservation techniques	73%	91%	88%	76%
Safety dimensions	73%	100%	100%	80%
Average	73%	92%	90%	76%

Prepared by: The authors

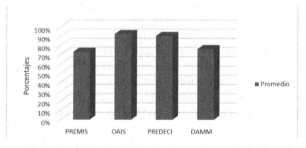

Fig. 1. Percentage of the effectiveness of digital preservation models. Prepared by: The authors

From the comparative analysis of the models studied in this research such as PREMIS, OAIS, PREDECI, DAMM, it is verified that OAIS of ISO 14721: 2003 meets different characteristics that will contribute to effectively in the elaboration of the new model to improve the preservation of academic production of the Higher Technological Institutes. Hence the OAIS model has 92%.

The OAIS reference model has been published as a recommendation of the CCSDS[1] and as iso14721:2003. OAIS focuses its activity on the long-term preservation of information in digital format, as a guarantee that it will be accessible in the future. (Dante, 2012).

---

[1] Consultative Committee for Space Data Systems.

In the OAIS model and its relationship with Information Representation, it serves as a functional model of a file system. It is not a metadata model in itself, but it defines different types of conceptual objects, and some of them are specifically defined to fulfill the purposes of preservation and access. Each type of information object is constructed from a simple generic model, in which the data object can be interpreted using the associated representation information (Giusti, 2014).

4   Audit and Certification of Preservation Repositories

4.1   Nestor Catalogue of Criteria for Trusted Digital Repositories

The Working Group Trusted Repositories – Certification working group produces the Catalogue of Criteria for Trusted Digital Repositories. Nestor is a research project in digital preservation and conservation. The working group has created this catalog where some judgments are presented to achieve Trusted Digital Repositories: based on national and international standards, such as DINI, the RLGOCLC report [14–16].

This catalog of criteria identifies and analyzes the organization in technical requirements security, information integrity, organizational framework, object management, uses the terminology of the OAIS reference model, despite having Germany funding has great international approval.

Nestor is a German project created with the mission of ensuring the preservation of digital resources in Germany and working with other institutions internationally to ensure access to global digital memory. Among its specific objectives is to serve as a point of union and communication to all parties working in Germany on the long-term preservation of electronic documents. Among its results is a thematic portal where more than 2000 publications on preservation are collected.

Its catalog for the creation of reliable repositories identifies criteria that facilitate the evaluation of repositories and is based on the reliability of the contents and the repository itself both at an organizational and technical level. Its objective is to ensure the preservation of the contents, stored as digital objects, in the long term.

Consider a repository as that institution that has taken responsibility for the long-term preservation and accessibility of digital objects by ensuring that they can be used in the future by a specific user community or group. The evaluation criteria that are proposed are articulated in three sections: organizational framework, management of objects, and infrastructure and security.

5   Methodology

For the development of this research, and evaluation of the digital preservation processes is carried out with an estimate of the current state and the determination of needs according to the catalog of criteria of secure repositories NESTOR. An analysis of the most used digital preservation models and the strategies, policies, techniques, standards on which they are based is carried out. A review of regulations, international and local laws of digital preservation is also carried out to support the elaboration of the model so that it is applicable in higher technological institutes of education. This project has a descriptive approach, sing IBM's SPSS statistical software, for the application of descriptive statistics and inferential statistics (ANOVA), in addition, to analyze variables on The Likert scale, which is very useful when working with evaluation instruments by experts such as Nestor [14].

For the validation of the model, the ANOVA technique was used, since it supports the comparison of the average importance assigned by each of the validating experts, in this way it was possible to know if there are statistically significant differences between the validation generated by each expert, or if there is a consensus regarding the validation of the model and its importance in the preservation of digital documents in the long term.

The study using the ANOVA technique allows obtaining a p-value (p-value) of approximately zero so that by setting a level of alpha statistical significance equal to 0.05 (5%) therefore, it is possible to conclude with a statistical confidence of 95% that the implementation of a Digital Document Preservation Model improves the long-term preservation of digital documents in higher education institutes.

6   Results

6.1   MPDL-ISTJV Long-Term Digital Preservation Model

The model that is called MPDL-ISTJV adopts environment and preservation functions of the OAIS model, in aspects of higher education institutions such as the technological Juan de Velasco, also addresses the preservation of the environment of creation of digital scientific collections and the ability to increase their preservation over time, as well as the administration of the digital archive in reliable external repositories with the establishment of future policies and agreements that guarantee the objective of this research by adding or reducing the necessary characteristics required by the new model. Then the postage and simplifications of the new model.

Functional Entity Intake
Reception of Submission. - According to its description in the OAIS model, it provides and facilitates the appropriate storage capacity from the Producer or the Administrator. To this entity is added subsumption of Verification of the Sending of the Data that are entered with the digital documents, this includes a corresponding authorization for its preservation, which complies with the necessary regulation of preservation of the institution that verifies the types of users according to the roles of the entities of the designated community are these administrators, educators, creators, and the general public, as well as the generation of the first original copy of the digital object to be preserved by verifying errors caused by active applications or corrupt media with errors in the reception of the original object.

In the Submission Reception Function the SIP can be delivered by different means of communication that need to comply with the specific legal regulations of access, validating that it is not a corrupt file, to incorporate into the OAIS file, placing income identifiers, as well as copyright, and when there is an error in the acquisition process request the forwarding of the package to the Producer.

Functional Entity-Quality Assurance

If conceived with a subfunction of the Sending Reception Function, the treatment of the digital object is the same as the OAIS model. This certifies that the SIP data transfer is successful through Cyclic Redundancy Checks (CRC) to the transient storage process. In the case of scientific products generated in IST, it is provided that the files to be transferred or their means of communication, do not have read/write errors, authenticating the formats according to the data received by the subsumption.

Verification of the Sending of the File: through audits attending to the integrity of the data, certifying the entry to match the file with the information model thus validating the integrity of the data.

Generate AIP: This function converts the SIP into AIP to prepare information based on rules, policies, and schemes like digital files.

Generation of Descriptive Information: A function that extracts descriptive data from the AIP, which in this case will be the archives of scientific knowledge (thesis), in addition to selecting descriptive information from other blocks that help administer data management, when performing the extraction/generation of metadata facilitates the retrieval of the archived digital object in the long term.

Coordination of Updates: Allows to manage the sending of AIPs of digital documents to Archive Storage and descriptive information to Data Management.

Storage Functional Entity

The Archive Storage entity is a primary function conceived within the OAIS model is responsible for storing information on the physical medium in one or more internal units that will contain digital documents. Saves the API received from the ingest guaranteeing integrity by verifying that the data when transferred is not damaged or has errors, duplicating digital objects and constantly sending inventory information to the administration to manage Access policies and help in the management of storage hierarchy, media replacement, and guaranteeing access to information in case of disasters.

Data Reception: Receives a request to stably store the AIP that comes from the Ingest, shows the frequency of retrieval of the data that forms the AIP, and passes to the error checking function.

Error Verification: Validates that the ingest API and its elements are without any error; thus, also verifies that no damage occurs in the data transfers within the storage processes. The hardware and software issues warnings of probable errors that are sent to the error registry to be reviewed by the store managers and correct to ensure their availability.

Storage Hierarchy Management: Places AIPs on the appropriate storage medium, placing security policies if necessary. It is responsible for the choice of the type of media, disposes of the mechanisms performing the physical transfer of the storage devices of the digital documents.

Media Replacement: This function is eliminated since the Disaster Recovery function is assigned this functionality.

Disaster Recovery: Duplicates, migrates, mobilizes refreshes the digital documents collected in the archive, and physically replicates the copy of the digital file on various removable media or by your transfer network system, these recovery rules are defined by the Administration.

Data Provider: Makes copies of AIPS collected to the entity accessing through an AIP request.

Storage Medium: Here the copy of the original digital file and its elements that accompany it of accepted repository processes is executed, on the reproduction, all the activities of access, management, and storage operations are made.

Coordination: This function is added to coordinate and directly organize replication actions of the original digital document processed in local Data Storage Medium with the external entity with whom transactions and replication processes of the API will be shared through the balance of techniques, policies, agreements, collaborative work alliances in replication of digital repositories in the network managing to guarantee its long-term presentation.

Functional Entity Data Management

The functional entity Data Management has as its primary activity to carry out processes of administration and custody of the descriptive or administrative information of the database that describes the digital documents to generate reports. Its operation is linked to the storage entity. Updates the information that is incorporated and offers reports if any data is modified or deleted. Generates reports of the various components of OAIS. The report request can be entity ingest, access or administration.

Generate Report: Generates reports of the stored digital documents, these can be viewed by their category, accesses, or provide descriptive data according to the request made by ingestion, access, and administration.

Perform Queries: The Access function makes a query request to this function that accesses the database to display a response for the requester.

Database Administrator: Responsible for the administration of database update policies; the administration who sends the rules to maintain the database integrates, responsible for providing storage components, in addition to taking care of the reception of the system update, before receiving descriptive information and requesting update with processes from ingestion and administration.

Receiving Database Update: The process of this function is merged with the Database Administrator, so it is removed from the schema.

Functional Entity Administration
This entity has functions and services to execute everything the support of the digital document and is the space of the internal and external interrelations of the model MPDL-ISTJV, determines agreements with the producer of the digital document Adding information, identifies data that is Add to the digital document, setting storage rules from documents at risk and listening responsibilities to requests for consultation of digital documents.

Acceptance Negotiation Function: Requests acceptable final reports to negotiate and with the producer proceed to the preservation of the digital document, makes the presentation of a calendar of sessions of agreed requests for information, establishing guidelines and precise resources of transfer and the acceptance of the SIPs to the MPDL-IESJV model.

Physical Access Control Function: According to archiving strategies, it contributes with components or physical elements that restrict or allow physical access to digital documents.

Establish Standards and Policies Function: You are responsible for creating, implementing, and protecting file system patterns, models, schemas, policies, and standards. Receives recommendations and proposals from the planning entity for the preservation of new standards for digital documents and the management of constant risk reports, returning to this entity objectives norms, migration policies of approved standards.

Audit Acceptance Function: Here you receive feedback from the AIP/SIP packages from the preservation planning, issue observations if the AIP/SIP records have been applied successfully in the intake, you will check that the AIP/SIP shipments are made with the shipping agreements, checking that the packages comply with the specifications of the file. It will verify that the information of the PDI is correct, clear, and autonomous of the assigned community.

File Information Update Function: Provides the necessary means to renew the information of the digital documents of the model.

Customer Service Function: It is the one that manages and maintains consumption accounts, creating billing data, and receiving payment from the client for used resources. The function that is decided to suppress since there is no billing for access to the pool of scientific knowledge.

Request Activation Function: Helps with the realization of the request for transmission, dissemination, or propagation of the information to the access entity.

Configuration Management System Function: Frequently observes digital documents in terms of technology, obeys the function of establishing standards and policies reinforcing the custody of the model file.

Functional Entity Preservation Planning
This function inspects the model environment, constitutes long-term preservation plans, certifies that the information collected is available and understandable to the community, monitors provenance technology, information policies, computer scenarios.

Development of Packaging Design and Migration Plans: Performs prototypes of implementation of management rules and policies through the development of designs of information packages before recommendations and suggestions on their application, suggests SIP/AIP examined and individualized, receives results of prototypes, prevention requirements, approved standards, migration objectives and sends all these issues to be treated in the function of the development of state res and prevention strategies returning this advice.

Designed Community Monitoring: Works with customers and producers and tracks service needs and demands and product technologies, such as advances in computing platforms, types of devices and media, information formats, package handling software. Surveys, frequent observations, constant community working groups are fundamental for the development of this function that fits from sending technological alerts, external data standards, prototype results to the monitoring function, and development of prevention strategies based on prototype requests.

Technology Monitoring: As the name implies, it monitors obsolete technologies that could affect the digital document in its computerized medium, at the same time it searches and tracks new technologies, hardware, and software, computer standards to renew the digital document in the software repository and prevent it from falling into obsolescence, receives a request for prototypes of the functions and returns technology alerts, external data standards, prototype results, and reports to the preservation strategies and standards development function.

Development of Preservation Strategies and Standards: Works with customers and producers and tracks the needs and demands of service and product technologies, such as advances in computing platforms, types of devices and media, information formats, package management software, to recommend proposals, having AIP/SIP revisions and templates of new AIP/SIP, migration packages and customization tips from other features to better manage the digital document in preservation planning.

Functional Entity Access
An entity that systematizes access to information, carries out the process of transmission of DIPs to users, facilitates services to consumers by placing and looking for the information to be presented to users.

Access Activities Coordinator Function: Provides various interfaces for retrieving digital documents through online services.

Generate DIP Function: Supports a propagation request, recovers the AIP of the functional entity temporary file storage making a duplicate to be processed, when necessary, immediately.

Give Answer Function: Responds and determines an authorization reproduction id of the digital document in deliveries to customers, when it makes an online delivery, it receives the response of the function coordinate access activities by arranging real-time transmission through communication rules.

The proposed model (see Fig. 2) defines different roles and responsibilities in the management of the digital archive. After exposing the research and verifying the environment based on the case studies interviewed, an evaluation based on Nestor is carried out and data is obtained on its computer systems and processes that allow an analysis of its flaws in the processes.

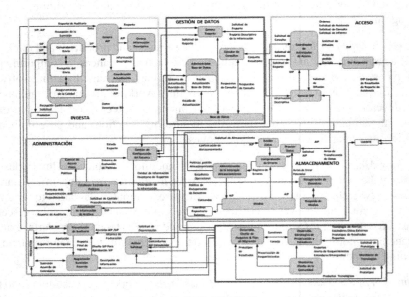

Fig. 2. Functional Entities MPDL-ISTJV. Prepared by: The authors

7 Conclusions

The different models proposed for digital preservation of documents in the long term have been studied, analyzing each of them and it is observed that the OAIS model complies with 92% complying with a degree of effectiveness in information security and the best preservation strategies, serving as a basis for the elaboration of the proposed model in technological higher education environments and that helps the assurance and management of the digital document.

When analyzing the laws, norms, rules in force at the national level on digital preservation of documents, it can be cited that they do not have the necessary scope to preserve scientific collections despite being obliged by legislation. The lack of regulations, policies put at risk the intellectual digital heritage of Technological Higher Education institutions.

The application of Nestor Criteria allowed measuring the level of integrity, availability, and accessibility of the academic-scientific production of the institution, identifying the needs and requirements for the elaboration of the long-term preservation model, verifying that there is a total lack of a recognizable process.

The elaboration of the conceptual model of long-term digital preservation of digital documents for Higher Technological Institutes, improves by 96% the long-term preservation processes on the initial scenario, having as its main task the assurance of digital scientific products through strategies, techniques, and preservation guidelines, since it is the heritage and evidence of the academic life of the institution and the contribution to the community and the country.

The evaluation of Nestor to certify repositories by experts allows establishing the importance of the MPDL-ISTJV model, according to the qualifications granted by each specialist the statistical confidence is 95%, allowing to verify that the implementation of the proposed model of Preservation of Digital Documents improves the long-term preservation of digital documents.

References

1. Alvarez-Wong, B.: Los repositorios digitales para la conservación, Un acercamiento a la preservación digital a largo plazo. Ciencias de la Información **48**(2), 15–22 (2017)
2. Anne, T.: Digitization and prevencion: global opportunites and cultural challenges. In: International Conference on Permanent Access to Digital Documentary Heritage, Vancouver (2012)
3. UNESCO: La educación inclusiva: el camino hacia el future. UNESCO, Ginebra (2003)
4. Leija, D.: Preservación digital distribuida y la colaboración interinstitucional. Facultad de Biblioteconomía y documentación, Barcelona (2017)
5. Asamblea Nacional: Ley del Sistema Nacional de Registro de Datos Publicos. Asamblea Nacional, Ecuador (2010)
6. Molina-Granja, F., Rodriguez, G.: The preservation of digital evidence and its admissibility in the court. Int. J. Electron. Secur. Digit. Forensics **9**(1), 1–18 (2017)
7. De Giusti, M.: Una metodología de evaluación de repositorios digitales para asegurar la preservación en el tiempo y el acceso a los contenidos. Universidad Nacional de La Plata, Argentina (2014)
8. Giménez, V.: Criterios ISO para la preservación digital de los documentos de archive. Universitat Politécnica de Valencia, España (2014)
9. CCSD, Reference Model for an Open Archival Information System (OAIS) 650.0-M-2. Consultative Committee for Space Data Systems, USA (2012)
10. Molina-Granja, F., Rodriguez, G.: Model for digital evidence preservation in criminal research institutions-PREDECI. Int. J. Electron. Secur. Digit. Forensics **9**(2), 150–166 (2017)
11. PREMIS. PREMIS Data Dictionary for Preservation Metadata, Version 3.0 (2020). https://www.loc.gov/standards/premis/v3/index.html
12. Tessella: Digital Preservation Maturity Model - White Paper (2013)
13. Preservica: Digital preservation maturity model (2021). https://preservica.com/resources/white-papers/digital-preservation-maturity-model
14. Nestor: Catalogue of Criteria for Trusted Digital Repositories. Version 2. Nestor working Group Trusted Repositories, Frankfurt (2009)
15. Dini, A.: Zertifikat Dokumenten-und Publikationsservice. Publikationsservice, Berlin (2007)
16. Research Libraries Group: RLG (2018). https://www.rlg.org/

Extending the Occupational Safety and Health Management System as a Knowledge Management System Through the Mixed-Reality Remote Audit

Mohd Fuad Mohd Isa[1], Nor Zairah Ab. Rahim[2](✉), Mohamad Syazli Fathi[2], and Rasimah Che Mohd Yusoff[2]

[1] Ministry of Human Resources, Putrajaya, Malaysia
[2] Universiti Teknologi Malaysia, Kuala Lumpur, Malaysia
nzairah@utm.my

Abstract. Auditing is one of the most important stages in evaluating the effectiveness of an Occupational Safety and Health Management System (OSHMS), which is also recognized as a Knowledge Management System (KMS). According to the International Labor Organization (ILO), the audit process is part of the evaluation element, where the auditor must evaluate the OSH performance. The traditional audit might not be able to be conducted due to the Covid-19 pandemic and the Movement Control Order (MCO) scenario, therefore the remote audit is being viewed as a viable solution to ensuring the audit process continues. The solution could also be utilized beyond the pandemic period as it may become one of the effective method for the audit process. The paper describes how the OSHMS can be remotely audited utilizing Mixed Reality (MR) applications in a design thinking manner. To test the approach, preliminary data was collected in an OSH office. The findings of this paper will aid stakeholders in the relevant context in making investment decisions for digitising their OSH audit process in order to create a future-ready ecosystem.

Keywords: OSHMS · KMS · Mixed Reality · Remote audit · Design thinking

1 Introduction

The World Health Organization (WHO) defines occupational safety and health (OSH) as including all aspects of workplace health and safety and focusing on primary hazard prevention [1]. OSH covers all staff safety and health measures as well as other activities. This includes workplace safety, occupational sicknesses, and health hazards, as well as human-centered design. The OHS management system consists of five (5) primary components: policy, organising, planning and implementation, assessment, and improvement action [2]. The OSH allows businesses to address worker safety concerns and employees to take responsibility for their own safety. In 2018, 37,436 occupational accidents occurred in Malaysia, compared to 36,661 in 2017 [3]. To reduce workplace

© Springer Nature Switzerland AG 2022
L. Uden et al. (Eds.): KMO 2022, CCIS 1593, pp. 270–278, 2022.
https://doi.org/10.1007/978-3-031-07920-7_21

accidents, researchers recommend more research on the best ways to communicate safety information to workers.

Authorities have imposed restrictions on social activities due of the ongoing COVID-19 outbreak. In most industries, this has an indirect impact on the economy and jobs. Employers also take important and safe steps to guarantee that the industrial workforce is not affected by the virus. The creation of Covid-19-related SOPs in the workplace improves the OSH management system in most sectors. During the Covid-19 pandemic, audits should be conducted to ensure that the OSH system is functioning properly.

Remote audit is a systematic, independent and documented processes for obtaining evidence without having the auditor nearby. The procedure could be carried out by accessing the computer from a different place [10]. Current ICTs must be supplemented with new technologies that enable remote collaboration, centralised proof gathering, and audit team management in order to migrate to a remote audit. [7] defines remote auditing as the process through which auditors use ICT and big data to review and report on data quality and compliance requirements, obtain electronic evidence, and communicate with auditees regardless of the auditor's physical location. This process fits the knowledge management systems (KMSs) definition where the remote audit platform provides organizations with processes and tools to capture, organize, and manage knowledge [14].

Only by carefully controlling interactions between technology systems and humans can effective safety be established. Virtual reality (VR) is a notion that has been around for 50 years. However, augmented reality (AR) technology combines virtual objects into the actual environment. AR technology's capabilities could increase the user's experience of virtual prototyping with real entities while retaining the virtual world's flexibility [4]. Mixed Reality (MR) is the blending of reality with virtual reality. Physical and digital goods can interact simultaneously in a new environment created by MR technology [5]. Figure 1 depicts MR's position as described by [6]. A review on other relevant studies [21] has been conducted to understand how can the OSHMS especially in the university context be remotely audited using Mixed Reality (MR).

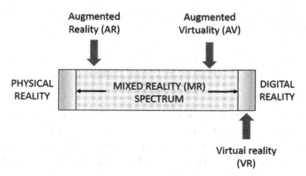

Fig. 1. Spectrum of mixed reality [6]

Thus this paper extended the work with a preliminary data collection in an OSH office. The design thinking method was utilized to examine the stakeholders' perception for the said solution. The rest of the paper is organized as follows: Sect. 2 discusses related research to the context of study. Section 3 describes the research methodology, which explains how the remote audit process being developed through design thinking approach. Then, the discussion of the context in Sect. 4. Section 5 concludes the paper.

2 Related Research

2.1 Occupational Safety and Health Management System (OSHMS) as a Knowledge Management System (KMS)

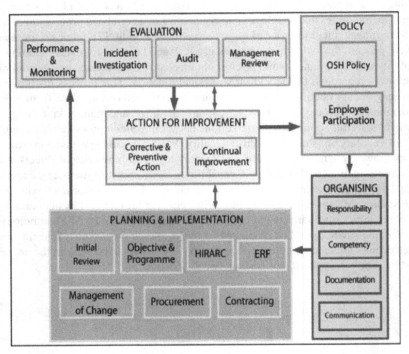

Fig. 2. OSHMS conceptual framework [2]

The national OSH scheme lead by DOSH is in accordance with ILO conventions and are harmonised in all legislation Royde et al. (2013). The World Health Organisation (WHO) states that occupational health and Occupational safety and health (OSH) encompasses all aspects of occupational health and safety and should place a strong emphasis on primary risk reduction. Management systems are commonly utilised in corporate decision-making and even inadvertently in everyday life, whether in the purchase of supplies, establishing a firm, or just selecting new furnishings. The OSHMS is classified as a KMS since it provides methods and tools for capturing, organising, and managing audit knowledge in the organisation. The OSHMS focuses on the most important OSH criteria, standards, and performance. The purpose of a KMS like this is to create a process for increasing risk assessment performance and preventing workplace accidents and incidents. It's a rational, step-by-step method for determining the correct tasks to complete in order to measure progress toward goals, how effectively they're being met, and where room for improvement can be found. It must be able to adapt to changes in the organization's business and statutory obligations. The system must include the main parts of policy, organization, planning, and implementation, as well as assessment and improvement actions. OSHMS with its sub element is shown in (Fig. 2).

OSH encompasses both worker and mode of operation safety and wellness programmes. This entails preventing job-related injuries, illnesses, and health risks, as well as creating work settings that prioritise people. The main preventive concept is the motivating premise behind emphasising high-level techniques for fighting hazards at work throughout the life cycle as a result of lower rates of injuries and illnesses [15].

2.2 Remote Audit

It was indicated earlier that the OSHMS is a KMS that should be adaptable to take account of changes in the sector of the company and to comply with legislation. Therefore, the implementation of remote audit should be considered especially in the pandemic era. The remote audit should be looking into the technological and behavioural aspects and is provided by the two key enabling elements of the remote audit, ICT and analytics.

These elements are depicted in Fig. 3. On-site and remote audit team members use ICT to interact with programme management and each other. Auditors use tools to collect and analyse data from the auditee's systems to assess internal controls and transactions. As technology and internet connectivity costs continue to plummet while budgets tighten, more internal audit specialists are turning to remote audit solutions. There are also cost savings for organisations that use remote auditing such as reduced travel and entertainment expenses [8].

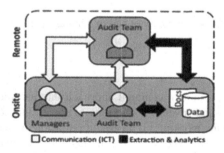

Fig. 3. Components of remote auditing [8]

2.3 Mixed Reality

Immersive technologies like MR have been utilised for teaching, risk monitoring, and preconstruction planning for over a decade. Immersive panoramas, according to [11], are a collection of panoramic pictures and construction site photos. Audio, video, and virtual 2D or 3D models were extended to provide a continuous immersive interface in such panoramic simulated worlds. Users can explore a 360-degree virtual world of a dynamic construction project while learning more about the project and work site.

The MR technology has come a long way. Despite the term "virtual reality" being used in the technology's description, 360-degree panoramic VR is closer to the left end of the spectrum. It's a popular way to visualise large construction sites with multiple levels of features. Like traditional virtual worlds, panoramic virtual reality can provide users with an immersive experience while presenting realistic and accurate simulations of the actual surroundings [12].

3   Methodology

The study applied the design thinking and POV approach in conducting the case study in testing the use of MR technology for remote audit as indicated in Fig. 4. A preliminary study in one of the OSH office was conducted by applying this approach.

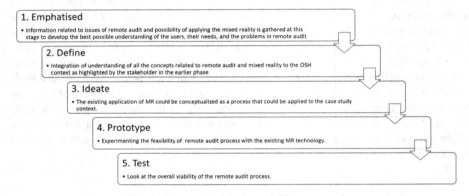

Fig. 4. Summary of design thinking approach

3.1   Design Thinking

Design thinking (DT) is a human-centered approach that uses design tools and mind-sets to develop creative and inventive solutions to social and commercial challenges [17]. DT involves students working on unstructured problems with no clear solutions. Aside from employing words and symbols, the DT method focuses on the following principles: empathising to understand user wants; identifying needs; conducting trials; prototyping; obtaining user input; and redesigning the process [18]. There is no single approach to pursue the design thinking process because there is no consistent description in literature. Many design process models have been established by Stanford Hasso Plattner Design School, IDEO, and Design Council. In all models, gathering knowledge, applying creative thinking skills, and being experienced were emphasised [19]. The four principles of design thinking are: (1) The human rule: No matter what the context, all design activity is social in nature, and any social innovation will bring us back to the "human-centric point of view". (2) The ambiguity rule: Ambiguity is inevitable, and it cannot be removed or oversimplified. Experimenting at the limits of your knowledge and ability is crucial in being able to see things differently. (3) The redesign rule: All design is redesign. While technology and social circumstances may change and evolve, basic human needs remain unchanged. We essentially only redesign the means of fulfilling these needs or reaching desired outcomes. (4) The tangibility rule: Making ideas tangible in the form of prototypes enables designers to communicate them more effectively. The design thinking method described in Kostrzewski [16] could be utilized to examine the stakeholders' perception in applying MR as the remote audit solutions.

3.2 Design Thinking Process and Instruments

The DT process can be broken down into five steps (empathize, define, ideate, prototype and test) [20, 22].

Phase 1: Empathize. Empathy is the foundation of design thinking. This phase gathers information on remote auditing and mixed reality to be used in the next stage to better understand the users, their demands, and the difficulties that underpin the product's development.

Phase 2: Define Action-based problem statements will be made after studying and synthesising empathy data. Problem circumstances are described as "User + User's Need + Insight" POV statements and defined as a problem statement. As outlined by the stakeholder in the prior phase, this includes comprehending remote audit and mixed reality concepts.

Phase 3: Ideate. It's time to start thinking about solutions. The ideation stage of the design thinking process is when the creativity happens. MR could now be conceived as a process that could be applied to the case study environment.

Phase 4: Prototype phase The design team exhibited product features to investigate problem solutions produced in the previous stage. It can be tested on a small group of persons outside the design team. This is an experimental phase to find the best solution to the challenges highlighted in the prior three stages. The solutions are implemented in the prototypes and tested one by one by the users, before being accepted, improved, and re-tested. By the end of this stage, the design team will have a deeper understanding of the product's limits and issues, as well as how real users will behave, think, and feel when interacting with the final product. The prototype is intended to investigate the process rather than the technology itself, as the technology employed is already available.

Phase 5: Test. In the testing phase, the user is able to experience the developed prototype in this case the whole remote audit process and give feedback to the designers. Solutions developed according to user feedback are evaluated and will be improved accordingly. The intention of this phase is to look at the overall viability of the remote audit process.

4 Finding and Discussion

The finding of the preliminary study is documented briefly in Table 1.

Table 1. Design thinking activity for remote audit

Steps	Activity	Outcome
Phase 1: Empathise	Interview with the OSH Unit Manager	Identification of issues related to audit especially during the MCO period
Phase 2: Define	Researcher outlined the problems based on feedback in Phase 1	Sharing of MR samples to suits the organization context
Phase 3: Ideate	Discussion with team members and stakeholders	Customization of process based on feedback in Phase 1 and 2 with the samples of existing MR
Phase 4: Prototype	Development of the process by integrating all the elements discussed and considered in the earlier phases	Technical specification identified and ready to be tested
Phase 5: Test	Running of the prototype in the proposed outlined	Identification of the viability of the process and getting feedback from the stakeholders

Although MR have been used for various safety-related applications such as training, hazard monitoring, and preconstruction planning, its application in audit process is still lacking. The design thinking approach of developing the process would be helpful to customize the process and extend the need of remote audit the OSH context. This will also extend the KMS capability of OSHMS making it more dynamic. The design thinking approach conducted for the preliminary study assisted both the researcher and also the stakeholders to understand the flow of the technology and how it could be feasible for the remote audit process. This understanding would prepare the researcher for the actual data collection while at the same time both parties could streamline the requirements for actual implementation from both the perspectives of the researcher and also the stakeholders.

Marzuki [8] was reported to have done the only remote audit study in Malaysia. The goal of this study is to find out how internal auditors felt about internal audit effectiveness throughout the MCO period in terms of technology, competency, time quality, client answers, and auditor attributes. All independent variables show a positive relationship with internal audit effectiveness, according to the data. Internal auditors should be given necessary resources and apply acceptable methodologies when executing audit tasks at irregular intervals, according to the findings [9]. Furthermore, establishing the essential determinants of internal audit effectiveness will aid auditors in determining the best tools and strategies for completing audit engagements.

5 Conclusions

OSH has a long history of employing simulation techniques. (a) accepted and proven product safety monitoring procedures (e.g. hydraulication laboratory stress testing), (b) role plays in OSH occupational safety simulation preparation, (c) backward-looking hazard analysis (e.g. causative and where and when justification and testing), and (d) non-respective, unexpected, incoherent testing of the goods [13]. VR has evolved into a human modelling platform for participating in many device domains with complicated 3D simulated environments during the last few decades. The technology has been applied in several contexts with various customization. Thus, the technologies evolution is now being proposed to be extended to the a KMS, in this context an OSHMS for remote audit solution. Similar concept and techniques could be much applied and beneficial to be conducted in the OSHMS audit. This paper could assist the stakeholders in the relevant context in their investment decision making towards digitizing their businesses for future ready ecosystem. Although the initial context of this paper is more generic, the specific scope of the study is only focused on the preliminary study which attempted to apply DT approach in testing the MR for the remote audit process. Appropriate case study protocol will be developed based on the findings from the preliminary study to prepare the researcher for the actual case studies that are proposed to be conducted in several other identified organizations.

References

1. Nickel, P., Lungfiel, A.: Improving occupational safety and health (OSH) in human-system interaction (HSI) through applications in virtual environments. Paper presented at the International Conference on Digital Human Modeling and Applications in Health, Safety, Ergonomics and Risk Management (2018)
2. DOSH: Guidelines on Occupational Safety and Health Management Systems (OSHMS) (2011). https://www.dosh.gov.my/index.php/legislation/guidelines/general/597-04-guidel ines-on-occupational-safety-and-health-management-systems-oshms/file
3. SOCSO: Annual Report 2018. Annual Report 2018 (2018). https://www.perkeso.gov.my/ images/laporan_tahunan/LAPORAN%20TAHUNAN%20_ANNUAL%20REPORT%202 018.pdf
4. Hou, L., Wang, X., Bernold, L., Love, P.E.: Using animated augmented reality to cognitively guide assembly. J. Comput. Civ. Eng. 27(5), 439–451 (2013)
5. Chi, H.-L., Kang, S.-C., Wang, X.: Research trends and opportunities of augmented reality applications in architecture, engineering, and construction. Autom. Constr. 33, 116–122 (2013)
6. Milgram, P., Kishino, F.: A taxonomy of mixed reality visual displays. IEICE Trans. Inf. Syst. 77(12), 1321–1329 (1994)
7. Teeter, R.A., Vasarhelyi, M.A.: Remote audit: a review of audit-enhancing information and communication technology literature. J. Emerg. Technol. Account. (2010)
8. Marzuki, H., Ayob, A., Naain, I.Z.M., Rahaizak, N.F.: Internal Audit Effectiveness During Movement Control Order (MCO) Period (2020)
9. Greiner, P., Bogatsch, T., Jahn, N., Martins, L., Linß, G., Notni, G.: Remote-audit and VR support in precision and mechanical engineering. Paper presented at the Photonics and Education in Measurement Science 2019 (2019)
10. Eulerich, M., Wagener, M., Wood, D.A.: Evidence on Internal Audit Effectiveness from Transitioning to Remote Audits because of COVID-19. Available at SSRN 3774050 (2021)
11. Pereira, R.E., Moud, H.I., Gheisari, M.: Using 360-degree interactive panoramas to develop virtual representation of construction sites. Paper presented at the Lean and Computing in Construction Congress (LC3): Volume ID Proceedings of the Joint Conference on Computing in Construction (JC3), 4–7 July 2017, Heraklion, Greece (2017)

12. La Salandra, A., Frajberg, D., Fraternali, P.: A virtual reality application for augmented panoramic mountain images. Virtual Reality **24**(1), 123–141 (2019). https://doi.org/10.1007/s10055-019-00385-x

13. Määttä, T.J.: Virtual environments in machinery safety analysis and participatory ergonomics. Hum. Factors Ergon. Manuf. Service Ind. **17**(5), 435–443 (2007)

14. Hwang, Y., Lin, H., Shin, D.: Knowledge system commitment and knowledge sharing intention: the role of personal information management motivation. Int. J. Inf. Manag. **39**, 220–227 (2018)

15. Hassan, N.A.: Implementation of a knowledge management system (KMS) in small and medium enterprises (SME). J. Inf. Knowl. Manag. (JIKM) **10**(1), 1–9 (2020)

16. Kostrzewski, M.: One design issue – many solutions. Different perspectives of design thinking – case study. In: Uden, L., Hadzima, B., Ting, I.-H. (eds.) KMO 2018. CCIS, vol. 877, pp. 179–190. Springer, Cham (2018). https://doi.org/10.1007/978-3-319-95204-8_16

17. Lor, R.: Design thinking in education: a critical review of literature. In: International Academic Conference on Social Sciences and Management/Asian Conference on Education and Psychology. Conference proceedings, Bangkok, Thailand, pp. 37–68 (2017)

18. Darbellay, F., Moody, Z., Lubart, T. (eds.): Creativity, Design Thinking and Interdisciplinarity. Springer, Singapore (2017). https://doi.org/10.1007/978-981-10-7524-7

19. Chesson, D.: Design thinker profile: creating and validating a scale for measuring design thinking capabilities (2017)

20. Henriksen, D., Richardson, C., Mehta, R.: Design thinking: a creative approach to educational problems of practice. Think. Skills Creat. **26**, 140–153 (2017)

21. Isa, M.F.M., Ab Rahim, N.Z., Fathi, M.S.B.: Review of remote audit in occupational safety and health management system through the mixed-reality spectrum. In: 2021 7th International Conference on Research and Innovation in Information Systems (ICRIIS) (2021)

22. Zainal, S., Yusoff, R.C.M., Abas, H., Yaacub, S., Zainuddin, N.M.: Review of design thinking approach in learning IoT programming. Int. J. Adv. Res. Future Ready Learn. Educ. **24**(1), 28–38 (2021)

Intelligent Science

YOLOv4-MobileNetV2-DW-LCARM:
A Real-Time Ship Detection Network

Puchun Xie[✉], Ran Tao[✉], Xin Luo, and Youqun Shi

School of Computer Science and Technology, Donghua University, Shanghai, China
617420561@qq.com, {taoran,xluo,yqshi}@dhu.edu.cn

Abstract. Ship detection is a key research task for ship identification, monitoring and management to ensure the safety of shipping lanes and harbour. Object detection methods based on computer vision and deep learning has the potential for real-time ship detection, but has the challenges of accuracy, real-time, and lack of high-quality ship datasets. This paper proposes an object detection network named YOLOv4-MobileNetV2-DW-LCARM for ship detection, which is a hybrid application of YOLOv4, MobileNetV2, Depthwise separable convolution and a proposed Lightweight Channel Attention Residual Module (LCARM). To verify the effectiveness of the network, we built a ship dataset with 10 categories and 20216 samples for model training, ablation experiments, and comparative experiments. Compared with YOLOv4, the results show that our network reduces the number of parameters by 82.58% and improves the forward inference speed by 53.6%, reaching the accuracy of 62.75% ArP@0.75 and 94% AP@0.5. The proposed network can be deployed on edge devices for real-time ship detection because it has 24.82 FPS of processing speed. The proposed dataset construction methods also contribute to similar object detection tasks.

Keyword: Ship detection · Object detection · YOLOv4 · Depthwise separable convolution · Data augmentation

1 Introduction

Ship detection is one of the most important research contents of ship identification, monitoring and management to ensure smooth waterways and safe harbors. The current ship detection methods have the following challenges [1–4]: Firstly, ship detection based on artificial observation and VHF (Very High Frequency) communication phone is difficult to accurately get ship information, position and traffic status under horizon and bad weather conditions, which will result in improper dispatching management and then lead to ship traffic accidents. Secondly, ship detection based on AIS (Automatic identification System) technology strongly relies on the signal equipment of the sender and the receiver, and is unable to identify ships without signal or illegal ships equipped with disguised signal generator. Thirdly, computer vision-based ship detection lacks high-quality ship datasets that meet practical requirements. Moreover, computer vision-based ship detection lacks accurate real-time classification algorithms that can be deployed on edge devices.

© Springer Nature Switzerland AG 2022
L. Uden et al. (Eds.): KMO 2022, CCIS 1593, pp. 281–293, 2022.
https://doi.org/10.1007/978-3-031-07920-7_22

YOLOv4 is a single-stage object detection network with good detection performance, which has the potential for real-time ship detection applications. However, YOLOv4 is relatively complex and requires high hardware costs. The purpose of this paper is to propose a computer vision-based method for ship detection with real-time performance and higher accuracy on edge devices. We try to optimize the YOLOv4 with good accuracy and real-time, thus reducing the hardware cost of applications to facilitate application promotion. In order to solve the problem of inadequate ship dataset, we build a ship dataset containing 10 categories and 20216 samples for model training. We also carry out manual data expansion, offline data augmentation and online data augmentation respectively.

The rest of the paper is organized as follows: section two reviews the existing achievements of ship detection and the related research of object detection based on deep learning. In section three, YOLOv4-MobileNetV2-DW-LCARM network is proposed and three improvements of YOLOv4 are described. Ship dataset construction and data augmentation are introduced in section four. Several experiments are also performed to demonstrate the effectiveness of the proposed method. Section five summarizes the research results of this paper.

2   Related Literature Review

There are many research achievements in the field of ship detection. Tang realized ship detection of satellite optical images by combining DNN and ELM with deep neural network [2]. Wang effectively detected ships from complex background SAR images by using variance weighted information entropy (VWIE) method to measure local differences between targets and their neighborhoods [3]. Yang proposed a rotating dense feature pyramid network (R-DFPN) framework, which could effectively detect ships in different scenes such as ocean and port [4].

The above traditional detection algorithm is difficult to achieve good accuracy and real time. It is an important direction to apply feature expression capability of convolutional neural network (CNN) to ship identification. Li, Mou et al. proposed a detection network HSV-NET for detecting high-resolution optical remote sensing images based on depth features [5]. This network is a single-stage, end-to-end target detection algorithm based on region perposal. HSV-NET achieves good accuracy and robustness of small target recognition, but it is only suitable for non-real-time optical remote sensing images. Yao et al. studied optical remote sensing images under complex background, and realized ship detection through CNN convolutional neural network and RPN regional suggestion network respectively [6]. Li et al. proposed a ship detection model in SAR images based on Faster-RCNN [7]. And this method strengthens the training effect through feature fusion and transfer learning. In 2021, Lee et al. proposed a deep learning based ship environment perception and recognition technology [8]. This method is based on YOLOv3 object detection network, which uses kalman filter to track the position of target ship. Li et al. proposed a target detection network SDVI based on YOLOv3 Tiny for real-time identification and positioning of six types of ships [9]. In this method, the author improves the backbone network of YOLOv3 by adding CBAM attention module, which improves the accuracy and achieves a good balance between speed and precision. Although CBAM has optimized the accuracy to some extent, the effect is limited.

The problem of poor feature extraction effect still exists due to the insufficient depth of YOLOv3 Tiny backbone network. Jiang et al. proposed a multi-channel fusion SAR image processing that makes full use of image information and network feature extraction capabilities [10]. YOLOv4 used by the authors achieves an average accuracy of 90.37% on The SAR ship detection dataset SSDD. The research of this paper is based on YOLOv4 and the improvements mainly involve: YOLOv4, MobileNetV2 and DW. A brief introduction will be given below.

2.1 YOLOv4

Object detection can be divided into one-stage method and two-stage method. Two-stage detection algorithm is based on Region Proposal. Among the two-stage detection algorithms, representative algorithms are R-CNN, Fast R-CNN and Faster R-CNN. One-stage object detection algorithm is based on regression object detection algorithm. This kind of algorithm has faster detection speed. Typical one-stage object detection algorithms are YOLO and SSD.

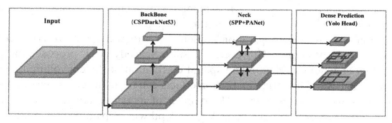

Fig. 1. YOLOv4 network diagram

One-stage YOLOv4 was proposed by Bochkovskiy et al. in 2020. Based on YOLOv3, YOLOv4 has made many improvements on the network [11]. Firstly, as shown in Fig. 1, in terms of backbone, YOLOv4 introduces the architecture of Cross Stage Partial Network (CSPNet) and CSPDarknet53 [12]. Secondly, in the neck network, YOLOv4 joins Spatial Pyramid Pooling module (SPP) and Path Aggregation Network (PANet) [13, 14]. SPP improves the receptive field by using three pooling cores of different sizes. PANet can transmit three feature information of different scales from bottom to top, integrating feature information to avoid information loss.

2.2 MobileNetV2

The requirement of object detection for accuracy makes the depth and scale of CNN increase continuously, which makes it difficult for edge equipment and mobile devices to support real-time computing. Therefore, CNN began to branch on the development of lightweight. Lightweight networks represented by ShuffleNet, SqueezeNet, MobileNet, Xception optimize the network structure and reduce the number of network parameters and computation while ensuring accuracy [15–18].

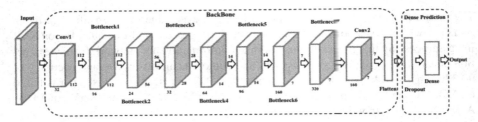

Fig. 2. MobileNetV2 network diagram

MobileNetV2 was proposed in 2018 by Mark Sandler [20] This network is designed to apply in mobile devices, and its structure is shown in Fig. 2.

2.3 Depthwise Separable Convolution (DW)

The development of lightweight networks provides us with a large number of lightweight network solutions, such as group convolution [16], depthwise separable convolution [20] and inverse residual block [15, 17, 20]. Among them, depthwise separable convolution is an important mean of model lightweight in this paper.

In general, a convolution operation implements a joint mapping of channel correlation and spatial correlation. However, Christian Szegedy et al. proposed an idea in Inception that channel correlation and spatial correlation of the convolution layer can be decouple [19]. Similar feature extraction effects can be achieved by mapping spatial and channel convolution separately. The number of model parameters can be significantly reduced. On this basis, shown as Fig. 3, depthwise separable convolution (DW) is generated, and its principle is to decouple a traditional convolution into depthwise convolutions and pointwise convolutions.

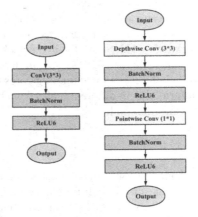

Fig. 3. Depthwise separable convolution (DW)

3 Methodology

3.1 An Improved YOLOv4 Network Structure

We designed an object detection network named YOLOv4-MobileNetV2-DW-LCARM for real-time ship detection. The network diagram and network structure are shown in Fig. 4 and 5.

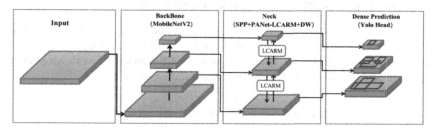

Fig. 4. YOLOv4-MobileNetV2-DW-LCARM network diagram

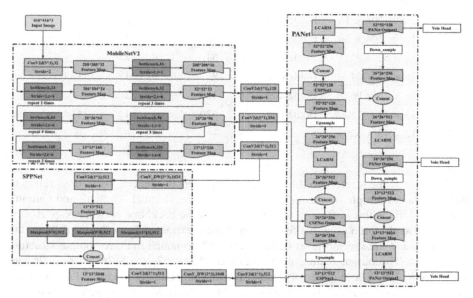

Fig. 5. YOLOv4-MobileNetV2-DW-LCARM network structure

The contributions of the proposed network are as follows:

(1) We replace the backbone of YOLOv4 (CSPDarkNet53) with MobileNetV2, reducing the amounts of parameters and computational complexity. At the same time, CSPNet, SPP and PANet are retained to ensure the accuracy of object detection.

(2) We further reduce the parameters of network to speed up forward calculation, by using depthwise separable convolution (represented as DW in the proposed network) to reconstruct standard 3 * 3 convolution in SPP and PANet.

(3) We propose a lightweight channel attention residual module (LCARM) which is applied to PANet to reduce the degradation and gradient dispersion of deep neural network, improving the high-dimensional feature extraction ability of the model.

3.2 Neural Network Backbone Network Optimization

Due to the excellent feature fusion ability of PANet and SPP, the network structure of these two parts is retained in this network. In order to meet the real-time ships detection on edge devices, we replace the backbone network CSPDarknet53 with MobilenetV2. The reconstructed backbone network structure is shown in Table 1.

Table 1. Revamped MobileNetV2 network structure

Layer	Input	Operator	t	Channel	n	Stride	CSP-output
1	$208 \times 208 \times 32$	Bottleneck	1	16	1	1	–
2	$208 \times 208 \times 16$	Bottleneck	6	24	2	2	–
3	$104 \times 104 \times 24$	Bottleneck	6	32	3	2	Output1
4	$52 \times 52 \times 32$	Bottleneck	6	64	4	2	–
5	$26 \times 26 \times 64$	Bottleneck	6	96	3	1	Output2
6	$26 \times 26 \times 96$	Bottleneck	6	160	3	2	–
7	$13 \times 13 \times 160$	Bottleneck	6	320	1	1	Output3
8	$13 \times 13 \times 320$	–	–	–	–	–	–

In Table 1, the n refers to the number of repeated Bottleneck layer, the t refers to the expansion multiple of channel dimension, and the Output1, Output2 and Output3 correspond to the three effective feature outputs of the backbone network respectively. In this network, three effective feature maps were extracted from the third layer, the fifth layer, and the seventh layer of MobileNetV2, to match the three-output structure of CSPNet. The output feature map sizes were $52 \times 52 \times 32$, $26 \times 26 \times 96$ and $13 \times 13 \times 320$. The number of channels in the input feature map of PANet in the original YOLOv4 network is 128, 256, and 512, which does not match the output of the backbone characteristic network after the replacement. Therefore, in this network, three convolution blocks with size 1 * 1 and step size 1 are respectively used to raise dimensions, so as to achieve the backbone network fusion without changing PANet.

3.3 Lightweight Network

As the spatial pyramid pooling module and the path aggregation network frequently stack standard convolution for feature extraction, the number of parameters in these two parts is relatively high, which affects the efficiency of forward calculation. In this paper, all standard convolutions in SPP module and PANet are replaced by depthwise separable convolution (DW) which reduce the number of parameters and computation cost. Compared with ordinary convolution, DW can reduce the number of computed parameters. As shown in Fig. 6, we assume that the size of upper output feature map is $F_s \times F_s \times P$ (F_s and P are the length and width of the feature map and the number of channels). Since the feature map of P channels need to match P convolution kernels for filtering, the parameters of the standard convolution kernels shown as Formula 1.

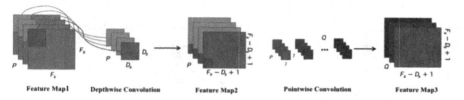

Fig. 6. Schematic diagram of depthwise separable convolution (DW)

Replacing ordinary convolution with DW can greatly reduce the number of model parameters. Suppose that P ordinary convolutions are replaced by P DW ($D_s \times D_s \times 1$) and Q pointwise convolutions ($1 \times 1 \times P$). So the number of the DW parameters is shown as Formula 1. The parameter ratio of DW and standard convolution is shown in Formula 2. In this network, all of the 3 * 3 convolutions in SPP and PANet are replaced by DW. As the channel Q of feature map is large, $1/Q$ can be ignored. By calculation, the number of parameters in the network is reduced to about one ninth of the original number.

$$Params(Conv) = D_s^2 * Q * P \tag{1}$$

$$Params(DW) = D_s^2 * P + P * Q \tag{2}$$

$$(D_s^2 * P + P * Q)/(D_s^2 * Q * P) = 1/Q + 1/D_s^2 \tag{3}$$

3.4 A Lightweight Channel Attention Residual Module (LCARM)

We designed a lightweight channel attention residual module (LCARM). Figure 7(a) is the original five-layer convolution feature extraction module of PANet, and Fig. 7(b) is the structure of the proposed LCARM.

The LCARM is applied to PANet to reduce the degradation and gradient dispersion of deep neural network, improving the capability and robustness of high-dimensional feature extraction. Firstly, LCARM replaces the original standard convolution with depth separable convolution, which effectively reduces the number of parameters of the model. Secondly, inspired by SENet, ILSVRC2017 classification task champion, we add channel attention SE-block to LCARM, further strengthening the correlation between channels [21]. Thirdly, in order to solve the problem of network degradation caused by network depth, LCARM adds a residual edge to alleviate this phenomenon.

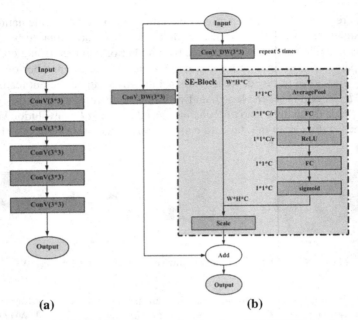

(a)   **(b)**

Fig. 7. (a) Original feature extraction structure. (b) LCARM structure

4   Experiments and Results

4.1   Dataset and Data Augmentation

We build a ship dataset containing 10 categories and 20216 samples for model training. The dataset includes ten ship categories with 20216 samples.

The dataset comes from three sources. First, we manually collected 10,756 surveillance camera images. Second, we manually extracted 2,754 ship images from MS COCO, Pascal VOC dataset [22, 23]. Third, we add 6,706 samples by means of offline data enhancement technology to generate equivalent random data based on existing data, enriching the distribution of training data. The dataset categories and dataset structure are shown in Table 2.

Our experiment uses offline Data Augmentation technology to generate equivalent random data based on existing data, enriching the distribution of training data. Partial offline data enhancement pictures are shown in Fig. 8.

In order to better make the expanded 2754 samples more like the actual camera monitoring pictures, the experiment simulated large-scale light changes which caused by environmental influences such as rain, fog, water vapor and sunshine, by adding noise (such as Gaussian blur) and color gamut distortion (such as RGB disturbance). Random flipping, translation and scaling are used to increase diversity of training samples, reducing the dependence of the model on some attributes.

Table 2. Composition and classification of dataset

Classification	Origin data	Manual collection	Offline enhancement	Total
Ore carrier	2199	14	56	2269
General cargo ship	1821	92	189	2102
Bulk cargo carrier	2145	4	10	2159
Container ship	1207	40	93	1340
Passenger ship	577	376	917	1870
Fishing boat	2226	0	0	2226
Vehicle carrier	319	168	768	1255
Sailboat	115	724	1716	2555
Tanker	104	448	1120	1672
Tug boat	43	788	1937	2768
Total	**10756**	**2754**	**6706**	**20216**

Fig. 8. Offline data augmentation examples

4.2   Results

In order to verify the effectiveness of the YOLOv4-MobileNetV2-DW-LCARM, ablation experiments and comparison experiments were performed. The computing environment is Intel CPU Core i5, GeForce GTX 1060 6g, Ubuntu18.04.6, and CUDA 10.0. The mAP@0.5 and mAP@0.75 were used as accuracy indicators, and the total parameters and FPS are used as scale and speed indicators (see Table 3).

Table 3. Ablation experiment results

Method	mAP@0.5	mAP@0.75	Total params	FPS
YOLOv4-DW-LCARM	93.19%	64.38%	36,512,413	16.18
YOLOv4-MobileNetV2-DW	90.36%	53.62%	10,801,149	25.66
YOLOv4-MobileNetV2-LCARM	91.68%	62.67%	18,012,989	22.42
YOLOv4-MobileNetV2-DW-LCARM*	78.7%	26.32%	11,211,325	24.82
YOLOv4-MobileNetV2-DW-LCARM	**94.0%**	**62.57%**	**11,211,325**	**24.82**

As shown in Table 3, the ablation experiment mainly studies the role of backbone (MobileNetV2), depthwise separable convolution (DW), light channel attention residual block module (LCARM) and data augmentation. The method with * indicates that the dataset is not enhanced.

To prove the effect of backbone MobileNetV2, we have designed the first ablation experiment. As shown in the first and fifth lines, when MobileNetV2 was used as the backbone network, the number of parameters decreased by about 69.3% and the FPS increased by 53.4%. The accuracy index mAP@0.75 decreased by 1.81%, while mAP@0.5 increased slightly. This ablation experiment indicates that MobileNetV2 is slightly lower than CSPDarkNet53 in feature extraction accuracy, but significantly accelerates in forward calculation speed.

In order to demonstrate the effect of LCARM on the network, the second ablation experiment is designed. As shown in the second and fifth lines, from mAP@0.5 and mAP@0.75, LCARM improves accuracy by 3.64% and 8.95%, respectively. LCARM effectively alleviates the degradation and gradient dispersion of deep neural network through attention mechanism and residual structure, improving network accuracy.

To demonstrate the effect of DW on the network, the third ablation experiment is designed. As shown in the third and fifth lines, this experiment replaces the 3 * 3 convolution in PANet and SPP (excluding the backbone network) with DW. This reduces the number of network parameters by 37.76%, and the detection frame rate increases by 2.4FPS.

In order to demonstrate the effect of data augmentation on detection, the fourth ablation experiment is designed. As shown in the fourth and fifth lines, the model trained on unenhanced datasets has a significant decline in accuracy, indicating that it's very necessary for self-built datasets with limited scale to enhance dataset.

In the comparison experiment, the difference in accuracy and speed between YOLOv4-MobileNetV2-DW-LCARM and other networks is studied. As shown in Table 4, compared with large-scale networks such as YOLOv3 and YOLOv4, the detection speed of YOLOv4-MobileNetV2-DW-LCARM have been greatly improved, with the FPS increased by 40.62% and 53.49% respectively. The number of parameters decreased by 81.9% and 82.52%. In terms of accuracy, compared with YOLOv3 and YOLOv4, the model proposed in this paper has a slight decline in mAP@0.75 and exceeds YOLOv4 in mAP@0.5 index. YOLOv4-MobileNetV2-DW-LCARM is much

Table 4. Ablation experiment results

Method	mAP@0.5	mAP@0.75	Total params	FPS
YOLOv3	92.79%	64.32%	61,949,149	17.65
YOLOv4	93.19%	64.98%	64,363,101	16.17
EfficientDet	69.02%	33.75%	3,874,217	30.12
YOLOv4-tiny	84.24%	33.36%	6,056,606	32.64
YOLOv4-MobileNetV2-DW-LCARM	**94.00%**	**62.57%**	**11,211,325**	24.82

more accurate than EfficientDet, YOLOv4-tiny. The detection effect comparison images of different networks are shown in Fig. 9.

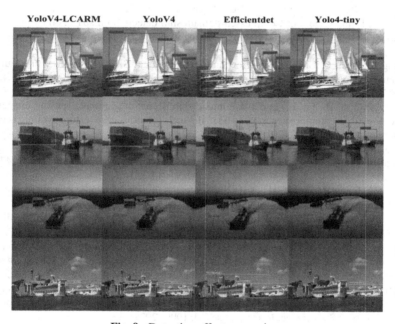

Fig. 9. Detection effect comparison

5   Conclusion

In order to solve the problems of slow detection speed, low identification accuracy and lack of ship dataset, we proposed YOLOV4-MobileNetV2-DW-LCARM network for real-time ship detection and a ship dataset construction method in this paper. Firstly, MobileNetV2 network is used to replace the backbone network of YOLOv4, reducing the number of network parameters. Secondly, by introducing DW to reconstruct SPP and PANet, we speed up the forward calculation. Thirdly, a LCARM is proposed and applied to PANet to improve the model's high-dimensional feature extraction capability and robustness. Fourthly, data augmentation is used on the dataset to improve the generalization ability of the model. The results of experiments show that the proposed YOLOv4-MobileNetV2-DW-LCARM can improve the computing speed while ensuring the accuracy of object detection. The proposed network and the ship dataset construction method also contribute to the design of similar object detection systems running on edge devices.

Acknowledgments. This research was supported by the National Key R&D Program of China under Grant No. 2020YFB1707700.

References s

1. Lecun, Y., Bengio, Y., Hinton, G.: Deep learning. Nature **521**(7553), 436 (2015)
2. Tang, J., Deng, C., et al.: Compressed-domain ship detection on spaceborne optical image using deep neural network and extreme learning machine. IEEE Trans. Geosci. Remote Sens. **53**(3), 1174–1185 (2015)
3. Wang, X., Chen, C.: Ship detection for complex background SAR images based on a multiscale variance weighted image entropy method. IEEE Geosci. Remote Sens. Lett. **14**(2), 184–187 (2017)
4. Yang, X., Sun, H., Fu, K., et al.: Automatic ship detection of remote sensing images from Google earth in complex scenes based on multi-scale rotation dense feature pyramid networks. Remote Sens. **10**(1), 132 (2018)
5. Li, Q., Mou, L., Liu, Q., et al.: HSF-Net: multiscale deep feature embedding for ship detection in optical remote sensing imagery. IEEE Trans. Geosci. Remote Sens. **56**(12), 7147–7161 (2018)
6. Yuan, Y., Jiang, Z., Zhang, H., et al.: Ship detection in optical remote sensing images based on deep convolutional neural networks. J. Appl. Remote Sens. **11**(4), 1 (2017)
7. Li, J., Qu, C., Shao, J.: Ship detection in SAR images based on an improved faster R-CNN. In: SAR in Big Data Era: Models, Methods & Applications. IEEE (2017)
8. Lee, W.-J., Roh, M.-I., Lee, H.-W., et al.: Detection and tracking for the awareness of surroundings of a ship based on deep learning. J. Comput. Des. Eng. **8**(5), 1407–1430 (2021)
9. Li, H., Deng, L., Yang, C., et al.: Enhanced YOLOv3 tiny network for real-time ship detection from visual image. IEEE Access **9**, 16692–16706 (2021)
10. Ma, Z.: High-speed lightweight ship detection algorithm based on YOLO-v4 for three-channels RGB SAR image. Remote Sens. **13**, 1909 (2021)
11. Bochkovskiy, A., Wang, C.Y., Liao, H.: YOLOv4: optimal speed and accuracy of object detection (2020)
12. Wang, C.Y., Liao, H., Wu, Y.H., et al.: CSPNet: a new backbone that can enhance learning capability of CNN. In: 2020 IEEE/CVF Conference on Computer Vision and Pattern Recognition Workshops (CVPRW). IEEE (2020)
13. He, K., Ren, S., et al.: Spatial pyramid pooling in deep convolutional networks for visual recognition. IEEE Trans. Pattern Anal. Mach. Intell. **37**(9), 1904–1916 (2015)
14. Liu, S., et al.: Path aggregation network for instance segmentation. IEEE (2018)
15. Zhang, X., Zhou, X., Lin, M., et al.: ShuffleNet: an extremely efficient convolutional neural network for mobile devices (2017)
16. Iandola, F.N., Han, S., Moskewicz, M.W., et al.: SqueezeNet: AlexNet-level accuracy with 50x fewer parameters and <0.5 MB model size (2016)

17. Howard, A.G., Zhu, M., Chen, B., et al.: MobileNets: efficient convolutional neural networks for mobile vision applications (2017)
18. Chollet, F.: Xception: deep learning with depthwise separable convolutions. In: 2017 IEEE Conference on Computer Vision and Pattern Recognition (CVPR). IEEE (2017)
19. Szegedy, C., Vanhoucke, V., Ioffe, S., et al.: Rethinking the inception architecture for computer vision, pp. 2818–2826. IEEE (2016)
20. Sandler, M., Howard, A., Zhu, M., et al.: MobileNetV2: inverted residuals and linear bottlenecks. In: Conference on Computer Vision and Pattern Recognition. IEEE (2018)
21. Jie, H., Li, S., Gang, S., et al.: Squeeze-and-excitation networks. IEEE Trans. Pattern Anal. Mach. Intell. (2017)
22. Veit, A., Matera, T., Neumann, L., et al.: COCO-text: dataset and benchmark for text detection and recognition in natural images (2016)
23. Everingham, M., Eslami, S., Gool, L.V., et al.: The Pascal visual object classes challenge: a retrospective. Int. J. Comput. Vis. **111**(1), 98–136 (2015)

Chatbots for News Delivery – Investigations into Intrinsic Motivation and User Engagement

Lukas Köb, Stephan Schlögl[(✉)] [iD], and Ellen Richter

Department of Management, Communication and IT, MCI – The Entrepreneurial School, Universitätsstraße 15, 6020 Innsbruck, Austria
stephan.schloegl@mci.edu

Abstract. The Internet has led to an unprecedented diversity in the news delivery sector. Today's news consumers no longer inform themselves through newspapers alone. Rather it is radio and TV and increasingly also newspaper websites, social media channels, and dedicated news apps, which give them a great choice in how to keep up with ongoing developments. In this context, much hope has recently been placed on so-called news chatbots as a novel delivery format. Yet, little is known about the suitability of these chatbots as a news medium. Hence, the work presented in this paper aimed to trigger respective investigations by focusing on intrinsic motivation to use news chatbots and the resulting user engagement. In an experimental study (n = 60) we compared a linear news delivery mode in the form of a one-way newsflash delivered by a chatbot with a conversational news delivery mode in the form of back-and-forth chatbot interactions. Results show that people feel less pressured and stressed in the conversational mode, while the linear mode had a negative effect on the intrinsic motivation to use the chatbot. Furthermore, we found that the conversational mode had a positive impact on user engagement.

Keywords: Media industry · News consumption · Chatbots · Intrinsic motivation · User engagement

1 Introduction

Driven by ongoing digital transformation efforts we see that *"the way news is gathered, the way it is distributed, sold, and paid for, and the way it is consumed and redistributed has changed"* [15, p. 25]. Hence, for news organisations to be successful, they need to quickly respond to the increasing audience fragmentation and growing competition fostered by digital, social, and mobile media platforms [9]. Responses have to include strategies on how to provide an attractive medium to young people, how to master the transformation in terms of penalisation and mobilisation and furthermore how to work effectively with third-party platforms [14]. In this respect, it is no longer sufficient to simply provide an

© Springer Nature Switzerland AG 2022
L. Uden et al. (Eds.): KMO 2022, CCIS 1593, pp. 294–305, 2022.
https://doi.org/10.1007/978-3-031-07920-7_23

online version of a once traditional print medium. News providers rather need a comprehensive digital strategy that is driven by ongoing consumer research and innovation [13]. Many established news companies have recognised this fact and thus experimented with so-called news chatbots and conversational journalism. Whether these chatbots are a suitable means to consume media and whether engagement differs between different interaction styles, however, is still unclear. Only if we know the extent to which and the form in which news chatbots are effective, can they be integrated into a media company's comprehensive news delivery strategy [4].

Building upon research by Hong and Oh [7], it was thus the goal of the work presented below to build a more profound understanding of the modern news audience. Our study aimed to explore the intrinsic motivation to use news chatbots and the user engagement different delivery modes may trigger. More precisely, we wanted to understand whether a conversational news delivery mode more positively affects intrinsic motivation and user engagement than a linear news delivery mode. Consequently, our study was driven by the following research question:

"What influence does conversational news delivery through chatbots have on users' intrinsic motivation to use and engage with news chatbots?"

Our report on this research endeavour begins in Sect. 2, with a brief discussion of the radical changes the news industry is going through due to ongoing digital transformation efforts, and why news chatbots, therefore, are on the rise. Then, Sect. 3 outlines our research design and respective methodology. Section 4 reports on the experiment results, whose relevance and limitations are discussed in Sect. 5. Finally, Sect. 6 concludes the paper and proposes some ideas for future research.

2   Developments in the Media Sector

Recent research has shown that society no longer consumes news in the conventional newspaper format[1,2,3,4] [12]. While in the past people used to follow a certain ritual of reading (mostly long) newspaper articles at very specific times during the day, today, news are absorbed mainly by chance and rather casually on the go. These habitual changes started approximately 20 years ago at the point when newspapers launched the first online news sites, complementing their traditional paper-based offerings. And already then, it seemed clear that

---

[1] Online: https://www.pewresearch.org/fact-tank/2019/05/16/facts-about-americans-and-facebook/ [accessed: January 30th 2022].

[2] Online: https://www.pewresearch.org/fact-tank/2017/06/12/growth-in-mobile-news-use-driven-by-older-adults/ [accessed: January 30th 2022].

[3] Online: https://www.pewresearch.org/internet/2010/03/01/understanding-the-participatory-news-consumer/ [accessed: January 30th 2022].

[4] Online: https://de.statista.com/statistik/daten/studie/171257/umfrage/normalerweise-genutzte-quelle-fuer-informationen/ [accessed: January 30th 2022].

for the younger generation it will be unlikely that they would develop the same newspaper reading habits as their parents had[5].

As research conducted by Huang [8] highlights, today's news consumption often serves as a temporary escape. Also, it was shown that news are increasingly consumed via instant messenger, especially by younger people [2,3,17], which explains why respective messaging and bot systems are continuously gaining momentum[6] and instant messaging and social network application usage keeps growing[7].

At the same time, a certain app saturation becomes apparent [16], for which experts increasingly talk about bots becoming *"the next big thing"* [6]. To this end, Microsoft CEO Satya Nadella convincingly proclaimed, during a famous keynote speech in 2016, that it is reasonable to assume that bots will replace apps[8]. Assuming this prediction holds, we stand at the beginning of a paradigm shift in smartphone usage – away from the static use of numerous different applications to dynamic, conversation-based interactions with companies and other institutions over only a few different messaging platforms. Messaging would thus become the ultimate meta-platform through which not only e-commerce would take place but potentially also news consumption. Consequently, *"newspapers are knee-deep in explorations of various online delivery channels and have shifted a substantial amount of their dwindling resources from their print editions to new devices, believing that younger readers will embrace these devices as new sources of news and information"* [4, p. 431]. News organisations also experiment with new delivery formats, which are more informal and collaborative and thus may better align with the modern *Zeitgeist* [9]. Here, news chatbots are said to have great potential, as they effectively respond to the three media challenges highlighted by Sehl et al. [14]; i.e. (1) they represent an attractive medium for young people; (2) they are flexible in terms of personalisation and mobility; and (3) they offer cross-platform availability.

3   Methodology

In order to explore the potential of chatbots as a means for news delivery, we compared two different delivery modes. That is, we had one chatbot which provided news headlines in a linear way (i.e., via a linear newsfeed), and another chatbot which provided the same news in a conversational format (i.e., via a conversational newsfeed). As expressed by our research question, the goal was to investigate whether conversational news delivery has a more positive effect on intrinsic user motivation and user engagement than linear news delivery.

---

[5] Online: https://www.pewresearch.org/politics/2002/06/09/publics-news-habits-little-changed-by-september-11/ [accessed: January 30th 2022].

[6] Online: https://www.businessinsider.com/the-messaging-app-report-2016-4-23?international=true&r=US&IR=T [accessed: January 30th 2022].

[7] Online: https://www.digitalnewsreport.org/survey/2018/the-rise-of-messaging-apps-for-news/ [accessed: January 30th 2022].

[8] Online: https://eu.usatoday.com/story/tech/news/2016/03/30/microsof-ceo-nadella-bots-new-apps/82431672/ [accessed: January 30th 2022].

3.1 Experiment Procedure, Measures and Data Collection

We used a between-subject design where participants were divided into two groups. One group received daily news notifications in the form of a one-way linear chatbot newsfeed (cf. Fig. 1). The other group received the same news but embedded in short automated chatbot conversations (cf. Fig. 2). Participants were informed that all the news they received were purely fictional so as to allow for an unbiased objective evaluation. Before starting the experiment, they were asked to complete a short questionnaire measuring intrinsic motivation with respect to chatbot use. Similar to Yin et al. [18], this motivation questionnaire was adapted from the Intrinsic Motivation Inventory (IMI) [11]. The used subscales included *Interest & Enjoyment, Perceived Competence, Value/Usefulness, Tension/Pressure,* as well as *Compatibility*, where the six items of *Interest & Enjoyment* were taken as a direct indicator of intrinsic motivation. The four items for *Perceived Competence* and the four for *Value/Usefulness* were considered positive, and the three for *Tension/Pressure* negative predictors. Finally, *Compatibility* used three items which we thought may also influence intrinsic motivation to use a news chatbot. All 20 questionnaire items used a 7-point Likert scale ranging from $1 = Not\,at\,all\,True$ to $7 = Very\,True$. The complete questionnaire is depicted in Tables 5 and 6, which may be found at the end of this paper.

In order to measure user engagement, we used the memorability method, which is commonly employed in marketing studies. Our postulation here was, that the better users can retain the news provided by the chatbot, the higher the engagement with the chatbot. As an evaluation instrument, we used a single choice test with ten questions about the fictional news provided by the chatbots.

Figure 3 illustrates the subsequent experimental procedure. The experiment took place over 7 days. First, participants were asked to install the respective chatbot on their smartphone. This installation took only a couple of seconds. As soon as the chatbot was activated, it provided all the necessary information about the study purpose and exact experiment procedure. Before delivering the first news item, the chatbot asked a participant to complete the above-described questionnaire regarding his/her subjectively perceived intrinsic motivation to use chatbots as a news source. Subsequently, participants could start the chatbot at any time so that the respective start time determined the general time of news reception over the next five days.

Conversational news consumption lasted no longer than five minutes, whereas linear news were sent once a day. On the sixth day, the chatbot asked participants to take the final test and to once more complete the questionnaire about their subjectively perceived intrinsic motivation. This time with a specific focus on the used news chatbot.

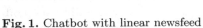

Fig. 1. Chatbot with linear newsfeed

Fig. 2. Chatbot with conversational newsfeed

3.2 Chatbots and Material

Chatbots were created using the Flow XO chatbot development platform[9] and made available via the Telegram instant messenger service[10]. Following the classification of Adamopoulou and Moussiades [1], they may be categorized as rule-based, closed-domain, interpersonal, informative chatbots. The motivation questionnaire and the memorability test were both built with Google Forms and made available via links sent through the chatbot.

3.3 Sampling

In general, we focused on young adults, aged between 20 and 35 years who have been growing up with digital technology and thus are likely to have a high affinity for digital products. Participation was entirely voluntary and in accordance with European data protection regulations (i.e., GDPR) including respective informed consent procedures. The sampling method as well as the data collection and analysis procedures were furthermore approved by the school's Ethics Commission.

---

[9] Online: https://flowxo.com/ [accessed: January 26th 2022].
[10] Online: https://telegram.org/ [accessed: January 26th 2022].

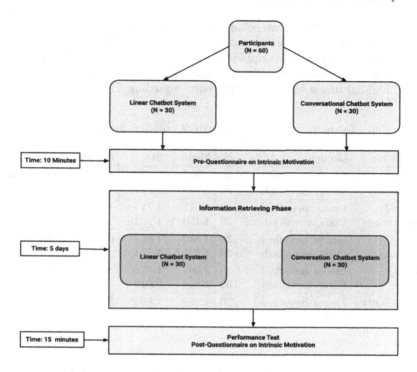

Fig. 3. Experiment procedure. Adapted from Yin et al. [18]

Through snowball sampling, we were able to recruit a total of 86 participants corresponding to this sample frame, who were assigned to the two different study groups; i.e. linear news delivery vs. conversational news delivery. 26 of those participants did not complete the initial questionnaire and were thus excluded from further analysis, which left us with a total of 30 valid data sets per group.

4   Results

Data analysis regarding intrinsic motivation to use news chatbots showed that conversational reporting differed from linear news delivery, especially in terms of perceived tension and pressure. That is, respondents felt more tense and pressured by linear news delivery, suggesting that people would feel more comfortable when news are embedded in conversations. Furthermore, when the report was delivered in short dialogues, respondents seemed to better remember the information provided, indicating higher engagement with the conversational news delivery mode.

To formally compare the intrinsic motivation of the two news delivery modes an ANCOVA analysis was conducted. It was used to measure the influence of each delivery mode on the motivational factors with additional consideration of the pre-test scores. The intention was to determine whether conversational reporting had a positive effect on intrinsic motivation. Hence the delivery mode was defined as independent variables, while all post-test dimension scores were defined as dependent variables. Table 1 summarizes the results of this co-variance analysis, highlighting a significant difference regarding *Tension/Pressure*.

Table 1. Co-variance analysis of post-test motivation

Dimensions	Groups	N	Mean	SD	F value	P value	η^2
Interest & Enjoyment	Linear newsflash	30	4.367	1.872	3.007	0.088	0.05
	Conv. newsflash	30	5.128	1.317			
Perceived Competence	Linear newsflash	30	3.617	1.714	1.746	0.192	0.33
	Conv. newsflash	30	4.150	1.152			
Value/ Usefulness	Linear newsflash	30	4.342	1.867	0.852	0.360	0.015
	Conv. newsflash	30	4.725	1.284			
Tension/ Pressure	Linear newsflash	30	2.667	1.718	1.020	0.05*	0.066
	Conv. newsflash	30	1.944	0.910			
Compatibility	Linear newsflash	30	4.289	1.893	2.541	0.116	0.043
	Conv. newsflash	30	4.933	1.288			

Note. *p <= 0.05

Subsequently, following Yin et al. [18], a linear regression analysis was carried out so as to determine which dimensions influenced intrinsic motivation to what extent. Here, the *Interest & Enjoyment* dimension acted as a direct measure for intrinsic motivation and thus was defined as dependent variable. All other dimensions (i.e., *Perceived Competence, Value/Usefulness, Tension/Pressure,* and *Compatibility*) depicted independent variables in our analysis. Tables 2 and 3 show the results of this regression analysis for each of the two news delivery modes.

Finally, as for user engagement, results show that conversational news delivery had a positive effect on user engagement. The mean scores for memorability in the performance test were significantly different, with a mean score in the conversational delivery mode of $M = 7.10(SD = 1.826)$ and $M = 4.97(SD = 2.456)$ in the linear delivery mode. A T-test analysis confirmed the significant difference between the two delivery modes (cf. Table 4).

5   Discussion and Limitations

The above-presented results indicate that conversational journalism has potential as people feel less pressured when receiving news via conversations, indicating the higher comfort of conversational journalism. In addition, people are better at remembering information embedded in short conversations, suggesting that chatbots that convey news in the form of a dialogue generate higher engagement and are thus more effective than linear news chatbots. This aligns

Table 2. Linear regression analysis for linear news delivery

Dimensions	Unstandardised	Standardised	Stand. error
(Constant)	0.977		0.515
Perceived Competence	0.121	0.111	0.101
Value/Usefulness	0.680***	0.678***	0.146
Tension/Pressure	−0.205*	−0.188*	0.089
Compatibility	0.127	0.129	0.162
R^2	0.871		
Adjusted R^2	0.850		
F (df = 4; 25)	4.226***		

*$p < 0.05$; ***$p < 0.001$

Table 3. Linear regression analysis for conversational news delivery

Dimensions	Unstandardised	Standardised	Stand. error
(Constant)	0.589		0.901
Perceived Competence	0.077	0.067	0.178
Perceived Value	0.554*	0.540*	0.202
Tension/Pressure	0.090	0.062	0.191
Compatibility	0.289	0.283	0.205
R^2	0.657		
Adjusted R^2	0.602		
F (df = 4; 25)	11.955***		

*$p < 0.05$; ***$p < 0.001$

with the findings of Marchionni [10] in the sense that conversational journalism holds potential and is promising for the future as well as with the work of Ford and Hutchinson [5], who showed that news chatbots are an attractive alternative to traditional journalism. They seem to be well suited for these modern, non-traditional news consumption habits, which sounds promising for media companies, as they may use news chatbots to build engagement with the seemingly lost audience of young readers [9].

As for our study, however, we need to highlight that the conversational capabilities our chatbot was equipped with were rather limited and the time frame during which the news were received was very short. Furthermore, the experimental setup was subject to uncontrolled, potentially confounding factors that may have affected the outcome; i.e., (1) it was not possible to control when and how participants consumed the news; (2) depending on when a participant started the chatbot, there were different news delivery times; (3) participants

Table 4. T-test of post-test memorability

Groups	N	Mean	SD	P value
Conversational newsflash	30	7.10	1.826	0.0
Linear newsflash	30	4.97	2.456	0.00

Table 5. Pre-Test Questionnaire on Intrinsic Motivation

Pre-Test Questionnaire: Intrinsic Motivation

Interest & Enjoyment

1. I think I will enjoy receiving information this way
2. Receiving information this way is fun
3. I think this is a boring way to receive information (R)
4. This way of receiving information will not hold my attention at all (R)
5. I would describe this way of receiving information as very interesting
6. I think this way of receiving information is quite enjoyable

Perceived Competence

1. I think I'm pretty good at gathering information that way
2. think I do pretty well at gathering information that way, compared to others
3. I am pretty skilled in this type of information gathering
4. his kind of information gathering is something I'm not very good at (R)

Value/Usefulness

1. I believe receiving information this way could be of some value to me
2. I think that receiving information this way is useful for acquiring information
3. I think receiving information this way could help me to be better informed
4. I believe receiving information this way could be beneficial for me

Tension/Pressure

1. I feel very tense while receiving information this way
2. I feel pressured while receiving information this way
3. I am very relaxed in this information receiving process (R)

Compatibility

1. Receiving information this way is compatible with all aspects of my life
2. I think that using the system fits well with the way I like to be informed
3. Receiving information this way fits into my lifestyle

(R) = Reversed Likert Scale

may have been distracted or stressed at the time when they received the news; and (4) there were no uniform smartphone settings. Despite these limitations, we believe for our findings to be valuable, as they show that news chatbots and conversational journalism have potential and that further research in this area is needed.

Table 6. Post-Test Questionnaire on Intrinsic Motivation

Post-Test Questionnaire: Intrinsic Motivation
Interest & Enjoyment
1. I enjoyed receiving information this way
2. Receiving information this way is fun
3. I thought this is a boring way to receive information (R)
4. This way of receiving information did not hold my attention at all (R)
5. I would describe this way of receiving information as very interesting
6. I think this way of receiving information is quite enjoyable
Perceived Competence
1. I think I am pretty good at this type of information gathering
2. I think I did pretty well at this type of information gathering, compared to others
3. I was pretty skilled in this type of information gathering
4. This kind of information gathering was something I'm not very good at (R)
Value/Usefulness
1. I believe receiving information this way could be of some value to me
2. I think that receiving information this way is useful for acquiring information.
3. I think receiving information this way could help me to be better informed
4. I believe receiving information this way could be beneficial for me
Tension/Pressure
1. I felt very annoyed receiving information this way
2. I felt pressured while I received information this way
3. I was very relaxed in this information receiving process (R)
Compatibility
1. Receiving information this way is compatible with all aspects of my life
2. I think that using the system fits well with the way I like to be informed
3. Receiving information this way fits into my lifestyle
(R) = Reversed Likert Scale

6   Conclusion and Future Work

Building upon Hong and Oh [7], our study aimed to deepen the understanding of contemporary news consumption and whether chatbot technology may be used to help news providers win back lost audiences. To this end, we reported on the results of an experiment-based survey which explored the *"newsfullness"* [4] of chatbots as a news delivery instrument. We focused on participants' intrinsic motivation to use these news chatbots and the user engagement they are able to trigger. Comparing two different news delivery modes, our results show that conversational news delivery makes people feel less pressured and stressed compared to linear news delivery and that, with linear reporting, tension and pressure negatively affect intrinsic usage motivation. Results, furthermore indicate that conversational journalism has a positive impact on user engagement. In this way, the outcomes confirm earlier research in that both news chatbots and conversational journalism have potential.

Given today's significantly changed news consumption habits, which were driven by the ongoing digitalization efforts over the last 30 years, it is reasonable to assume that the newspaper industry needs to find new ways to engage with its readership. Respective providers need to keep pace with technological and socio-demographic progress so as to remain competitive. Here, the continuous growth of smartphone technology offers a platform through which chatbots could establish themselves as a modern way to engage with news consumers. While our study outlined two concrete advantages chatbots bring to the table (i.e., increased intrinsic motivation to use and increased user engagement), more research, particular focusing on technological, economic, social, and psychological factors of chatbot use, is required so as to grasp the full potential as well as the challenges this technology might hold for the news industry.

References

1. Adamopoulou, E., Moussiades, L.: Chatbots: history, technology, and applications. Mach. Learn. Appl. **2**, 100006 (2020)
2. Batra, B.: News communication through Whatsapp. Int. J. Inf. Futuristic Res. **3**(10), 3725–3733 (2016)
3. Bipat, T., Wilson, T., Kurniawan, O., Choi, Y.J.S., Starbird, K.: It is not all fun and games: breaking news consumption on snapchat. In: Proceedings of the 52nd Hawaii International Conference on System Sciences (2019)
4. Chyi, H.I., Chadha, M.: News on new devices: Is multi-platform news consumption a reality? Journalism Pract. **6**(4), 431–449 (2012)
5. Ford, H., Hutchinson, J.: Newsbots that mediate journalist and audience relationships. Digit. Journalism **7**(8), 1013–1031 (2019)
6. Gentsch, P.: AI in Marketing, Sales and Service: How Marketers Without a Data Science Degree can Use AI, Big Data and Bots. Springer, Cham (2018). https://doi.org/10.1007/978-3-319-89957-2
7. Hong, H., Oh, H.J.: Utilizing bots for sustainable news business: understanding users' perspectives of news bots in the age of social media. Sustainability **12**(16), 6515 (2020)
8. Huang, E.: The causes of youths' low news consumption and strategies for making youths happy news consumers. Convergence **15**(1), 105–122 (2009)
9. Jones, B., Jones, R.: Public service chatbots: automating conversation with BBC news. Digit. Journalism **7**(8), 1032–1053 (2019)
10. Marchionni, D.: Conversational journalism in practice: a case study of the Seattle times' 2010 Pulitzer prize for breaking news reporting. Digit. Journalism **1**(2), 252–269 (2013)
11. McAuley, E., Duncan, T., Tammen, V.V.: Psychometric properties of the intrinsic motivation inventory in a competitive sport setting: a confirmatory factor analysis. Res. Quart. Exerc. Sport **60**(1), 48–58 (1989)
12. Nelson, J.L., Lei, R.F.: The effect of digital platforms on news audience behavior. Digit. Journalism **6**(5), 619–633 (2018)
13. Pavlik, J.V.: Innovation and the future of journalism. Digit. Journalism **1**(2), 181–193 (2013)
14. Sehl, A., Cornia, A., Nielsen, R.K.: Public service news and digital media. Reuters Institute Reports (2016)

15. Tong, J., Lo, S.H.: Digital Technology and Journalism. Springer, Cham (2017). https://doi.org/10.1007/978-3-319-55026-8
16. Van Doorn, M., Duivestein, S.: The bot effect: 'friending your brand'. Report. Applied Innovation Exchange, SogetiLabs (2016)
17. Vázquez-Herrero, J., Negreira-Rey, M.C., López-García, X.: Let's dance the news! how the news media are adapting to the logic of tiktok. Journalism 1464884920969092 (2020)
18. Yin, J., Goh, T.T., Yang, B., Xiaobin, Y.: Conversation technology with micro-learning: the impact of chatbot-based learning on students' learning motivation and performance. J. Educ. Comput. Res. **59**(1), 154–177 (2021)

Agent-Based Vector-Label Propagation for Explaining Social Network Structures

Valerio Bellandi[1], Paolo Ceravolo[1(✉)], Ernesto Damiani[2],
and Samira Maghool[1(✉)]

[1] Università degli Studi di Milano (UNIMI), Milan, Italy
{valerio.bellandi,paolo.ceravolo,samira.maghool}@unimi.it
[2] Khalifa University (KUST), Abu Dhabi, UAE
ernesto.damiani@kustar.ac.ae

Abstract. Even though Social Network Analysis is quite helpful in studying the structural properties of interconnected systems, real-world networks reveal much more hidden characteristics from interacting domain-specific features. In this study, we designed an Agent-based Vector-label PRopagation Algorithm (AVPRA), which captures both structural properties and domain-specific features of a given network by assigning vectors of features to constituting agents. Experimental analysis proves that our algorithm is accurate in revealing the structural properties of a network in an explainable fashion. Furthermore, the resulting vector-labels are suitable for downstream machine learning tasks.

Keywords: Vector-label propagation · Social network analysis · Explainability

1 Introduction

Social network analysis (SNA) has been largely applied to study the interaction patterns and emergent conditions of a wide variety of systems [1,8,9,27]. Thanks to an abstract representation, where the connections between specific elements of a system, termed nodes or agents when they are capable of active functions, are spotted out, SNA can be applied to multiple domains. The behavior of the system, in terms of communication, propagation, and evolution of the connections is effectively captured by SNA metrics. However, approaches based on SNA have been criticized for their *structural determinism* [6,14], i.e. emphasizing the topology of the network or the position of a node but eliding features that are exogenous to it. This intrinsic limit appears clear considering the representation used in SNA makes different properties of the system captured by the same measures. Different phenomena generating similar network structures are accounted for in a similar way, losing their original distinction. For example, two nodes may have the same centrality value but be connected to different communities. Two communities may have the same density but have been generated by interactions of different kinds.

© Springer Nature Switzerland AG 2022
L. Uden et al. (Eds.): KMO 2022, CCIS 1593, pp. 306–317, 2022.
https://doi.org/10.1007/978-3-031-07920-7_24

The connection between the structural properties of the network and other features of the system is typically studied in separated stages. For example, in link prediction, it is common to use supervised learning to verify the capacity of domain-specific features in predicting the formation of links [15]. More recently, deep learning procedures made it feasible to handle feature spaces of very large size. The structural features of the network and domain-specific features of the systems can be fused to input learning procedures able to predict the emergence of specific conditions such as the social influence of agents [25] or the consolidation of communities in the network [22]. Although these approaches reach high levels of accuracy, they require to pipeline multiple tasks and carry significant computational complexity as every single task has to process the entire network.

Label propagation algorithms adopt a *local view*, incorporating domain-specific features directly in the procedures used for navigating the network space [26]. The general idea is the labels initially assigned to the nodes are propagated through the network following its edges. The propagation of a label to a node is based on the labels in its neighborhood, typically at a one-hop distance. A simple approach is to conform to the majority of the observed labels. Multiple iterations allow moving from the local optimum to approximations of the global optimum. Time complexity range between linear to exponential time, depending on the density of the network. The approach is naturally decentralized, with single-pass computation at the local level, i.e., per node at each iteration. The labels propagated in the network can capture different features such as the closest community of an agent [16] or the semantic annotation of social media content [33]. However, most label propagation algorithms deal with a single label per node. This provides a one-dimensional view of how domain-specific features spread in the network. But a single label may be insufficient to describe the features characterizing an agent. Vector-label propagation algorithms have been recently proposed to support a multi-dimensional representation of the features insisting on a node [29]. These approaches are useful for enriching our ability to represent the features space but are not necessarily able to capture the structure of the network.

In our work, we introduce a new vector-label propagation algorithm and we demonstrate its ability to capture both *domain-specific* and *structural properties* of the network. The proposed algorithm is named Agent-based Vector-label PRopagation Algorithm (AVPRA). It uses an agent-based computing approach to construct the vector of labels of nodes. Nodes are implemented as agents that can update their vectors unifying the vectors of the agents connected to them. During the unification process, agents assign to the labels a belonging coefficient that has to reflect their relative importance in the updated agent. We propose an approach for computing belonging coefficients that reflect both the relative frequency of labels and the position of the node in the network. In Sect. 2 we present the related works and motivate our proposal. In Sect. 3 we define the proposed algorithm. Section 4, contains the elaboration of experiments procedure and the evaluation of our algorithm.

2   Related Works

Label Propagation (LP) refers to a family of algorithms for predicting the labels of previously unlabeled nodes of a network [7]. Inspired by epidemic spreading, labels are propagated on nodes based on the labels observed in their neighborhood, until convergence is reached. Different from other SNA algorithms that adopt a global view, i.e. decision procedures are based on an overall evaluation of network proprieties, LP is naturally constructed on local decisions. The approach has been proven to be scalable and robust. It has computational complexity equal to $O(t(n + m))$, where n is the number of nodes, m is the number of edges, and t is the number of iterations before convergence.

The most complete survey on LP algorithms is provided in [16], it effectively presents the properties that characterize variants of LP algorithms. A key design point is related to the decision strategy adopted for propagating labels. This operation is referred as the *update rule*, in the earliest variant of the algorithm, it assigns to a node the label with maximum frequency among the nodes in its neighborhood. When multiple labels have equal frequency a random selection is operated. This random choice has been identified as a major source of instability, since different executions of the algorithm may result in different label assignments. To overcome this issue multiple variants of the update rule have been proposed. Using the degree of nodes [19], their clustering coefficient [30], structural similarity [32], or more complex metrics [21,28,31] it is possible to significantly reduce random selection related inaccuracies. Indeed these criteria identify the most *influential nodes* and can also be exploited to decide the order in which nodes are updated or the initialization of the labels in the network [2].

Still, the fact a single label is elected to represent a node is limitative. Labels could be adopted for describing any feature of the nodes and, in general, the association between features and nodes is not univocal. The preferences, the attitudes, or the properties a node have may require multiple labels to be described.

Our approach is similar to the one proposed in [17], the updating rule assigns to each node the union of the labels in its neighborhood, weighted based on a belonging coefficient. A major difference is related to the agent-based organization of our algorithm that allows to implement the updating rule based on multiple factors, ranging from label frequency to node distance, or other domain-specific factors. Another important difference is connected to the output of our algorithm that returns a *vector* compatible with the input format used in many machine learning algorithms, to favor the pipeline of our algorithm with other data analytics tasks. This *vector-label* is of fixed length for all nodes. It includes all the labels observed in the network, varying their belonging coefficient based on the structural properties of the network.

3   Defining the Algorithm

3.1   The Proposed Approach

In [17] the belonging coefficient is a measure parametrized on the number of communities to be detected. In our concept, the belonging coefficient is instead a measure of the *diffusibility/accumulability* of the labels of the nodes, depending on the distances with other nodes the network embed and on their frequency. To encode the diffusibility of all the features used in the network in all nodes, the *vector-label* has to include all of them, while the *belonging coefficient* accounts for their incidence in a node. Also, vectors have a fixed length. A big advantage of this approach is that, at the end of the propagation procedure, all the nodes of the network can be positioned in a same feature space, with the belonging coefficients describing the incidence of features into nodes. Other data analytics procedures, notably machine learning, can this way be exploited to interpret the vectors and solve different analytics tasks.

In accordance with the local nature of LP strategies, we designed our algorithm as an *agent-based model* where all the nodes of the network are interpreted as agents with a memory about their interactions with other nodes and with a bounded rationality for updating their memory. Considering the evolving nature of vector-labels, we iterate propagation up to the point in that changes in the belonging coefficients are negligible. Here, the optimal number of iterations for terminating the algorithm is an important problem to solve but our experiments show this number is low, close to the diameter of the network, as discussed in Sect. 4.4. Our algorithm, removing the random selection of labels, removes one important source of instability of traditional LP algorithms. Instability can still be generated by the ordering of the updates. This problem can be mitigated by averaging over enough possible variations in order to get more representative results for the belonging coefficient of labels, as discussed in Sect. 5.

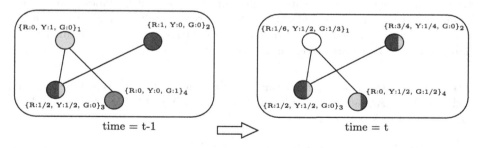

Fig. 1. The schematic view of the evolution of features composing the assigned vector-label to each node i at the transition of time $t-1 \longrightarrow t$. The left sub figure, represents the state of vector-label at time $t-1$, while the right one demonstrate the next timestamp of states for the same configuration. The vector-label contains the weight of three existing unique labels green (G), red (R) and yellow (Y) in the system. The propagation is demonstrated by the composition of features as weighted mixed colors. (Color figure online)

3.2   General Definitions

Agent-Based Propagation. We imagine labels can flow into the network and agents track their incidence. In AVPRA, the initial assigned vector-label $\mathbf{VL}_i(t)$ of agent $n_i \in \mathbf{N}$ is evolved in subsequent iterations getting $\mathbf{VL}_i(t+1)$, $\mathbf{VL}_i(t+2)$, ..., $\mathbf{VL}_i(t_s)$, where s is the stationary state. According to this view, modeling nodes as interacting agents play a decisive role in progressing the propagation. The agents are assumed semi-intelligent and act in response to the encountered situations. They are able to adopt different strategies in receiving or rejecting a label flowed from the neighborhood according to specific conditions [11,23]. This way the algorithm can control global effects, such as the termination condition, selecting the optimal s, or the computational costs of a specific execution, keeping $s \leq \alpha$.

Synchronous Updating. Concerning the dynamics of a network consisting of intelligent agents, in each iteration, large number of agents get impressed by cascading changes started from one-hop or multi-hop neighbors. To avoid conflicts in propagating the updates, in our algorithm the agents get updated synchronously. The vector-label of n_i, $\mathbf{VL}_i(t)$, is obtained from the vector-labels of it neighbours $\mathbf{VL}_{j \in \Gamma(i)}(t-1)$. Denoting the iteration preceding t as $t-1$ and the neighbours of a agent n_i as $\Gamma(i)$. At a given timestamp, all of the agents interact with their neighborhood and get updated simultaneously.

Initialization. In AVPRA, the semi-intelligent agents are labeled by a d-dimensional vectors, with $d = card(L)$, where L is the set of unique diffusible labels in the network. A vector-label can then be specified by $\mathbf{VL}[l_1, ..., l_d]$ with a position for each label $l \in L$ and a belonging coefficient $b : l \rightarrow [0,1]$. The labels may encode any features of the agents such as the list of favorite songs, the list of assigned projects, or other attributes. The L set is fixed at the initialization and cannot be changed except by re-initializing the algorithm. Some of the agents of the network must be assigned to valued vector-labels but not all the labels in a vector-label must be valued, and not all the agents have to start with valued vector-labels. The key requirement is the vector-labels assigned to nodes of network during initialisation reflect real properties of them acting as agents.

Updating Rule. The updating rule specifies how vector-labels are updated at each iteration. At each time step t, the $b(l)$ of the $\mathbf{VL}_i[l](t)$ can be updated by aggregating the k neighbors' $\mathbf{VL}_{j \in \Gamma(i)}[l](t-1)$.

$$\mathbf{VL}_i[l](t) = w_1 \mathbf{VL}_i[l](t) + w_2 \sum_{j \in \Gamma(i)} \mathbf{VL}_{j \in \Gamma(i)}[l](t-1) \qquad (1)$$

where the w_1 and w_2 are the weight of current assigned labels of n_i and the weight of $\Gamma(i)$ respectively. In a basic scenario, $w_1 = w_2 = \frac{1}{k+1}$, hence, for all the common elements in $\mathbf{VL}_i$ and $\mathbf{VL}_j$ vectors, n_i increase the value of the given element l unconditionally by the inverse of the carnality of $\Gamma(i)$. The core logic of our algorithm is presented in the pseudocode 1.

Algorithm 1. Agent-based Vector-label PRopagation Algorithm (AVPRA)

Require: Adjacency matrix $(A_{i,j})$, initial attributes in $d-dimensional$ labels VL to
each agent.
  for t in Timesteps **do**
    for i in $A_{i,j}$ **do**
      At each time step t, for all agents in $A_{i,j}$, run the model
      for k in VL_i **do**
        if $A_{i,j} == 1$ **then**
          $VL_i[d] = Updatefunc(VL_i[d], VL_j[d])$
        end if
      end for
    end for
  end for

Termination. The termination of the AVPRA algorithm is achieved when the
system reaches an iteration s where vector-labels are stationary. This implies, the
variations on the b values in L, referred as $|\delta L|$, must be less than p. We name
p the *negligibly threshold*, a free parameter to define according to the studied
problem.

As an illustrative example of our proposal, Fig. 1 proposes a schematic network containing four agents with three initial distinct features red (R), yellow (Y) and green (G). The vector-label for agent n_i at time $t - 1$ is as
$\{R, Y, G\}_i = \{l_1, l_2, l_3\}_i$, containing the weights of all unique features. The
updated vector-label at time t is created as a combination of its neighbors'
vector-labels at time $t - 1$, according to the update rule. For instance, using
Eq. 1, n_2 at time t is described by the vector $\{R, Y, G\}_2 = \{\frac{3}{4}, \frac{1}{4}, 0\}_2$. Given by
the union of its vector and the vector of its neighbour n_3 at time $t - 1$.

4 Experimental Analysis

4.1 Experimental Design

Our experimental analysis aims to demonstrate AVPRA can capture the structural properties of a network and characterise each agent by domain-specific
features. If this assumption is demonstrated we can consider our algorithm as
an effective instrument to encode domain-specific and structural properties of
network nodes into vectors that can feed subsequent analytical tasks. Using synthetically generated data, to better control the parameters of the experiments,
we used AVPRA to generate vector-labels and trained a classification algorithm
to identify the communities of the network based on vector-labels.

Community detection is a fundamental problem in studying networks that
reveals both topological and functional relationships between different components of a system. A measure often used to identify communities is modularity,
an indicator of how nodes tend to partition a network. The goal of community detection is then algorithmically translated into finding communities that

maximize modularity. Different approaches are discussed in the literature, the interested reader is referred to [10, 12, 13].

In this work, the community detection problem is addressed in a different way. We trained a classifier using the vector-labels generated by our algorithm as feature vectors, while the communities identified by state-of-the-art community detection algorithms are used as the ground truth. A classifier can then learn to map vector-labels and communities. The evaluation of the classification algorithm provides us with interesting insights. The accuracy obtained by the classifier is a measure of how well vector-labels capture the structural organization of the network. The accuracy trend with increased number of iterations allows us to study the conditions to get a stationary state s.

4.2   Generated Data

In our experiment, we consider the initial **VL**s as the list of equally-weighted 10-top liked songs assigned to each node of the synthetic network we generated. Using the *The million songs* dataset [3] we can guarantee the cluster of songs are following a real distribution. In the following iterations ($t > 0$), these **VL**s get updated following Eq. 1. Vectors are assigned to seed agents distributed in the synthetic network following a homophily principle [24] and power-law degree distribution [20]. In other words, the data generation procedure makes use of a mapping function connecting the **VL**$_i$ to each agent n_i according to its distance to other agents. Our goal is to model a network where "agents in the same community get the most similar vector-labels at the initialization". Table 1 presents some characteristics of two synthetic networks we generated for our experiments. The two networks are similar in terms of diameter and average path length but different in clustering coefficient and degree distribution. This way the experimental results report on the impact these different characteristics have on the capacity vector-labels have in encoding the modularity of the network.

Table 1. Key characteristics of the synthetic networks Net. 1 and Net. 2

Network	Degree		Betweenness		Diameter		Clustering Coefficient	
Net. 1	Min.	3	Min.	0	Radius	4	Min.	0
	Mean	5.98	Mean	–	Average path length	3.637865	Mean	0.338
	Max.	96	Max.	97811.73	Diameter	6	Max.	1
Net. 2	Min.	3	Min.	0	Radius	4	Min.	0
	Mean	5.978	Mean	–	Average path length	3.48832	Mean	0.15
	Max.	127	Max.	114598.33	Diameter	6	Max.	1

4.3   Experimental Procedure

In this section, the steps we followed to execute our experimental assessment are presented to clarify the procedure we adopted.

Step 1 Two synthetic networks are generated using $N = 1000$ nodes. Node's degrees are heterogeneous and follow the scale-free property of real-world networks[1]. We assume the agents are located on the nodes of this network and are interacting by edges.

Step 2 Vector-labels are generated selecting the 10-top liked songs for users, selecting from the global set of 16 songs in *The million songs* dataset [3]. Therefore we created the 16-dimensional vectors, $\mathbf{VL}[l_1, ..., l_{16}]$, with 10 non-zero elements assigned to each seed agent. Since we get 10 liked songs in the vector-label of each agent, at $t = 0$ the weight of all features is equal to 0.1 and the summation of these weights is 1.

Step 3 Using the Louvain algorithm [5] we detect the communities existing in the synthetic networks. The communities are the result of the distribution of the edges connecting nodes.

Step 4 A mapping function assign labels to agents considering the homophily principle [24]. The function first measure the similarity of vector-labels, then assign the vector-labels to agents favouring the assignment of similar vectors to agents in the same community.

Step 5 The AVPRA algorithm is executed. Iteration by iteration the belonging coefficients of vector-labels get updated following Eq. 1. For instance, in one of the trials, the $\mathbf{VL}_5(t = 0)$ is the initially assigned vector-label to agent n_5 which evolved at the 18th time step as $\mathbf{VL}_5(t = 18)$:

$$\mathbf{VL}_5(t_0) = [0.1, 0.1, 0, 0, 0.1, 0.1, 0.1, 0.1, 0, 0.1, 0, 0.1, 0, 0.1, 0.1, 0],$$
$$\mathbf{VL}_5(t_{18}) = [0.003308, 0.086863, 0.084958, 0.086338, 0.080669, 0.027699, 0.08074,$$
$$0.082326, 0.076636, 0.011632, 0.086938, 0.042238, 0.005815].$$

We proceed with these simulations until we get the stationary state s which satisfy the negligibility threshold, $p = |0.001|$.

Step 6 A Random Forest classifier [4] is trained using the vector-labels generated by AVPRA and the communities detected by the Louvain algorithm [5] as ground truth labels.

Step 7 The evaluation of the learning procedure is used to assess the capability of the vector-labels generated by AVPRA in encoding the structural properties of the network, together with the domain-specific features characterising agents.

4.4   Experimental Results

Following the procedure elaborated in Sect. 4.3, we run AVPRA and store the vector-labels at each iteration for the two network configurations introduced in Sect. 4.2. A Random Forest classifier [4] is then trained with in input the vector-labels obtained at each iteration and the community assigned to each node by the Louvain algorithm [5] as the ground truth labels. To evaluate our

---

[1] The networks are created using the `powerlaw_cluster_graph` function of `NetworkX` `package` 2, which is based on Holme and Kim algorithm [18].

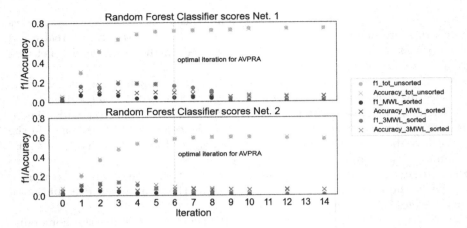

Fig. 2. F1 score and Accuracy of Random Forest classifier implemented on the evolving VLs, using the Louvain modularity classes as ground truth labels. Starting from initial Vector-Labels, the optimal scores are reached at the dashed line annotated by *optimal iteration= 6 for the AVPRA*. The results of two sets of experiments on different network configurations (Net1 and Net2) with depicted characteristic in Table 1 are presented.

idea we compare the accuracy obtained by AVRPA with the results of two other functional approaches. The first approach input the classifier using the Most-Weighted Label (MWL) only. This approach is similar to the *majority voting* strategy used in the original LP algorithm. The second approach selects the three labels related to the most-weighted belonging coefficients resulting from the **VL**s. We call this approach 3MWL. Figure 2 demonstrates the results obtained by AVPRA in terms of *accuracy* and *F1-score* outperform the other approaches. Getting *accuracy* = 0.74 and $f1$ = 0.75 with Net. 1 and *accuracy* = 0.60 and $f1$ = 0.62 with Net. 2. respectively. The optimal number of iterations is roughly 6 with both Net 1 and Net 2, a value very close to the diameter of those networks. Tables 2 Compares the AVPRA achieved performance score using the Logistic Regression and Random Forest as classifiers, with the other embedding algorithms implemented on the Net.1 and Net.2 respectively for the community detection task.

5   Discussion

SNA algorithms effectively measure the structure of systems that can be represented in terms of networks. However, real-life networks are not only described by their structural properties. The features agents have in common or that make them distinguishable from the other agents are also key elements to be considered in studying and explaining the behavior of this network.

Our algorithm was designed with the idea of taking a *holistic approach* in label propagation as all the features inherent to a network are used in labeling.

Table 2. The comparison of performance scores of the AVPRA implemented on the Net. 1 and Net. 2 with Deepwalk and Node2vec algorithms using Logistic Regression and Random Forest classifiers for the community detection task considering the Louvain algorithm as the ground truth labels.

Algorithm	Net. 1		Net. 2		Classifier
	fl-score	Accuracy	fl-score	Accuracy	
Deepwalk	0.645	0.645	0.49	0.49	LR
Deepwalk	0.615	0.615	0.44	0.44	RF
Node2vec (p = 0.25, q = 4)	0.53	0.53	0.425	0.425	LR
Node2vec (p = 0.25, q = 4)	0.575	0.575	0.465	0.465	RF
Node2vec (p = 1, q = 1)	0.525	0.525	0.435	0.435	LR
Node2vec (p = 1, q = 1)	0.625	0.625	0.455	0.455	RF
Node2vec (p = 0.1, q = 1)	0.55	0.555	0.425	0.425	LR
Node2vec (p = 0.1, q = 1)	0.545	0.545	0.465	0.465	RF
AVPRA	**0.75**	**0.74**	**0.62**	**0.6**	RF

All the agents are described by all the features while their incidence is modeled by the *belonging coefficient* influenced by neighborhood agents. The principle is oriented to measure the *diffusability of features* in the network. The vector-labels generated are intended to include both features inherent to the agent and features that have the potential to be inherent. The proposed approach inherits the properties of *agent-based computation* with low computational costs in a single iteration and increasing accuracy with increased number of iterations, with the possibility to modulate complexity and accuracy according to the application needs. Also, the holistic approach helps in reducing the instabilities problems of LP, such as ordering and random selection, by updating and averaging for each agent all the labels of the network, avoiding this way to remove or limit the propagation flow.

The experiment proposed in Sect. 4.4 demonstrated our approach can capture the *structural properties of the network*. At the same time, our method returns a *characterization of the agents* explaining their position and the distance from other agents. For example, if n_1 is equally distant from n_2 and n_3 our **VL**s can explain this could be due to positional similarities and clarifies the equal distance does not imply an equal set of shared features. In a simple example, considering $n_1 = [1, 0, 0]$, $n_2 = [0, 1, 0]$ and, $n_3 = [0, 0, 1]$ and acquiring the cosine similarity as distance measuring, although the n_1 is equally distant from the other two, n_2 and n_3 convey different features.

6 Conclusion

In the presented paper we introduced the Agent-based Vector-label PRopagation Algorithm (AVPRA) and explored its ability in capturing the specific characters of agents in a network. The design principles and procedures of the algorithm are presented and discussed. The experimental analysis we proposed demonstrates this approach can obtain accurate and explainable results in encoding the structural properties of a network. Future work will further study the properties of the algorithm.

Acknowledgements. This work was supported by the Università degli Studi di Milano under the Seal of Excellence (SoE) SEED 2020 Project POPULITE - POPUlist Language in ITalian political Elites (Project ID 1090).

References

1. Arafeh, M., Ceravolo, P., Mourad, A., Damiani, E., Bellini, E.: Ontology based recommender system using social network data. Future Gener. Comput. Syst. **115**, 769–779 (2021)
2. Azaouzi, M., Romdhane, L.B.: An evidential influence-based label propagation algorithm for distributed community detection in social networks. Procedia Comput. Sci. **112**, 407–416 (2017)
3. Bertin-Mahieux, T., Ellis, D.P., Whitman, B., Lamere, P.: The million song dataset. In: Proceedings of the 12th International Conference on Music Information Retrieval (ISMIR 2011) (2011)
4. Biau, G., Scornet, E.: A random forest guided tour. TEST **25**(2), 197–227 (2016). https://doi.org/10.1007/s11749-016-0481-7
5. Blondel, V.D., Guillaume, J.L., Lambiotte, R., Lefebvre, E.: Fast unfolding of communities in large networks **2008**(10), P10008 (2008). https://doi.org/10.1088/1742-5468/2008/10/p10008
6. Borgatti, S.P., Halgin, D.S.: On network theory. Organ. Sci. **22**(5), 1168–1181 (2011)
7. Brahim, L., Loubna, B., Ali, I.: A literature survey on label propagation for community detection. In: 2021 Fifth International Conference On Intelligent Computing in Data Sciences (ICDS), pp. 1–7. IEEE (2021)
8. Camacho, D., Panizo-LLedot, Á., Bello-Orgaz, G., Gonzalez-Pardo, A., Cambria, E.: The four dimensions of social network analysis: an overview of research methods, applications, and software tools. Inf. Fusion **63**, 88–120 (2020)
9. Ceravolo, P., Guerretti, S.: Testing social network metrics for measuring electoral success in the Italian municipal campaign of 2011. In: 2013 International Conference on Cloud and Green Computing, pp. 342–347. IEEE (2013)
10. Clauset, A., Newman, M.E., Moore, C.: Finding community structure in very large networks. Phys. Rev. E **70**(6), 066111 (2004)
11. Cremonini, M., Maghool, S.: The dynamical formation of ephemeral groups on networks and their effects on epidemics spreading. Sci. Rep. **12**(1), 1–10 (2022)
12. Danon, L., Diaz-Guilera, A., Duch, J., Arenas, A.: Comparing community structure identification. J. Stat. Mech. Theory Exp. **2005**(09), P09008 (2005)
13. Duch, J., Arenas, A.: Community detection in complex networks using extremal optimization. Physical review E **72**(2), 027104 (2005)
14. Emirbayer, M., Goodwin, J.: Network analysis, culture, and the problem of agency. Am. J. Sociol. **99**(6), 1411–1454 (1994)

15. van Engelen, J.E., Boekhout, H.D., Takes, F.W.: Explainable and efficient link prediction in real-world network data. In: Boström, H., Knobbe, A., Soares, C., Papapetrou, P. (eds.) IDA 2016. LNCS, vol. 9897, pp. 295–307. Springer, Cham (2016). https://doi.org/10.1007/978-3-319-46349-0_26
16. Garza, S.E., Schaeffer, S.E.: Community detection with the label propagation algorithm: a survey. Physica A Stat. Mech. Appl. **534**, 122058 (2019)
17. Gregory, S.: Finding overlapping communities in networks by label propagation. New J. Phys. **12**(10), 103018 (2010)
18. Holme, P., Kim, B.J.: Growing scale-free networks with tunable clustering. Phys. Rev. E **65**(2), 026107 (2002)
19. Jokar, E., Mosleh, M.: Community detection in social networks based on improved label propagation algorithm and balanced link density. Phys. Lett. A **383**(8), 718–727 (2019)
20. László, B.A.: Linked: How Everything is Connected to Everything Else and What IT MEANS FOR Business, Science, and Everyday Life. Basic Books (2014)
21. Li, Q., Zhou, T., Lü, L., Chen, D.: Identifying influential spreaders by weighted LeaderRank. Physica A Stat. Mech. Appl. **404**, 47–55 (2014)
22. Long, F., Ning, N., Song, C., Wu, B.: Strengthening social networks analysis by networks fusion. In: Proceedings of the 2019 IEEE/ACM International Conference on Advances in Social Networks Analysis and Mining, pp. 460–463 (2019)
23. Maghool, S., Maleki-Jirsaraei, N., Cremonini, M.: The coevolution of contagion and behavior with increasing and decreasing awareness. PloS One **14**(12), e0225447 (2019)
24. McPherson, M., Smith-Lovin, L., Cook, J.M.: Birds of a feather: homophily in social networks. Annu. Rev. Sociol. **27**(1), 415–444 (2001)
25. Qiu, J., Tang, J., Ma, H., Dong, Y., Wang, K., Tang, J.: DeepInf: social influence prediction with deep learning. In: Proceedings of the 24th ACM SIGKDD International Conference on Knowledge Discovery and Data Mining, pp. 2110–2119 (2018)
26. Raghavan, U.N., Albert, R., Kumara, S.: Near linear time algorithm to detect community structures in large-scale networks. Phys. Rev. E **76**(3), 036106 (2007)
27. Scott, J.: Social network analysis. Sociology **22**(1), 109–127 (1988)
28. Sun, H., Huang, J., Zhong, X., Liu, K., Zou, J., Song, Q.: Label propagation with-degree neighborhood impact for network community detection. Comput. Intell. Neurosci. **2014** (2014)
29. Wu, Z.H., Lin, Y.F., Gregory, S., Wan, H.Y., Tian, S.F.: Balanced multi-label propagation for overlapping community detection in social networks. J. Comput. Sci. Technol. **27**(3), 468–479 (2012)
30. Xie, J., Szymanski, B.K., Liu, X.: SLPA: uncovering overlapping communities in social networks via a speaker-listener interaction dynamic process. In: 2011 IEEE 11th International Conference on Data Mining Workshops, pp. 344–349. IEEE (2011)
31. Xing, Y., Meng, F., Zhou, Y., Zhu, M., Shi, M., Sun, G.: A node influence based label propagation algorithm for community detection in networks. The Scientific World Journal 2014 (2014)
32. Xu, X., Yuruk, N., Feng, Z., Schweiger, T.A.: SCAN: a structural clustering algorithm for networks. In: Proceedings of the 13th ACM SIGKDD International Conference on Knowledge Discovery and Data Mining, pp. 824–833 (2007)
33. Zoidi, O., Fotiadou, E., Nikolaidis, N., Pitas, I.: Graph-based label propagation in digital media: a review. ACM Comput. Surv. (CSUR) **47**(3), 1–35 (2015)

AI and New Trends in KM

An Asymmetric Parallel Residual Convolutional Neural Network for Pen-Holding Gesture Recognition

Jinyang Ding[✉], Ran Tao[✉], Xin Luo, and Xiangyang Feng

School of Computer Science and Technology, Donghua University, Shanghai, China
2202514@mail.dhu.edu.cn, {taoran,xluo,fengxy}@dhu.edu.cn

Abstract. Based on deep residual structure, attention mechanism, and CNN, we propose an asymmetric parallel residual convolutional neural network for pen-holding gesture recognition in this paper. To verify the effectiveness of the network, we build a pen-holding gestures dataset containing 923 images of 7 classes, and quadruple the training set by using data augmentation technology. The experimental results show that the accuracy of the propose network reaches 76.22% on basic pen-holding gestures dataset, and 82.16% on the augmentation pen-holding gestures dataset. The network and the dataset construction method proposed in this paper can be used to build a pen-holding gesture recognition system, and have reference value for similar recognition tasks without high-quality public datasets.

Keywords: Residual structure · Attention mechanism · Convolutional neural network · Parallel network · Pen-holding gesture recognition

1 Introduction

Nowadays, there is a widespread problem of non-standard pen-holding gesture among primary and secondary school students. The incorrect pen-holding gesture causes the rising proportion of students' myopia year after year, which hinders the development of calligraphy education and physical and mental health of students [1, 2]. At the same time, with the rapid development of deep learning, gesture recognition has been an active research field with a wide range of applications, including classroom teaching [3], human-computer interaction [4], sign language communication [5] and so on. In the aspect of gesture recognition, the research of pen-holding gesture recognition has innovation and application value.

Owing to the strong feature extraction and classification capabilities of convolutional neural networks, which train and learn the local and full features of input images, the problem of insufficient feature extraction caused by manual feature extraction can be solved. Deep learning has shown great advantages in computer vision tasks, such as image classification [6], target detection [7] and semantic segmentation [8].

According to the different methods of gesture data acquisition, gesture recognition can be divided into gesture recognition based on depth sensors such as data gloves

© Springer Nature Switzerland AG 2022
L. Uden et al. (Eds.): KMO 2022, CCIS 1593, pp. 321–333, 2022.
https://doi.org/10.1007/978-3-031-07920-7_25

[1, 9, 10] and gesture recognition based on computer vision [11]. The gesture recognition method based on computer vision has low cost and simple operation, which is also the research method used in this paper. In gesture recognition based on computer vision, the key step is to segment the hand area. In an uncontrolled environment, it is difficult to segment gestures accurately due to skin color, environmental color, lighting and shadow changes.

In this paper, we proposed an asymmetric parallel network based on a deep learning framework for pen-holding gesture recognition (as shown in Fig. 1). The network consists of two stages: gesture segmentation and gesture recognition. In stage 1, we input a RGB image first and segment gestures by skin color segmentation (also called "pretreatment"). In the second stage, we send RGB images and segment feature maps into the network for training and classification.

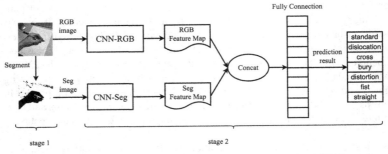

Fig. 1. Schematic diagram of the overall structure of APCNN.

The APCNN deals with the feature representations of RGB images and skin color segmentation respectively, and fuses the features before classification into the fully connected layer. In the CNN-RGB sub-network, spatial pyramid pooling block and hybrid coordinated attention module are used to solve the problem of insufficient feature extraction. Aiming at the problem of less data samples, we adopt the online and offline data augmentation methods proposed in HGR-Net [11] to improve the ability of the network.

Next, we will introduce the related research works in Sect. 2. In Sect. 3, we will describe the proposed network structure. The experimental results will be discussed in Sect. 4. Finally, the paper will be summarized in Sect. 5.

2   Related Work

2.1   Gesture Segmentation

Gesture segmentation has been used in many computer vision applications such as gesture tracking and gesture recognition. There are two main approaches for gesture segmentation: pixel-based and region-based. The pixel-based segmentation method classifies each pixel into skin class or non-skin class through skin detection method [12].

In computer vision, the color space of an image includes RGB, HSV and YCbCr, etc. The RGB color space is the most widely used, and the YCbCr color space provides the best distinction between skin and non-skin pixels. The threshold-based segmentation technique relies on the color space, and the threshold range of skin color in the YCbCr color space proposed by Basilio et al. [13]. Kolkur et al. [14] considered the color parameter range and combination range of RGB, HSV and YCbCr color spaces to distinguish skin pixels and non-skin pixels better.

2.2 Gesture Recognition

Gesture segmentation usually has several stages: data acquisition, preprocessing, segmentation, feature extraction and classification. Maharani et al. [15] discussed two methods for gesture recognition using K-means clustering and supporting vector machine (SVM) with directed acyclic graph decision, respectively, using depth images as input. Liu et al. [16] extracted features by drawing concentric circular scan lines (CCSL) and linear discriminant analysis (LDA) algorithm according to the center of the palm, and proposed a weighted k-nearest neighbor (W-KNN) algorithm to achieve real-time gesture classification and recognition. Rosalina et al. [17] used gesture segmentation, Gaussian blur and morphology to preprocess the image, and performed gesture recognition through artificial neural network.

In the traditional gesture recognition method, there are some problems such as insufficient feature extraction and cumbersome processing. Due to the feature extraction and classification capabilities of convolutional neural networks, deep learning has great advantages in the field of gesture recognition. Adithya et al. [18] constructed an efficient deep convolutional neural network architecture. Better results are obtained under complex and uncontrolled background conditions. Pinto [19] and others input the images after skin color segmentation and morphological processing into the CNN network for training. Islam [20] and others used data augmentation to improve the accuracy of CNN classification. A two-channel CNN architecture was proposed in [11, 21]. The original image and the preprocessed or segmented image are used as bimodal inputs to train the network with two segments of the same structure, and feature fusion is performed before the fully connected layer to improve the performance of the network by fusing multiple features.

2.3 Spatial Pyramid Pooling

There has been a technical problem in common CNN structures: the need to fix the size of the input image (e.g., 224 × 224). For example, in the CNN structure of image classification, the number of features of the fully connected layer is fixed, also called that the size of the feature map output by the convolution operation is fixed, so the image size of the input network needs to be fixed. When applied to a dataset containing images of arbitrary size, it is necessary to preprocess the image by clipping, scaling or stretching [8], which will also lead to the loss of some information of the original image and reduce the accuracy of image recognition. Spatial Pyramid Pooling (SPP) in SPPNet [22] solves this problem very well. For feature matrices of different sizes, SPP generates fixed-size output through multiple layers of pooling, where the size of the pooling kernel is proportional to the size of the image.

2.4 Attention Mechanism

Attention mechanism [23] has been developed in computer vision for many years. By using gating mechanisms such as soft-max or sigmoid, attention mechanism can selectively emphasize salient features and suppress unimportant features, so as to capture and utilize visual features better to reduce the complexity of the model. The SENet network proposed by Hu et al. [24] contains squeezing and excitation modules. This module is used to learn the channel attention of convolutional layers, providing an end-to-end training paradigm for the learning of attention mechanisms. Wang et al. [25] proposed an Efficient Channel Attention (ECA), which effectively implements a local cross-channel interaction strategy without dimensionality reduction through one-dimensional convolution. This appropriate cross-modal interaction can reduce the complexity of the model and maintain performance significantly. Woo et al. [26] proposed a Convolutional Block Attention Module (CBAM), which infers attention weights sequentially along two independent dimensions, channel and space. Channel attention mechanisms such as SENet usually ignore location information, and Hou et al. [27] proposed a Coordinate Attention (CA). The channel attention is decomposed into two one-dimensional feature encoding processes, and the location information is embedded into the channel attention by aggregating features from two directions, which has a simple structure and can be flexibly applied to the classical mobile network.

3   Asymmetric Parallel Residual Convolutional Neural Network

For pen-holding gesture recognition, we designed a two-stage network. The network structure diagram is shown in Fig. 2, where conv represents convolution operation of different channels, SPPB represents spatial pyramid pooling block, HCAM represents hybrid coordination attention block, concat means that the two sub-networks fuse the feature map through the splicing operation, and FC is the fully connected layer.

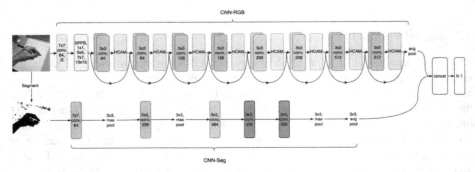

Fig. 2. Asymmetric parallel residual convolution network structure diagram

We preprocess the image in the stage of gesture segmentation. Firstly, we segment the skin color from the original RGB image. Then convert the RGB color space to YCrCb and HSV color space and segment the skin color on the specified threshold. After combining the two, median filtering and morphological closing operation are used to reduce the image noise respectively. In the stage of gesture recognition, there is a dual-channel asymmetric parallel network structure based on convolutional neural network and deep residual structure.

The input of the parallel network comprises two parts, an RGB original image and a segmented feature image. The CNN-RGB branch network with a deep residual structure is used to train the RGB image, and the CNN-Seg branch of a shallow convolutional neural network is used to learn the segmented feature. Then we fuse the features learned by the two branch networks before a fully connected layer, Finally, the classification is realized by the soft-max classifier. The following, in the first subsection, we introduce the spatial pyramid pooling block. The hybrid coordinated attention module proposed in this paper is described in the second subsection, and the network structure will be explained in detail in the third subsection.

3.1   Spatial Pyramid Pooling Block

The multi-scale pooling operation can extract spatial feature information of different sizes, which is robust to object deformation and spatial layout changes. According to the idea of SPP [22], we build a module with two layers of convolution operations and a 4-level Spatial Pyramid Pooling Block (SPPB), as shown in Fig. 3.

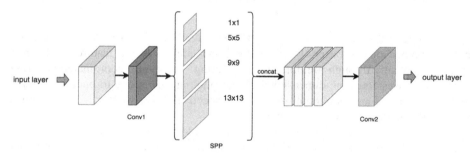

Fig. 3. Spatial pyramid pooling block structure.

Firstly, the input feature matrix is subjected to dimension reduction by convolution operation, and the size of the convolution kernel is 1×1. The number of channels is one half of the input feature matrix. After that, the multi-scale pooling operation is performed, and the sizes of the pooling cores are respectively $1 \times 1, 5 \times 5, 7 \times 7, 13 \times 13$. The step size is one half of the pooling kernel, and the feature maps are spliced after pooling. After spatial pyramid pooling, the dimension of the feature matrix will increase exponentially. In order to reduce the number of parameters and adapt to the subsequent network structure, we use a 1×1 convolution operation to adjust the number of channels of the feature matrix so that its output is the same as the number of channels input to the SPPB. We replace the single maximum pooling in the backbone network of ResNet [28] with SPPB, which can retain more feature context information.

3.2 Hybrid Coordinated Attention Module

Attention mechanisms [24–26] have been shown to enable networks to pay more attention to specific areas, thereby improving image recognition. For purpose of improving the recognition accuracy of the network model, we proposed a Hybrid Coordinate Attention Module (HCAM), as shown in Fig. 4.

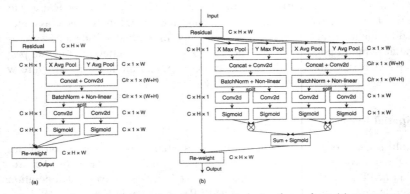

Fig. 4. Coordinated attention versus hybrid coordinated attention, where (a) represents coordinated attention and (B) represents hybrid coordinated attention.

To improve the structure of the coordinated attention [27], We add the maximum pooling branch on the basis of avg pooling, and emphasize the features of interest more significantly through multiplicative weighting. The hybrid coordinated attention mechanism uses four one-dimensional global pooling operations to encode features along the vertical and horizontal directions respectively, which effectively integrates spatial information into the attention map.

In the process of coordinating information embedding, we add a maximum pooling encoding process. Specifically, for a given input X, we use two spatial range pooling kernels $(H, 1)$ and $(1, W)$, each channel is encoded along the horizontal and vertical coordinates, respectively. The output of the c-th channel at height H can be expressed as

$$z_c^h(h) = \max_{0 \leq i < W} x_c(h, i) \tag{1}$$

Likewise, the output of the c-th channel at width w is

$$z_c^w(w) = \max_{0 \leq j < H} x_c(j, w) \tag{2}$$

The two transformations aggregate features along two spatial directions respectively, which can retain location information along different spatial directions and help the network locate the object of interest more accurately. For the encoded features, our processing is the same as that of CA. After aggregation and convolution transformation, we split and convolute the feature map to expand the dimensions. The attention weight output by average pooling is g_c^h and g_c^w, the weight of attention output by max-pooling is t_c^h and t_c^w. We multiply and add the attention weights separately to generate the hybrid weights w, which can be expressed as

$$w = \sigma\left(\left(g_c^h(i) \times g_c^w(j)\right) + \left(t_c^h(i) \times t_c^w(j)\right)\right) \tag{3}$$

Among σ is the sigmoid function. Finally, the output Y of our attention block can be written as

$$y_c(i,j) = x_c(i,j) \times w \tag{4}$$

3.3 The Proposed Asymmetric Parallel Network Structure

The network structure of the APCNN is shown in Table 1.

Table 1. APCNN network structure

CNN-RGB				CNN-Seg		
Name	Output	20-layers	36-layers	Input	320×320	Layers
input	320×320	–		input	320×320	–
conv1	160×160	7×7, 64, stride 2		conv1	79×79	11×11, 64, stride 4
conv2	160×160	7×7, 32, stride 1		pool1	39×39	max, 3×3, stride 4
spp	160×160	$k \times k$, stride $k/2$, $k = 1, 5, 9, 13$		conv2	39×39	5×5, 192, stride 1
conv3	160×160	7×7, 64, stride 1		pool2	19×19	max, 3×3, stride 4
conv4_x	160×160	$\begin{bmatrix} 3 \times 3, 64 \\ 3 \times 3, 64 \end{bmatrix} \times 2$	$\begin{bmatrix} 3 \times 3, 64 \\ 3 \times 3, 64 \end{bmatrix} \times 3$	conv3	19×19	3×3, 384, stride 1
conv5_x	80×80	$\begin{bmatrix} 3 \times 3, 128 \\ 3 \times 3, 128 \end{bmatrix} \times 2$	$\begin{bmatrix} 3 \times 3, 128 \\ 3 \times 3, 128 \end{bmatrix} \times 4$	conv4	19×19	3×3, 256, stride 1
conv6_x	40×40	$\begin{bmatrix} 3 \times 3, 256 \\ 3 \times 3, 256 \end{bmatrix} \times 2$	$\begin{bmatrix} 3 \times 3, 256 \\ 3 \times 3, 256 \end{bmatrix} \times 6$	conv5	19×19	3×3, 512, stride 1
conv7_x	20×20	$\begin{bmatrix} 3 \times 3, 512 \\ 3 \times 3, 512 \end{bmatrix} \times 2$	$\begin{bmatrix} 3 \times 3, 512 \\ 3 \times 3, 512 \end{bmatrix} \times 3$	pool2	9×9	max, 3×3, stride 2
pool	1×1	average pool		pool3	1×1	avg, 1×1
concat, 7-d fc, softmax						

The network is divided into two network branches, CNN-RGB and CNN-Seg. CNN-RGB is a network structure based on ResNet [28], and CNN-Seg is based on the network structure of AlexNet [6]. For the segmented image, a shallow network is used to fit the data to achieve the effect of reducing the number of parameters and improving the performance of the model under the condition of ensuring the recognition accuracy.

The sub-network (CNN-RGB) with RGB images as input is a deep CNN (CNN-RGB20) with 20 layers of convolutional layers and fully connected layers, which is constructed by using the residual structure. At the same time, we construct a CNN network (CNN-RGB36) with 36 layers by stacking the residual blocks.

4   Experiment and Analysis

4.1   Dataset Establishment and Experimental Settings

At present, because there is no publicly available dataset for pen-holding gestures, we have collected Pen-holding gesture images from human eye angles in sitting posture under different backgrounds, lighting and other conditions, and established a total of 923 basic pen-holding gesture datasets, the number of each class is 135, 139, 88, 97, 80, 162, 222. Some of the dataset are shown in Fig. 5.

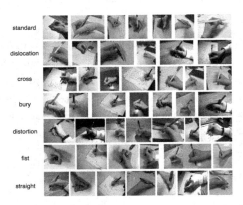

Fig. 5. Pen-holding gesture dataset, including seven pen gestures: standard, dislocation, cross, bury, distortion, fist and straight

In order to solve the problem that the number of datasets is small and biased, we use the method of online and offline data augmentation proposed in HGR-Net [11] to prevent overfitting and improve the generalization ability of the network. Our offline data augmentations include 20/90° rotations and vertical/horizontal flips, and with these operations, we have increased the training set by a factor of 4. Online data augmentation is to enhance the data in the network training process by randomly applying color perturbation, random rotation and random perspective in the network training process. In the experiments in this paper, we divided the training data and the validation data by the ratio of 8:2.

Our experiments were performed on Ubuntu 20.04 with NVIDIA Quadro RTX 4000 8 GB RAM GPU, CUDA 11.3, cuDNN 8.2.1. In the process of building the model, we use python 3.7 as the programming language and pytorch 1.10.0 as the open-source deep learning framework. When training the network, we use the cross-entropy loss as the loss function and Adam as the optimizer. The learning rate is initialized to 0.001, $\beta_1 = 0.9$, $\beta_2 = 0.999$. The number of iterations for network training is 64.

4.2 Ablation Experiment of Spatial Pyramid Pooling Block

In order to explore the effectiveness of the spatial pyramid pooling module for the pen-holding gesture recognition network, we conducted comparative experiments on the original residual networks ResNet18 and ResNet34, CNN-RGB (including 20-layer and 36-layer) embedded in the SPPB. The comparison results are shown in Table 2.

Table 2. Recognition rate comparison of spatial pyramid pooling block

Method	Input	Accuracy
ResNet18 [28]	RGB	68.11%
CNN-RGB20 (with sppb)	RGB	**69.73%**
ResNet34 [28]	RGB	66.49%
CNN-RGB36 (with sppb)	RGB	68.65%

It can be seen from Table 2 that the recognition accuracy of CNN-RGB20 embedded in the SPPB is 1.62% higher than ResNet18, indicating that the SPPB can retain more abundant context feature information, which is helpful to improve the recognition accuracy of the model. By comparing ResNet18 and ResNet34 with CNN-RGB20 and CNN-RGB36 embedding SPPB, deeper networks do not achieve higher recognition accuracy due to possible overfitting and gradient disappearance problems.

4.3 Ablation Experiment of Hybrid Coordinated Attention Module

In order to verify that the HCAM proposed in this paper can improve the network recognition performance, we embed the CA and the HCAM into ResNet18 and the subnetwork CNN-RGB20 in this paper respectively for comparative experiments, and the comparison results are shown in Table 3.

It can be seen from Table 3 that due to different image sizes and insufficient feature extraction, the recognition accuracy of the ResNet18 network embedded with CA does not increase but decreases, while the ResNet18 network embedded with HCAM is slightly higher than ResNet18. After the attention module is embedded in the CNN-RGB20 subnetwork proposed in this paper, the recognition accuracy of the model is 5.94% higher than that of the ResNet network. It is shown that the HCAM can enable the network to learn specific gesture areas and improve the performance of the model.

In order to show the effect of the attention module more intuitively, we use Grad-CAM++ [29] to visualize the feature maps generated by ResNet18, the ResNet18 network

Table 3. Comparison of recognition rate of hybrid coordinated attention module

Method	Input	Accuracy
ResNet18 [28]	RGB	68.11%
ResNet18 (with ca)	RGB	65.95%
ResNet18 (with hcam)	RGB	68.65%
CNN-RGB20 (with ca)	RGB	71.35%
CNN-RGB20 (with hcam)	RGB	**74.05%**

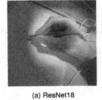 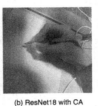 

(a) ResNet18   (b) ResNet18 with CA   (c) ResNet18 with HCAM

Fig. 6. Visualization of feature maps of models with different attention methods.

embedded with CA and HCAM, as shown in Fig. 6. Obviously, our hybrid coordinated attention module can help the model better locate the gesture areas of interest.

As shown in Fig. 6, Picture (a) only focuses on the middle area of the finger, Picture (b) focuses on most areas of the hand, but the focus areas are scattered. While the hybrid coordinated attention module proposed in this paper, Picture (c), it pays attention to the key areas, such as the way the hand holds the pen and the fingertips.

4.4   Comparative Experiment of Different Network

In order to verify the recognition effect of the asymmetric parallel network structure proposed in this paper, we use the classic networks AlexNet and ResNet18 for experiments, and we also build ResNet18 as a parallel network. Finally, we also apply the data augmentation technology to our model experiments, and the comparison results are shown in Table 4.

It can be seen from Table 4 that by comparing the results of ResNet18 and ResNet18 constructed as a parallel network, the application of deep network training to the segmented feature map will affect the overall recognition accuracy. Compared with CNN-RGB20, the recognition accuracy of the proposed 20-layer asymmetric parallel network APCNN20 is improved by 2.17%, and the recognition accuracy of the model reaches 82.16% after data augmentation. The above experiments show the effectiveness of our network, which is robust to pen-holding gesture recognition.

Table 4. Comparison of recognition rate of different network

Method	Input	Accuracy
AlexNet [6]	RGB	56.45%
ResNet18 [28]	RGB	68.11%
CNN-RGB20 (with hcam)	RGB	74.05%
ResNet18 [28]	RGB & Seg	54.05%
APCNN20 (ours)	RGB & Seg	**76.22%**
APCNN20* (ours)	RGB & Seg	82.16%

5 Conclusions

In this paper, we proposed an asymmetric parallel residual convolutional neural network and a pen-holding gestures dataset construction method for pen-holding gesture recognition. The experimental results show that the hybrid use of deep residual structure, attention mechanism, and convolutional neural networks can effectively perform pen-holding gesture recognition, and the data enhancement method can further improve the recognition accuracy. The asymmetric parallel network and the dataset construction method proposed in this paper can be used to build a pen-holding gesture recognition system, and are helpful to resolve similar gesture classification tasks. In the future, we will focus on reducing model complexity, increasing the speed of model inference, and achieving effective recognition performance in real scenarios.

Acknowledgments. This research was supported by the National Key R&D Program of China under Grant No. 2020YFB1707700.

References

1. Murata, K.G.A., Gotoh, K.: Effects of pen holding posture on handwriting motion. Adv. Soc. Organ. Factors **12**, 469–478 (2014)
2. Schwellnus, H., et al.: Effect of pencil grasp on the speed and legibility of handwriting in children. Am. J. Occup. Ther. **66**(6), 718–726 (2012)
3. Kim, Y., Soyata, T., Behnagh, R.F.: Towards emotionally aware AI smart classroom: current issues and directions for engineering and education. IEEE Access **6**, 5308–5331 (2018). https://doi.org/10.1109/ACCESS.2018.2791861
4. Xu, P.: A real-time hand gesture recognition and human-computer interaction system. arXiv preprint arXiv:1704.07296 (2017)
5. Cheok, M.J., Omar, Z., Jaward, M.H.: A review of hand gesture and sign language recognition techniques. Int. J. Mach. Learn. Cybern. **10**(1), 131–153 (2017). https://doi.org/10.1007/s13042-017-0705-5
6. Krizhevsky, A., Sutskever, I., Hinton, G.E.: ImageNet classification with deep convolutional neural networks. Commun. ACM **60**(6), 84–90 (2017)

7. Zhao, Z., Zheng, P., Xu, S., Wu, X.: Object detection with deep learning: a review. IEEE Trans. Neural Netw. Learn. Syst. **30**(11), 3212–3232 (2019). https://doi.org/10.1109/TNNLS.2018.2876865

8. Hao, S., Zhou, Y., Guo, Y.: A brief survey on semantic segmentation with deep learning. Neurocomputing **406**, 302–321 (2020)

9. Usachokcharoen, P., Washizawa, Y., Pasupa, K.: Sign language recognition with microsoft Kinect's depth and colour sensors. In: 2015 IEEE International Conference on Signal and Image Processing Applications (ICSIPA), pp. 186–190 (2015). https://doi.org/10.1109/ICSIPA.2015.7412187

10. Liang, H., Yuan, J., Thalmann, D.: Parsing the hand in depth images. IEEE Trans. Multimed. **16**(5), 1241–1253 (2014). https://doi.org/10.1109/TMM.2014.2306177

11. Dadashzadeh, A., et al.: HGR-Net: a fusion network for hand gesture segmentation and recognition. IET Comput. Vis. **13**(8), 700–707 (2019)

12. Naji, S., Jalab, H.A., Kareem, S.A.: A survey on skin detection in colored images. Artif. Intell. Rev. **52**(2), 1041–1087 (2019). https://doi.org/10.1007/s10462-018-9664-9

13. Basilio, J.A.M., et al.: Explicit image detection using YCbCr space color model as skin detection. In: Applications of Mathematics and Computer Engineering, pp. 123–128 (2011)

14. Kolkur, S., et al.: Human skin detection using RGB, HSV and YCbCr color models. arXiv preprint arXiv:1708.02694 (2017)

15. Maharani, D.A., Fakhrurroja, H., Riyanto, Machbub, C.: Hand gesture recognition using K-means clustering and support vector machine. In: 2018 IEEE Symposium on Computer Applications & Industrial Electronics (ISCAIE), pp. 1–6 (2018). https://doi.org/10.1109/ISCAIE.2018.8405435

16. Liu, Y., Wang, X., Yan, K.: Hand gesture recognition based on concentric circular scan lines and weighted K-nearest neighbor algorithm. Multimed. Tools Appl. **77**(1), 209–223 (2016). https://doi.org/10.1007/s11042-016-4265-6

17. Rosalina, Yusnita, L., Hadisukmana, N., Wahyu, R.B., Roestam, R., Wahyu, Y.: Implementation of real-time static hand gesture recognition using artificial neural network. In: 2017 4th International Conference on Computer Applications and Information Processing Technology (CAIPT), pp. 1–6 (2017). https://doi.org/10.1109/CAIPT.2017.8320692

18. Adithya, V., Rajesh, R.: A deep convolutional neural network approach for static hand gesture recognition. Procedia Comput. Sci. **171**, 2353–2361 (2020)

19. Pinto, R.F., et al.: Static hand gesture recognition based on convolutional neural networks. J. Electr. Comput. Eng. **2019** (2019). APA

20. Islam, M.Z., et al.: Static hand gesture recognition using convolutional neural network with data augmentation. In: 2019 Joint 8th International Conference on Informatics, Electronics & Vision (ICIEV) and 2019 3rd International Conference on Imaging, Vision & Pattern Recognition (icIVPR). IEEE (2019)

21. Gao, Q., Liu, J., Zhaojie, J., Li, Y., Tian, L.: Static hand gesture recognition with parallel CNNs for space human-robot interaction. In: Huang, YongAn, Hao, Wu., Liu, H., Yin, Z. (eds.) ICIRA 2017. LNCS (LNAI), vol. 10462, pp. 462–473. Springer, Cham (2017). https://doi.org/10.1007/978-3-319-65289-4_44

22. He, K., Zhang, X., Ren, S., Sun, J.: Spatial pyramid pooling in deep convolutional networks for visual recognition. IEEE Trans. Pattern Anal. Mach. Intell. **37**(9), 1904–1916 (2015). https://doi.org/10.1109/TPAMI.2015.2389824

23. Vaswani, A., et al.: Attention is all you need. In: Advances in Neural Information Processing Systems (2017)

24. Hu, J., Shen, L., Sun, G.: Squeeze-and-excitation networks. In: Proceedings of the IEEE Conference on Computer Vision and Pattern Recognition (2018)

25. Wang, Q., Wu, B., Zhu, P., Li, P., Zuo, W., Hu, Q.: ECA-Net: efficient channel attention for deep convolutional neural networks. In: 2020 IEEE/CVF Conference on Computer Vision and Pattern Recognition (CVPR), pp. 11531–11539 (2020). https://doi.org/10.1109/CVPR42 600.2020.01155
26. Woo, S., Park, J., Lee, J.-Y., Kweon, I.S.: CBAM: convolutional block attention module. In: Ferrari, V., Hebert, M., Sminchisescu, C., Weiss, Y. (eds.) ECCV 2018. LNCS, vol. 11211, pp. 3–19. Springer, Cham (2018). https://doi.org/10.1007/978-3-030-01234-2_1
27. Hou, Q., Zhou, D., Feng, J.: Coordinate attention for efficient mobile network design. In: Proceedings of the IEEE/CVF Conference on Computer Vision and Pattern Recognition (2021)
28. He, K., et al.: Deep residual learning for image recognition. In: Proceedings of the IEEE Conference on Computer Vision and Pattern Recognition (2016)
29. Chattopadhay, A., Sarkar, A., Howlader, P., Balasubramanian, V.N.: Grad-CAM++: generalized gradient-based visual explanations for deep convolutional networks. In: 2018 IEEE Winter Conference on Applications of Computer Vision (WACV), pp. 839–847 (2018). https://doi.org/10.1109/WACV.2018.00097

Plausible 6G Futures: Scenarios for the Future MNO Business Environment in the 6G Era

Yukie Ikezumi[1], Mikkel Stein Knudsen[1(✉)], and Jari Kaivo-oja[1,2]

[1] Finland Futures Research Centre, Turku School of Economics, University of Turku, Turku, Finland
mikkel.knudsen@utu.fi
[2] Kazimieras Simonavičius University, Vilnius, Lithuania

Abstract. The paper explores plausible scenarios for the business environment of mobile network operators (MNOs) after the eventual rollout of 6G. The 6G era is characterized by multi-dimensional uncertainty, as neither the technology nor the business landscape is yet in place. However, futures research methods and scenarios help alleviate uncertainty and provide futures knowledge about plausible developments. Using environmental scanning and expert interviews, the paper presents four scenarios for MNOs based on the assumed rate of change for the sector (transformative vs. conservative) and the market success of the incumbents (continued rise vs. fall). Underneath the scenarios is a shared base of assumptions for which the experts converged; these assumptions of changing market configurations provide a useful synopsis of current expert consensus for 6G business futures.

Keywords: 6G · Mobile network operators · Futures research · Strategic foresight · Scenarios · Knowledge management

1 Introduction

Mobile communication networks is the backbone of the modern digitalized society. The mobile wireless communication sector is therefore a sector of profound strategic and societal importance, as well as an economically important sector on its own. In recent years, the academic community has taken a growing interest in the sector's business models and their viability. Ahokangas and Matinmikko-Blue [1] note that in 2020 alone, over 60 research papers on business models in the mobile communications domain were published in the SCOPUS database.

Ahokangas and Matinmikko-Blue further note that with the current introduction of 5G-technology, the sector is now facing disruption in regulative, business, and technology domains. As 5G-technology enters the mainstream, technology research interest has already turned its eyes to the next generation of mobile wireless technology, 6G (see e.g. [2–6]). 6G, as established in 2019 in the IMT-2030 Standard, aims to provide both a revolutionary user experience and offer a new set of sensory information and experiences [4]. It will be a combined system composed of multiple different networks: local, mobile cellular, ocean, satellites, and other'as yet undefined' networks.

L. Uden et al. (Eds.): KMO 2022, CCIS 1593, pp. 334–346, 2022.
https://doi.org/10.1007/978-3-031-07920-7_26

At the time of this writing, the commercial deployment of 5G is still in its infancy, and potentially disrupting waves caused by it are yet to be absorbed. The 6G-technology, which supposedly will replace it, is still at the conceptual research stage and far from reaching the market. An assessment of the mobile wireless business world in the 6G era is therefore heavily characterized by what Heger and Rohrbeck [7] term "multi-dimensional uncertainty".

However, strategic foresight methods may help us reduce the domain of the unknowable [8] and provide ways of alleviating decision-making under uncertainty. Despite knowledge management actions, there are always certain risks and uncertainties. Scenario analysis remains the most popular method of strategic foresight [7, 9] with scenarios defined as challenging descriptions of alternative future states ("futures") relevant to a strategic decision and representative of plausible developments in the external world [9]. This paper explores plausible futures for the business environment of mobile network operators in the 6G era through the use of scenarios. Hitherto, there has been very limited work on 6G business models [10]. The paper, therefore, provides a valuable contribution to a novel field, and its findings can serve as important assistance for corporate and societal decision-makers, who are tasked with the tough job of making anticipative decisions before the full effect of 6G is known. Scenarios can help decision-makers to manage risks and uncertainties in organizations.

This paper is a condensed and reworked version of an M.Sc.-thesis in Futures Research at the University of Turku [11]. For further considerations regarding methodology and an expanded discussion of findings, we kindly refer readers hereto.

2 Background

Market research firms estimate the current global telecom market size at above $1.65 trillion annually [12] – topping the annual GDP of all but 10 countries in the world. As data and traffic increase all the time, the market is estimated to grow accordingly (well beyond the estimated global GDP growth).

The field of mobile infrastructure companies is a subfield of the larger mobile wireless industry, but it is a lucrative niche with an almost closed ecosystem. The technological nature of the field with radio spectrum handling as well as the high capital intensity has made it very difficult to enter for new market players. In 2018, just four global companies – Huawei (China), Ericsson (Sweden), Nokia (Finland), and ZTE (China) – combined for more than 90 pct. of the global mobile base station vendor market [13]. The market of mobile network operators (MNOs) is more diffused, but many countries or regions have local monopolies or oligopolies. Furthermore, the largest operators in the world are, indeed, very large – China Mobile has more than 950 million subscribers (Dec. 2021, [14]), more than 12% of the global population.

How the 6G era will unfold is guaranteed to affect billions of consumers. It could also have radical effects on global and regional economies. The case of Nokia serves as a good example of how rapid changes in the mobile communications ecosystem can dramatically impact even a national economy. Nokia's share of Finland's GDP went from 1 pct. to 4%. in just five years, and in the year 2000 the one company represented *half* of the national GDP growth [15, 16]. At its most influential peak in 2003, Nokia contributed almost 25% of all corporate taxes paid in Finland; in just another five years this figure dropped below 5% [15].

For both companies and society in Finland, preparedness and knowledge-based analysis for these kinds of changes are surely preferable. Also, for investment framework and investment strategy, such scenario analyses are valuable. Performed global Big Data analytics with 5G and 6G trend analytics reveals that after 2016 general global interest in 5G technology solutions has increased dramatically, but the global interest in 6G technology solutions is still at a low level. Noticeably, however, in India, there is already quite much national interest in 6G technology [17].

The Coming 6G Era

The history of the mobile communications systems is dominated by 10-year cycles: Each of the preceding five generations of systems (1G, 2G, 3G, 4G, and 5G) have taken about 10 years from concept to commercial application [4]. Keeping up with this tradition suggests that 6G systems will be standardized with deployments starting already before 2030 [5]. Like with 5G, the goal of 6G is to increase the respective capability by a factor of 10–100 compared to the previous mobile generation upgrade [18].

For each of the previous generations of systems, the ability to grow capacity have been dictated by the three fundamental dimensions of the spectrum, spectral efficiency and spatial reuse [5]. These dimensions are also expected to shape the technological characteristics of 6G. Potential revolutions in wireless communication with 6G pertain to e.g. terahertz communication, reconfigurable intelligent surfaces, and artificial intelligence [3]. AI-empowered 6G is in itself expected to provide an almost endless series of new features over the coming decades (for more projections on the emergent technologies, see [2–5, 19]).

MNO Business Models

There has been growing interest in the business models of mobile network operators (MNOs) and other elements composing the mobile wireless industry ecosystem [1]. At the end of the 2000s, the emergence of smartphones and device- and operating system (OS)-based platforms and related app store-based business models fundamentally altered the value configuration of the mobile communications world, leaving MNOs with the "dumb pipe"-threat of being marginalized in the value configuration [20]. The telecommunication industry today is still seeking ways to expand its connectivity provider role [10], and *"MNOs worldwide are reinventing their businesses to better position against digital transformation and take them beyond the service provider role"* [21]. This current industry sector's attempt to reinvent its business model provides an important lens for anticipating future threats and opportunities.

Futures Research and Strategic Foresight

The future is by definition unknowable. Features of technology, economics, market demand, and geopolitics for which we have no present certainty will shape the future of the 6G era. It is thus characterized by 'multi-dimensional uncertainty' [7].

However, with futures research methods and strategic foresight, it is possible to reduce the domain of the unknown [8], probe plausible developments, and provide partial clarity about possible futures. Futures research is the *'systematic exploration of what might be'* [18] and its methods can be useful for capturing various strong signals about plausible futures and transmit these into systematic and actionable information for decision-makers facing uncertainty in the present.

Remarkably, some other prominent initial attempts to handle the multi-sided uncertainty of 6G and capture plausible 6G futures also lean strongly on futures research methods, from scenario building to causal layered analysis (CLA) [10, 19, 22], despite originating in engineering and technology-focused contexts.

Here we use the traditional futures research method of scenario building and scenario analysis.

3 Methodology

Data Collection
This paper applies two main sources of data collection: (1) Environment scanning, and (2) Expert Interviews. These knowledge management phases of scenario building provide a preliminary base for detailed 6G scenarios. In this study, scenarios are limited to explorative scenarios [9, p. 13)].

Environment scanning facilitated the preliminary data collection. Environmental scanning is the central input of futures research, and all futurists perform it in one way or another in their work [23, 24]. The primary data collection comes from a set of eight semi-structured expert interviews with representatives of MNO (Orange, Telefonica), vendors (Nokia (2), Huawei (2), Samsung), and an independent editor of a major trade news media [11]. Several of the company representatives have also published academically on 6G. All interview participants have deep knowledge and insider views as incumbent players in the mobile wireless industry, and they were all able to convey key predictions for future market developments. All interviews were conducted during the first half of 2021.

Data Analysis and Scenario Building
The process of data analysis and scenario building here follows a 'light' version of the eight steps proposed by Schwartz [25]: (1) Identify Focal Issue or Decision, (2) Key forces in the local environment, (3) Driving forces, (4) Rank by importance and uncertainty, (5) Selecting scenario logics, (6) Fleshing out the scenarios, (7) Implications, and (8) Selection of leading indicators and signposts.

The focal issue is the future operating environment of mobile network operators (MNOs) after the arrival of 6G.

4 Results

Analysis of Drivers of Changes
64 important driving forces for the development of the mobile wireless industry were identified through environmental scanning and expert interviews (full list in [11]). The driving forces are categorized according to the PESTEC-classification (Political (6), Economic (11), Social (14), Technological (21), Environmental (4), and Cultural (8) forces; for information on the PESTEC-method, see e.g. [26]).

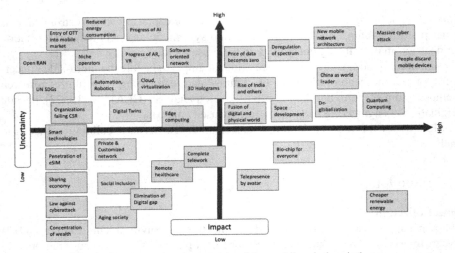

Fig. 1. Impact-uncertainty matrix of the mobile wireless industry.

To elicit the impactful driving forces among collected information, an impact-uncertainty matrix is used. The identified forces are sorted on the impact-uncertainty matrix by assessing each item based on these two points: (1) How impactful would this driving force be on the future development of the mobile wireless industry? (2) What is the probability of its occurrence?

The impact-uncertainty matrix of the mobile wireless industry is illustrated in Fig. 1. The authors provide the assessment of each driver, although heavily influenced by collected data. Driving forces in the top left quadrant, i.e. high impact, high probability drivers (HIHPs), include those emphasized by most experts as indispensable when considering the future of the mobile wireless world:

i.   New entrants into the market are inevitable. Mega IT companies and over-the-top (OTT) providers are most likely to enter the market successfully.
ii. Meaningful collaboration with the new competitors and different industries is imperative.
iii. New content and new applications based on AI, AR, VR, and holograms are awaited.
iv. Sustainability goals such as the UN SDGs need to be incorporated within the development of 6G.
v.   Network architecture will be different from today (e.g. Open RAN).

The top right quadrant of high impact, high-probability driving forces (HILPs) include a complete revision of the mobile network architecture, a massive cyberattack, and the potential development that people increasingly discard their mobile devices.

Scenario Cross Matrix

The scenario cross matrix is constructed based on the identified driving forces and centered around the aforementioned HIHPs, for which there were no divergent opinions picked up among the expert interviewees [9, p. 25].

The purpose of the scenario matrix (Fig. 2 below) is to illustrate plausible futures for MNOs in the forthcoming 6G era. The matrix is constructed with two axes: The x-axis represents continued growth for the current market oligopoly ('Rise') or a fall from today's strengths ('Fall'). The y-axis represents transformative market disruptions, that is either a fundamental change in business models ('Transformative') or a more or less continuation of the current situation ('Conservative').

The viewpoint to determine these elements is whether incumbent players in the market, who are responsible for the current rigid and oligopolistic structure, may keep the current mode of operations or not. Based on these elements, finally, tailored preliminary limited scenario narratives of each quadrant are generated. In our paper, we are not presenting scenario numbers of alternative business models. It would complete the current analysis as the Numbers-Narratives paradigm suggests to do [27].

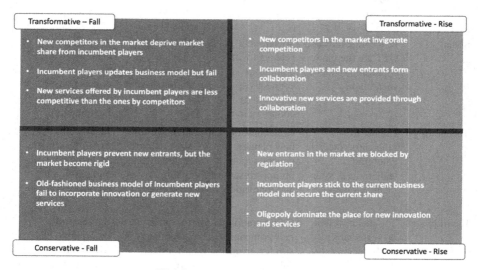

Fig. 2. Key elements in scenarios

Scenario Narratives

Narratives for the four scenarios help exemplify key developments. The target year of the four scenarios is set to be 2035, where we, based on the patterns observed with previous generations of mobile systems, expect the contours of the 6G landscape to have started to settle.

Furthermore, to elaborate on the difference between each scenario, the main characteristics of each one are picked up and organized per PESTEC fields. Table 1 below shows the summary of distinctive flavors of each scenario per PESTEC categories.

Table 1. PESTEC for each scenario storyline

Scenarios	"Good ideas. Actions don't follow along"	"Fluid, dynamic, and collaborative"	"Thus passes the glory of the world"	"Leave it to the professional"
X-Axis	*Transformative*	*Transformative*	*Conservative*	*Conservative*
Y-Axis	*Fall*	*Rise*	*Fall*	*Rise*
Political	Spectrum regulations loosened, new entrants are favored by governments	Spectrum regulations loosened, but fair competition is secured by policies	Spectrum regulations unchanged, the current players keep the majority of spectrum	Spectrum regulations unchanged, the current players keep the majority of spectrum
Economic	ICT companies and OTT and smaller players enter the market	Collaboration with a variety of industries progress	No new frontiers are to be developed. Market is locked	Status quo - new entrants are not arriving in the market
Social	ICT companies and OTT are the main solution provider to social issues	Social inclusion is achieved with ubiquitous connectivity achieved by collaborations	Unable to provide solutions to digital divide	Social inclusion is achieved with ubiquitous connectivity achieved solely by incumbents
Technology	Unable to efficiently integrate emerging technologies after many attempts	Collaboration with new players generate more optimized service and innovation	Incumbents stick to current technologies, ignore emerging technologies	Incumbents evolve existing networks by leveraging AI and past track record
Environment	Too much weight on sustainability goals decrease the profit of incumbents	Collaboration with new companies to aim for greener solutions	Profit for incumbents is prioritized over sustainability goals	Successfully incorporate UN SDGs into the development of 6G
Culture	End-users aggressively seek new experiences, AR/VR/Holograms become a norm	End-users aggressively seek new experiences, AR/VR/Holograms become a norm	Rebound from too digitalized world is seen	End-users aggressively seek new experiences, AR/VR/Holograms become a norm

A Shared Narrative of Assumptions – Base Background of Each Scenario

Although each scenario has different characteristics, several assumptions are common in all of these scenarios. By the year 2035, it is expected that 6G commercial deployments are steadily progressing and users are expecting versatile services through 6G. For example, end-users are enjoying hyper-fast, novel experiences empowered by emerging technologies such as AR, VR, and 3D Holograms. Social Network Services (SNS) are still commonly used but platforms are reinvented with these immersive technologies. These technologies are not only entertaining end-users but also various industries are reliant on the super-fast connectivity in the time of 6G. Enterprise sectors desire flexible and customized networks catering to different business demands. Autonomous driving cars are now occupying half of the fleet worldwide. Passenger vehicles are autonomously driven, empowered by AI, and mobility of 6G with the highest reliability.

Penetration of ultra-fast 6G service has eliminated the digital divide between rural and urban areas and equal public services such as health treatment and education are offered remotely.

6G networks, therefore, need to be more flexible and dynamic compared to the previous generations to cater to the diverse demand of users. As defined in the 6G visions and targets, 6G is built on completely virtualized environments except for radio antennas. Furthermore, computing functions are offset to peripheral, edge devices rather than at the cluster of central servers located in the centralized network centers.

Narrative for Scenario 1 – "Good Ideas, Actions Don't Follow Along"

To invigorate the market, governments in many countries loosened the regulation of spectrum assignment to invite new competitors into the mobile wireless market. New spectrum supported in 6G are equally allocated to existing MNOs and new entrants, making the frequency band per one operator smaller. This movement devasted the businesses of existing major companies in the mobile wireless industry.

Mega ICT companies such as Google or Amazon, along with Over-The-Top (OTT) media companies acquired frequency bands and embarked upon the mobile wireless business. With massive computing power at the existing cloud and virtualization platform, they are succeeding in managing 6G mobile networks at virtualized platforms efficiently. Furthermore, with AI-empowered algorithms combined with their big data, they are now providing flexible, customized, and competitive data subscription plans catering to each mobile user. Smaller companies are also actively entering the market, aiming to fulfill the niche demands of small enterprises.

Amid such competition, the conventional major companies of MNOs and network infrastructure vendors are finding it hard to cater their services to the various demands of users. Conventional MNOs still provide nationwide networks for 4G and 5G to keep the backward compatibility. However, such legacy assets have become a burden as the maintenance cost and effort are enormous. Network infrastructure vendors are also struggling as the revenue of selling dedicated hardware has decreased significantly due to virtualization.

To address this situation, MNOs try to offer content over AR, VR, and holograms dedicated only to their subscribers, to no avail. Giant ICT companies have already acquired most of the promising start-ups specializing in media contents creation to offer innovative content based on AI and big data. MNOs are unable to lower subscription fees as the maintenance cost of nationwide networks including 4G and 5G is enormous.

In this scenario, previous giants in the mobile wireless industry are unable to find competitive edges over powerful new entrants.

Narrative of Scenario 2 – "Fluid, Dynamic, and Collaborative"

Prior to the 6G commercial launch, governments loosened regulations on spectrum use to allure new competitors. The major MNOs and network infrastructure vendors had long anticipated this lower barrier of entry and proactively sought collaboration with new entrants. Network infrastructure vendors proactively approached top ICT companies who provide general cloud services. Up to 5G, network infrastructure is built on special hardware or partly virtualized platform with support from OEM vendors. To mitigate R&D costs, collaboration with OTT companies to develop a new set of virtualization infrastructure and AI algorithms suitable for mobile networks is active.

6G networks are run on smaller-scaled edge servers. This new network architecture has brought new business cases to enterprise customers. Huge network centers gradually disappear and small "network centers" are configured easily on the premises of enterprise users. With this model, MNOs have reduced the running cost of network centers significantly.

Sustainable and less-energy consuming devices are another key factor of 6G. Vendors are inventing new radio antennas with great energy efficiency or the capability of self-generating energy from natural resources such as wind and solar power. Also, radio antennas made of new materials such as algae and fungi are gaining attention. Space development is also becoming an important source of new business development. For example, in the year 2023, Nokia installed the first-ever 4G cellular network on the moon in the collaboration with NASA. The moon cellular network was upgraded to 5G after several years, and now it is being upgraded to a 6G network. Cellular systems on the moon and beyond are a good investment for the future.

In this scenario, collaboration with new competitors and different industries than the mobile wireless industry are inevitable and the key to success. The effort to find meaningful collaborations would be critical for incumbent MNOs and vendors to survive.

Narrative of Scenario 3 – "Thus Passes the Glory of the World"

In 2035, the commercial deployment of 6G networks has been progressing. MNOs are investing a large amount of money into the advertisement of their services in an attempt to steal subscribers from rival MNOs, however, the new subscriptions are just growing at a sluggish pace.

With vigorous or even aggressive lobby to politicians, incumbent major MNOs and network infrastructure vendors have succeeded in blocking new entrants into the market. At the same time, they are struggling to renew their business models and increase their revenue. The mobile wireless market has already been mature since the time of 4G or 5G. The share of the pie is limited, and MNOs are unable to find a way to drastically increase their subscription base. Existing MNOs are just stealing subscribers from each other and failing to find an innovative source of new revenue.

Network infrastructure vendors are also facing a hard time. As the new network architecture of 6G is more and more reliant on software, their previous business models to sell both software and dedicated hardware are no longer profitable in the 6G era.

Both MNOs and network infrastructure vendors have lived in a closed ecosystem. The tight financials of existing players have failed to nourish a place for innovations and services. They are busy with maintaining the current market share and do not have the affluent energy to invest in emerging technologies. Furthermore, many of such companies are not successful in achieving UN SDGs. Energy consumption of mobile wireless products has not been much improved from the previous generations.

With such a background, the mobile fee in the 6G era has been critically expensive, as MNOs are trying to translate their investment cost onto mobile subscription fees. Frustrations of users are accumulating and the backlash against such an ever-continuing oligopoly by a subset of incumbent players has moved governments in many countries to consider new regulations to cap the growing subscription fees. Additionally, researches for a new generation of mobile wireless technologies are now strictly controlled by governmental bodies to avoid future dominance of the market by incumbents.

In this scenario, the players in the mobile wireless market manage to maintain their regimes and continue to dominate the market. However, the effort to keep the oligopoly has invited the deadlock of the market without a buffer for future growth.

Narrative of Scenario 4 – "Leave it to the Professional"
In the year 2035, people are fully enjoying experiences through novel technologies of AR, VR, 3D Holograms over their mobile devices. Nowadays mobile phones are less seen among users, but smaller and more sophisticated wearable devices in the form of glasses, bracelets, or small chips attached to the skin are becoming common. Not only entertainment, but most of the infrastructure required for basic living is also now built on the ultra-fast, reliable networks of 6G. Until this day, major corporations of MNOs and network infrastructure companies had vigorously lobbied to politicians to block new entrants to the market to defend their existing market share. The effort paid off, and spectrum regulations remain unchanged for the past 15 years. It means that it is extremely challenging for new competitors to enter the market.

In the bubble unthreatened by new competitors, key players in the industry have set out new projects to become a key revenue source in the 6G era - they have determined UN SDGs to be the key enabler of success. As most of the densely populated terrestrial areas are already covered by the existing mobile wireless networks, the industry has decided to feed its way into the excavation of new coverage areas. This goes beyond terrestrial areas and expands into the sea, mountains, and spaces. Vendors have acquired start-ups and small-scaled companies specializing in new raw materials to develop radio heads with new materials sustainable even in extreme-conditioned areas.

Both MNOs and network infrastructure vendors have made a great investment in the application of artificial intelligence (AI). AI is now succeeding in managing fluid and dynamic networks efficiently. With the intelligence accumulated by machine learning of AI, network operations are optimized to consume minimum power. User subscription fees are also dynamic, based on the demands of users. Especially enterprise users have their requirements in performance and a customized network catering to each demand is desired. AI-based, flexible virtual solutions can answer the demand for more personalized networks.

In this scenario, the structure of the mobile wireless industry remains unchanged from the time of 5G. The key enabler is the use of AI for optimization, and how companies find a profitable source of revenue in the mature market. The possible areas to be explored are the extreme surface of the earth, space, and how the industry responds to the Sustainable Development Goals (SDGs).

5   Discussion and Conclusions

Over the next 10 years, the technological and business ecosystemic landscape of 6G technology will be shaped. For companies involved in the mobile communications sector, a lot is riding on getting the development right – the market value of the sector is roughly the GDP numbers of South Korea or Russia, and the sector has a history of rapidly changing value configurations. At the same time, any attempt at looking ahead must consider the multi-dimensional uncertainty, as markets are shifting and the technology involved is still at a conceptual stage. Scenario analysis (with logical explorations) is one important method to grasp plausible futures under this uncertainty and risks.

Through environmental scanning and expert interviews, we have elicited important information about plausible futures for mobile network operators (MNOs) in the 6G era. Experts' opinions converged offering us a shared base of assumptions:

New entrants (likely tech giants or OTT-providers) inevitably enters the market. Collaboration and coopetition with new market players is imperative. Emerging technologies such as AI, AR, VR, and 3D holograms shifts the market for content. 6G development needs to incorporate the green transition and sustainability concerns (e.g. UN SDGs). Network architecture is markedly different from today, e.g. with Open RAN.

This shared base of professional expert assumptions gives important clues about the most plausible developments for the 6G era. For the MNOs, four scenarios are created through two axes of x) transformative vs. conservative rate of change in the sector, and y) continued rise vs. fall of market incumbents. We followed the logic of the traditional scenario cross approach.

Fleshing out scenarios – here titled *"Good ideas. Actions don't follow along"*, *"Fluid, dynamic, and collaborative"*, *"Thus passes the glory of the world"*, and *"Leave it to the professional"* – also assists in identifying important signposts, signaling where the development is headed in the future.

In our case, a very important signpost is the political handling of spectrum regulation, which is very important for setting the barriers of entry for new market participants. Previous research suggests that spectrum regulation of emerging mobile technologies tends to lean too heavily on past experiences (regulation of previous generations of mobile systems), even when this leads to suboptimal policies [28, 29]. As foresight can help us sketch plausible transformations, we might suggest increased use of foresight for mobile communication regulation too. This strategic suggestion is highly relevant because the regulatory environment in each country provides enablers and barriers for future technological development.

In general, our paper provides a very early look at driving forces shaping the 6G environment. As industry and society start setting their eyes on this potential and feasible future, this information can serve as important assistance. A very important aspect of the relevance of such narrative stories has been underlined by various scholars among them Nobel Prize winner Robert J. Stiller [30]. In this study, our narrative scenario stories were based on the well-established knowledge management method of environment scanning.

Acknowledgements. This study has received financial support from the Strategic Research Council at the Academy of Finland [grant nos. 335980, 335989]. Professor, Dr. Jari Kaivo-oja gratefully acknowledge financial support from the Research Council of Lithuania (LMTLT) and the European Regional Development Fund implementing the project "Platforms of Big Data Foresight (PLATBIDAFO)" (project No. 01.2.2-LMT-K-718-02-0019).

References

1. Ahokangas, P., Matinmikko-Blue, M.: Introduction to special issue "mobile communications and novel business models". Sustainability **13**(2), 674 (2021)
2. Bariah, L., et al.: A prospective look: key enabling technologies, applications and open research topics in 6G networks. IEEE Access **8**, 174792–174820 (2020)
3. Dang, S., Amin, O., Shihada, B., Alouini, M.-S.: What should 6G be? Nat. Electron. **3**, 20–29 (2020)
4. Lu, Y., Zheng, X.: 6G: a survey on technologies, scenarios, challenges and the related issues. J. Ind. Inf. Integr. **19**, 100158 (2020)
5. Visnawathan, H., Mogensen, P.: Communications in the 6G era. IEEE Access **8**, 57063–57074 (2020)
6. Bhat, J.R., Alqahtani, S.A.: 6G ecosystem: current status and future perspective. IEEE Access **9**, 43134–43167 (2021)
7. Heger, T., Rohrbeck, R.: Strategic foresight for collaborative exploration of new business fields. Technol. Forecast. Soc. Change **79**(5), 819–831 (2012)
8. Gordon, T.J., Glenn, J.C., Jakil, A.: Frontiers of futures research: what's next? Technol. Forecast. Soc. Change **72**(9), 1064–1069 (2005)
9. Nekkers, J.: Developing scenarios. In: van der Duin, P. (ed.) Foresight in Organizations. Methods and Tools, pp. 11–39. Routledge, New York (2016)
10. Schwarz, J.O., Ram, C., Rohrbeck, R.: Combining scenario planning and business wargaming to better anticipate future competitive dynamics. Futures **105**, 133–142 (2019)
11. Yrjölä, S., Ahokangas, P., Matinmikko-Blue, M.: Sustainability as a challenge and a driver for novel ecosystemic 6G business scenarios. Sustainability **12**(21), 8951 (2020)
12. Ikezumi, Y.: Mobile wireless business world in the 6G era. M.Sc. thesis, Finland Futures Research Centre, University of Turku (2021). https://urn.fi/URN:NBN:fi-fe2021092847338
13. Grand View Research. Telecom Market Size, Share & Trends Analysis Report By Service Type (Mobile Data Services, Machine-to-Machine Services), By Transmission (Wireline, Wireless), By End-use, By Region, And Segment Forecasts, 2021–2028 (2021). https://www.grandviewresearch.com/industry-analysis/global-telecom-services-market
14. Statista. Mobile base station vendor market share worldwide from 2019 to 2021 (2021). https://www.statista.com/statistics/1134472/global-mobile-base-station-vendor-market-share/
15. China Mobile. Monthly Customer Data (2022). https://www.chinamobileltd.com/en/ir/operation_m.php
16. Google Trends. 5G, 6G - Explore - Google Trends, 29 January 2022. https://trends.google.com/trends/explore?date=all&q=5G,6G

17. Ali-Yrkkö, J.: The role of Nokia in the finnish economy. In: Ali-Yrkkö, J. (ed.) Nokia and Finland in a Sea of Change. ETLA. The Research Institute of the Finnish Economy (2010)
18. Porter, M.E., Sölvell, Ö.: Finland and Nokia: Creating the World's Most Competitive Economy. Harvard Business School Case 702-427 (2002)
19. Chowdhury, M.Z., Shahjalal, M.R., Ahmed, S., Jang, Y.M.: 6G wireless communication systems: applications, requirements, technologies, challenges and research directions. IEEE Open J. Commun. Soc. 1, 957–975 (2020)
20. Stanoevska-Slabeva, K., Wozniak, T.: Opportunities and threats by mobile platforms: the (new) role of mobile network operators. In: 2010 14th International Conference on Intelligence in Next Generation Networks. IEEE Xplore (2010)
21. Yrjöla, S., Ahokangas, P., Matinmikko-Blue, M.: Platform-based business models in future mobile operator business. J. Bus. Models 9(4), 67–93 (2021)
22. 6G Flagship. White Paper on Business of 6G (2020). https://www.oulu.fi/6gflagship/6g-white-paper-business-of-6g
23. Gordon, T.J.: The methods of future research. Ann. Am. Acad. Polit. Soc. Sci. 522, 25–35 (1992)
24. Gordon, T.J., Glenn, J.C.: Environmental scanning. In: The Millenium Project, Futures Research Methodology – V30 (2009)
25. Schwartz, P.: The art of the long view: planning for the future in an uncertain world (1996)
26. Heinonen, S., Ruotsalainen, J.: Futures clinique—method for promoting futures learning and provoking radical futures. Eur. J. Futures Res. 1(1), 1–11 (2013). https://doi.org/10.1007/s40309-013-0007-4
27. Damodaran, A.: Narrative and Numbers. The Value of Stories in Business. Columbia Business School Publishing (2017)
28. Bauer, J.M., Bohlin, E.: Regulation and innovation in 5G markets. Telecommun. Policy 46(4), 102260 (2021)
29. Briglauer, W., Camarda, E.M., Vogelsang, I.: Path dependencies versus efficiencies in regulation: evidence from "old" and "new" broadband markets in the EU. Telecommun. Policy 43(8), 101825 (2019)
30. Shiller, R.: Narrative Economics: How Stories Go Viral and Drive Major Economic Events. Princeton University Press, Princeton (2019)

A Lightweight Facial Expression Recognition Network Based on Dense Connections

XiaoKang Xu$^{(\boxtimes)}$, Ran Tao$^{(\boxtimes)}$, Xiangyang Feng, and Ming Zhu

School of Computer Science and Technology, Donghua University, Shanghai, China
2223144261@qq.com, {taoran,fengxy,zhuming}@dhu.edu.cn

Abstract. Facial expression is one of the most representative signals for human emotional states and intentions. Facial expression recognition has attracted increasing attention in academia and industry, and has been wide used in robotics, intelligent security, medical monitoring, educational evaluation, driving fatigue monitoring, etc. This paper proposes a lightweight network Dense-MobileNet. In which, a DenseDW-block for feature reuse is designed and embedded into MobileNetV1 for better accuracy and less computation. The width selection and comparison experiments are used on the widely used Real-World Affective Face Database (RAF-DB) to choose the best network parameters and to validate the effectiveness of the proposed Dense-MobileNet. The results show that: 1) Among the three proposed sub networks Dense-MobileNet-1, Dense-MobileNet-2, Dense-MobileNet-3, the Dense-MobileNet-2 has the best accuracy of 82.4%. 2) Comparing with MobileNetV1, the recognition accuracy of our model is improved by 2.5%, the number of parameters is reduced by 45.7%, and the amount of computation is reduced by 66.73%. As a lightweight network with better accuracy and less computation, the proposed Dense-MobileNet is suitable for facial expression recognition on mobile terminals and edge devices. The proposed DenseDW-block serving as a feature reuse module can be used to design or optimize similar CNN to improve accuracy and accelerate computation.

Keywords: MobileNetV1 · DenseNet · Facial expression recognition · Lightweight

1 Introduction

Facial expressions are one of the most representative signals for humans to express their emotional states and intentions [1]. As a research hotspot in the field of computer vision and human-computer interaction, facial expression recognition has a wide range of application areas, including intelligent security [2], educational assessment [3], driving fatigue monitoring [4], and expression recognition can be applied to knowledge management in various scenarios, for example, medical expert system [5] uses expression recognition for expression data collection and analysis of patients. Enterprise expert system [6] uses expression recognition to analyze the emotion of enterprise employees, accumulate a set of knowledge systems, and make behavioral predictions. Based on a large number of cross-cultural studies, the famous psychologist Ekman [7] defined six

© Springer Nature Switzerland AG 2022
L. Uden et al. (Eds.): KMO 2022, CCIS 1593, pp. 347–359, 2022.
https://doi.org/10.1007/978-3-031-07920-7_27

basic facial expressions common to all human races and cultures: happiness, disgust, anger, surprise, sadness and fear, and the research on facial expression recognition based on these six facial expressions has also started in the field of computer vision.

Facial Expression recognition methods are mainly divided into two directions. One is traditional methods, which mainly use Shallow Learning or hand-designed features, such as Local Binary Pattern (LBP) [8], Local Phase Quantization (LPQ) [9], Principal Component Analysis (PCA) [10] and Gabor filter [11], etc. However, traditional methods are subject to human interference factors, which can lead to inadequate feature extraction and ultimately inaccurate classification. The other is Deep Learning. Convolutional neural network (CNN) extracts the deeper features of facial expressions by constructing multiple convolutional layers, which avoids the error of human extraction and having strong robustness. Since AlexNet [12] won the image classification competition in 2012, more excellent network models have been proposed. These network models achieved very good results in the face expression recognition task by effectively increasing the depth, width, residual (VGG [13], GoogLeNet [14], ResNet [15], etc.), but have the disadvantages of large model, deep network, and slow computation. In practical application scenarios, facial expression recognition often has high real time requirements, especially on mobile terminals and edge devices. However, the current lightweight network models often reduce the amount of model parameters and computation by sacrificing accuracy (MobileNetV1 [16], MobiExpressNet [17], etc.). It is meaningful to propose a model with higher recognition accuracy and less model parameters. In this paper, we propose a lightweight network model Dense-MobileNet based on dense connections. The main contributions of this paper are listed as follows:

1. To design a lightweight block, DenseDW-block, for feature reuse. Experiments show that DenseDW-block has less parameters and computation while maintaining better feature extraction capabilities.
2. To optimize MobileNetV1 by embedding DenseDW-block and propose a light-weight network model Dense-MobileNet, we design three sub networks (Dense-MobileNet-1, Dense-MobileNet-2, Dense-MobileNet-3) and conduct width comparison experiments on these sub networks. The results reveal that all of them reduce the number of parameters and calculations with Dense-MobileNet-2 which has the best overall performance.
3. We compare Dense-MobileNet-2 with other methods such as MobileNetV1. Results show that the recognition accuracy of Dense-MobileNet-2 is improved by 2.5%, the number of parameters is reduced by 45.7%, and the amount of calculation is reduced by 66.73% compared with MobileNetV1.

The rest of this paper is organized as follows. The second section describes related work of Facial Expression Recognition; the third section introduces the structure of Dense-MobileNet and the method in this paper; the fourth section analyzes the experimental results; the experiments are summarized in Sect. 5.

2   Related Work

2.1   Image-Based Facial Expression Recognition

Image-based facial expression recognition task has been one of the long-term research topics in the field of computer vision. In recent years, many facial expression datasets have also been proposed, such as CK+ [18], FER2013 [19], RAF-DB [20], etc. And Deep Learning is widely used to feature extraction in expression recognition tasks. In 2015, He Kaiming's team proposed ResNet [15], which uses the residual structure to effectively increase the depth of the network and avoid the problem of deep network degradation. Huang et al. [21] proposed a gridded attention mechanism and built an end-to-end facial expression recognition model with ResNet as the backbone network, and achieved good results on the CK+ dataset, but the model is large and not suitable for real-time recognition scenarios. Hu et al. [22] proposed a lightweight multi-scale attention network, which extracted facial expression feature information through multi-scale convolution, and fused these features to expand the receptive field, thereby improving the recognition ability of the network. Shane et al. [17] proposed a new lightweight deep learning model MobiExpressNet, which made the model lightweight through the method of depthwise separable convolution and fast downsampling. Although the model is very lightweight, the recognition accuracy needs improvement. Cugu et al. [23] used knowledge distillation to lighten the CNN network model, effectively reducing the size of the model, and conducted experiments on the CK+ and Oulu-CASIA datasets. The results show that the model is fast but the accuracy is lower than the state of art. In summary, the accuracy of facial expression recognition is getting higher and higher, but the deep convolutional neural network model is too large for mobile terminals and edge devices. And the current lightweight convolutional neural network has low recognition accuracy. Therefore, in the case of ensuring that the model has good recognition ability, it is a very meaningful research topic to lighten the model with guaranteed recognition accuracy.

2.2   MobileNetV1

MobileNetV1 [17] is a lightweight convolutional neural network proposed by the Google team. Its advantage is that the number of parameters is very small compared with other mainstream neural networks, so it can be applied in mobile terminals or edge devices. The main convolution method of MobileNetV1 is depthwise separable convolution, and it decomposes the convolution into two separate layers. The first layer is depthwise convolution, which has a convolutional filter of size $D \times D$ to each input channel. The second layer is 1×1 convolution, called pointwise convolution, which combines the filtered channels to produce output with N channels. The number of depthwise separable convolutional parameters is $(\frac{1}{N} + \frac{1}{D^2})$ times smaller than the normal convolution with the same filter size and output channels. Because N is much larger than D, the number of parameters reduced by the depthwise separable convolution is approximately D^2 times that of the normal convolution, as shown in Fig. 1.

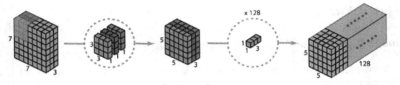

Fig. 1. Depthwise separable convolution [16].

2.3 DenseNet

DenseNet [24] minimizes the number of parameters by dense connectivity and stacking with several narrow convolutional layers. DenseNet is mainly divided into two parts: dense blocks and transition layers. Dense block contains multiple tightly connected convolutional layers, and each layer accepts feature maps from all previous layers, as shown in Fig. 2. The other part is the transition layer. The transition layer consists of 1 × 1 convolution and 2 × 2 max pooling and it connects two dense blocks and reduces the dimensionality of feature maps. There is no dense link between two dense fasts. DenseNet establishes connections between different layers, which improves the efficiency of information and gradient transmission in the network. Each layer in the dense block can directly obtain gradient information from the loss function and the input signal.

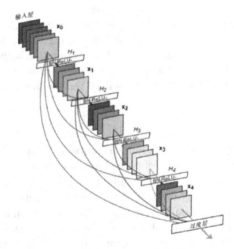

Fig. 2. Dense block [18].

3   Lightweight Expression Recognition Network Based on Dense Connections

In order to perform expression recognition on edge devices and mobile devices, this paper designs an improved MobileNetV1 lightweight network model, Dense-MobileNet.

The feature extraction of our model is mainly composed of lightweight block (DenseDW-block) proposed by this paper and Depthwise Separable Convolution block (DWblock). The input of the overall network is the facial expression image, and the output is the expression classification. The structure is shown in Fig. 3.

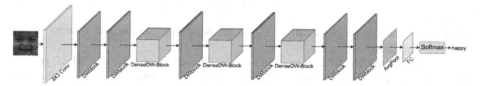

Fig. 3. The structure of Dense-MobileNet. This figure shows the exact position of DenseDW-block and DWblock in Dense-MoblieNet.

3.1 DenseDW-Block

This paper combines the idea of dense connectivity in DenseNet with deep separable convolution, and designs a lightweight module DenseDW-block, shown in Fig. 4. In the figure, 'concat' represents the operation of splicing feature map channel;

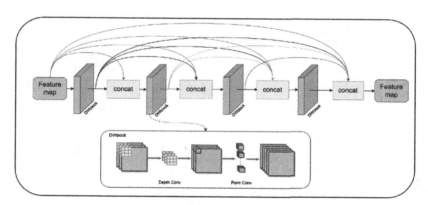

Fig. 4. The structure of DenseDW-block.

The DenseDW-block module contains four depthwise separable convolution blocks (DWblock). The output of each DWblock is feature map with k channels. In the DenseDW-block, we introduce direct connections from any DWblock to all subsequent DWblock. Finally, the output of the entire module is a feature map with $5 \times k$ channels. We define hyperparameter k as width of DenseDW-block. Therefore, the ith DWblock in DenseDW-block accepts the output of all previous DWblocks as input:

$$x_i = H_i([x_0, x_1, \ldots, x_{i-1}])i \in (0, 4] \tag{1}$$

where $[x_0, x_1, \ldots, x_{i-1}]$ represents the feature map splicing from the 0th DWblock to the $i - 1$th DWblock, i means the ith DWblock, $i \in (0, 4]$, and H_i represents the nonlinear transformation of the ith DWblock.

We define $H_i(x)$ as a composite function of two consecutive operations: 1. 3×3 depthwise convolution, batch normalization (BN), and the ReLu activation function. 2. 1×1 Point convolution, batch normalization (BN) and ReLu activation functions, as shown in Eq. (2):

$$H_i(x) = G_i(F_i(x)) \tag{2}$$

F_i represents depthwise convolution, G_i means point convolution and x refers to the input feature maps.

DenseDW-block has advantages of narrow width and less parameters, which greatly reduces the amount of computation and parameters of the module, and achieves the goal of lightweight. At the same time, feature reuse improves the efficiency of feature maps, so DenseDW-block still maintains a great feature extraction ability.

3.2   Dense-MobileNet

This paper compares the network structures of MobileNetV1 (Fig. 5(a)) and Dense-MobileNet (Fig. 5(b)) to clearly demonstrate the improvements. As shown in Fig. 5.

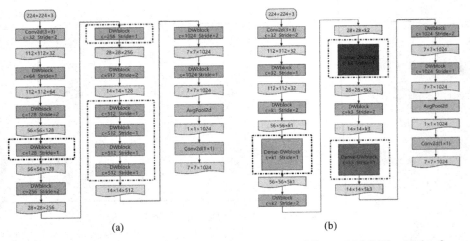

(a)   (b)

Fig. 5. (a) The structure of MobileNetV1. (b) The structure of Dense-MobileNet. (Color figure online)

The overall improvement idea is listed as follows: 1. The part of the convolutional layers in MobileNetV1 is replaced by three DenseDW-blocks with width of k_1, k_2 and k_3, as shown in Fig. 5(a), and the convolutional layers in the red, blue, and green boxes are replaced by DenseDW-blocks of corresponding colors in (b). 2. A DWblock with 2 strides is saved between the two DenseDW-blocks as a transition layer, and this paper narrows the width of DWblocks for reducing parameters. 3. Modify the classification number of the fully connected layer to the number of RAF-DB dataset types. According to the different width of DenseDW-blocks, we design three sub networks with different width combination of DenseDW-blocks. They are listed as follows: 1. Dense-MobileNet-1 with DenseDW-block widths of 16, 32, and 64; 2. Dense-MobileNet-2 with DenseDW-block widths of 24, 48 and 96; 3. Dense-MobileNet-3 with DenseDW-block widths of 32, 64 and 128; the setting of the width combination refers to the network structure of MobileNetV1. The specific structure is shown in Table 1, where k_1, k_2 and k_3 represent the width of the DenseDW-blocks embedded in Dense-MobileNet. The output of the i th ($i = 1, 2, 3$) DenseDW-block is W $\times$ H $\times$ $5k_i$, and W and H are the width and height of feature maps, respectively High, $5k_i$ means five times the number of channels of feature maps k_i; 3×3 depth conv means 3×3 depth convolution; 1×1 wise conv means point convolution.

Table 1. The structure of Dense-MobileNet.

Input	Operator	Dense-MobileNet-1 ($k_1 = 16, k_2 = 32, k_3 = 64$)	Dense-MobileNet-2 ($k_1 = 24, k_2 = 48, k_3 = 96$)	Dense-MobileNet-3 ($k_1 = 32, k_2 = 64, k_3 = 128$)
$224 \times 224 \times 3$	Conv 2d (stride = 2)	3×3 conv	3×3 conv	3×3 conv
$112 \times 112 \times 32$	Dwblock (stride = 1)	$\begin{bmatrix} 3 \times 3 \text{ depth conv} \\ 1 \times 1 \text{ wise conv} \end{bmatrix}$	$\begin{bmatrix} 3 \times 3 \text{ depth conv} \\ 1 \times 1 \text{ wise conv} \end{bmatrix}$	$\begin{bmatrix} 3 \times 3 \text{ depth conv} \\ 1 \times 1 \text{ wise conv} \end{bmatrix}$
$112 \times 112 \times 32$	Dwblock (stride = 2)	$\begin{bmatrix} 3 \times 3 \text{ depth conv} \\ 1 \times 1 \text{ wise conv} \end{bmatrix}$	$\begin{bmatrix} 3 \times 3 \text{ depth conv} \\ 1 \times 1 \text{ wise conv} \end{bmatrix}$	$\begin{bmatrix} 3 \times 3 \text{ depth conv} \\ 1 \times 1 \text{ wise conv} \end{bmatrix}$
$56 \times 56 \times k_1$	DenseDW-block (stride = 1)	$\begin{bmatrix} 3 \times 3 \text{ depth conv} \\ 1 \times 1 \text{ wise conv} \end{bmatrix} \times 4$	$\begin{bmatrix} 3 \times 3 \text{ depth conv} \\ 1 \times 1 \text{ wise conv} \end{bmatrix} \times 4$	$\begin{bmatrix} 3 \times 3 \text{ depth conv} \\ 1 \times 1 \text{ wise conv} \end{bmatrix} \times 4$
$56 \times 56 \times 5k_1$	Dwblock (stride = 2)	$\begin{bmatrix} 3 \times 3 \text{ depth conv} \\ 1 \times 1 \text{ wise conv} \end{bmatrix}$	$\begin{bmatrix} 3 \times 3 \text{ depth conv} \\ 1 \times 1 \text{ wise conv} \end{bmatrix}$	$\begin{bmatrix} 3 \times 3 \text{ depth conv} \\ 1 \times 1 \text{ wise conv} \end{bmatrix}$
$28 \times 28 \times k_2$	DenseDW-block (stride = 1)	$\begin{bmatrix} 3 \times 3 \text{ depth conv} \\ 1 \times 1 \text{ wise conv} \end{bmatrix} \times 4$	$\begin{bmatrix} 3 \times 3 \text{ depth conv} \\ 1 \times 1 \text{ wise conv} \end{bmatrix} \times 4$	$\begin{bmatrix} 3 \times 3 \text{ depth conv} \\ 1 \times 1 \text{ wise conv} \end{bmatrix} \times 4$
$28 \times 28 \times 5k_2$	Dwblock (stride = 2)	$\begin{bmatrix} 3 \times 3 \text{ depth conv} \\ 1 \times 1 \text{ wise conv} \end{bmatrix}$	$\begin{bmatrix} 3 \times 3 \text{ depth conv} \\ 1 \times 1 \text{ wise conv} \end{bmatrix}$	$\begin{bmatrix} 3 \times 3 \text{ depth conv} \\ 1 \times 1 \text{ wise conv} \end{bmatrix}$
$14 \times 14 \times k_3$	DenseDW-block (stride = 1)	$\begin{bmatrix} 3 \times 3 \text{ depth conv} \\ 1 \times 1 \text{ wise conv} \end{bmatrix} \times 4$	$\begin{bmatrix} 3 \times 3 \text{ depth conv} \\ 1 \times 1 \text{ wise conv} \end{bmatrix} \times 4$	$\begin{bmatrix} 3 \times 3 \text{ depth conv} \\ 1 \times 1 \text{ wise conv} \end{bmatrix} \times 4$
$14 \times 14 \times 5k_3$	Dwblock (stride = 2)	$\begin{bmatrix} 3 \times 3 \text{ depth conv} \\ 1 \times 1 \text{ wise conv} \end{bmatrix}$	$\begin{bmatrix} 3 \times 3 \text{ depth conv} \\ 1 \times 1 \text{ wise conv} \end{bmatrix}$	$\begin{bmatrix} 3 \times 3 \text{ depth conv} \\ 1 \times 1 \text{ wise conv} \end{bmatrix}$
$7 \times 7 \times 1024$	Dwblock (stride = 1)	$\begin{bmatrix} 3 \times 3 \text{ depth conv} \\ 1 \times 1 \text{ wise conv} \end{bmatrix}$	$\begin{bmatrix} 3 \times 3 \text{ depth conv} \\ 1 \times 1 \text{ wise conv} \end{bmatrix}$	$\begin{bmatrix} 3 \times 3 \text{ depth conv} \\ 1 \times 1 \text{ wise conv} \end{bmatrix}$
$7 \times 7 \times 1024$	AvgPool			
$1 \times 1 \times 1024$	FC/Softmax			

4 Experiments

4.1 Experimental Environment

To verify the effectiveness of our model, this paper validates it on the RAF-DB dataset. The GPU used in our experiments is NVIDIA GeForce GTX 1060 6 GB RAM, CUDA 11.3. The framework of Deep Learning used in our experiments is Pytorch 1.10.0, and the programming language is Python 3.7.

4.2 Experimental Dataset and Experimental Setup

Experimental Dataset: The Real-World Affective Face Database (RAF-DB) is a facial expression dataset released by Li et al. [21]. The dataset contains about 30,000 facial images that vary widely in subjects' age, gender and ethnicity, head pose, lighting conditions, occlusions, and more. For the simplicity of the experiment, we use a partial dataset with 7 classes of basic emotions, including 12,271 images in the training data and 3,068 images in the validating data.

Dataset preprocessing: The experiments do not use pre-training parameters, and this paper makes Data Augmentation on the dataset before training. The image size of the input data set is uniformly 224×224, and each training set image is flipped horizontally once, and the images are standardized channel by channel, which can speed up the convergence of the model.

Experimental setup: To illustrate that the effectiveness of Dense-MobileNet comes from the network design rather than different parameter settings or training strategies, this paper uses the same settings when training different networks. This paper uses cross-entropy loss as the loss function and Adam as the optimizer. The learning rate is initialized to 0.01 at the beginning of training, and in the experiment, the learning rate is reduced by ten times after every 20 rounds, which are 0.01, 0.001, and 0.0001. The number of iterations for network training is set to 60, and the batch size of each batch is 16.

4.3 Comparison Experiment

We conduct three comparison experiments on the RAF dataset: Dense-MobileNet width comparison experiments, Dense-MobileNet-2 and MobileNetV1 comparison experiment, and Dense-MobileNet-2 comparison experiments with other models.

4.3.1 Dense-MobileNet Width Comparison Experiments

This paper makes width comparison experiments to compare three sub networks in Table 1 to obtain the best performance of Dense-MobileNet. Table 2 is the comparison of the accuracy, parameter amount, and calculation amount of the above three networks on the RAF-DB dataset. It shows that all three Dense-MobileNets have less parameters and lower computational complexity. Especially, Dense-MobileNet-1 has the least parameters with lowest accuracy rate, indicating that the width of Dense-MobileNet-1 is too small and the extracted features are not rich enough, which impairs the recognition ability of Dense-MobileNet-1. Dense-MobileNet-3 has the most parameters in three Dense-MobileNets, however, its recognition ability is not as good as Dense-MobileNet-2 with fewer parameters, which means that the feature utilization rate of Dense-MobileNet-3 is lower than that of Dense-MobileNet-2. To sum up, in the three networks, Dense-MobileNet-2 has lower parameters and better recognition ability, so it has the best overall performance. Figure 6 shows that the prediction results of Dense-MobileNet-2.

Table 2. Dense-MobileNet width comparison experiment.

Method	Params	Flops	Accuracy
Dense-MobileNet-1	1.49×10^6	143.33M	79.7%
Dense-MobileNet-2	1.74×10^6	193.87M	82.4%
Dense-MobileNet-3	2.04×10^6	258.46M	82.2%

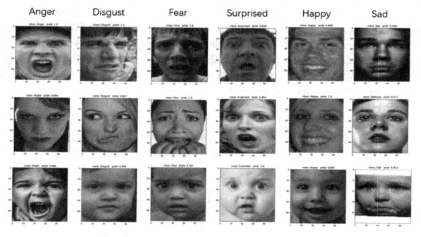

Fig. 6. Dense-MobileNet-2 prediction results.

4.3.2 Dense-MobileNet-2 and MobileNetV1 Comparison Experiment

Results in the previous subsection show that Dense-MobileNet-2 has the best overall performance. The model in this paper is improved on MobileNetV1, so we compare Dense-MobileNet-2 and MobileNetV1, which can better illustrate the effectiveness of our method. Table 3 is a comparison result of MobileNetV1 and Dense-MobileNet-2.

Table 3. Comparison result of Dense-MobileNet-2 and MobleNetv1.

Method	Params	Flops	Accuracy	Size
MobileNetV1	3.21×10^6	582.85M	79.9%	12.3 MB
Dense-MobileNet-2	$\mathbf{1.74 \times 10^6}$	**193.87M**	**82.4%**	**7.02 MB**

Result in Table 3 shows that accuracy of Dense-MobileNet-2 is improved by 2.5%, the number of parameters is reduced by 45.7%, the number of calculations is reduced by 66.73%, and the final model size is reduced by 42.92% compared with MobileNetV1. These results mean that the embedding of DenseDW-block not only reduces the width of the network model to achieve light weight, but also improves the recognition ability of the network. The reason for this is that a small number of feature maps generated by each DWblock can be accessed by subsequent DWblocks, and the continuous accumulation of feature maps makes the whole network obtain rich information with better recognition capability. By reducing the number of channels (widths), the number of parameters and the amount of computation can be greatly reduced, thus achieving lightweighting.

Figure 7 shows a large fluctuation during model training, because the learning rate is larger in the first 20 epochs. The learning rate decreases at the 20th epoch, so the accuracy of Dense-MobileNet-2 and MobileNetV1 begin to gradually stabilize. As the learning rate decreases, Dense-MobileNet-2 starts to show better performance, and the accuracy and loss values are better than MobileNetV1 and remain stable. This reflects the superiority of the model in this paper.

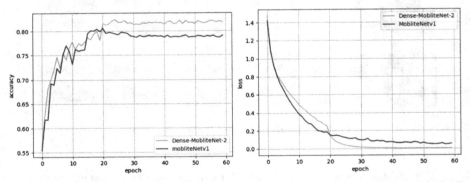

Fig. 7. The experimental parameter changes of Dense-MobileNet-2 and MobileNetv1 on the RAF-DB dataset. The left image is the comparison of accuracy, and right image is the comparison of loss.

4.3.3 Dense-MobileNet-2 and Other Models

In order to verify the effectiveness of the method in this paper, we compare Dense-MobileNet-2 with other different methods, including accuracy, parameter amount, computation amount and model size.

Table 4. Experimental comparison of Dense-MobileNet-2 and other models.

Method	Params	Flops	Accuracy	Size
AlexNet	4.44×10^7	698.87M	70.1%	89.4 MB
ResNet50	2.26×10^7	4218.88M	78.7%	97.7 MB
MobileNetV2 [25]	2.23×10^6	318.97M	**82.6%**	8.74 MB
MobileNetV3 [26]	4.21×10^6	226.44M	80.5%	16.2 MB
Dense-MobileNet-2	**1.74×10^6**	**193.87M**	82.4%	**7.02 MB**

As shown in Table 4, compared with the traditional deep network AlexNet and ResNet50, the parameters of our model are reduced by an order of magnitude, and Dense-MobileNet-2 has better recognition ability. Compared with MobileNetV3, our model still shows better comprehensive ability. Although the accuracy of our model is reduced by 0.2% compared with MobileNetV2, parameters are reduced by 22%, and size is reduced by 1.72 MB, indicating that out model is more lightweight and efficient, and is more suitable for real-time expression recognition scenes.

5 Conclusion

This paper proposes a lightweight network Dense-MobileNet for facial expression recognition tasks. Firstly, a DenseDW-block for feature reuse is designed and embedded into MobileNetV1 for better accuracy and less computation. Secondly, three sub networks Dense-MobileNet-1, Dense-MobileNet-2, Dense-MobileNet-3 are proposed for choose the best network parameters. Finally, the width selection and comparison experiments are used on the RAF-DB dataset. The results show that: 1) In the three sub networks, the Dense-MobileNet-2 has the best accuracy of 82.4%. 2) Compared with MobileNetV1, the recognition accuracy of our model is improved by 2.5%, and the number of parameters is reduced by 45.7%. These reflect the effectiveness of our method. And with better accuracy and less computation, Dense-MobileNet is suitable for facial expression recognition on mobile terminals and edge devices. In the future, we will conduct dynamic facial expression recognition based on this study.

Acknowledgments. This research was supported by the National Key R&D Program of China under Grant No. 2020YFB1707700.

References

1. Darwin, C.: The expression of the emotions in man and animals. Portable Darwin **123**(1), 146 (2012)
2. Li, Z., et al.: Intelligent facial emotion recognition and semantic-based topic detection for a humanoid robot. Expert Syst. Appl. **40**(13), 5160–5168 (2013)
3. Sheng, C., et al.: A study on classroom teaching based on dynamic identification of students' emotions. China Educ. Informatization **13**, 4 (2019). (in Chinese)

4. Liu, Z, Peng, Y., Hu, W.: Driver fatigue detection based on deeply-learned facial expression representation. In: 2018 IEEE International Conference on Information and Automation (ICIA), p. 102723. IEEE (2019)

5. Jingjing, W., Wushan, C., Zhiwen, D., et al.: Research on multidimensional expert system based on facial expression and physiological parameters. Int. J. Res. Eng. Sci. 5(5), 46–50 (2017)

6. Sekin, A.A., Bychkova, N.A.: Designing an expert system for recognizing the emotional state of an enterprise employee. In: EPJ Web of Conferences, vol. 248, p. 03002. EDP Sciences (2021)

7. Ekman, P.: Constants across cultures in the face and emotion. J. Pers. Soc. Psychol. 17(2), 124–129 (1971)

8. Liu, Y., et al.: Facial expression recognition with PCA and LBP features extracting from active facial patches. In: IEEE International Conference on Real-Time Computing & Robotics. IEEE (2016)

9. Zhang, B., Liu, G., Xie, G.: Facial expression recognition using LBP and LPQ based on Gabor wavelet transform. In: 2016 2nd IEEE International Conference on Computer and Communications (ICCC). IEEE (2016)

10. Mohammadi, M.R., Fatemizadeh, E., Mahoor, M.H.: PCA-based dictionary building for accurate facial expression recognition via sparse representation. J. Vis. Commun. Image Represent. 25(5), 1082–1092 (2014)

11. Mahmood, M., Jalal, A., Evans, H.A.: Facial expression recognition in image sequences using 1D transform and Gabor wavelet transform. In: 2018 International Conference on Applied and Engineering Mathematics (ICAEM) (2018)

12. Technicolor T, Related S, Technicolor T, et al.: ImageNet classification with deep convolutional neural networks

13. Simonyan, K., Zisserman, A.: Very deep convolutional networks for large-scale image recognition. Comput. Sci. (2014)

14. Szegedy, C., Liu, W., Jia, Y., et al.: Going deeper with convolutions. IEEE Computer Society (2014)

15. He, K., Zhang, X., Ren, S., et al.: Deep residual learning for image recognition. In: 2016 IEEE Conference on Computer Vision and Pattern Recognition (CVPR) (2016)

16. Howard, A.G., Zhu, M., Chen, B., et al.: MobileNets: efficient convolutional neural networks for mobile vision applications (2017)

17. Cotter, S.F.: MobiExpressNet: a deep learning network for face expression recognition on smart phones. In: 2020 IEEE International Conference on Consumer Electronics (ICCE). IEEE (2020)

18. Lucey, P., Cohn, J.F., Kanade, T., et al.: The extended cohn-kanade dataset (CK+): a complete dataset for action unit and emotion-specified expression. In: Computer Vision & Pattern Recognition Workshops. IEEE (2010)

19. Challenges in representation learning: a report on three machine learning contests. Neural Netw. Off. J. Int. Neural Netw. Soc. (2015)

20. Li, S., Deng, W., Du, J.P.: Reliable crowdsourcing and deep locality-preserving learning for expression recognition in the wild. In: 2017 IEEE Conference on Computer Vision and Pattern Recognition (CVPR). IEEE (2017)

21. Qha, B., Cha, B., Xw, A., et al.: Facial expression recognition with grid-wise attention and visual transformer. Inf. Sci. 580, 35–54 (2021)

22. Hu, Z., Yan, C.: Lightweight multi-scale network with attention for facial expression recognition. In: 2021 4th International Conference on Advanced Electronic Materials, Computers and Software Engineering (AEMCSE), pp. 695–698 (2021). https://doi.org/10.1109/AEMCSE51986.2021.00143

23. Cugu, I., Sener, E., Akbas, E.: MicroExpNet: an extremely small and fast model for expression recognition from face images. In: 2019 Ninth International Conference on Image Processing Theory, Tools and Applications (IPTA) (2019)

24. Huang, G., Liu, Z., Van Der Maaten, L., et al.: Densely connected convolutional networks. IEEE Computer Society (2016)

25. Sandler, M., Howard, A., Zhu, M., et al.: MobileNetV2: inverted residuals and linear bottlenecks. In: 2018 IEEE/CVF Conference on Computer Vision and Pattern Recognition (CVPR). IEEE (2018)

26. Howard, A., Sandler, M., Chen, B., et al.: Searching for MobileNetV3. In: 2019 IEEE/CVF International Conference on Computer Vision (ICCV). IEEE (2020)

Investigating the Potential of AutoML as an Instrument for Fostering AI Adoption in SMEs

Stephan Olsowski, Stephan Schlögl$^{(\boxtimes)}$ (iD), Ellen Richter, and Reinhard Bernsteiner (iD)

Department of Management, Communication and IT, MCI – The Entrepreneurial School, Universitätsstraße 15, 6020 Innsbruck, Austria
stephan.schloegl@mci.edu

Abstract. Artificial Intelligence (AI) has emerged as a mature and value-adding technology in business. Yet, its adoption is often challenging, due to both a lack of financial resources as well as staff. Particularly small and mid-sized enterprises (SME) risk to be left behind. AutoML, an instrument that helps automate certain AI tasks and thus reduces the need for dedicated staff, promises to overcome some of these AI adoption challenges. Investigating this problem space, the given paper reports on the results of a study exploring AI strategies, initiatives and obstacles SMEs in Germany, Austria and Switzerland face, and how AutoML may help with them. Results from an interview study with representatives from 12 different manufacturing companies suggest that AutoML can facilitate AI adoption, especially to overcome limited data science expertise and to enable prototyping. In this, it may further support strategic decision-making and create awareness for AI-driven innovation. Yet, a basic level of AI majority is required for AutoML to tap its full potential.

Keywords: Artificial Intelligence · AI readiness · AutoML · SME

1 Introduction

Throughout the last decade, Machine Learning (ML) and Artificial Intelligence (AI) have come a long way in demonstrating their value to industry. While in 2015, just about 10% of companies used ML [41], it is expected that by 2024 75% of companies will have operating ML and AI solutions incorporated into their business activities[1]. Respective examples can be found in almost any industry, ranging from anomaly detection and demand forecasting, to image recognition and natural language processing [38]. AI is increasingly considered a general-purpose technology that has the potential to change the nature of business value chains [6]. Charran and Sweetman [7] as well as Vicario and Coleman [48] thus

---

[1] Online: https://www.gartner.com/smarterwithgartner/2-megatrends-dominate-the-gartner-hype-cycle-for-artificial-intelligence-2020/ [accessed: January 14th 2022].

© Springer Nature Switzerland AG 2022
L. Uden et al. (Eds.): KMO 2022, CCIS 1593, pp. 360–371, 2022.
https://doi.org/10.1007/978-3-031-07920-7_28

conclude, that the use of relevant Data Science (DS) methods has become a significant competitive advantage for companies of the 21st century.

Yet, not all companies equally embrace ML. There is evidence that small and medium-sized enterprises (SME) significantly lag behind [5,32]. Here, one of the main challenges is seen in the attraction of talent [9]. Ever since Harvard Business Review named DS the *"sexiest job of the 21st century"* [11], demand has been growing [28]. And this trend is likely to continue, as data-generating application domains, such as the Internet of Things, Smart Cities, as well as Smart Factories, are just about to become mainstream [28,48].

AutoML (i.e., Automated Machine Learning) could help SMEs overcome some of these challenges. It automates the creation process of an AI solution and thus decreases the demand for full-fledged DS personnel [1]. Although previous studies have addressed SME-specific challenges in AI adoption [5,21,42], little is known about the use of AutoML. Hence, the work presented in this paper aimed to close this knowledge gap by investigating the following research question:

"To what extent can AutoML offerings improve the AI readiness of SMEs?"

We start our report of this investigation with Sect. 2, discussing some theoretical background and related work on AutoML and the use of AI and ML in SMEs. Next, Sect. 3 describes our research approach and Sect. 4 outlines and reflects upon our results. Hereinafter, Sect. 5 identifies areas in which AutoML may help with AI adoption. Finally, Sect. 6 concludes the paper with a summary, some limitations and recommendations for future research directions.

2   Theoretical Background and Related Work

Related previous work on the adoption of AI is often based on the Technology-Organization-Environment (TOE) framework [45] and the Diffusion of Innovation (DOI) theory [2,37]. While DOI theory focuses on social processes and technology characteristics [40], the TOE framework describes the adoption of new technological innovations, based on the three factors *Technology, Organization* and *Environment* [45]. Although the two theories aim to describe the same phenomenon, both take a slightly different perspective and thus are frequently used in a complementary fashion [33].

Another way of defining a company's strategy concerning the use of AI is its AI readiness score. The term AI readiness was coined by Alsheibani et al. as *"the preparedness of organizations to implement change involving applications and technology related to AI"* [2, p. 3]. Its underlying evaluation model is subdivide into five relevant categories (i.e., *Strategic Alignment, Resources, Knowledge, Culture* and *Data*) and as such describes the relevant foundations which increase the likelihood of a successful AI adoption [22].

ML approaches, which represent the core of an AI product or service, require an iterative development process [3,12,36], where data needs to be discovered, sourced, cleaned, managed and versioned so as to support a given use case [3]. These activities require people from different backgrounds (e.g., domain experts, data scientists, ML engineers, software developers, etc.) to collaborate and work with different tools (e.g., *Jupyter Notebook* and *JupyterLab*[2], *Google Collaboratory*[3], etc.) [50,51]. Some of these tasks, such as data cleaning, data labeling, feature engineering, ML-model selection or hyperparameter tuning[4], are very repetitive and time-consuming [51]. As a result, it is estimated that data scientists spend approx. 60%–80% of their time cleaning and organizing data [31,53]. More so, optimizing hyperparameter settings and ML model selection are recurrent activities, which are based on a mixture of past experiences, trial and error and rule of thumb [20]. As such it is not only very time consuming, but may also lead to sub-optimal ML algorithm configurations [53].

This is where AutoML may be considered a viable future alternative, as it tries to automate the creation of ML solutions. In a way, it may be described as a computing framework [52], which solves the *"fundamental problems of deciding which machine learning algorithm to use on a given data set, whether and how to pre-process its features, and how to set all hyperparameters"* [15, p. 2]. AutoML can thus be seen as a large-scale optimization problem, where different ML models are tested, their hyperparameters be set and their data be pre-processed according to the particularities and requirements of a given ML model [53]. Given the number and variability of hyperparameters, this generates a very large and complex search space for the optimization problem [14,44,53]. Additionally, dependencies between data preparation and algorithm selection complicate the optimization problem [30,34]. When successfully implemented, however, it has been shown that AutoML can perform as well as human experts [19,44], which may lead to significantly shortened development times [44,46].

3   Methodology

Given the novelty of AutoML our investigations started with AI readiness, from which we then extrapolated potential benefits of using AutoML. Semi-structured expert interviews were chosen as an analysis instrument, and Jöhnk et al.'s AI readiness framework [22] as an anchor point. As the framework offers 18 different AI-adoption factors (clustered in 5 categories), it served as a solid foundation, ensuring systematic coverage of the topic while allowing for deviations and further examinations in individual interviews.

---

[2] Online: https://jupyter.org/ [accessed: January 14th 2022].
[3] Online: https://colab.research.google.com/ [accessed: January 14th 2022].
[4] Note: Hyperparameters define the working of the ML algorithm and through this significantly influence the performance of the algorithm for a given ML problem.

3.1   Sampling and Recruitment

In order to identify viable interview partners it was decided to focus on SMEs as defined by the EU (i.e., less than 250 employees and a yearly turnover below EUR 250 million[5]). In addition the following restrictions were imposed:

1. In order to streamline AI application scenarios and available data sources, we focused on the manufacturing domain.
2. To control for potential cultural bias, we limited participation to companies from the DACH (i.e., Germany, Austria and Switzerland) region.
3. Start-ups were excluded as it was assumed that they would have a general dexterity in using modern technology involving data, analytics, and AI.
4. Companies from the field of robotics were excluded since AI is assumed to be at the core of their business.
5. Finally, so as to avoid elite bias (cf. [27, p. 264]), employees of all hierarchy levels were approached.

These restrictions helped narrow the sample while assuring adequate internal representation [26, p. 100]. Respective recruitment and the interviews took place over a period of 11 weeks. First, eligible companies that corresponded to the above criteria were researched. Subsequently, representatives of qualifying companies were contacted via LinkedIn or email and asked for their participation. Participation was entirely voluntary and in accordance with European data protection regulations (i.e., GDPR) including respective informed consent procedures. This sampling method as well as subsequent data collection and analysis procedures (cf. Sect. 3.2) were furthermore approved by the school's Ethics Commission.

3.2   Data Collection and Analysis

Interviews were conducted via Microsoft Teams. They lasted between 29 and 45 min and were subsequently transcribed following a de-naturalized transcription protocol. All of them started with a short introduction to the research topic, outlining the structure of the interview, followed by a short definition of AI and some exemplary application scenarios for ML. In order to analyse the transcripts, we used the MAXQDA software package[6] and applied Mayring's approach to qualitative content analysis [25]. Both deductive and inductive coding was used, where the former had its roots in the AI readiness framework [22] as well as in literature on AutoML and AI adoption challenges. After grouping the codes into sub-codes and main categories, they underwent two revisions. The first revision took place before analyzing the interviews and focused on the relevance and logic of the category definition and the coding rules. The second revision was conducted after analyzing half of the interviews and evaluated whether codes

---

[5] Online: https://ec.europa.eu/growth/smes/sme-definition_en [accessed: January 14th 2022].

[6] Online: https://www.maxqda.com/ [accessed: January 14th 2022].

covered all important aspects of the generated content. To assure reliability of results, an intra-coder agreement was calculated based on two randomly selected interviews, which were re-coded one week after the initial coding. Comparison showed a 89% agreement pointing to a high coding reliability.

3.3   Sample Description

Through the sampling strategy described in Sect. 3.1 we were able to recruit interview partners from 12 different SMEs (C1–C12) in Austria, Germany and Switzerland. Participating companies were classified according to the scheme outlined by Magoulas [23]. It distinguishes between companies which currently do not have any deliberate use of AI (*None*; $n = 0$), companies which are currently evaluating the potential use of AI through the definition of use cases and first proof of concepts (*Evaluating*; $n = 7$), companies which currently explore, summarize and analyze their data and build ML model prototypes (*Analyzing*; $n = 2$), and finally companies which already have productive AI solutions (*Production*; $n = 3$).

4   Findings

The following summarizes our findings and reflects upon their validity in light of previous work. The analysis ranges from companys' AI readiness to different drivers and challenges that impact the use of AI, and finally leads to a discussion on whether AutoML may be able to facilitate AI adoption.

4.1   Strategy and Management

Despite the general perception that SMEs approach new technologies rather hesitantly [32,49], a majority of the companies we talked to were in favor of using AI in business settings. In fact, half of them (i.e., C2, C3, C4, C5, C6, C11) have already included it in their company strategy, although this orientation towards AI is mostly long-term and does so far only play a minor role. To this end, P2 described AI as a *"lighthouse project"* (C2) deemed essential for the long-term survival of the company. For C4 AI was so deeply integrated into the activities of the company, that it is considered a rather universal *"tool"*, which may be employed to help with various different uses cases. These strategic orientations were mainly based on the economic expectations that would result from the use of the technology. They ranged from being less dependent on qualified personnel (C5), to the reduction of production down-times (C1, C6) and the development of new, renewed, or unique products and services (C2, C9). However, not all of the interviewed companies were willing to go down this path. While for some (C8, C9, C10) AI currently represents a topic which is being monitored and evaluated but not (yet) part of the company strategy, it has for others not yet reached the relevance to be included into strategic planning (C7, C12).

Consistent with findings from Ghobakhloo et al. [18] and Fuller-Love [17] we found that the strategic orientation towards the use of AI was often highly influenced by the managing director. That is, his/her awareness of AI (C7, C11), his/her vision for the future of the company (C3, C5, C6), as well as his/her previous experiences (C5) seemed to have a direct influence on the strategic positioning of the technology. For example, the representative of C5 noted that *"if the managing director is not open-minded, then it's relatively simple: there's no money, and such projects and ideas are not supported. I think [the decision for AI] in SMEs is very much influenced by the managing director"*. On the other hand, if the managing director is enthusiastic about using AI, he/she may pave the way by assigning funds, creating a supportive environment and giving the topic a high priority. An example for this may be found in the attitude of the managing director of C6, who developed a graphical strategy map for the digitalization of the company. The map did not only break down the different milestones and projects required for the digital future but also considered training and development towards a more data-driven and technology-friendly company culture.

Furthermore, the interviews showed that promoters and opponents are not always equally distributed. In some of the participating companies AI initiatives were triggered by management (C1, C3, C6) whereas in others they were driven by employees (C2, C7, C9, C12). And while lack of management support was perceived to slow down AI initiatives (C1, C9, C12) (see also [8]), it did not necessarily prevent small-scale experiments, even in cases where available time resources were limited and relevant expertise, in particular with respect to DS, was missing (C7).

4.2   Use Case Discovery and Solution Development

Participating companies seemed to have a rather clear vision of the kind of uses cases AI would be able to help them with. They mostly emerged from a mix between business and market demands (C2, C4, C5, C7, C9) or the knowledge about the implementation of a similar use case in another company (C2, C10, C7). Alternatively, C11 and C12 were approached by technology vendors and consulting companies who pitched concrete company-specific use cases to them. While this confirms previous work in that many smaller companies do require only little assistance in identifying suitable use cases for AI [39], it also shows that they sometimes lack the knowledge to grasp the full potential the technology may offer [5]. As for AI development and integration, the required cooperation between DS and domain experts, as already outlined by Passi and Jackson [35], as well as the challenges of ML model development, as noted by Studer et al. [43], were dominant interview topics. Here, the representative of C2 argued that planing an AI project from beginning to end, following a plan-driven development approach, is rather difficult. Thus, the use and consequent improvement of AI prototypes, as suggested by Tuggener et al. [46], was preferred by several of the participating companies (C3, C4, C9), although lack of resources may often interfere with regular and comprehensive evaluations (C7).

4.3   Available Resources

Confirming previous research [29], participating companies reported on limited financial resources for investments in AI. Here it is particular the often insecure outcome of AI initiatives (C2, C7, C9, C10, C11) which makes it difficult to justify expenses. The representative of C2, for example, explained that there is willingness to spend money on potential solutions *"if the overall business case is right. It has to fit the overall product and the market. If that's the case, then they wouldn't hesitate to make larger investments. But you have to be able to present the whole thing beforehand, which is certainly not easy [...]."*. Here it would help if companies could *"calculate [the utility of AI] as linearly as possible"* (C2, C5, C7, C10, C12). Yet, they still struggle with uncertainties connected to the expected market demand (C2), the quality of available AI solutions (C2, C4) as well as uncertainties regarding the complexity and length of the development process (C2, C7) (see also [24,47]). To this end, C4 pointed out that no calculation will ever account for all risks attached to an AI project and emphasized that until an ML model is built, there exists no certainty that it delivers the desired results.

Next to available financial resources, the existing IT infrastructure is considered an important prerequisite for dealing with AI and its data requirements. The results of Coleman et al. [9] suggest that SMEs often struggle to cover the required expertise related to setting up, configuring, and maintaining relevant infrastructure building blocks such as servers, databases, sensors, and respective software, and therefore may rely on external IT support. Interviews confirmed this general assumption, yet we have also observed significant ambitions to establish in-house expertise (C1, C2, C4, C6, C8, C10, C12), at least with individual staff members (C7, C9, C11). And while on-premise hardware solutions were perceived to often be unrealistic, cloud services for storage as well as computing power increasingly help strengthen a company's AI capabilities [4].

The ML and DS field, on the other hand, remains a bottleneck. Only two of the companies we talked to had a dedicated position in one of these fields (C4, C9). Many of the others (C2, C5, C6, C8, C9, C10) aim to expand their DS workforce in the future. Yet, the challenge lies in forming a respective team as *"one person is not really a critical mass to be able to accompany such a fast changing technology"* (P5).

4.4   People and Company Culture

People and company culture are said to have a significant impact on the success of an AI project [16]. While the majority of the companies we talked to considered themselves as innovative and constantly searching for ways to adapt and improve their products, we found differences in employees' attitudes. That is, with those companies which reported to apply AI in order to drive product innovation (C2, C4, C7, C9), AI was approached openly. On the other hand, with those companies which aimed to integrate AI into their business processes, interviews pointed towards distrust and fear among employees. They were particularly afraid of job loss (C11, C3), mistrusted the reliability of AI solutions

(C3) or had the feeling of being constantly monitored (C1). The representative of C10 explained that most of this skepticism among employees was fueled by the assumption that *"computers will [at some point] govern us all [...] and take our jobs away"*. This underlines the importance of respective change management initiatives, to create awareness among employees and openly tackle existing fears (C6). Furthermore, the role of the managing director as a leading figure (C5, C6), the importance to identify innovation supporters across the company (C4, C6) as well as the need to clearly explain the necessity for change (C10) and thus give employees a clear perspective (C11) were deemed important ingredients for a successful AI integration.

4.5 Data

Although all participating companies had realized the importance of data-driven decision making, the collection and use of relevant data for the development and training of ML models remains a great challenge (C1, C2, C3, C5, C6, C7, C8, C9). Often, companies put high expectations into open-access online data sets, but were disappointed as they were mostly unsuitable for their specific use cases (C2, C7). Furthermore, companies tend to forget about data structure and quality. As predicted by Earley [13], many of them, even the ones that had already gathered data, were struggling due to issues around incompatible data gathering devices and formats (C1, C2), consequent data silos (C10, C11), a lack of proper annotation schemes (C6) and manual data gathering processes (C4, C6, C11). Finally, although the availability of given AI use cases seemed to help gather the right data, none of the participating companies had so far established data management practices which would help assure data quality.

5 The Potential Impact of AutoML

From the above presented results we may draw some conclusions as to the potential role AutoML could play in helping with AI adoption challenges.

First, regarding the build-up and maintenance of ML and DS expertise, AutoML provides significant support in model building. It can enable employees to focus on formatting and structuring the data, and on monitoring and fine-tuning systems. Such may foster a company's expertise without the need for hiring additional personnel. In a way, this allows for democratizing ML capabilities among ordinary employees (see aso Crisan and Fiore-Gartland [10]).

Second, AutoML supports prototyping and thus the exploration of potential AI capabilities. As we have seen with several participating companies (C1, C7, C9, C12), it is often difficult to convince management of the opportunities AI may hold. Prototypes generated with AutoML help compare different use cases [10], showcase concrete solution approaches and consequently convince management of its benefits.

Third, AutoML-based prototypes can be used as a starting point for profitability calculations. Several sources [24, 39, 47] as well as some of our participants (C2, C4, C7), underlined this difficulty of calculating the ROI of an AI investment. By creating first prototypes, which test the available data and provide an initial estimation of the type of results that can be expected, more confidence can be put into an AI initiative. One may still not achieve absolute certainty regarding the financial evaluation of an AI investment, but according to Ulrich and Bachlechner [47] any insights that inform the discussion on the benefits of AI are considered useful.

Finally, AutoML generated prototypes also provide valuable insights concerning the required data, required ML modeling steps and consequently the associated effort an AI initiative has to undergo.

Despite these potential benefits, it should be emphasized that AutoML does not make the work of experienced ML experts obsolete. Although it can reduce the need for dedicated DS personnel, sporadic expert input is still needed. And while AutoML may help increase the AI readiness of companies, it should also be noted, that a basic level of AI awareness as well as relevant data so as to start exploring different ML use cases, are required for it to be effective.

6   Conclusions, Limitations and Future Work

In summary, our results indicate that AutoML can improve the AI readiness of SMEs, at least in some areas. Its potential help is perceived most strongly in setting up in-house ML expertise, both through democratizing ML capabilities and by making the work of an ML expert more efficient. Furthermore, AutoML-generated prototypes can increase AI readiness as a communication tool. They can be used to inform management on the potential of AI and to bring more certainty into respective profitability assessments.

While these results may underline the potential benefits of AutoML as a means to foster AI adoption among SMEs, the rather small sample of 12 participating companies, and their self-expressed openness for innovation, inhibits generalization. Hence, we call for more studies in this field so as to verify our findings. To this end, it may be interesting to investigate other industry sectors or to accompany a concrete AI adoption process and focus on context-specific peculiarities of AutoML implementations.

References

1. Abbassi, A., Kitchens, B., Faizan, A.: The risks of AutoML and how to avoid them (2019). https://hbr.org/2019/10/the-risks-of-automl-and-how-to-avoid-them
2. Alsheibani, S., Cheung, Y., Messom, C.: Artificial intelligence adoption: AI-readiness at firm-level. In: Proceedings of the Twenty-Second Pacific Asia Conference on Information Systems (PACIS), p. 37 (2018)
3. Amershi, S., et al.: Software engineering for machine learning: a case study. In: 2019 IEEE/ACM 41st International Conference on Software Engineering: Software Engineering in Practice (ICSE-SEIP), pp. 291–300. IEEE (2019). https://doi.org/10.1109/ICSE-SEIP.2019.00042
4. Assante, D., Castro, M., Hamburg, I., Martin, S.: The use of cloud computing in SMEs. Procedia Comput. Sci. **83**, 1207–1212 (2016)

5. Bauer, M., van Dinther, C., Kiefer, D.: Machine learning in SME: an empirical study on enablers and success factors. In: AMCIS 2020 Proceedings (2020)
6. Brynjolfsson, E., McAfee, A.: The business of artificial intelligence: What it can - and cannot - do for your organization (2017). https://hbr.org/2017/07/the-business-of-artificial-intelligence
7. Charran, E., Sweetman, S.: AI maturity and organizations: Understanding AI maturity (2020)
8. Chatterjee, S., Rana, N.P., Dwivedi, Y.K., Baabdullah, A.M.: Understanding AI adoption in manufacturing and production firms using an integrated tam-toe model. Technol. Forecast. Soc. Change **170**, 120880 (2021). https://doi.org/10.1016/j.techfore.2021.120880
9. Coleman, S., Göb, R., Manco, G., Pievatolo, A., Tort-Martorell, X., Reis, M.S.: How can SMEs benefit from big data? Challenges and a path forward. Qual. Reliab. Eng. Int. **32**(6), 2151–2164 (2016)
10. Crisan, A., Fiore-Gartland, B.: Fits and starts: enterprise use of AutoML and the role of humans in the loop. In: Proceedings of the 2021 CHI Conference on Human Factors in Computing Systems, pp. 1–15 (2021)
11. Davenport, T.H., Patil, D.J.: Data scientist: the sexiest job of the 21st century. Harv. Bus. Rev. (2012). https://hbr.org/2012/10/data-scientist-the-sexiest-job-of-the-21st-century
12. Domingos, P.: A few useful things to know about machine learning. Commun. ACM **55**(10), 78–87 (2012). https://doi.org/10.1145/2347736.2347755
13. Earley, S.: There is no AI without IA. IT Prof. **18**(3), 58–64 (2016)
14. Feurer, M., Hutter, F.: Hyperparameter optimization. In: Hutter, F., Kotthoff, L., Vanschoren, J. (eds.) Automated Machine Learning. TSSCML, pp. 3–33. Springer, Cham (2019). https://doi.org/10.1007/978-3-030-05318-5_1
15. Feurer, M., Klein, A., Eggensperger, K., Springenberg, J.T., Blum, M., Hutter, F.: Auto-sklearn: efficient and robust automated machine learning. In: Hutter, F., Kotthoff, L., Vanschoren, J. (eds.) Automated Machine Learning. TSSCML, pp. 113–134. Springer, Cham (2019). https://doi.org/10.1007/978-3-030-05318-5_6
16. Fountaine, T., McCarthy, B., Saleh, T.: Building the AI-powered organization: technology isn't the biggest challenge. Culture is. Harv. Bus. Rev. **97**(4), 62–73 (2019)
17. Fuller-Love, N.: Management development in small firms. Int. J. Manage. Rev. **8**(3), 175–190 (2006). https://doi.org/10.1111/j.1468-2370.2006.00125.x
18. Ghobakhloo, M., Hong, T.S., Sabouri, M.S., Zulkifli, N.: Strategies for successful information technology adoption in small and medium-sized enterprises. Information **3**(1), 36–67 (2012). https://doi.org/10.3390/info3010036
19. Hanussek, M., Blohm, M., Kintz, M.: Can AutoML outperform humans? An evaluation on popular OpenML datasets using AutoML benchmark. In: AIRC 2020 Conference Proceedings (2020)
20. Hill, C., Bellamy, R., Erickson, T., Burnett, M.: Trials and tribulations of developers of intelligent systems: a field study. In: 2016 IEEE Symposium on Visual Languages and Human-Centric Computing, pp. 162–170. IEEE, Piscataway (2016). https://doi.org/10.1109/VLHCC.2016.7739680
21. Iftikhar, N., Nordbjerg, F.E.: Adopting artificial intelligence in Danish SMEs - barriers to become a data driven company, its solutions and benefits. In: Proceedings of the 2nd International Conference on Innovative Intelligent Industrial Production and Logistics (IN4PL 2021) (2021)
22. Jöhnk, J., Weißert, M., Wyrtki, K.: Ready or not, AI comes–an interview study of organizational AI readiness factors. Bus. Inf. Syst. Eng. **63**(1), 5–20 (2021)

23. Magoulas, R., Swoyer, S.: AI-adoption in the enterprise 2020 (2020)
24. Mannar, K.: The ROI of AI (2019). https://www.accenture.com/us-en/insights/artificial-intelligence/roi-artificial-intelligence
25. Mayring, P.: Qualitative content analysis. Forum Qual. Soc. Res. **1**(2), 159–176 (2000)
26. Merkens, H.: Stichproben bei qualitativen studien. In: Friebertshäuser, B., Prengel, A. (eds.) Handbuch Qualitative Forschungsmethoden in der Erziehungswissenschaft, pp. 97–106. Weinheim/München: Juventa. journal=Zeitschrift für Pädagogik, München (1998)
27. Miles, M.B., Huberman, A.M.: Organization Change: Theory and Practice. SAGE, New Delhi (1994)
28. Miller, S., Debbie, H.: The quant crunch: how the demand for data science skills is disrupting the job market (2017)
29. Mittal, S., Khan, M.A., Romero, D., Wuest, T.: A critical review of smart manufacturing and industry 4.0 maturity models: implications for small and medium-sized enterprises (SMEs). J. Manuf. Syst. **49**, 194–214 (2018). https://doi.org/10.1016/j.jmsy.2018.10.005
30. Mohr, F., Wever, M., Hüllermeier, E.: Ml-plan: automated machine learning via hierarchical planning. Mach. Learn. **107**(8–10), 1495–1515 (2018). https://doi.org/10.1007/s10994-018-5735-z
31. Muller, M., et al.: How data science workers work with data. In: Brewster, S., Fitzpatrick, G., Cox, A., Kostakos, V. (eds.) Proceedings of the 2019 CHI Conference on Human Factors in Computing Systems. pp. 1–15. ACM, New York (2019). https://doi.org/10.1145/3290605.3300356
32. OECD: The digital transformation of SMEs (2021). https://doi.org/10.1787/20780990
33. Oliveira, T., Fraga, M.: Literature review of information technology adoption models at firm level. Electron. J. Inf. Syst. Eval. **14**(1), 110–121 (2011)
34. Olson, R.S., Bartley, N., Urbanowicz, R.J., Moore, J.H.: Evaluation of a tree-based pipeline optimization tool for automating data science. In: Neumann, F. (ed.) Proceedings of the Genetic and Evolutionary Computation Conference 2016, pp. 485–492. ACM, New York (2016). https://doi.org/10.1145/2908812.2908918
35. Passi, S., Jackson, S.J.: Trust in data science: collaboration, translation, and accountability in corporate data science projects. In: Proceedings of the ACM on Human-Computer Interaction, vol. 2, issue number (CSCW), pp. 1–28 (2018)
36. Patel, K., Fogarty, J., Landay, J.A., Harrison, B.: Investigating statistical machine learning as a tool for software development. In: Czerwinski, M. (ed.) Proceedings of the SIGCHI Conference on Human Factors in Computing Systems, p. 667. ACM Digital Library, ACM, New York (2008). https://doi.org/10.1145/1357054.1357160
37. Pumplun, L., Tauchert, C., Heidt, M.: A new organizational chassis for artificial intelligence - exploring organizational readiness factors. In: Proceedings of the 27th European Conference on Information Systems, Stockholm-Uppsala, Sweden (2019)
38. Purdy, M., Daugherty, P.: Why artificial intelligence is the future of growth (2016)
39. Reder, B.: Studie machine learning/deep learning 2019 (2019)
40. Rogers, E.M.: Diffusion of Innovations, 4th edn. Free Press, New York (1995)
41. Rowsell-Jones, A., Howard, C.: 2019 CIO survey: CIOS have awoken to the importance of AI (2019). https://www.gartner.com/en/documents/3897266/2019-cio-survey-cios-have-awoken-to-the-importance-of-ai

42. Schlögl, S., Postulka, C., Bernsteiner, R., Ploder, C.: Artificial intelligence tool penetration in business: adoption, challenges and fears. In: Uden, L., Ting, I.-H., Corchado, J.M. (eds.) KMO 2019. CCIS, vol. 1027, pp. 259–270. Springer, Cham (2019). https://doi.org/10.1007/978-3-030-21451-7_22

43. Studer, S., et al.: Towards CRISP-ML(Q): a machine learning process model with quality assurance methodology. Mach. Learn. Knowl. Extr. **3**(2), 392–413 (2021). https://doi.org/10.3390/make3020020

44. Swearingen, T., Drevo, W., Cyphers, B., Cuesta-Infante, A., Ross, A., Veeramachaneni, K.: ATM: a distributed, collaborative, scalable system for automated machine learning. In: Nie, J.Y., Obradovic, Z., Suzumura, T., Ghosh, R., Nambiar, R., Wang, C. (eds.) 2017 IEEE International Conference on Big Data, pp. 151–162. IEEE, Piscataway (2017). https://doi.org/10.1109/BigData.2017.8257923

45. Tornatzky, L., Fleischer, M.: The Process of Technology Innovation. Lexington Books, Lexington (1990)

46. Tuggener, L., et al.: Automated machine learning in practice: state of the art and recent results. In: Geiger, M. (ed.) 6th Swiss Conference on Data Science, pp. 31–36. IEEE, Piscataway (2019). https://doi.org/10.1109/SDS.2019.00-11

47. Ulrich, M., Bachlechner, D.: Wirtschaftliche bewertung von ki in der praxis – status quo, methodische ansätze und handlungsempfehlungen. HMD Praxis der Wirtschaftsinformatik **57**(1), 46–59 (2020). https://doi.org/10.1365/s40702-019-00576-9

48. Vicario, G., Coleman, S.: A review of data science in business and industry and a future view. Appl. Stoch. Models Bus. Ind. **36**(1), 6–18 (2020)

49. Vossen, G., Lechtenbörger, J., Fekete, D.: Big data in kleinen und mittleren unternehmen: Eine empirische bestandsaufnahme. Technical report, Arbeitsberichte des Instituts für Wirtschaftsinformatik. Münster (2015)

50. Wang, D., et al.: How much automation does a data scientist want? arXiv preprint arXiv:2101.03970 (2021)

51. Wang, D., et al.: Human-AI collaboration in data science. In: Proceedings of the ACM on Human-Computer Interaction, vol. 3, issue number (CSCW), pp. 1–24 (2019). https://doi.org/10.1145/3359313

52. Yao, Q., et al.: Taking human out of learning applications: a survey on automated machine learning. arXiv preprint arXiv:2101.03970 (2018)

53. Zöller, M.A., Huber, M.F.: Benchmark and survey of automated machine learning frameworks. J. Artif. Intell. Res. **70**, 409–474 (2021)

Artificial Intelligence, Case Study: Detection of Diabetic Retinopathy Through a Neuronal Networks in Citizens of Bogotá-Colombia

Diego Alejandro Barragán Vargas[1]([✉]), Ricardo Alirio Gonzalez Bustamante[2], and Roberto Ferro Escobar[1]

[1] Universidad Distrital Francisco José de Caldas, Bogotá, Colombia
dabarraganv@correo.udistrital.edu.co, rferro@udistrital.edu.co
[2] Universidad ECCI, Bogotá, Colombia
rgonzalezb@ecci.edu.co

Abstract. This document shows a brief history and a simple definition of artificial intelligence, to observe the concept of artificial neural networks in order to observe the case of diabetic retinopathy in Colombia, to understand the factors that facilitate this disease, it will also be studied the classification of healthy people and patients with the condition through a supervised artificial neural network that was explored and studied with different architectures in which the hidden layers, the training algorithm, the transfer function and the number of neurons were varied, where it was observed that the Levenberg-Marquadt method was the most suitable for the classification of affected patients, due to the speed of the algorithm in the training and validation of the data, which had a more agile response time than the algorithms with optimization of gradient descent, likewise it was visualized that by having a reduced number of neurons in l. The hidden part layers help to reduce the error, reduce the computational load of the system and when complemented with a suitable objective function such as logsig, it allows an approximation to the desired answer. For the diabetic retinopathy problem, it was observed that the best architecture is ARC [30 1], which has 31 neurons, since it has the lowest validation error of 24%.

Keywords: Government · Governance · Artificial intelligence · Smart City

1 Introduction

With the development of human civilization, cities saw a significant increase in population, which allowed an expansion in the urban and demographic processes, however this development generated new problems in important areas such as environmental, social, economic, political and technological, which led us to think of possible solutions, such as the improvement of cities in different concepts, to convert them into so-called smart cities, all with the aim of making them green, livable, innovative and harmonious, with the main perception, a wide range in its interoperability, in the management of participation with people to understand their needs and a greater depth with intelligence [1, 2], the above is possible, thanks to the development of information technologies and communication (ICT), which allowed the evolution of the internet, with a significant improvement in the connections It is from mobile devices, to implement growing practices such as the Internet of Things (IOT) [3].

Smart Cities can be observed, such as the use of applied technologies of intelligent computing, to make various public services and infrastructure infrastructure components more intelligent, interconnected and efficient [4], as well as the idea of an intelligent city, it is the sustainable development of its urban area, to significantly improve the quality of life of its citizens [5], this can be achieved using the concepts of governance and government, which allow adequate policies for an implementation and direction corresponding to the ICT management, with respect to the public restrictions present, around the desired behavior in the digital sphere with citizens [6], giving an opportunity to technologies to carry out exchanges between government organizations, with private companies, which allows the use of other concepts such as "e-government", which provides the basis to encourage positive effects ivos within the public administrations derived from the use of ICT in the different contexts of public action [7].

From the above, there is another concept necessary for the success of an intelligent city such as the "Intelligent Government", which is intertwined with a good government, which allows the application of transparent, fair, participatory rules that are linked to the government, for a constant progress with technology [8]. However, this concept is also based on the inhabitants, who are the central axis of the project, since electronic governance is focused on the provision of services that the residents of a country want, this is done through ICT, which goes marking a desired archetype in the evaluated area [9, 10].

Artificial intelligence (AI) has now become a multidisciplinary field, it is defined in several ways, an example of this was John McCarthy, a computer scientist in 1979, who coined the term Artificial Intelligence (AI) to define it as "the science and engineering of making intelligent machines" [11], in computer science is defined as machines that manifest a certain way of thinking; it can be said that the AI was born from a philosophical study of human science having as uncertainty the finding of objects capable of imitating the nature of human thought [12], there are other definitions proposed by various speakers such as Eugene Charniak who commented on AI as "Study of the mental faculties through the use of computational models", Marvin Minsky said that "Artificial Intelligence is the construction of computer programs that perform tasks, for the moment, executed efficiently by the human being because they demand high mental processes. level such as: perceptual learning, organization of memory and critical reasoning" [13].

Artificial intelligence has some basic principles that are applied in all the branches that use it, which are:

- Self-learning capacity.
- A dynamic interaction with the user.
- Must have a good reaction in real time
- Must have autonomy [12].

2 Neuronal Networks

Are the networks that try to imitate the structure and behavior of biological neurons in the stage of processing information, using learning models that seek to solve different problems, likewise are a set of mathematical algorithms that find non-linear relationships between sets of data, generally neural networks are used in trends prediction fields and as respective classifiers of data sets.

There are several methods among which two stand out in a particular way:

- Supervised networks: These are techniques for extracting data, taking into account the input-output relationship to store these relationships in mathematical equations, these networks can be used in predictions or in decision-making.
- Unsupervised networks: These are techniques for the classification, organization and visualization of large data sets without requiring external influence, these are networks developed by Professor Teuvo Kohonen [14, 25].

The multilayer perceptron neural network (MLP), is part of the supervised networks, this network is a model formalized by Rumelhart, Hinton and Williams (1986), in which the network learns the association that exists between a set of input patterns and its corresponding outputs. An MLP is composed of an input layer, an output layer and one or more hidden layers, in this type of models the connections between nodes always go from the neurons of a certain layer, to the neurons of the next layer, that is why that the information is always transmitted from the input layer to the output layer [15] (Fig. 1).

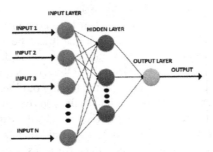

Fig. 1. Architecture of an MLP network.

The input pattern p, can be expressed as a vector $p_x : x_{p1}, \ldots, x_{pi}, \ldots, x_{pn}$, this is transferred through the weights W_{ij} from the input layer to the hidden layer, the net input that a hidden neuron receives j, net_{pj}, is:

$$net_{pj} = \sum_{i=j}^{N} w_{ij} x_{ij} + \theta_j \tag{1}$$

where θ is the threshold of the neuron that is assumed to be a weight associated with a fictitious neuron with an output value equal to 1. It should be taken into account that the neurons in the intermediate layer transform the received signals by applying a function of activation, to obtain in this way an output value [15]:

$$b_{pj} = f\left(net_{pj}\right) \tag{2}$$

where b_{pj} is the output value of the neuron j.

The value b_{pj} is transferred through the weights V_{kj} towards the output layer:

$$net_{pk} = \sum_{j=1}^{L} V_{kj}b_{pj} + \theta_k \tag{3}$$

In the output layer the same operation is performed as in the previous layer, the neurons of this last layer provide the output, y_{pk}, of the network:

$$Y_{pk} = f\left(net_{pk}\right) \tag{4}$$

3   Data on Diabetic Retinopathy in Latin America and Colombia

According to the guidelines of the International Diabetes Federation 2015, there are 415 million people in the world with diabetes, of these, more than a third will develop some form of diabetic retinopathy throughout their lives. It is estimated that currently people with eye damage from diabetes are more than 93 million in the world [16]. This number is likely to increase as a result of global population aging, urbanization, the high prevalence of obesity, and sedentary lifestyles. The improvement in the treatment of diabetes has decreased macrovascular mortality, so that patients live long enough to develop RD (Diabetic Retinopathy) [17, 18].

In the American National Health and Nutrition Examination Survey, 28.5% of diabetic patients had some degree of RD, and 4.4% had diabetic retinopathy that affected vision [19]. Similar prevalence estimates have been observed in other developed countries [30]. Latin America is not the exception. It was estimated that by the year 2000 there were 13.3 million people with RD and for the year 2030 this figure will increase to 33 million, which represents an increase of 148%.

In Colombia, cases of diabetic retinopathy have increased from one year to the next, reporting a prevalence of 12.86 per 100,000 inhabitants in 2012 and 19.76 in 2017. When disaggregating the information by sex, there is a prevalence estimated for women of 10.41/100,000 in 2012 and 19.51 in 2017, presenting an increase of 9.1/100,000 in the six years analyzed. On the other hand, men reported a prevalence of 9.20/100,000 in 2012 and 16.06 in 2017, with an increase of 6.86 per 100,000 inhabitants in the six years [17, 18] (Fig. 2).

Regarding the estimated prevalence of diabetic retinopathy in the departments of Colombia, it is evident that Bogotá, Valle, Norte de Santander, Antioquia and Santander have the highest prevalences (17,30–24.18/100,000) for the period 2012–2017. In contrast to San Andrés, Vichada and Vaupés that report the lowest prevalences for the same period (0.39–1.35/100,000). When comparing the prevalence of 2012 with that of 2017, it is observed that Cundinamarca shows an increase in the prevalence of 22.61/100,000,

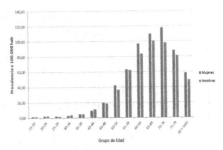

Fig. 2. Prevalence of diabetic retinopathy by age groups and sexes in Colombia, 2014 [23].

followed by Valle with an increase of 18.34 and Caldas with an increase of 14.72 per 100,000 inhabitants [17, 18].

When comparing the number of cases of diabetic retinopathy in patients diagnosed with diabetes by department for the year 2014, it is obtained that Valle (538.57), Cundinamarca (526.03), Bogotá (496.92), Antioquia (458,24) and Santander (397.84) recorded the highest rates of diabetic retinopathy per 100,000 diabetic people. In contrast to Guainía (43,63), San Andrés (23,71) and Vichada (0,00) that present the lowest rates in the country (Fig. 3).

Fig. 3. Rate of diabetic retinopathy in patients with diabetes. Colombia, 2014 [24].

4   Proposal of a Neural Network Sorting

We proceeded to design a MLP neural network as a classifier, because the inputs and outputs of the problem are known, as well as serving to start with a correct training of the network, since knowing the data facilitates a follow-up process by means of the comparison of the training error that is the analyzed data of the system, with respect to the validation error that is the data analyzed by the neural network, for this a set of data taken from the repository of the University of California in Irving was used, where we have (Table 1):

Table 1. Diabetic retinopathy

Database	Output
Diabetic retinopathy	Class 1: "Suffers disease" Class 2: "Do not suffer"

The following steps were taken into account for the design:

- Have a cross validation where the data is collected (random pair (x, y) and take a percentage for validation and another percentage to train).
- It is advisable to use 80% to 70% of the data to train, these are chosen from the database acquired from the repository of the University of California [26].
- It is advisable to use 30% to 20% of the data to validate, these are taken from the acquired database [26].
- It is important that the data number is greater than 10 times the size of the problem.

It is important to mention that the data set of the University of California contains features extracted from Messidor's set of images that serve to predict whether an image contains signs of diabetic retinopathy or not [26]. In the database, 19 entries were taken into account and an output that in order is exposed to show the information indicated [26]:

Table 2. Meaning of each entry and exit of the database [25]

Input 1	Binary result of the quality evaluation, having 0 as a bad quality and 1 as a sufficient quality
Input 2	Indicates a binary result of the preselection where 1 is a severe retinal anomaly and 0 that has no abnormalities
Input (3–8)	Results of the detection of Microaneurysms
Input (9–16)	They contain the same ticket information (3–8), but with different analysis
Input 17	It shows the information obtained from the Euclidean distance from the center of the macula and the center of the optical disc, this input provides important information about the patient's condition
Input 18	Indicates the diameter of the optical disc
Input 19	Indicates the binary result of the AM/FM based classification
Output	Shows the final result of the analysis of the entries. If the result is, it means that the patient contains signs of diabetic retinopathy, if the result is 0, it means that there are no signs of diabetic retinopathy

It proceeds to show the minimum and maximum values of each of the entries placed in the database having:

Table 3. Maximum and minimum of each entry

Input 1	Minimum value = 0 Maximum value = 1
Input 2	Minimum value = 0 Maximum value = 1
Input 3	Minimum value = 1 Maximum value = 151
Input 4	Minimum value = 1 Maximum value = 132
Input 5	Minimum value = 1 Maximum value = 120
Input 6	Minimum value = 1 Maximum value = 105
Input 7	Minimum value = 1 Maximum value = 97
Input 8	Minimum value = 1 V Maximum value = 89
Input 9	Minimum value = 0,35 Maximum value = 404
Input 10	Minimum value = 0 Maximum value = 167,17
Input 11	Minimum value = 0 Maximum value = 106,07
Input 12	Minimum value = 0 Maximum value = 60
Input 13	Minimum value = 0 Maximum value = 51,42
Input 14	Minimum value = 0 Maximum value = 20,09
Input 15	Minimum value = 0 Maximum value = 6
Input 16	Minimum value = 0 Maximum value = 3,08
Input 17	Minimum value = 0,37 Maximum value = 0,59
Input 18	Minimum value = 0,06 Maximum value = 0,22
Input 19	Minimum value = 0 Maximum value = 1

We proceeded to normalize the data having:

$$V_n = \frac{V - V_{min}}{V_{max} - V_{min}}$$

Obtaining the normalized data and knowing the entries, we proceeded to load the file and generate the partition of the data to evaluate one part as training and another part as validation, in order to perform cross validation (Fig. 4).

```
close all; clear all; clc
load('NORMALIZACION.mat'); %Carga del fichero normalizado
cont = 0;
%%------------------------Datos Entrenamiento-------------
x = NORMALIZACION(1:900,1:19)';        %%Matriz de entradas
y = NORMALIZACION(1:900,20)';          %%Matriz de salidas
%%------------------------Datos Validación--------------
xx = NORMALIZACION(901:1151,1:19)'; %%Matriz de entradas
yy = NORMALIZACION(901:1151,20)';   %%Matriz de salidas
nets = [];
```

Fig. 4. File upload and partition of Matlab data

It must be taken into account that the file "dataset.mat" is a matrix of size 1151×20, which results in 23020 data that would be 100% of information for the problem, so it was taken into account for the respective validation of data and training the following:

Training Data
For the input matrix, a total of 17,100 data was chosen, equivalent to approximately 74.28% of the total data. For the output matrix, a total of 900 was chosen, which is equivalent to 78.19% of the total data.

Validation Data
For the input matrix, a total of 4750 data were chosen, equivalent to 20.63% of the total data. For the output matrix, a total of 250 data was chosen, equivalent to 21.72% of the total data. Observing Table 2 and carrying out the respective standardization, we proceeded to create and train the network having (Fig. 5):

```
for h=1:50
%% Creación y Entrenamiento de la red
PR = [0 1;0 1;0 1;0 1;0 1;0 1;0 1;0 1;0 1;0 1;0 1;0 1;0 1;0 1;0 1;0 1;0 1;0 1;0 1];
ARC = [2 2 2 1];
net=newff(PR,ARC,{'logsig' 'logsig' 'logsig' 'logsig'},'traingda','learngdm','mse');
[net,tr] = train(net,x,y);
```

Fig. 5. Creation and training of the network

In this it can be seen that the PR matrix has the maximums and minimums of each input of the problem. Likewise, the ARC matrix is an array that shows the size of each

layer and in the creation of the feed-forward back-propagation network, the 'logsig' neuronal function was used, with the gradient slope training method with adaptive learning
rate backpropagation called 'traingda', likewise a learning function was used for the bias
of 'learngdm' and a performance function, by default that is the 'mse' (Fig. 6).

After creating and training the network, we proceeded to validate by means of the
calculation of the error, having:

```
[Y] = sim(net,xx);
cont =0;
for i=1:length(Y)
    if Y(i)<0.5
        Y(i)=0;
    else
        Y(i)=1;
    end
    if Y(i)==yy(i)
        cont = cont+1;
    end
end
errorpercent(h)= (250-cont)*100/250
nets = [nets ; net];
end
```

Fig. 6. Error validation

Then proceeded to generate the respective graph of the error and save the respective
files that will show the saved architecture, having (Fig. 7):

```
figure;
hist(errorpercent);
set (gca,'fontsize',12);
title('Error de validación');
xlabel('Porcentaje de error');
ylabel('Repeticiones');
print('NET.png','-dpng','-r300');
save('NET.mat','errorpercent','nets','ARC');
```

Fig. 7. Creating figures and generating tables for errors

5   Results

We proceed to corroborate, varying the respective hidden layers and neurons, at the same
time proceeding to choose the best architecture in each layer having the following order:

We proceed to show the best architecture per layer with the activation function
"logsig" which are the architectures highlighted in yellow and the gradient slope training
method with adaptive learning rate "traingda", backpropagation. The best architectures
for one, two and three hidden layers were:

In Fig. 8 it can be seen that the validation error has a maximum of 41%, a minimum
of 30% and an average of 36%, which shows that it is not a very good network to classify.

In Fig. 9 it can be seen that the validation error has a maximum of 42%, a minimum
of 28% and an average of 36%, which shows that it is not a very good network to classify.

The best architecture of this experiment (Table 4) was found in the neural network
with four hidden layers observing the following:

Table 4. Architecture with the "TRAINGDA" training method and "logsig" activation function.

SIZE	# NEURONS	MSE	ERROR OF VALIDATION (%)			REGRESSION
			MIN	MED	M¡ X	
[1 1]	2	0,221	28	38	50	0,356
[5 1]	6	0,210	30	36	41	0,428
[10 1]	11	0,216	32	36	41	0,425
[1 1 1]	3	0,203	28	40	50	0,445
[5 1 1]	7	0,204	28	35	42	0,437
[5 5 1]	11	0,193	30	48	46	0,481
[10 5 1]	16	0,211	31	45	42	0,405
[10 10 1]	21	0,214	30	38	44	0,407
[1 1 1 1]	4	0,198	28	36	50	0,457
[5 5 5 1]	16	0,212	30	38	50	0,397
[10 10 10 1]	31	0,200	30	34	42	0,446
[20 15 10 1]	46	0,197	28	34	44	0,459
[30 15 10 1]	56	0,186	31	37	42	0,507
[30 30 30 1]	61	0,203	28	40	44	0,447
[50 40 20 1]	111	0,191	30	35	45	0,483
[1 1 1 1 1]	5	0,249	30	35	50	0,091
[2 2 2 2 1]	9	0,244	31	39	50	0,183
[5 5 5 5 1]	21	0,195	30	39	50	0,469
[10 10 10 10 1]	41	0,185	28	34	41	0,513
[20 20 20 20 1]	81	0,205	30	37	43	0,448
[30 25 20 15 1]	91	0,189	30	36	43	0.491
[40 30 20 10 1]	91	0,202	30	35	39	0,442

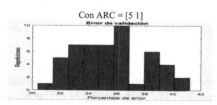

Con ARC = [5 1]

Fig. 8. Validation error with the best architecture of a hidden layer

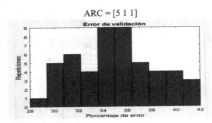

Fig. 9. Validation error with the best architecture of two hidden layers

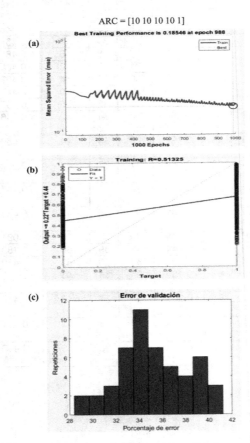

Fig. 10. (a) Mean square error, (b) R = 0.513 and (c) validation error for four hidden layers architecture

Figure 10 shows the best result obtained with the "traingda" training method and the "logsig" activation function. The best result was obtained, using four hidden layers where the best behavior of the validation error was had, with a linear regression of 0.513, with a training error of 0.185.

Now we change the transfer function of the neural network that was previously "logsig" to "purelin", which is a linear function and the same training algorithm is left ("traingda"), observing:

Table 5. Architecture with the "TRAINGDA" training method and "purelin" activation function.

Size	#Neurons	MSE	ERROR OF VALIDATION(%)			REGRESSION
			MIN	MED	Mₗ X	
[1 1]	2	0,214	28	32	40	0,384
[5 1]	6	0,209	28	30	28	0,384
[10 1]	11	0,211	26	30	35	0,396
[1 1 1]	3	0,225	28	32	42	0,317
[5 5 1]	11	0,208	29	31	38	0,411
[10 10 1]	21	0,203	29	32	39	0,426

The best architectures found when simulating were:

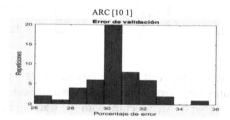

Fig. 11. Validation error for a hidden layer architecture

In Fig. 11 it can be seen that the validation error has a maximum of 35%, a minimum of 26% and an average of 31%, which shows a notable improvement over the architecture tested previously (Table 4), however, it is better to continue testing architectures, to observe to what extent you can decrease the validation error.

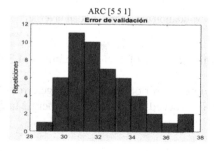

Fig. 12. Validation error for two hidden layer architecture.

Figure 12 shows that the validation error increased slightly, with a minimum of 29%, an average of 32%, with a maximum of 37%.

Now we proceed to analyze the activation function "tansig" having:

Table 6. Architecture with the "TRAINGDA" training method and "tansig" activation function.

Tamaòo	#Neuronas	MSE	ERROR DE VALIDACI" N(%)			REGRESI" N
			MIN	MED	M¡ X	
[1 1]	2	0,202	30	40	50	0,445
[5 1]	6	0,202	26	32	40	0,441
[10 1]	11	0,195	27	33	36	0,485
[1 1 1]	3	0,194	30	35	50	0,481
[5 5 1]	11	0,195	26	35	42	0,489
[10 10 1]	21	0,191	26	33	42	0,489

The best architectures will proceed to show below, taking into account their performance mainly in the validation error, since this is what indicates how close it is, with respect to the real data. Table 6. Architecture with the training method "TRAINGDA" and activation function "tansig".

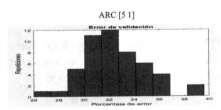

Fig. 13. Validation error for a hidden layer architecture

Figure 13 shows a minimum error of 26%, a maximum of 39% and a mean error of 32%.

Figure 14 shows a minimum error of 26%, an average error of 33% and a maximum error of 41%. Now we will proceed to use the Levenberg Marquadt method with the logsig function having:

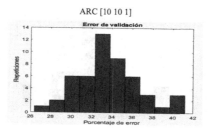

Fig. 14. Validation error for two hidden layer architecture

Table 7. Architecture with the "TRAINLM" training method and "logsig" activation function.

SIZE	#Neurons	MSE	ERROR OF VALIDATION(%)			REGRESSION
			MIN	MED	M¡ X	
[1 1]	2	0,155	26	26	26	0,611
[5 1]	6	0,108	22	29	35	0,756
[10 1]	11	0,053	24	29	35	0,893
[20 1]	21	0,038	26	30	34	0,922
[30 1]	31	0,025	24	30	36	0,949
[40 1]	41	0,025	25	30	50	0,948

Next, we proceed to show the histograms of each of the architectures of Table 6 having:

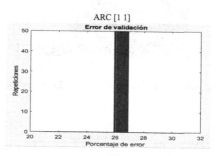

Fig. 15. Validation error for a hidden layer architecture

In Fig. 15, the validation error was shown to be 26%, only one bar shows the histogram because this architecture has a single neuron in its hidden layer.

Figure 16 shows the validation error, which had a minimum of 21%, an average of 29% and a maximum of 34%.

In Fig. 17 the validation error had a minimum of 24%, an average of 29% and a maximum of 35%.

Figure 18 shows a validation error with a maximum of 35%, a minimum of 26% and an average of 30%.

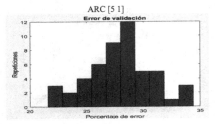

Fig. 16. Validation error for a hidden layer architecture.

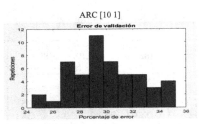

Fig. 17. Validation error for a hidden layer architecture

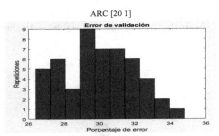

Fig. 18. Validation error for a hidden layer architecture

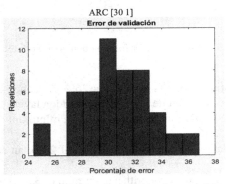

Fig. 19. Validation error for a hidden layer architecture

In Fig. 19, a validation error is shown with a minimum of 24%, an average of 30% and a maximum of 37%.

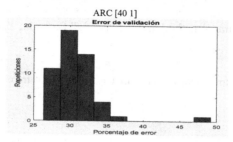

Fig. 20. Validation error for architecture of a hidden layer

Figure 20 shows the validation error with a minimum of 25%, an average of 30% and a maximum of 50%.

Finally, we will proceed to test with the gradient descent training method "traingd", having:

Table 8. Architecture with the "TRAINGD" training method and "logsig" activation function.

SIZE	#N	MSE	ERROR OF VALIDATION(%)			REG
			MIN	MEDIO	M¡ X	
[1 1]	2	0,264	39	50	60	0,113
[5 1]	6	0,260	36	50	60	0,056
[10 1]	11	0,308	35	45	60	0,144
[20 1]	21	0,4597	35	45	60	0,058
[30 1]	31	0,252	35	45	50	0.024
[40 1]	41	0,254	39	50	60	0,092

Table 7 shows that the validation error is very high, its mean square error also and its linear regression tends to 0, so it is discarded immediately.

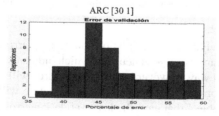

Fig. 21. Validation error for a hidden layer architecture

Figure 21 shows the validation error with a minimum of 35%, an average of 45% and a maximum of 60%.

6   Analysis of Results

From Table 3 the data of the architectures with four hidden layers was chosen since it was observed by means of the histograms representing the minor validation error with the "traingda" training method and the "logsig" function; You have the following information:

Table 9. Architecture of four hidden layers with the "TRAINGD" training method and "logsig" activation function.

Four hidden layers		
Neurons	Etraining	Evalidation
5	0,249	0,3
9	0,244	0,31
21	0,195	0,3
41	0,185	0,28
81	0,205	0,3
91	0,189	0,3
91	0,202	0,3

When plotting the data of the number of neurons in the face of validation and training errors, we have:

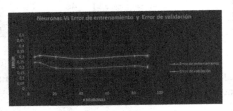

Fig. 22. Number of neurons vs training error and validation error.

It is observed through Fig. 22 that validation and training errors tend to be constant in the presence of a significant increase in neurons, which indicates that the neural network is classifying in a correct way, however, other architectures will be analyzed to observe if a minor validation error can be generated, the architecture will now be tested with a hidden layer shown in Table 4 that gave the least validation error with the same training method, but now using the "purelin" function that is linear (Table 10).

The data in Table 9 show a similar error of validation against the training error, so it is observed that the classification of the neural network is similar, with respect to the data of the architectures tested in Table 8 and it is necessary to review other architectures.

Table 10. Architecture of a hidden layer with the "TRAINGD" training method and "purelin" activation function.

A hidden layer		
Neurons	Etraining	Evalidation
2	0,214	0,28
6	0,209	0,28
11	0,211	0,26

Now we proceed to use another activation function with the same training method, the function used was "tansig" and the data obtained from the simulation can be visualized in Table 5, from this information the architecture was chosen with a hidden layer that showed a lower validation error, to visualize it having (Table 11):

Table 11. Architecture of a hidden layer with the "TRAINGD" training method and "tansig" activation function

A hidden layer		
Neurons	Etraining	Evalidation
2	0,202	0,3
6	0,202	0,26
11	0,195	0,27

From the table it can be seen that the difference between the training error and the validation error decreases slightly, so the architecture is similar in the classification, taking into account this will now proceed to analyze the other data obtained with other methods of training.

Now we are going to proceed to analyze the data of the architectures generated by means of the training method of Levenberg-Marquatd that in Matlab has the acronym "trainlm" with the activation function "logsig" that are in Table 6, in this observe that the best architecture with a layer and is ARC [30 1], we proceed to graph the data of the architectures with a hidden layer to observe the behavior of the validation error regarding the training error, having (Table 12):

Having the validation error and the training error are (Fig. 23):

The architectures made with the Levenberg Marquadt method showed better results in the validation errors, being this finally the one chosen for the analysis of the classification of diabetic retinopathy.

Table 12. Architecture of a hidden layer with the "TRAINLM" training method and "logsig" activation function

A hidden layer		
Neurons	Etraining	Evalidation
2	0,155	0,26
6	0,108	0,22
11	0,053	0,24
21	0,038	0,26
31	0,025	0,24
41	0,025	0,25

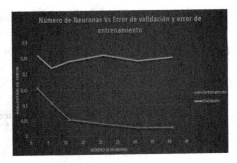

Fig. 23. Number of neurons vs training error and validation error.

7 Conclusions

- It was observed that learning methods based on gradient descent have the problem that they can be located at a local minimum (Fig. 24) and not at a global minimum (Fig. 25), given that they tend to converge more rapidly.
- It was observed that using more hidden layers increases the possibility of finding local minimums, so it is necessary to train the same neural network more times in order to find the global minimum.
- The method with a higher validation error was the "traingd", because it has a greater facility in locating in the local minimums.
- It was observed that sometimes the neural network was trained in a very short time, this happened because the network fell to a local minimum.
- The Levenberg-Marquartd method allowed us to correctly classify the exposed cases of diabetic retinopathy, it was observed on some occasions that the neuronal network was trained very quickly, but producing a lot of validation errors, this is because the network fell into a local minimum.
- Currently hospitals in Colombia have a great potential for the acquisition of patient data in order to help in the diagnosis, however, these are not well explored and several important factors in the life of the patient that can end are regularly omitted. In a bad

result, health centers are often in large cities that do not meet the demand of the rural population and citizens often from these remote places have to travel to the capital, leaving as a discussion the deep use of tools such as neural networks to support the specialist in their diagnostic results and serve to implement tools such as telemedicine that are of great help to the country.

- As future work, readers are asked to analyze the data with unsupervised neural networks and Bayesian neural networks to observe possible training methods and algorithms that improve the classification, decrease the validation error and perform the simulation in less time.

Fig. 24. Local minimum

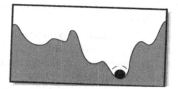

Fig. 25. Global minimum

References

1. Chen, M., Zheng, Y.: Construction of intelligent city evaluation system based on entropy model, p. 5 (2017)
2. Güel, J.M.F.: Ciudades inteligentes, la mitificación de las nuevas tecnologías como respuesta a los retos de las ciudades contemporáneas, p. 12 (2015)
3. Bernabeu, M.A.C., Mazón, J.-N., Sánchez, D.G.: Open data y turismo. Implicaciones para la gestión turística en ciudades y destinos turísticos inteligentes, vol. 15, p. 30 (2018)
4. Madakam, S., Ramaswamy, R.: 100 new smart cities (India's smart vision), p. 6 (2015)
5. de Avila Muñoz, L., Sanchez, S.G.: Destinos turísticos inteligentes, p. 10 (2015)
6. Signes, E.S., Merino, B.R., Vera, J.M.B., Puig, M.A.B.: La necesidad de un plan director para ciudades turísticas inteligentes. propuestas metodológicas basadas en la participación-acción, vol. 16, p. 18 (2018)
7. Criado, J.I., Gil-García, J.R.: Gobierno electrónico, gestión y políticas públicas estado actual y tendencias futuras en am´erica latina, p. 46 (2013)
8. Lopes, N.V.: Smart governance: a key factor for smart cities implementation, p. 6 (2017)

9. Das, R.K., Misra, H.: Smart city and E-governance: exploring the connect in the context of local development in India, p. 2 (2017)

10. Silvia, E., et al.: Gobernanza digital, mejora de procesos de gestión y calidad de software, p. 6 (2018)

11. Srivastava, S., Bisht, A.: Safety and security in smart cities using artificial intelligence-a review, p. 4 (2017)

12. Serna, A., Acevedo, E., Serna, E.: Principios de la inteligencia artificial en las ciencias computacionales, vol. 3, p. 8 (2017)

13. Pereira, W.: Desafíos de la inteligencia artificial bioinspirada con algoritmos genéticos, vol. 20, p. 27 (2017)

14. Pérez Ramírez, F.O., Castaño, H.F.: Las redes neuronales y la evaluación del riesgo de crédito, vol. 6, p. 15 (2007)

15. Viana, C.P.: Son más corruptos los países menos abiertos a los mercados internacionales, p. 35 (2011)

16. International Federation od Diabetics: Retinopathy of Prematurity - Latin America Guidelines (2017)

17. Nishimura, R., et al.: Mortality trends in type 1 diabetes. The Allegheny County (Pennsylvania) Registry 1965–1999. Diabetes Care **24**(5), 823–827 (2001)

18. Yau, J.W.: Global prevalence and major risk factors of diabetic retinopathy. Diabetes Care **35**(3), 556–564 (2012)

19. Zhang, X., et al.: Prevalence of diabetic retinopathy in the United States, 2005–2008. JAMA **304**(6), 649–656 (2012)

20. von-Bischhoffshausen, F.B., et al.: Planning diabetic retinopathy services - lessons from Latin America. Community Eye Health **75**, 14–16 (2011)

21. Sivaprasad, S.: Prevalence of diabetic retinopathy in various ethnic groups: a worldwide perspective. Surv. Ophthalmol. **57**(4), 347–370 (2012)

22. Leske, M.C.: Causes of visual loss and their risk factors: an incidence summary from the Barbados Eye Studies. Rev. Panam. Salud Publica. **27**(4), 259–267 (2010)

23. MINSALUD: Análisis de salud de situación de salud visual en Colombia en 2016, convenio 519 de 2015, p. 82 (2016)

24. MINSALUD: Análisis de salud de situación de salud visual en Colombia en 2016, convenio 519 de 2015, p. 84 (2016)

25. Wannakam, K., Jiriwibhakorn, S.: Evaluation of generation system reliability using adaptive neuro-fuzzy inference system (ANFIS) and artificial neuronal networks (ANNs). In: International Review of Electrical Engineering (IREE) (2018)

26. Antal, B., Hadju, A.: An ensemble-based system for automatic screening of diabetic retinopathy, p. 32 (2014)

Author Index